AMERICAN ART DECO

Jacques Schnier "Two Dancers," bronze group, 15 in. (38 cm) high, 1931 (collection John P. Axelrod)

ALASTAIR DUNCAN

AMERICAN ART DECO

HARRY N. ABRAMS, INC.,
PUBLISHERS, NEW YORK

TO NICHOLAS

Library of Congress Cataloging-in-Publication Data

Duncan, Alastair, 1942–
    American art deco.

    Bibliography: p.
    Includes index.
    1. Art deco—United States.   2. Art, Modern—
20th century—United States.   I. Title.
N6512.5.A7D86   1986   709'.73   86–3561
ISBN 0–8109–1850–1

Published in 1986 by Harry N. Abrams,
Incorporated, New York. All rights reserved. No part
of the contents of this book may be reproduced
without the written permission of the publishers

Times Mirror Books

Printed and bound in Japan

CONTENTS

ACKNOWLEDGMENTS

My very sincere gratitude to the many who provided ready assistance and information in the compilation of this book.

These, in alphabetical order, include Lynn Abbie, Herbert S. Adler, the Art Institute of Chicago (Sheryl Bailey), the Atlantic Richfield Company, the Auburn-Duesenberg Museum (Gregg Buttermore), the Avery Library (Janet Parks, Harriet Stratis, and Jay Hendricks), John P. Axelrod, Bob Barrett, Becket Associates, Joseph Duci Bella, Bill Benedict, Michael Bleichfeld, Richard Bohl, Frederick Brandt, Walter Scott Braznell, Carla Breeze, Brookgreen Gardens (Robin A. Salmon), The Brooklyn Museum (Diane Pilgrim and Christopher Wilk), Dr. Annella Brown, the Buffalo and Erie County Historical Society (Thomas Payne), the Butler Library (Alison Scott), Barbara B. Capitman, The Carnegie Institute (Phillip M. Johnston), Charles H. Carpenter, Jr., the Catalina Island Museum Society (Patricia Anne Moore), Irwin S. Chanin, the Chicago Historical Society (Sharon S. Darling, Wim de Wit, Zabra Clark, and Robert Breugmann), Christie's New York and Geneva (David Robinson, Peter L. Daly, Karin L. Willis, Mary-Beth McCaffrey, Leslie Weckstein, Carol Haggerty, Hans Nadelhoffer, Sue Fiamma, Debi Jackson, Georges de Bartha, Axelle Thijssen, and Joseph Siejack), the Chrysler Museum (Nancy O. Merrill), the Cincinnati Art Museum (Karen Zukowski), the Cleveland Institute of Art (Dennis Buck and Roberta A. Hubbard), the Cleveland Museum of Art (Henry Hawley), Joyce Colton, the Cooper-Hewitt Museum (Elaine E. Dee, David McFadden, Timothy Rub, William Clagett, Derek Ostergard, Margaret Luchars, Sarah A. Seggerman, Scott Hyde, and Cathy Martinez), The Corning Museum of Glass (Priscilla Price and Jane Spillman), the Cowan Pottery Museum (Victoria F. Peltz), the Cranbrook Academy of Art (Susan Waller), Michael Crowe, the Dallas Historical Society (Peggy Riddle), William Davis, Jr., Anthony de Lorenzo, Monroe Denton, the Detroit Institute of Arts (Patricia K. Lawrence and Mary Ann Wilkinson), Martin Diamond, Martin Eidelberg, Richard Farnan, Carl U. Fauster, Mark Feldman, Catherine A. Fitch, Barry Friedman, Denis Gallion, Vernon Gay, Laurie Gentile, Vicky Gold, Robert Goodman, David Halpern, Rita Hanke, David Hanks, Hedrich-Blessing (William Thompkins), Tony Heinsbergen, Terry Helgesen, Lloyd Herman (the Renwick Gallery), Adam C. Heyman, Peter Hill, William Hill, Hirschl and Adler (Susan Menconi), the Indianapolis Museum of Art (Janet Feemster), Inglett-Watson (Dan Inglett and Gene Watson), Carl Y. Iri, James J. Jennewein, the Jordan-Volpe Gallery (Todd Volpe), Randy Juster, Muriel Karasik, Duny B. Katzman, Grace Keating, Ronald and Lee Keno, Vicki Levi, Sydney and Frances Lewis, the Library of Congress (Ford Peatros), Miles Lourie, Michael and Wendy Lubin, Mark MacDonald, Mrs. Malatesta, Donald McCormick, the Metropolitan Museum of Art (Craig Miller, Linda G. Lawson, and Andrew Spahr), Allen Michaan, Randal Michelson, the Minnesota Museum of Art (Gloria Kittleson), Daniel Morris,

Alan Moss, the Museum of the City of New York (Jennifer Bright), Jan Nadelman, Victor Nardini, the National Museum of American Art (Dr. Elizabeth Broun, Tom Bower, Patricia C. Geeson, Barbara Nosanow, and Rachel M. Allen), Albert Nesle, the Newark Museum (Ulysses G. Dietz), the Niagara Mohawk Power Corporation (James M. Cosgrove), the Northwest Architectural Archives: University of Minnesota (Alan Lathrop and Susan Brown), the Norton Gallery and School of Art, the Museum of Art of Ogunquit (Henry Strater), John Perricault, Pflueger Associates (Debra Huskisson), Russell P. Phillips, Maxime Polack, the Queen's Museum (Eileen Shepherd), Don Reed, Anthony Robins, the Rockefeller Center (Anita McGurn and James Reed), the Rockwell Museum (Bobby Rockwell and Michael Duty), Joseph Rosenburg, William Rothschild, Christine Roussel, the Saint Louis Art Museum (Christina H. Nelson), the San Francisco Public Library (Gladys Hanson and Patricia Akre), Robert Schoelkopf, Viktor Schreckengost, Arlene Palmer Schwind, Severance Hall (Denise Horstman and Timothy D. Parkinson), Amy Freedman Sharak, Julius Shulman, Sotheby's New York (Jacqueline Samols and Amy Murphy), Jewel Stern, John Stern, the Steuben Glass Company (Chloë Zerwick), William Straus, David Stravitz, Richard Striner, the Tampa Museum (Rebecca L. Wilson), Jeffrey Thier, Tiffany & Co. (John Loring and Kathy Murtha), Kaz Tsuruta, Susan Tunick, Charles Uht, the University Art Museum: University of California at Santa Barbara (Professor David Gebhard and Gavin Townsend), Elayne Varian, William Warmus, George H. Waterman III, William T. Weber, Larry Whiteley, the Whitney Museum of American Art (Jody Erdman), Carol Willis, Robert Winter, Diane Wolf, the Mitchell Wolfson, Jr., Collection of Decorative and Propaganda Arts (Stephen Greengard, Carol Alper, and Mercedes A. Quiroga), the Yale University Art Gallery (Patricia Kane and Karen Davies), and Larry Zim.

Particular thanks is extended to the following for special assistance: Randy Juster, whose many photographs attest admirably to his abilities as a photographer and his broad knowledge of American Art Deco architecture; Katherine C. Kurland, for innumerable hours of research, much of it tedious; Alan Moss, for his readiness to share information in a field in which he has long been an acknowledged authority; Timothy Rub, for the selfless manner in which he offered invaluable archival and photographic sources which would otherwise have been missed; and Alice, my wife, for both her expert advice on American sculpture and her support through three years of research. Thanks, also, to Donald Deskey and Viktor Schreckengost for their comments on various sections of the text. Finally, the book is a tribute to the pioneer research by Karen Davies, whose 1983 exhibition catalogue for the Yale University Art Gallery, *At Home in Manhattan*, provided, in part, the impetus for this book.

T he term "Art Deco," as is now well known, comes from the title of the celebrated exhibition of decorative and industrial arts held in Paris in 1925: 1'Exposition Internationale des Arts Décoratifs et Industriels Modernes. It was not a term used at the time, however. In the 1920s and 1930s contemporary design was known as Art Moderne in France and Moderne or Modernistic in the United States. The expression "Art Deco" was not coined until 1968, as the title of a book by Bevis Hillier on the decorative arts of the 1920s and 1930s. It is a useful term, as long as one remembers that no single phrase can possibly describe all the interrelated forces at play in the art of the era.[1] The field is simply too broad and the sources too manifold and complex.

Decorative arts in the period between the Wars drew not only on contemporary themes, but also on practically every historical influence from the Egyptian mania that swept Paris after Carter's discovery of Tutankhamun's tomb in 1922, to the science fiction of Buck Rogers in which a Depression-racked American public sought refuge a decade later – a range which has been described as "from the ancient past to the distant future."[2]

The 1920s Neoclassical refinement of Emile Jacques Ruhlmann, the asceticism of Le Corbusier and Walter Gropius, the youthful exuberance of the Wiener Werkstätte, and the wrought-iron floral excesses of Edgar Brandt defy any attempt to classify them together. Likewise, the crisp angularities of Charles Rennie Mackintosh and Josef Hoffmann, the organic forms of Hector Guimard's and Victor Horta's Art Nouveau, the botanical symbolism of Emile Gallé, and the analytic geometry of Cubism – in all of which one can find antecedents of the decorative arts of the post-World War 1 era – were unrelated, often irreconcilable, forces in the world of art at the turn of the century. Nevertheless Hillier's "Art Deco" remains our only shorthand description of the decorative arts of the years between the Wars.

For the purposes of this book, Art Deco incorporates the two principal movements that dominated the European decorative arts in the first quarter of this century, both of which, with modifications, formed the nucleus of later parallel movements in the United States. The first of these, chronologically, was the movement spawned in the early years of the century in Austria and Germany as an alternative to the faltering *Jugendstil*. Based on Germanic logic and geometry, in

Below

René Paul Chambellan panel in carved stone, 13 in. (33 cm) high, on the facade of the Stewart & Company Building, 5th Avenue and 56th Street, New York, 1929 (Warren & Wetmore, architects) (photo Wurts Bros. Archives, Museum of the City of New York)

contrast to Art Nouveau's litany of flowers and maidens in neighboring France, it placed emphasis on functional design applicable to mass production.[3] Ornament was given only secondary status. This movement was the forerunner of the strain of Art Deco that took root in the decorative arts in the United States in the late 1920s. Its crisp, angular functionalism earned it at the time the label "Modernism," and that is how it is referred to in the following text.

The second principal decorative movement, and the one that is today most readily identified as Art Deco, was the highly colorful and playful style which ruled Paris in the immediate post-World War 1 years. Were it not for the 1914-18 hiatus, this movement would have played itself out a lot sooner, but it is seen now as an extension, rather than the antithesis, of the Art Nouveau vernacular which its disciples had set out to eradicate. It provided the last splendidly self-indulgent decorative style, a style designed, according to a recent critic, "for luxury and leisure, for comfort and conviviality. It is an exciting style and should, like the archetypal drink of the period, the cocktail, be enjoyed while it is still laughing at you".[4] Identified in the text as early French Art Deco, the style arrived in the United States before the older, more austere, Austrian/German variation.

The term "American Art Deco," as used in the title of this book, covers items made in the United States both by American-born designers and by European designers who settled in the USA between the early 1900s and the 1930s.

The application to American design in the 1920s and 1930s of the two Art Deco strains described above – the Art Deco of France and the Modernism of Germany and Austria – fell into two distinct categories: first, architecture, and, secondly, the broad spectrum of the decorative (i.e., applied) arts. As will become evident, vanguard European decorative art was interpreted differently in these two fields, both of which then underwent pronounced modifications of their own in the wake of the stock market crash of October, 1929. The impact of the Crash cannot be overstated. Among its influences on the decorative arts was the creation of the profession of industrial designer, which, in turn, led to a vast project of product redesign, carefully staged to restimulate consumer buying in the 1930s.

Although some highly ornamental French motifs were recreated on American ceramics and glass vases and on the occasional piece of furniture, French Art Deco ornamentation aligned itself far more closely with American architecture in the 1920s than it did with any disciplines within the decorative arts. This was largely because architecture's advances in the United States preceded those of the decorative arts by five to seven years. In 1923-25, when the skyscraper boom began in earnest, the only distinctly modern, and therefore appropriate, decorative style on which the architect could draw to embellish his set-backs and entrance lobbies, was that of the Paris *Salon*. In America, quite simply, no modern style existed.

The safe, proven way to dress a building would have been to continue with the traditional period-revivalism of Cass Gilbert's Woolworth Building in New York, or Hood and Howells' Chicago Tribune Tower, but America's new generation of architects, spearheaded by firms such as Voorhees, Gmelin & Walker, and

Below

Morgan, Walls, & Clements (architects) bronze panel, lobby, Richfield Oil Company Building, Los Angeles, 1928-9 (photo Randy Juster)

Right

Frank Lloyd Wright living room in the Ennis-Brown house, 2607 Glendower Avenue, Los Angeles; 16 in. (40.6 cm) hollow concrete blocks with repeating geometric pattern. The house, designed in 1924 for Charles W. Ennis, changed hands several times before it was purchased by G. Oliver Brown in 1968 (photo Julius Shulman)

Right

E. H. Faile & Co. (architects) elevator doors in nickel, bronze, and brass; Goelet Building, 608 5th Avenue, New York, 1930. Illustrated in *Metalcraft*, March 1932, p. 108 (photo Randy Juster)

Far right

Wirt Rowland (architect) elevator doors, Penobscot Building (also known as the City National Bank Building), 1356 Griswold Fort, Detroit, c. 1930 (photo Randy Juster)

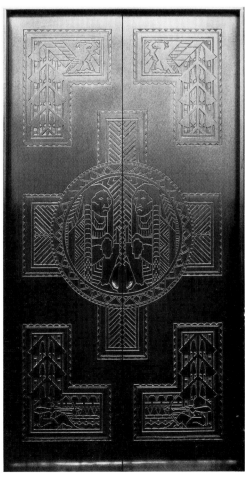

individuals such as William Van Alen, rejected these as inappropriate to the twentieth-century structure. In place of historicism, up-to-the-minute colorful geometric and floral abstractions of the French capital were introduced – chevrons, arcs, sunbursts, maidens, flower sprays, and the ubiquitous *biche* (doe). That America had not developed its own grammar of Modernist ornament does not appear to have troubled anybody. In matters of decoration and fashion, anything from Paris carried, as it always had, authority.

Architectural motifs were therefore plucked directly from the objects at the Salon des Artistes Décorateurs and the Salon d'Automne in the immediate post-World War 1 years for transposition on to the friezes of America's new buildings. Parisian Art Deco borrowings became America's most readily identifiable decorative vernacular of the 1920s, and one which it continued to use long after the style had become hackneyed and outdated in its country of origin.

This transplanted ornamentation associated itself most forcefully with the skyscraper, so much so that its disappearance, from the early 1930s, was bound up directly with the demise of the tall building. While in fashion, however, it shared the skyscraper's romance and celebrity.

The tall commercial building personified the country's buoyant mood in the 1920s. The cathedrals of commerce which rose so rapidly to scrape the skies were monuments to man's ingenuity and energy. They showed, above all, that capitalism worked. They were also uniquely American, an irrefutable proof of America's leadership in engineering technology. An entranced populace watched as the battle for the world's tallest building was waged, first in Chicago, and then in New York.

Walter Chrysler's enshrinement of his first box of tools in a glass case on the 71st floor of the Chrysler Building was seen by many at the time as an idealistic, rather than a self-glorifying gesture. Likewise, the project to moor dirigibles on the top of the Empire State Building was seen as further evidence of man's ability to tame his environment. Even though uncontrollable wind factors caused the idea to be rapidly abandoned, the fact remained that only in America could it even have been contemplated.

As much as any other architect, Hugh Ferriss popularized the emerging tall building in a series of architectural renderings which logged its evolution within the limits laid down by the 1916 New York Zoning Laws. A renderer by profession, Ferriss applied a highly individual and romantic style to the depiction of soaring, terraced structures which, by the mid-1920s, were concentrated into multilevel futuristic inner cities. In an exhibition at John Wanamaker's in New York in 1925 to celebrate New York's tercentenary, Ferriss displayed a range of renderings of multiple structures of the immediate future, including a fantastic vision of "Apartments on Bridges," which a critic described as "a view which quite outdoes anything Jules Verne figured out for terrestrial terminals."[5] In 1929, a few months before the stock market crash which precipitated a sharp retreat from Verne's utopian world, Ferriss published a selection of his architectural drawings under the apocryphal title, *The Metropolis of Tomorrow*. It was not to be.

Contemporary architectural reviews indicate that several important voices had been gathering force within the architectural community against the wisdom of

Below

Hugh Ferriss perspective of the proposed Majestic Hotel, corner 72nd Street and Central Park West, New York, for the Chanin Architectural Office, charcoal on board, 1930 (photo Irwin S. Chanin)

linking the profession's future so closely to the whims of the property developer and his rollercoaster world of commerce. Frank Lloyd Wright especially crusaded constantly in the 1920s and 1930s against the evils of the skyscraper. His authority to speak on the subject was strengthened by the fact that he had witnessed first-hand the conception of the world's first tall building, the Wainwright, while a trainee in Louis Sullivan's offices as far back as 1890.[6] Wright took special exception to the manner in which skyscrapers had been allowed to proliferate in, and therefore to congest, the inner city. In an article entitled *The Tyranny of the Skyscraper,* he wrote,

They are monotonous. They no longer startle or amuse. Verticality is already stale; vertigo has given way to nausea; perpendicularity is changed by corrugation of various sorts, some wholly crosswise, some crosswise at the sides with perpendicularity at the center, yet all remaining "envelopes". The types of envelope wearily reiterate the artificial setback, or are forced back for effect, with now and then a flight that has no meaning.[7]

Wright's summary was predictable: skyscrapers had no higher ideal than profit. His disenchantment would no doubt have carried more weight had it not come at a moment of relative inactivity and obscurity in his own career.

Echoing Wright's misgivings, Lewis Mumford, the Skyline critic of *The New Yorker,* noted in 1931, in response to the recently announced plans for the towering 70-story RCA building to cap the Rockefeller Center project, that the scheme was, at the very least, unhygienic; that the millionaires who were to occupy offices in the new building would seriously compromise their health by living in such close proximity to other millionaires![8]

Wright and Mumford were not entirely wrong. When the economy unraveled in the aftermath of the stock market crash, the skyscraper, its prized monument, faltered. As businesses foundered, the rentable spaces in these vast structures fell vacant. Two of New York's most spectacular surviving landmarks, the Empire State Building and Rockefeller Center (neither of which, incidentally, would have been constructed had the owners not been forced to honor contracts signed *before* the 1929 crash), suffered in the 1930s the consequences of the previous decade's boundless optimism. Both remained largely empty for years. The Empire State Building was referred to disparagingly as "The Empty State Building" and Rockefeller Center, scarcely a year after it had opened in 1933, became the butt of innumerable jokes. It was even sued by a local realtor for demoralizing the neighborhood's mid-town property market![9] Today, the wealth of artistic talent represented in the complex, on both its interior and exterior, makes the thought of its initial reverses incredible.

As the skyscraper tottered, so too did the fortunes of its Modernist decoration. Momentum slowed throughout the 1930s and architectural ornamentation slipped from favor, viewed as an unwanted extravagance in a new age of austerity. Except for Rockefeller Center, as noted, nothing as lavish as the Chrysler Building in New York or the Guaranty Building in Detroit was even contemplated. In architecture, Art Deco's moment at center stage had passed, though French-inspired ornamentation continued to find its way on to American buildings even into the 1940s. Its later application, however, was perfunctory and uninspired. As the most recent decorative style to have been applied to architecture, it was selected by force of habit for factories, store fronts, and the marquees on movie theaters. A more sympathetic hearing for the apostles of rationality sprang up in its place, which, in turn, ushered in the 1930s streamlined aesthetic in architecture. The early French Art Deco style, however, had in its moment of glory provided America with the legacy of rich architectural ornamentation shown in this book.

The early French Art Deco style had appealed to the emotions; its late 1920s Modernist successor appealed to the intellect. If the geometric angularities of the previous five years had only hinted at the machine's impending emergence, now it had arrived. The traditional artist-designers of Paris, such as Emile Jacques Ruhlmann, Jules Leleu, and Süe et Mare, faced a new and contradictory brand of Modernism after 1925, one which advocated functionalism, mass production, and new materials appropriate to the new age; in short, France's first authentic twentieth-century style.

It was this second phase of the French Art Deco movement which in the late 1920s helped to establish the Modernist decorative arts in the United States. This time, however, France's role was not that of pioneer. Long before the sharply functional furnishings of the French vanguard architect Pierre Chareau were first seen in 1928 at the New York department stores,[10] northern European immigrants such as Bruno Paul and Lucian Bernhard, from Germany, and Joseph Urban, Paul Frankl, and Wolfgang and Pola Hoffmann, from Austria, had been working hard to promote the same ideology in their adopted country. The arrival of the later French examples simply reinforced the foundations already laid.

Other immigrants, both in the 1920s and earlier, included, from Germany, Peter Müller-Munk, Walter von Nessen, and Wilhelm Hunt Diederich; from Hungary, Ilonka and Mariska Karasz; from Poland, Elie Nadelman; from Russia, William Zorach, Boris Lovet-Lorski, and Alexander Archipenko; from Denmark, Erik Magnussen; from Sweden, Carl Milles; from Finland, Eliel Saarinen; and from France, Jules Bouy, Gaston Lachaise, and Robert Laurent. Their reasons for selecting the United States were diverse: they included an escape from economic hardship and political oppression, and the chance of a fresh beginning in the New World.

For the immigrant artist-designer joining ranks with the handful of aspiring local Modernists, progress was uneven, not only because, in many instances, he or she was a new disciple to Modernism's cause (and had not, therefore, developed a consistent style or body of work with which to promote him or herself), but also because of the country's deep-rooted conservatism and corresponding resistance to change. The critic Helen Appleton Read traced the issue in a 1927 article,

The modern movement has taken a stronger hold in Europe than here, owing to the fact that the Europeans have been willing to experiment. Europeans were not so sure as we were that the decorative arts were dead and buried and that the best anyone could get, if he could not afford originals, were expert copies of the antique. It is curious that the inquiring American mind should have developed this rapid spirit of antiquarianism and so remained insensible and even hostile to the new spirit of design.[11]

The reasons why Modernism met with initial resistance in America remain complex.[12] The country was enjoying unprecedented prosperity in the 1920s due to its advanced technology and aggressive brand of marketing, which brought the most recent innovations of science to the householder far more quickly than in any other part of the world. The citizen only slightly better off than average became the proud owner of a host of ultramodern home appliances, including a piano or automatic piano player ($500) a radio ($150), a talking machine ($50), and, towards 1930, the replacement of his icebox with a $200 refrigerator from General Electric. His greatest possession by far, however, was his automobile, which like everything else, was paid for by installments.[13] If all these objects, in addition to the airplane in which he flew, and the tall building in which he worked, were so unequivocally new, both in their design and appearance, why did he cling so tenaciously to the past in his choice of home furnishings? This paradox was examined in 1925 by the critic Richardson Wright.

We live in an age of motor cars, radio and air transportation, and yet we are satisfied to have houses that were created to suit ages when none of these improvements were dreamed of. We listen to radio in a Louis XVI living room, drive our motors up to early Italian villas and land our airplanes in gardens that might have been laid out by Le Nôtre. Why not chuck the whole bundle of ancient sticks and create styles of our own, styles suitable to the age in which we live?[14]

Wright, who had recently returned from the 1925 Exposition Internationale, where, like so many of his compatriots, he had been outraged by "the most serious and sustained exhibition of bad taste the world has ever seen,"[15] felt that

Left

Waid & Corbett (architects) perspective of the proposed 80-story Metropolitan Life Insurance Company, North Building, 1 Madison Avenue, New York, c. 1930 (photo the Metropolitan Life Insurance Company)

America's disinclination to bring Modernism into the home was readily explained by the country's youthfulness.

People kick over the traces when they become surfeited. In England and on the Continent artists and craftsmen are surfeited with the past and with tradition. They have had to live with them so long. Consequently they are inclined to throw tradition out the window. We, on the other hand, are too young a people to be surfeited. We are so young that we are the most conservative nation on the face of the globe. We cling to what little traditions we possess. One of these days we may become so bored with early American furniture that we'll do something desperate, but that day is still far off.[16]

Wright's reasoning, common to the period, seems simplistic today. Part of the reason for Modernism's initial poor showing was the harried and fractured manner in which it was presented to the buying public. Another factor was that much Modernist design was of inferior quality. Also overlooked, in large part, was the fact that many of the people attracted to the new idiom could not bear the cost of throwing out their Louis XV and XVI reproductions to start afresh. Later sociologists saw this apparent rejection of Modernist home furnishings as stemming from the country's need to keep one foot firmly in the past, part of its insecurity about where it was going, and why. Some traced the cause of this 1920s anxiety to man's realization, following the 1914-18 War, that there would never again be a localized conflict, that man had signaled his own universal destruction by his mastery of science and technology. None of the theories which were postulated could, however, fully explain the incongruity of 1920s skyscrapers filled, floor by floor, with eighteenth-century-style desks and chairs.

In the decorative arts, the Modernist, too eager in his attempt to be in the vanguard of the movement's growth in America, faced an early barrage of criticism, much of it warranted. Mary Fenton Roberts noted, in what was far from an isolated rebuke,

Modernistic art came like a parade, waving banners, shouting, laughing somewhat hysterically; at first ignoring the past, filling the present, snatching at the future. It *would* stand alone, there must be no links anywhere; take it or leave it, was the motto. And the result was that people were bewildered or antagonized, feeling their beautiful background of the past blotted out, and with nothing to look forward to but furniture and decoration that seemed determined to leave them without physical comfort or peace of mind.[17]

Throughout all the early controversy, Richard R. Bach, who had organized the 1926 traveling Museum exhibition of items from the 1925 Exposition Internationale, played the role of Modernism's protector, rushing into print whenever necessary to explain the inexperience and youthful excesses of his protégé. In 1928, for example, pointing out the disparity of quality evident in the exhibits by local and foreign entrants at the Macy's International Exhibition of Art in Industry, he wrote, "To compare the American and the foreign rooms is, we hope, forbidden, for this is something we should not like to do; one cannot compare a youth of sixteen with a man of forty-five."[18] A year later, during the Industrial Arts exhibition at the Metropolitan Museum of Art, he again defended the new movement:

If the new style now taking shape wherever we look can be proved reasonable, we need not be troubled because its voice is cracked, its color pitched too high, its apperception a

Above

Peter Müller-Munk 3-piece tea service, silver, c. 1929. Illustrated in *Creative Art*, Vol. 5, 1929, p. 711

bit vague. These are the marks of adolescence which may be just as reasonable as they are raucous; modulation comes with maturity and this style of today is but a quarter-century old.[19]

Related to Modernism's uneven progress was the fact that its application within the different disciplines of the decorative arts also varied. The sparkling new designs which were introduced in the fields of silver, sculpture, ceramics, and textiles, for example, often matched those by the premier Europeans of the time. In furniture, however, models were frequently too garish or gimmicky; in glass, they were mostly nondescript; and in jewelry, in large part non-existent. The reasons for this discrepancy depended on the amount of resistance that the Modernist faced from the traditionalist in his field – both manufacturer and consumer – and on the extent of his own creativity. The early models produced by the Modernist furniture designers were seen to be in such bad taste that they fortified the position of the period-revival manufacturer. In silver, conversely, the Modernist designer, either because he understood better the conservative nature of his market, or because he was less adventuresome, created models which did not offend the conservative taste of his clientele. For a while, at least until the American critics and public had learned to distinguish between good and bad design, the apologists of Modernism took refuge behind the statement that modern art lent itself very well to some disciplines, but not at all to others.

Unlike his French and German counterparts, the American artist-designer had no Beaux-Arts tradition to fall back on. Until the late 1920s, when American Modernist designers had to band together to promote their works through the American Designers' Gallery, AUDAC, and Contempora, there were no annual exhibitions to match the Paris Salon, the German Werkbund, or the Austrian Hagenbund. Had it not been for the ground-breaking efforts of individuals such as John Cotton Dana, Director-Founder of the Newark Museum, as early as 1910, to promote progressive European design through traveling museum shows, and the later Industrial Art Exhibitions at the Metropolitan Museum of Art in New York, Modernism in the USA would have existed in a vacuum until the 1926 traveling Museum exhibition of items from the 1925 Exposition Internationale. Even the American department stores, which could have learned from the large Parisian *maisons* – Au Printemps, Le Louvre, Au Bon Marché, and Les Galeries Lafayette – how to establish themselves as arbiters of taste by controlling their manufacturers and thereby their products, vacillated until they were thrown into the Modernist arena with everybody else in 1927 and 1928. Most stores showed their disdain for the aspiring local Modernist designer by manufacturing a range of inexpensive copies of the European masterpieces which they had shown in their inaugural exhibitions (a form of plagiarism which so outraged the Europeans that they refused to participate in future American shows), rather than to pursue an alternative national style.

Government and private financial support, so vital to the establishment and growth of European design schools such as the Bauhaus and the Wiener Werkstätte, was likewise absent in the United States until the New Deal Public Works of Art programmes were implemented, beginning in 1933. In short, the pioneer Modernist designer in America found himself in a bind; nobody expressed interest in sponsoring his cause until it had established itself, but it could not establish itself without such sponsorship.

Also, unlike his 1920s Parisian counterpart who could draw on the private patronage of contemporary art collectors such as Jacques Doucet, Jeanne Lanvin, and Coco Chanel for both work and income, the American Modernist designer's struggle for acceptance was piecemeal and hard-fought. In sculpture particularly, the road ahead was blocked by the arch-conservative National Sculpture Society, whose sanction largely determined the allocation of all commissions for public or corporate statuary. The meager press coverage of the initial one-man shows of John Storrs and William Zorach (one an abstract sculptor, the other a rebel against the medium's traditional materials), appear now to have been conspiratorial.

Of the few American patrons of Modernist design, almost all pursued their interest in Europe rather than at home. In 1927, for example, Templeton Crocker of the California banking family retained Jean-Michel Frank in Paris to assemble a team of that city's top designers to furnish his San Francisco duplex penthouse in the modern idiom rather than sponsor local designers.[20] Frank won a similar commission from Nelson Rockefeller shortly thereafter, just before Donald Deskey's designs for Radio City Music Hall and S. L. "Roxy" Rothafel's apartment above it brought to the country's attention the quality of contemporary design available right at home.

Another prosperous New York collector, George Blumenthal, had earlier ignored local talent when he commissioned Armand-Albert Rateau, a French decorator, to furnish his Park Avenue townhouse and indoor swimming pool. Only one collector, Glendon Allvine, appears to have had the temerity to patronize members of the vanguard New York Modernist movement. Allvine visited Europe in 1927, and was introduced to the architecture of Le Corbusier, Gropius, and Mallet-Stevens. Two years later he retained the California architect, Warren Shephard Matthews, to apply the same Modernist principles to the house which he planned to build in Long Beach, Long Island.[21] This, on its completion in 1929, was hailed in the press as "America's First Modernistic Home East of the Rockies."[22] Newspapers gave the completed project generous coverage, one critic noting that "automobiles drive down the street with occupants striving to accustom their vision to this new and strange composition of cement situated on the edge of the Atlantic Ocean," (Le Corbusier's earlier avant-garde house at Auteuil, near Paris, had evoked similar comments in the French press.) For furnishings to complement the stark architectural boldness of his house, Allvine searched out participants at the American Designers' Gallery, including Donald Deskey, Paul Frankl, Walter von Nessen, and Ruth Reeves.[23]

Changing social mores in the 1920s precipitated a range of new products in the field of home appliances. Related to this was the new status of the American woman, who lost a measure of her old-fashioned femininity both in the manner in which she dressed and in the way she decorated her house. Interiors lost their previous softness. The new look allowed for a practical no-frills lifestyle, in keeping with the fact that domestic help was less easily available and the houseowner herself often had to do the housework. Allied to this was the fact that more people

Above

Boris Lovet-Lorski group in Belgian black marble, 17 in. (43.2 cm) high, inscribed BORIS LOVET-LORSKI, c. 1928 (private collection)

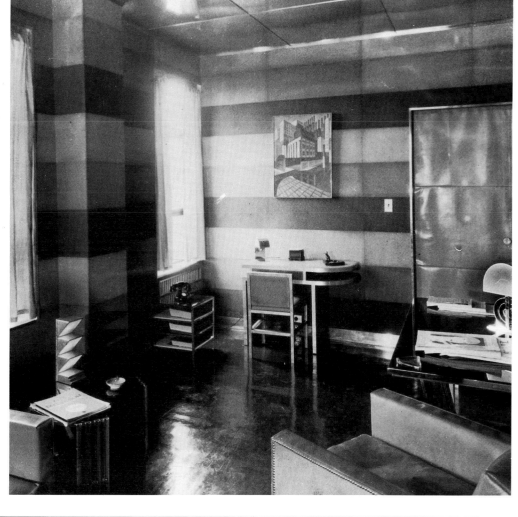

Right

Donald Deskey apartment for Mr. and Mrs. Adam
Gimbel, New York, c. 1929

Below

Donald Deskey furniture for the lobby of Radio City
Music Hall; carpet by Ruth Reeves, sculpture by
William Zorach, c. 1931

began to stay in the city during the week, living in small apartments which required space-saving, multipurpose furnishings. Product designers responded with a range of easy-to-clean diningroom/kitchen and bedroom/livingroom modular units. Home entertainment was adjusted accordingly, the informal cocktail party came into vogue, replacing the traditional luncheon, tea dance, and formal dinner party (all requiring lots of room and domestic help). A range of drink-related furnishings – bar stools, cocktail tables and shakers, etc. – came on to the market even during Prohibition, which had the unexpected effect of glamorizing drinking, rather than the reverse. The chic young woman now joined her consort in smoking openly to show her urbane sophistication. The market responded with a series of stylish smoking accessories – ashstands, bar lighters, and the like. These in turn drew the attention of the emerging industrial designer, who responded with durable materials that were proof against untended cigarettes and spilled alcohol. Donald Deskey traced his initial choice of plastic for furniture design to this need: "I used plastics for the first time as a table top in a room I designed for a private client, and chose that material because of its resistance to cigarette burns and because it was the only suitable material that could withstand the alcoholic concoctions of that era."[24]

Designers of these accessories for the urban home soon drew on the city's premier image, the skyscraper, as an appropriate design concept, the terraced form providing the inspiration for a host of home furnishings and appliances until 1930. But the Depression put an end to skyscraper imagery, with its capitalist connotations which seemed inappropriate to the new age.

A fresh image was needed to stimulate both industry and the buying public. The "streamline" shape, symbolizing forward movement, industrial progress, and hope for economic revival, became the accepted form for a wide range of products.

In general, decoration was pared down as the drive to reduce production costs accelerated. Handcrafting, already on the decline, had now become altogether too expensive. Simplicity and standardization were the keynotes of the new Modernism. American designers concentrated on the production of machine-made articles in quantity, at reasonable prices, which would still satisfy a high aesthetic standard. An old adage was recalled: "It is what is left out that makes a work of art." The machine, for so long a silent partner in all this, was venerated in the exhibition "Machine Art" at the Museum of Modern Art in 1934. The public came in droves to reconsider the aesthetic value of such mundane items as ball bearings, kitchen sinks, plate warmers and carpet sweepers.

Since 1980, a dozen or so Art Deco societies have sprung up in the United States to focus the public's attention on its rich 1920s heritage.[25] Some of these, such as the New York and Chicago chapters, are well established, generating newsletters, symposia, and walking tours for the enthusiast. Others are just beginning. This concentration on the Art Deco era, and particularly on its architecture, has helped local preservation leagues in their battle to protect endangered buildings and, in the case of South Miami Beach, entire districts. Local preservationists and landmark commissions (where they exist) are now working more effectively to

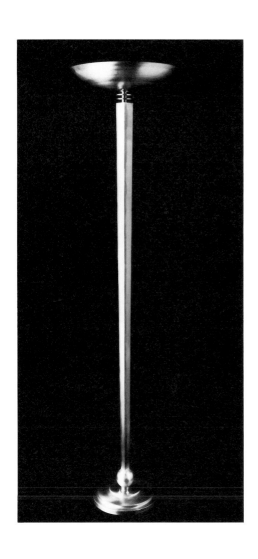

slow the previous rate of attrition, not only on the scale of Radio City Music Hall, which was threatened with demolition in the late 1970s, but on other, smaller, period classics such as neighborhood diners, gas stations, and theaters. Once a building is designated, it is completely protected from demolition or unapproved alterations to its exterior or interior public spaces. Another safeguard is for a building to be placed on the National Register of Historic Places. This, though it does not in itself guarantee survival (especially for structures less than fifty years old), provides a potential property developer with attractive preservation tax incentives not to make changes.

A poignant reminder of the present revival in the popularity of Art Deco is given by Donald McCormick, who designed the Mid-Continent Petroleum gas station in Sapulpa, Oklahoma, around 1928/29. In recounting his choice of modern design and materials for the commission, McCormick, now retired, noted in a recent telephone conversation that he had completed the project over a weekend, and thought no more about it.[26] Only its growing celebrity in the last few years has forced him to accept the hard reality that he is now associated in the public's mind more with this gas station than with *all* his other works spanning forty years as a respected Tulsa architect!

Left

Archibald Taylor torchère in silvered metal, copper, and bronze, 1938-39 (collection Denis Gallion and Daniel Morris)

Right

Lee Lawrie, in collaboration with Leon V. Solon (colorist) three limestone figures, "Light," "Wisdom," and "Sound," main entrance, RCA Building, Rockefeller Center (photo Wurts Bros. Archives, Museum of the City of New York)

☰ EXHIBITIONS ☰

T he Modernist movement in America emerged directly from the 1925 Exposition Internationale des Arts Décoratifs et Industriels Modernes in Paris. The Exposition had been a long time coming; its conception is traceable to 1907 when the German Werkbund was established with a charter to further the interrelationship between architects, craftsmen, artists, and industry.[1] Design in France was at that time at a standstill, and the French authorities saw the need to stimulate local designers by pitting them against their German counterparts. In 1912 plans were made for an exposition to be staged in Paris three years later, but these plans were preempted by the advent of World War I. Germany's position in 1919 became more complicated; whereas its modern design movement was still dominant in Europe, it was now a conquered enemy nation, and chauvinist overtones were evident in France's attempt to resurrect the exposition. In 1922 the date was finally set for April-October 1925.

This was ostensibly and by name an international exhibition, but Germany's invitation came too late to allow her industrial designers and design schools, most notably the Bauhaus and the Werkbund, adequate time to prepare themselves. Thus the Germans – the original inspiration for the entire event – did not participate.

The United States was another to decline, for the reason (as given by the Secretary of Commerce Herbert Hoover) that American designers could not meet the entry requirements: "Works admitted to the Exposition must show new inspiration and real originality. They must be executed and presented by artisans, artists, manufacturers, who have created the models, and by editors, whose work belongs to modern decorative and industrial art. Reproductions, imitations, and counterfeits of ancient styles will be strictly prohibited."[2] Hoover did, however, see the necessity for the American manufacturing industry to keep abreast of European developments, and appointed a committee to visit and report on the Exposition, naming Professor Charles R. Richards, Director of the American Association of Museums, to head a delegation of 108 representatives from the costume, textile, jewelry, silver, lighting, furniture, wallpaper, glass, ceramics, graphic arts, and construction industries.[3]

Comment, official and private, flowed back to the United States as the delegates worked their way through the fifty-five acres on which the Exposition was

Right

75th Anniversary exhibition, Marshall Field & Co., Chicago, 1927 bedroom ensemble manufactured by the American Furniture Novelty Company. Illustrated in *Good Furniture Magazine*, December 1927, p. 86

assembled in the heart of the French capital. Stretching from the Champs-Elysées on the Right Bank across the Alexandre III bridge to the Hôtel des Invalides on the Left, the exhibition resembled a glittering fairyland or, as one critic wrote, a giant Coney Island.[4] The orgy of colors and shapes of one's first glance soon yielded, however, to the realization that beneath the colorful veneer lay less than one had expected. According to the same critic,

The Exposition des Arts Décoratifs at Paris, it is commonly agreed, is not the outstanding success it was thought it would be. It is tremendously spectacular, it is massive in acreage, it is all that, but it isn't moving designers, interior designers, architects, or manufacturers to cast off the shackles of classic tradition and put on the *habillements* of what for a more exact term we call modern art. No one, so far as we have heard, who has visited the exposition has been proselyted to the belief that what is old is totally out of date and bad, and what is new is good – because it is new.[5]

Among American commentators the consensus was overwhelmingly negative, except for the single dissenting opinion of Charles Richards. Censure was aimed at both the buildings and the decorative arts which they housed. The architecture represented, in sum, a conglomeration of ill-proportioned rectangles and triangles traced, ironically, against the silhouettes of the Louvre, Tuileries, and Invalides "which, like silent disapproving ghosts, stood in the distance."[6]

The buildings, at least, would soon be gone, the world of good taste salvaged by the demolition crew which descended on the site at the Exposition's closure. No such radical remedy, however, occurred to the critics concerning the modern decorative arts which they had seen, and their warnings, in this respect, were therefore more strident. Reminding its readers that "to be different is not necessarily to be fine . . .," an editorial in *The American Magazine of Art* dismissed the majority of the objects at the Exposition as "clumsy, gross, ugly, violating in many instances those principles to which design for ages has conformed – grace of line, balance, color harmony, orderly arrangement, rhythm, repetition. The reaction apparently sought is shock, the effect that of naive barbarity. . . . Insincerity is almost always transparent, and art which does not ring true will never endure."[7] The real danger was that the new mode would somehow penetrate France's borders to arrive unchecked on America's shores: "What a pity if, because France dictates it, we must discard our fine old Colonial and accept instead chairs which would seem to have been cut from barrels, sideboards that resemble Pullman buffets, china that would seem to have been decorated by accident. And why should we? Art is not only a factor in but the measure of civilization."

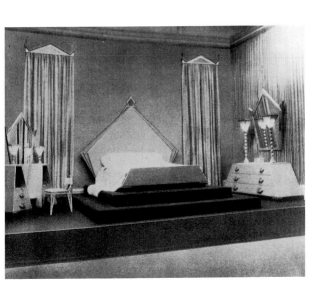

Even more alarmed was Ellow H. Hostache, who wrote of "this bastard offspring of anaemic artisanship and efficient salesmanship . . . the dictatorship of ornament."[8] He concluded: "The entire Exposition might be described as a futile gesture – if not a hopelessly lost opportunity for helpful accomplishment."

It was left to Charles Richards to provide a better sense of perspective and moderation. Dismissing the Exposition's gaudiest buildings and objects as opportunistic, he stressed the participation of many of France's foremost architects and designers in the Modernist movement, while reminding his audience that Americans were still artistically immature and dependent for their culture on Europe's leadership.[9]

Today it seems that Richards and the Exposition's detractors were not so far apart as they might have thought. Richards was encouraged by the best that he had seen, the others depressed and outraged by the worst. Both sides agreed that the Exposition's conditions of entry – that no design could show *any* traditional influence – placed an unrealistic limitation on the exhibitors, almost forcing them towards the abnormal and impractical.[10]

Sixty years later the harshness of the American reviews is astonishing. For one thing, the Exposition's most readily identifiable ornamental excesses – stylized flowers, zigzags, and angular sunbursts – found their way on to, and into, countless American buildings within five years, the very buildings which provided the USA with its architectural supremacy in that period. For another, it is hard to comprehend the press's antagonism as one identifies in contemporary illustrations so many of the items which are today considered by American museum curators and collectors to be masterpieces of twentieth-century design.

One of Richards' responsibilities as Director of the American Association of Museums was the selection of items from the Exposition for inclusion in a traveling exhibition to visit museums in the USA the following year. This would allow the American public, including the manufacturers and designers who had been unable to go to Paris, to judge the modern movement for themselves. Four hundred examples in every category of the industrial decorative arts were chosen, nearly all lent directly by the artists themselves.

The 1926 traveling loan exhibition was not the first on modern European decorative arts to take place in the USA. A few unrelated shows had been staged earlier, most notably that of Joseph Urban's work at the Wiener Werkstätte in America Gallery in New York in 1922.[11] At the Newark Museum, largely under the energetic stewardship of John Cotton Dana, there had been a series of shows on the modern movement since 1912, including two on modern German applied arts (1912 and 1922), textiles (1914), and, in 1926, a mini-show of the 1925 Exposition.[12] In autumn 1925, F. Schumacher and Co. in New York took the lead with its installation of a room in the modern French taste furnished by Dubocq, Brandt, Lalique, and Follot.[13]

Professor Richards' 1926 traveling loan exhibition opened its eight-city tour in Boston, before continuing to New York. Anticipating public distaste, Joseph Breck, Assistant Director of Decorative Arts at the Metropolitan Museum of Art, begged patience from his readers in the Museum Bulletin:

For the past twenty-five years and more a new style in decoration has been developing in Europe. It has thrown overboard the copy and the pastiche which the topsy-turvy nineteenth century in the throes of industrialism substituted for original creation. It strives to embody old principles in new forms of beauty, and to meet new conditions of living with frankness and understanding. The "historic styles" were not created overnight, and, doubtless, considerable time must elapse before this "modern style" takes definite shape.[14]

Today, as one scans the list of participants in the Exhibition catalogue, it is interesting to note that roughly half of them have slipped into oblivion, casualties, no doubt, of the public distaste to which Breck referred.[15]

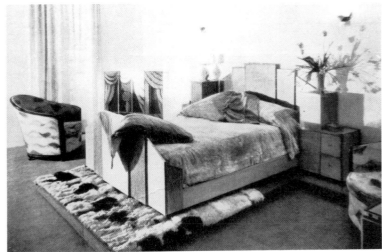

Above, left

"A selected collection of objects from the International Exposition of Modern Decorative and Industrial Art," The Metropolitan Museum of Art, New York, 1926 view of the main gallery, showing works by French designers, including Edgar Brandt, Jean Dunand, and Georges Hoentschel (photo The Metropolitan Museum of Art)

Above, right

"Exposition of Modern French Decorative Art," Lord & Taylor, New York, 1928 one of five rooms designed by Lord & Taylor's department of modern decoration. Illustrated in *House and Garden*, May 1928, p. 9

The 1926 exhibition at the Metropolitan sparked off a race among the American department stores to introduce the new aesthetic to the marketplace. No fewer than thirty-six exhibitions were staged in cities throughout the country within as many months (see Appendix), some limited to a single ensemble, others to an entire floor. As in Europe, the retailer capitalized on the museum's leadership. Shipments of prime European Modernist furnishings by the period's most prestigious designers – Ruhlmann, Leleu, Chareau, Hoffmann, Puiforcat, etc. – were sped across the Atlantic as the rush for the consumer market intensified. Notable among the few Americans to purchase furniture directly from Parisian sources at the time was Templeton Crocker, of the California banking family, who in 1927 commissioned Jean Michel Frank to furnish his duplex penthouse in San Francisco.

For the department store, the new vogue provided a much-needed break in the cycle of "period" styles which rotated from year to year. Even though the public's initial response to the new style was ambivalent, its potential was too great to be ignored. The haphazard manner in which art moderne furnishings flooded the American market alarmed several of the Modernists themselves. Kem Weber, for example, cried out against the lack of control and comprehension in the way one installation was put together, "half-baked, untrained, adaptation with shallow superficial surface appearance."[16] Few Americans were as discerning as Weber, however, and the stampede continued.

It was in 1928 that the European Modernist movement reached full bloom in the USA. In that same year the battle lines were firmly drawn, on the one hand, between the department stores and the museums and, on the other, between the stores themselves, in the race to dominate the new fashion. In twelve short months, a profusion of exhibitions were staged by retailers nationwide. Of these, two bear special mention: Lord & Taylor and R. H. Macy's, both in New York City.

At Lord & Taylor responsibility for the "Exposition of Modern French Decorative Art" fell on the capable shoulders of Dorothy Shaver, Director of Fashion and Decoration.[17] The commercial risks inherent in the show, soon forgotten in the blaze of publicity afforded its opening in February 1928, were later recalled in the firm's correspondence: "Lord & Taylor in 1928 gambled $100,000 on importing a collection of modern French furniture and art (including some of the first Picassos,

Derains, Braques, and Utrillos exhibited in this country). Presented with the flourish of a Theater Guild premiere – red carpets on the sidewalk, blazing floodlights – it was a sensation – and the effect of the exhibition was electric."[18] Displayed alongside those of the French were five Modernist rooms designed and manufactured entirely by the firm's own staff.

The Macy's exhibition, organized by Virginia Hamill and Lee Simonson, comprised fifteen rooms similarly furnished by both foreign and domestic artist-designers. Five hundred works by 300-odd entrants from six nations were included. Strangely, this vast venture, accompanied by a comprehensive catalogue,[19] was given only two weeks – May 14-26 – in the store's calendar. Josef Hoffmann summarized the exhibition's goal in his introduction to the Austrian section in the catalogue:

The modern man of culture, with his up-to-date attire, with his motor cars, railways, airplanes, is a living proof of the fact that the power of creative art has not gone from our time. Just as it would be ridiculous to walk down Fifth Avenue in an antique suit of armor, be it ever so fine, it is ridiculous to tolerate all these used-up, out-of-place copies of old styles on our buildings, furniture, and all the little things we use. It is our duty to break with the habit.[20]

The first exhibition of the American Designers' Gallery was held in the Chase Bank Building at 145 West 57th Street, New York, in the autumn of 1928.[21] Unlike the mixed reviews which accompanied the majority of the exhibitions listed in the Appendix, press sentiment was now united in its praise – in large part, it seems, because this was billed as the first *all*-American exhibition. Certainly all the exhibitors had been actively involved in some way in the Modernist movement in the USA, but suddenly it was perceived as cohesive and mature. As one critic wrote, "I at once had a feeling that the new movement had struck its pace. It had quieted down a little, was no longer shaking a frenzied mane or foaming at the mouth. Here I found men and women gathered together who had something to say, who were not administering stinging reproofs to the past or sneering at lovers of ancient beauty."[22]

The exhibition consisted of ten complete interiors with additional displays of "accessories." Thirty-six designers and artists participated, including the Gallery's fifteen full members: Biddle, Deskey, Wolfgang Hoffmann, Hood, Reiss, Ryther, Herman Rosse, Kahn, Karasz, Locher, Poor, Reeves, Simonson, Urban, and Walker.[23] Others, whose entries drew praise, included Archipenko, Heaton, Esherik, Frankl, Kantack, Müller-Munk, and Steichen. Following its opening in New York, the exhibition traveled to department stores in ten cities, and a further two shows were added in early 1929 by the artists, buoyed by the broad response to their "noble" experiment.[24]

The American Designers' Gallery's second, and final, exhibition was staged in 1929. Most of the thirty-eight exhibitors had participated the previous year. The new emphasis, outlined in the introduction to the show's catalogue, was on "affordable" and "livable" furniture.[25]

The critics now apparently appeased, if not won over, by the first exhibition, the next target was the buying public. For them the American Designers' Gallery displayed six rooms at prices ranging from $700 to $1,200, many furnished,

Above

American Designers' Gallery, New York, 1928 entrance hall ensemble by Robert Locher; maple, metal, and glass. Illustrated in *Good Furniture Magazine,* January 1929, p. 43; and *The American Architect,* December 5, 1928, p. 753

appropriately, in inexpensive synthetic materials such as Fabrikoid and rayon.[26] Gone was Urban's tantalizing black "Repose" bedroom and Rosse's lacquered Monel metal dining-room of the inaugural show; in their place were furnishings for general distribution through retail outlets.[27]

The Metropolitan Museum of Art contributed further to the concept of All-Americanism with its 1929 exhibition, "The Architect and the Industrial Arts."[28] A subtle new emphasis was introduced, one which aligned the architect of the twentieth-century building with its interior. The modern architect, familiar with the period's new materials and style, would lead where others did not. Robert W. deForest, President of the Metropolitan, was unequivocal in his criticism of the principal offender – the American furniture manufacturer – whose creations, in form and color, were "an affront to man and God."[29]

Rooms were shown by a hierarchy of American architects: Hood, Kahn, Saarinen, Schoen, Solon, Walker, Fitzhugh, Root, and Urban.[30] Special attention was paid to the effective use of new materials, such as rubber, aluminum, Fabrikoid, Vitrolite, and rayon, in a dozen model *ensembles* ranging from an apartment house loggia (Hood) to a backyard garden (Kahn).[31] The exhibition was heralded as a major advance, the Museum's neutrality providing the most suitable forum for an objective analysis of modern industrial art and its alliance with the householder's needs. In all, the talents of 150 individual craftsmen and firms were brought to bear by the nine participating architects.

Only one dissenting voice seems to have been raised, that of Douglas Haskell, who wrote,

One expected to find that these architects, who among them have built some of our finest skyscrapers, had designed or chosen tables, chairs, desks, bath-tubs, closets, walls, floors, windows, and whatnot, of a kind that could be industrially fabricated, and had arranged them in rooms so excellent and compelling that manufacturers would have been given an entirely new sense of what to produce for the current market . . . [but] the architects here have failed in imagination. Instead of envisioning the idea, *Industrial Art, 1929*, they have simply followed the other groups of interior decorators and the department stores in arranging one more set of fashionable modern rooms. Is this because the architects are so much professional men, and their clients all from Park Avenue? Very well: Bow down, bow down, before the upper middle classes – and pray that the good strokes in design may eventually filter through to the rest.[32]

History, it must be noted, has largely proved Mr. Haskell wrong. It is the "Park Avenue set" who finance the experiments that make mass production an ultimate economic reality.

The American Union of Decorative Arts and Craftsmen (AUDAC) passed like a meteor through twentieth-century American design, shining fiercely for two short years before abruptly disappearing. Its inaugural show at the Grand Central Palace, New York, in March 1930, contained only six furnished rooms by as many designers;[33] a year later its second, and final, exhibition at the Brooklyn Museum incorporated the works of 90 of the 114 active members listed in the modest accompanying catalogue.[34] The onset of the Depression delayed an intended third annual show, after which it was more or less permanently shelved. AUDAC did, however, leave an indelible mark on the design philosophy of the period, forcing its members, through their participation in the Brooklyn show, to focus on

Below

Joseph Urban conservatory, exhibition of "The Architect and the Industrial Arts," The Metropolitan Museum of Art, New York, 1929. Illustrated in *Good Furniture Magazine*, March 1929, p. 119; *The American Architect*, March 5, 1929, p. 318; *Design*, Vol. 31, 1929/30, p. 115; and *The American Magazine of Art*, Vol. 20, 1929, p. 206 (photo Butler Library, Columbia University)

Left

John Wellborn Root sketch of a woman's bedroom, exhibition of "The Architect and the Industrial Arts," The Metropolitan Museum of Art, New York, 1929 (photo the Chicago Historical Society)

Left

John Wellborn Root woman's bedroom, exhibition of "The Architect and the Industrial Arts," The Metropolitan Museum of Art, New York, 1929. Illustrated in *The American Magazine of Art*, Vol. 20, 1929, pp. 207-8; and *Good Furniture Magazine*, March 1929, p. 120 (photo The Metropolitan Museum of Art)

Left

Raymond M. Hood, in collaboration with Harry V.K. Henderson (design) business executive's office, aluminum furniture, exhibition of "The Architect and the Industrial Arts," The Metropolitan Museum of Art, New York, 1929. Illustrated in *Good Furniture Magazine*, March 1929, p. 125; *The American Architect*, March 5, 1929, p. 319; *Metalcraft*, March 1929, p. 135; and *The American Magazine of Art*, Vol. 20, 1929, p. 211

Right

"The Architect and the Industrial Arts," *The
Metropolitan Museum of Art, New York, 1929* formal
portrait of 8 of the 9 participants (John Wellborn Root
missing); *standing:* Raymond M. Hood, Eugene
Schoen, and Ely Jacques Kahn; *seated:* Ralph T.
Walker, Armistead Fitzhugh, Eliel Saarinen, Leon V.
Solon, and Joseph Urban (photo The Metropolitan
Museum of Art)

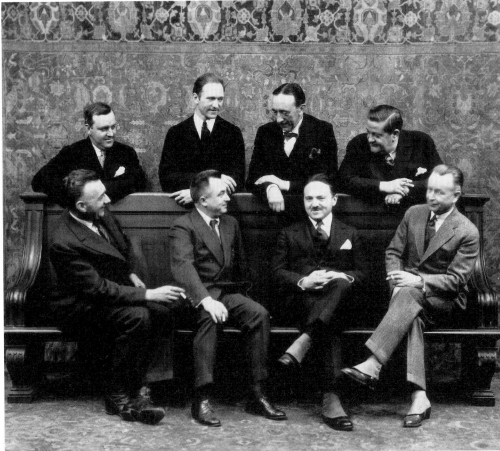

Right

"The Architect and the Industrial Arts," *The
Metropolitan Museum of Art, New York, 1929* informal
photograph of 8 of the 9 participants (John Wellborn
Root missing); *standing:* Ralph T. Walker, Armistead
Fitzhugh, Leon V. Solon, and Joseph Urban; *seated:*
Eugene Schoen, Raymond M. Hood, Ely Jacques
Kahn, and Eliel Saarinen (photo Butler Library,
Columbia University)

the union of industry and art in a manner not otherwise available. In addition, Lee Simonson, AUDAC's president,[35] pressed continually for a distinct national style (rather than pseudo-European styles), further sharpening the focus for many of the immigrant designers in the group who were searching for a new direction.

The 1931 Brooklyn Museum exhibition represented the pinnacle of industrial design in the period under discussion. Included was the work of a stellar group of artist-designers: Weber, Von Nessen, Winold and Henriette Reiss, Russel Wright, Frankl, Reeves, Deskey, Loebel, Pola and Wolfgang Hoffmann, Ilonka Karasz, Saarinen, Schoen, Urban, and many others of comparable talent.[36] The critic Donald McGregor provided an even-handed assessment: "The entire exhibit gives one plenty of food for thought. We cannot dismiss all contemporary effort and original use of materials and individual design with a shrug of the shoulders and a muttered word 'Modern'."[37]

The name of Contempora, which was formed in 1929, was chosen to identify its members as furniture and interior designers in the "modern" manner. Under the directorship of Paul Lester Wiener were several noted contemporary artists and designers: Bruno Paul, Lucian Bernhard, Rockwell Kent, and Paul Poiret (full members) and Vally Wieselthier, Joseph Sinel, and Julius Klinger (associated artists).[38] Like AUDAC a year later, Contempora became a short-lived association of prominent artists. Unlike AUDAC, however, which fell victim to the stock market crash, Contempora appears to have contributed to its own demise, not through lack of talent – its members were prodigiously talented – but by its arcane charter.

Contempora staged its first (and last) exhibition at the Art Center, New York, in June 1929.[39] The accompanying catalogue defined the group's principal philosophy, which was that the sum of the whole (the interior) is more important than its individual parts. To illustrate this point, seven "harmonized rooms" by Paul, Bernhard, Kent, and Poiret were displayed, variation in each made possible by the selection of any one of six harmonized color schemes.[40] The critics, predictably, railed against this specter of standardization, even regimentation.[41] Also questioned was the exhibition's imposition of "foreign" interior design on the American home. (Of the group of designers represented, only Kent and Sinel were strictly American.) And what justification was there for entire rooms composed by Kent (an artist) and Klinger (a poster designer)? In short, the project as a whole seemed rather rushed and jumbled, less successful than its individual parts. Only one exhibit received universal acclaim: thirty renderings and photographs of Erich Mendelsohn's most recent streamlined architecture – a guest exhibit.[42]

Infrequent articles on Contempora's completed commissions – for example, a residence for Mrs. Alma Wertheim in Washington Mews, New York City, and the Contempora offices themselves[43] – appeared in the decorative art reviews until 1933, after which the artists pursued their individual careers.

By 1930 the department stores' commitment to the new style was spent; after four years it was simply no longer newsworthy. The momentum reverted to the museum, in particular the Metropolitan Museum of Art, which continued in the early 1930s to stage exhibitions of contemporary design. Now, however, the emphasis shifted increasingly from the "decorative" to the "industrial" or

Below

Paul Poiret woman's bedroom, furniture in two shades of Fabrikoid, walls in two tones of mauve, "Exposition of Art and Industry," Contempora, New York, 1929. Illustrated in *Good Furniture Magazine*, August 1929, p. 72

"machine" arts.[44] Joining in this mission was the newly founded Museum of Modern Art.

The Museum of Modern Art held two exhibitions organized by Philip Johnson in 1933 and 1934 which focused sharply on modern industrial design. The first, and smaller, compared the 1900 design idiom with that of 1933. The Art Nouveau organisms of Louis Comfort Tiffany and Hector Guimard were juxtaposed with the unornamented, sleek functionalism of the moment. Certainly no clearer measure of the distance covered by the Industrial Revolution could have been attempted in pitting the avant-garde aesthetic of one era against that of another.

It was the 1934 exhibition, however, which aroused the public's interest. Entitled "Machine Art," its goal was to "end the divorce between industry and culture."[45] The show's machine-made exhibits were divided into six categories: industrial units, household and office equipment, kitchenware, house furnishings and accessories, scientific instruments, laboratory glass and porcelain. Despite the mundane subject matter, the exhibition surprised viewers with the quality of design and the technical precision evident in the works of the participating American engineers and technologists. New York in 1934 was at the midpoint of the first flowering of the American industrial design movement, and the exhibition showed clearly the gains already made. Although a self-aligning ball bearing or outboard propeller could not touch an emotional chord, they did draw respect for their purity and functionalism.

Another exhibition on Art and the Machine was held in April 1934 by the National Alliance of Art and Industry, Inc., on the 62nd floor of Rockefeller Center.[46] Entitled "The Industrial Arts Exposition," the show included a selection of consumer items similar to that at the Museum of Modern Art by industrial designers such as Deskey, Dreyfuss, Van Doren, Loewy, Wright, Sakier, and Jensen.

The exhibition of Contemporary American Industrial Art at the Metropolitan Museum of Art in 1934 allowed some sharp comparisons with the by now celebrated 1929 Contemporary Design Exhibition held in the same rooms. That it comprised a similar giant team effort between industry, architects, and manufacturers was in itself an achievement if one considers the difficulties of coordinating the works and temperaments of more than 200 participants. Of specific interest, however, was the visible effect of the precipitous collapse of the American economy which had occurred in the interim. The 1929 show was conceived and staged before the Wall Street crash; the 1934 event took place five years into the subsequent period of austerity.

A contemporary critic recalled the mood of the earlier show.

There was money to burn. We had, according to our great thinkers, reversed for all time the previous history of economics and had discovered that there could be no end to prosperity. All the schemes therefore were based on that glittering assumption. Everyone was going to have even more money next year than last. Rooms that would not have disgraced the home of the most ostentatious of millionaires were offered as the proper thing for the humblest citizen. The keynote was gorgeousness.

In 1934 the story is different. We have been through five years of depression and the whole system is now geared to a rigid economy. Misguided observers might suppose that the design of the architect and his allied industrial designer would suffer thereby. The contrary is the case. The dictates of economy required that the designer get down to some sort of reality and offer things that are within the reach of the most limited budget.

As a result, the visitor to the Metropolitan Museum today will see things that he can not only pay for but can take to his heart and learn to love. Gone is the self-consciously clever design of five years ago . . .[47]

The 1934 exhibition consisted of three main galleries, each divided into rooms which housed the works of an astonishing 237 exhibitors. The terms of entry were precise: no item could have been exhibited previously, and all items had to have been designed for "quantity manufacture," in other words, mass production. Many of the items were therefore designed expressly for the exhibition, a fact that contributed greatly to the freshness and, therefore, success which the show enjoyed.[48]

Left

Gilbert Rohde corner of a music room, Exhibition of Contemporary American Industrial Art, The Metropolitan Museum of Art, New York, 1934, including piano by Steinway & Sons; table and chair by Warren McArthur; rug by Nelson S. Fink of V'Soske Shops; and floor lamp by Mutual Sunset Lamp Mfg. Company. Illustrated in *The Architectural Forum*, December 1934, p. 417

I t is a common misconception that American Modernist furniture took its inspiration from France. Those searching for lavish sharkskin or Macassar ebony veneers trimmed with ivory will look in vain. The original source was Germany, a fact later obscured by the attention showered on France at the 1925 Exposition Internationale.[1]

The movement towards Modernism made rapid progress in Germany from the turn of the century, a key factor being the formation of a chain of technical schools (*Kunstgewerbeschüle*) which sprang up all over the country following the foundation by the Duke of Hesse of a craft colony in Darmstadt in 1900. In 1908 the *Deutsche Werkbund* was established to foster a closer working relationship between artist and manufacturer. It applied its resources to the creation of artistic objects for the average home appropriate to modern usage, a project that gave further stimulation to *Kunstgewerbeschüle*. A complete break from *Jugendstil* and the historic styles, the latter identified especially by the Hohenzollern heaviness which had cast its blight on German taste for a full generation, led to the earliest attempts at a modern decorative style. The straight line became, for the first time, a source of beauty.

In 1910, Munich artisans participated at the Salon d'Automne in Paris. From all accounts, including those of the French, the Munich display was the most cohesive of the entire exhibition, showing a new consistency of spirit and a new sense of unity and order. Only M. Verneuil, the editor of *Art et Décoration*, took exception, his point of view being that the dissimilarity of the two nations made it unlikely that the Munich work would ever be acceptable to the French. Yet examination of the periodical *Dekorative Kunst* between 1910 and 1914 shows that precedence in modern decorative arts clearly belonged to the Germans. One interior by Bruno Paul in 1911, for example, was distinctly in the modern manner, and even compares favorably with interiors designed twenty years later. The buildings and exhibition halls designed by Gropius, Lossow, Kuhne and the Belgian Van de Velde in 1914 for the Deutsche Werkbund Exhibition in Cologne showed again, in comparison with those presented by the French at the Exposition Internationale eleven years later, how far ahead the Germans were.

The formation of the Bauhaus by Walter Gropius in 1919 consolidated earlier German developments towards a twentieth-century style. The School exerted an enormous influence far beyond Germany even after it moved from Weimar, in 1925, to Dessau. Several of its leading lights, including Gropius and his assistant director, László Moholy-Nagy, found their way later to the United States,[2] where the Bauhaus doctrine was embraced enthusiastically. Two other Germans exerted an influence on the American furniture designer in the late 1920s. Lucian Bernhard, an architect, decorator, and furniture designer, organized the 1929 Contempora exhibition in New York,[3] in addition to acting as a publicist for the new movement.[4] His compatriot, Bruno Paul, the Director of the State Schools of Fine and Applied Arts in Germany, achieved acclaim at the exhibition mounted by R. H. Macy's in 1928. His wood dining room was judged thoroughly modern, not only in form, but for its introduction of contrasting color combinations.[5] At the same time, appreciation for the earlier metal furniture prototypes of Marcel Breuer and Mies van der Rohe was growing in the United States, as elsewhere.[6]

In France, the modern furniture movement — that identified today as "Art Deco" — proved in reality to be an extension of the very style which it had set out to eradicate, Art Nouveau. Whereas the tortuous sinuosities of Guimard's buffets had disappeared, the preoccupation with ornamentation persisted, only now carefully harnessed within the Modernist's creed that an object's function must determine its form. The French Art Deco movement would have reached full bloom by 1920 if World War I had not intervened. Ruhlmann, for example, designed some of his most celebrated "Art Deco" creations as early as 1916. Other classic Art Deco designs by Iribe, Follot, and Mère also predate the outbreak of war.

As it was, the style lingered on until the 1925 Exposition Internationale, which formed a fitting capstone to a brief, but glowing, chapter in the history of world furniture. By 1927 the Parisian Art Deco ébénistes — Ruhlmann, Leleu, Süe et Mare, and Joubert et Petit — were scrambling for survival against a new generation of furniture designers, spearheaded by architects such as Mallet-Stevens, Perriand, Lurcat, Moreau, Chareau, and Le Bourgeois, who in varying degrees espoused Le Corbusier's spartan philosophies concerning the function of a twentieth-century home. It was to this new Parisian group, which was consolidated in 1930 under the banner of the Union des Artistes Modernes (U.A.M.), that the American furniture designers looked for inspiration in the late 1920s, not to the outmoded cabinetmakers in the same city. Given a choice between the Baroque of Ruhlmann and the Neoclassical purism of Mallet-Stevens, the American public opted unhesitatingly for the latter.[7]

The French Art Deco wood furniture movement of the 1920-25 era had remained unknown in America, and when it was first seen in the 1926 traveling museum exhibition of items from the 1925 Exposition, and then again in 1927 and 1928 at the department stores, it was viewed as alien, a Gallic eccentricity unsuited to local taste. One suite of furniture, made by Lord & Taylor as an inexpensive alternative to the costly French original, met with justifiable censure from one critic:

By practically copying Ruhlmann, as was the case in a bedroom group recently shown, we are doing positive harm. Not only was this set lacking in the intrinsic charm of the original, but by doing this we are discouraging the initiative and creative talents of our

Below

Robert Winthrop Chanler 2-panel screen; painted canvas, 60 x 77in. (152.4 x 195.6cm), 1920-25. A selection of other Chanler screens are illustrated in *House & Garden*, June 1922, p. 66 (photo Christie's, New York)

American furniture designers. While this type of furniture may be very good for France, it is alien to our shores, and has no relation to our life. Why not then let our art express our time, which is distinct, unique and different from all that has gone before?[8]

What was there, within the framework of America's own earlier furniture, from which the Modernist could draw inspiration? In effect, nothing beyond the simplicity of the Colonial Style. The 1920s American householder lived with a pastiche of earlier styles, both European (especially English: Jacobean, Sheraton, Chippendale, Adam, etc.) and American (Colonial, Duncan Phyfe, the Victorian Gothic and Rococo revival styles, Eastlake, Mission). Reproduction credenzas, buffets, escritoires, and tester beds vied for the public's eye and pocketbook.

Even Tiffany Studios got into the act, exhibiting a sixteenth-century-style Hispano-Moresque room at the 1926 Art-in-Trades Club of New York Show at the Waldorf-Astoria Hotel. Alongside was a Louis XIV drawing-room by F.A. Belmont, of Philadelphia. Both were cordially reviewed by contemporary critics. Another critic did, however, show mild consternation that modern copies of eighteenth-century English dining chairs, designed originally to accommodate hoopskirts, remained unchanged despite the fact that ladies' fashions had radically changed. Paul Frankl was another who denounced the decorators that perpetuated this traditionalism:

If these same decorators saw a woman in crinolines trying to cross Fifth Avenue they would turn to one another and say: "She can't wear such clothes nowadays. There isn't space nor time for her balloonish outfit." But these same observers think nothing of placing a Louis Seize chair, a massive Tudor chest or carved and gilded Medici bed in a modern American home – pieces of furniture that no more belong in our present day environment than the beplumed, corseted and crinolined lady in traffic-glutted Fifth Avenue.[9]

Frankl was the first to try to remedy the situation, his skyscraper bookcases establishing him both as America's pioneer Modernist and as the first furniture designer to align himself with contemporary architecture. Inspired by the setback contours of the buildings which soared above his New York gallery, Frankl explained in 1927 the space-saving concept behind the new form.

In my own creations for the modern American home, I have kept within the architectural spirit of our time. The straight line is the most important feature. They call my chests of drawers, my dressing tables, my bookcases, "Skyscraper" – to which I blushingly bow. Why not skyscraper furniture? After all, space is as much at a premium within the home as it is outside of it. Why have a bookcase take up half your floor in squat, rigid formality when your bookcase can rise toward the ceiling in vertical, pyramidic beauty with an inviting informality that should go with books people actually read.[10]

Made of California redwood, usually with red or black lacquered trim and interiors in turquoise blue or green, Frankl's skyscraper furniture is viewed today as a forceful and novel expression of late 1920s urban taste.[11] Curiously, for works which received wide international attention, if not acclaim, at the time, the cabinetry of these pieces is invariably poor, the doors and drawers sloppily fitted.

Two other furniture designers adopted the skyscraper form, Kem Weber and J.B. Peters,[12] both from Los Angeles. Within four years, however, the concept was viewed as spurious, even by Frankl himself, who in 1932 abruptly reversed his

Below

Warren McArthur table, chromium-plated metal and glass, 31 in. (78.7 cm) high, 1930s (collection Denis Gallion and Daniel Morris)

earlier philosophy, "The skyscraper, considered America's outstanding contribution to the present day civilization, is but a passing fad. The tallest of them, the Empire State, is but the tombstone on the grave of the era that built it . . . . Skyscrapers are monuments to the greedy."[13] Frankl's skyscraper designs had, however, addressed a major issue confronting the interior decorator in the late 1920s — the shortage of urban living space. As Charles Richards explained in 1929,

A large fraction of us live in cities where room becomes more and more at a premium. This has made the apartment house our typical living arrangement, with the constant tendency to smaller and fewer rooms. Furthermore, household service, because of higher wages and changed social attitudes, becomes increasingly difficult to afford. All these things require that we have fewer and smaller pieces of furniture. We no longer have space for the *chaise longue* or for couches. We must put up with fewer great chairs or tables. What furniture we have must function effectively.[14]

The working population's switch in lifestyle from suburban houses to city tenements led to a revolution in furniture design. Confined living spaces required drastic new solutions. For a start, rooms had to be combined: bedroom-livingroom, diningroom-kitchen, etc. Furniture also had to become multipurpose: sofas transformed at nightfall into beds, center tables became desks, their pedestal feet designed to house filing cabinets and bookshelves. Gilbert Rohde, more than any other designer, applied himself to this issue, incorporating radios into side tables and bookshelves into the sides and backs of settees. His 1929 "Rotorette" table was especially successful, its drum form enclosing a revolving four-part celarette: one for books, two for glass stemware, and one for bottles. When the drum was in a locked position, only the bookshelves were visible; unlocked, the interior revolved to allow its owner to toast a speedy end to Prohibition.[15] Kem Weber also concentrated on the problems of confined living. His display in the 1928 R.H. Macy's exhibition consisted of a lounge-bedroom with 2-in-1 furniture. Another scheme, for one-room women's apartments by Wolfgang and Pola Hoffmann, included a combination desk, dressing table, and bookcase unit.[16]

The issue of space quickly drew the American architect's attention, bringing him squarely into conflict with the interior designer and furniture maker. The architect's solution was to eliminate various types of furniture entirely. For example, built-in closets would remove the need for wardrobes and chests of drawers, and recessed mural bookshelves would replace bookcases; this applied also to other traditional pieces of furniture. The designers and manufacturers of furniture awoke to the realization that their professions faced obsolescence if they did not respond positively, and in short order.

Another issue addressed by the architect was the "servant problem," judged by some social observers at the time as a challenge to the very fiber of civilization itself. In his effort to help the modern housewife, the architect removed furniture moldings and wall cornices — both "dust-catchers" requiring periodic cleaning — from his designs for interiors.

A modern style of architecture was seen to call for modern furnishings, and it was this that let the architect into the interiors of the buildings he designed. Official

Below

W.J. Campbell "Climax" cocktail smoker; chromium-plated metal, manufactured by the Climax Machinery Company, Indianapolis, 26¼in. (66.7cm) high, 1934. Henry Dreyfuss incorporated a similar model in the cocktail lounges on his locomotive, The Twentieth Century Limited (collection Denis Gallion and Daniel Morris)

Left

Paul Theodore Frankl pair of bookcases; "skyscraper" design, California redwood with nickel-plated steel trim, 90in. (228.6cm) high, late 1920s. Illustrated in *New Dimensions*, Paul T. Frankl, Payson & Clarke, New York, 1928, p. 22; and *The Arts*, March 1928, p. 154. A similar model is illustrated in *Art et Décoration*, Janvier 1928, p. 54 (collection The Cincinnati Art Museum, gift of the Estate of Mrs. James M. Hutton II, 1969.417-418)

Below, left

Paul Theodore Frankl pair of chest-of-drawers; "skyscraper" design, wood with ebonized trim and green lacquer interiors, 77in. (195.6cm) high (collection John P. Axelrod)

Below, right

Paul Theodore Frankl bookcase; "skyscraper" design, ebonized wood with red lacquer trim, 27½in. (69.8cm) high. Illustrated in *New Dimensions*, Paul T. Frankl, Payson & Clarke, New York, 1928, p. 36. Similar models are illustrated in *House & Garden*, February 1928, p. 60; and *The American Architect*, February 5, 1928, p. 183 (collection The Cincinnati Art Museum, gift of the Estate of Mrs. James M. Hutton II, 169.409)

Right

Paul Theodore Frankl desk; red lacquer with silver leaf drawers and silvered handles, 33in. (83.8cm) high, c. 1927. The model is known as a "puzzle" desk due to the asymetrical placement of the drawers and the concealed seat. Similar models are illustrated in *House & Garden*, February 1927, p. 140; *Vogue*, March 15, 1927, p. 84; and *New Dimensions*, Paul T. Frankl, Payson & Clarke, New York, 1928, #33, unpaginated (collection Mitchell Wolfson, Jr., Miami-Dade Community College)

Below, left

Paul Theodore Frankl man's cabinet; red and black lacquered wood with gold- and silver-plated metal discs, silver leaf trim at the top, gold trim at the foot, mahogany interior, c. 1930. Illustrated in *House & Garden*, April 1930, p. 83 (collection Michael and Wendy Lubin)

Below, right

Paul Theodore Frankl dressing table bench; lacquer on wood, 23½in. (59.7cm) high. Illustrated in *Good Furniture Magazine*, September 1927, p. 119 (collection Mr. & Mrs. Goodman)

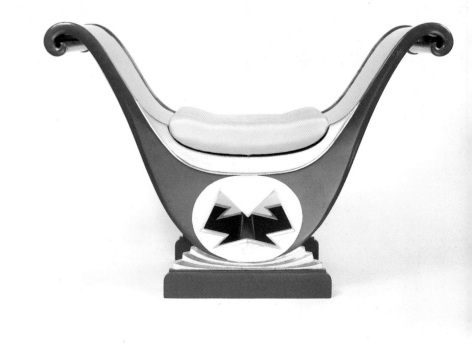

sanction was granted by the Metropolitan Museum of Art with its 1929 exhibition, "The Architect and the Industrial Arts." Included were nine prominent architects, both vintage (Urban, Hood, Saarinen) and of the moment (Kahn), all with the brief to design a modern interior setting comprised of standardized *metal* units.[17] The designer and manufacturer, after years of full participation in the Museum's Industrial Art exhibitions, were suddenly banished, if not entirely (in the case of the designer), then to a footnote in the show's accompanying catalogue. The critics applauded this development. As Helen Appleton Read noted in *Vogue*,

Because any genuine and vital contemporary decoration is inevitably related to contemporary living conditions, which, in physical demonstration, means architecture, it was attacking the problem from the right angle to ask architects, rather than decorators and *ensembliers*, to design the interiors and their accessories. The problems of contemporary decoration are basically and indissolubly bound up with architecture, as, also, it must not be forgotten, they are bound up with mass production. Hence the significance of the title of this year's exhibition, "The Architect and the Industrial Arts," in its suggestion that only through the partnership of the architect and the industrial arts can a genuine twentieth-century style be developed.[18]

Others were even more insistent that the architect was the only one who could integrate successfully the modern building and its interior. According to an article in *The American Architect*, "It will be far more satisfactory for all if the development of a modern style is left solely in the hands of the architect. After all, the designs in which manufacturers produce their products are dependent on architecture. The designers employed by manufacturers must get inspiration from the architects."[19]

By 1930 the architect was enjoying his newly enhanced status as an "*interior* architect." Many responded enthusiastically to this extension of their traditional profession. Some, such as Lescaze and Root, limited themselves to the interiors of their own buildings; others, including Schoen, Reiss, and Rosse, expanded into the realm of the interior decorator and created successful prototypes that went into mass production.

The 1929 exhibition at the Metropolitan Museum brought legitimacy to the cause of metal in the public's mind. The endorsement of the nation's most prestigious art institution, and that of a selection of America's most famous architects, could not easily be discounted. A substantial number of metal furnishings had been displayed the previous year by both AUDAC and the American Designers' Gallery, in addition to department stores across the country. These, however, had been largely understood to represent the *future*. The Metropolitan Museum's exhibition brought it all that much closer.

The American designers' early inability to make metal furniture attractive manifested itself in attempts to make it look like something else. A popular ploy was to cover it with paint grained in imitation of wood. Alternatively, the metal frame was entirely concealed by the upholstery. By the mid-1920s three practical difficulties still had to be eliminated: metal furniture, in the manner of Napoleonic brass and iron beds, was too heavy for everyday use; it was generally uncomfortable; and its sharp edges caused cut skin and torn clothes.[20]

Only when designers began to comprehend that their designs for metal furnishings were to be manufactured by machine, rather than by hand, was proper attention paid to the correct, i.e., non-wood, form. The designers had to learn to be true to the nature of metal as they had previously been to that of wood. It had its own distinct aesthetic "in true harmony with a swiftly moving world, which seeks to rid itself of non-essentials and has no time for the useless frippery of life."[21]

When metal finally became respectable in the USA, a full five years after it had established itself in Europe, its acceptance was relatively quick and pervasive. The absence of any other contemporary wood furniture style – such as that of Ruhlmann, Leleu, and Follot in France – facilitated its introduction into the American home for those who had tired of standard reproduction "period" furniture.

In 1930, Paul Frankl promoted the cause of metal in a book called *Form and Re-Form*.

Its advantages over wood are tremendous. Metal is not only stronger, but also more pliant than wood. Metal furniture is not subject to warping or cracking; is fire-resistant; and, if properly dimensioned, no heavier than the same piece executed in wood. Aluminum pieces are much lighter. The future success of modern furniture depends entirely upon the ability of the designer to cope with this new material. Metal furniture has been condemned by our critics as being cold, impersonal, inhuman. If this criticism were just, I would join them in banishing it forever from the American home. As a matter of fact, metal is among the most malleable of media.[22]

In the same year, an editorial in *Retailing* magazine – one of the furniture industry's unofficial mouthpieces – chronicled metal's ascendancy:

If historians and sociologists of the future who have taken seriously the custom of categorizing stages of civilization by denominations such as the "ice age" or the "stone age" will seek an appropriate title for the current period they will very likely determine upon "the age of metal." And they would very largely be true, particularly as regards architecture and its auxiliary, home furnishings. The increasing importance of metal home furnishings is now beyond dispute . . . metal bedroom furnishings are on the upswing in various quarters already.[23]

Despite metal's onslaught, wood continued to retain adherents, as it does today. Its innate beauty and warmth could not be matched either by chromium or by aluminum, or by the synthetic materials which began to reach the market in the late 1920s – Formica, Bakelite, Micarta, etc. A fresh batch of highly grained exotic veneers helped to draw the eye in a way that a tubular metal chair frame could not. Paradoxically, it was the same cry of functionalism which had ushered in metal that helped the proponents of wood. The large surface areas on Modernist furniture – rectangular chair backs and sides, for example – showed off the natural grain far better than did period-style furniture, cluttered as it was with carved moldings and/or floral marquetry decoration. If a subtle design accent was sought, this could be achieved by borders of contrasting wood veneers or inlaid metal bands. Popular American woods were harewood, birch, white holly, maple, and walnut, the last two often burled. Imported were such French favorites as palisander and zebrawood.[24]

Who were the leaders of the Modernist furniture movement in America? The

Left

Pittsburgh Plate Glass Company armchair; glass, metal, and upholstered cushion, unsigned, 29¼in. (74.2cm) high (collection Carnegie Institute, DuPuy Fund)

Opposite, above left

Eugene Schoen bench; tiger maple with ivory trim, upholstered by Paul Rodier in a cotton and rayon brocade, manufactured by Schmieg, Hungate & Kotzian, 1926 (collection John Loring)

Opposite, above right

Raymond M. Hood table; black glass, steel, wrought iron, brass, and brass-plated steel, 29⅞in. (75.9cm) high, designed for the Rex Cole showrooms, Brooklyn, c. 1931. Illustrated in *Raymond M. Hood*, Arthur Tappan North, New York, 1931, p. 101; and *Raymond M. Hood*, Robert A. M. Stern, Rizzoli, New York, 1982, p. 64, #5 (collection Alan Moss, Ltd.)

Opposite, below left

Elsie de Wolfe side chair; Lucite, wood, and upholstery, 33⅝in. (85.4cm) high, c. 1939. Illustrated in *Mackintosh to Mollino, Fifty Years of Chair Design*, exhibition catalogue, Barry Friedman Ltd., New York, 1984, p. 52 (collection Barry Friedman, Ltd.)

Opposite, below right

Abel Faidy settee, "skyscraper" design, for the Charles and Ruth Singleton penthouse, 1244 Stone Street, Chicago, 1927. Illustrated in *Chicago Furniture Art, Craft and Industry 1833-1983*, Sharon Darling, W. W. Norton, New York, 1984, color plate section, p. 194 ff. (photo The Chicago Historical Society)

Above, right

Eliel Saarinen pair of side chairs manufactured by the Company of Mastercraftsmen; fir with black ocher paint, red horsehair upholstery, 37⅜in. (94.9cm) high, 1929-30. Illustrated in *Design in America: The Cranbrook Vision 1925-1950*, exhibition catalogue, The Detroit Institute of Arts and The Metropolitan Museum of Art, Harry N. Abrams, New York, 1983, p. 90 (collection The Cranbrook Academy of Art/Museum, photo The Detroit Institute of Arts)

Right

Eliel Saarinen pair of armchairs and table designed for the Saarinen house, Cranbrook, manufactured by Tor Berglund; greenhart, African walnut, rosewood, and maple veneers with silk and linen upholstery, 30¾in. (78.1cm) height of chairs, 26in. (66cm) height of table. Illustrated in *Design in America: The Cranbrook Vision 1925-1950*, exhibition catalogue, The Detroit Institute of Arts and The Metropolitan Museum of Art, Harry N. Abrams, New York, 1983, p. 95 (collection The Cranbrook Academy of Art/Museum, photo The Detroit Institute of Arts)

Below, right

Ely Jacques Kahn and Eliel Saarinen sketch of a chair for the Richard Hudnut shop, 693 5th Avenue, New York; crayon on paper. Interior views of the shop are illustrated in *Interior Architecture and Decoration*, June 1931, pp. 137-8; and *The Architectural Forum*, October 1931, pp. 420-1 (photo Avery Library, Columbia University)

Below, far right

Ely Jacques Kahn and Eliel Saarinen sketch of a chair for the Richard Hudnut shop, 693 5th Avenue, New York; colored crayon on paper, 1930 (photo Avery Library, Columbia University)

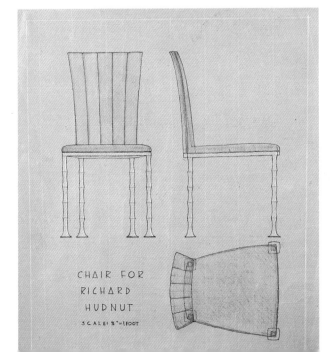

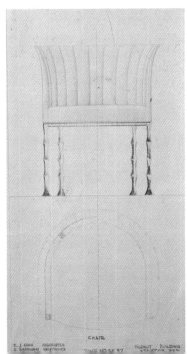

CHAIR FOR
RICHARD
HUDNUT
SCALE 3"=1 FOOT

twenty-seven discussed below were in the vanguard, yet many other designers participated, their works then, as now, anonymous. The large furniture manufacturers, in particular, kept the names of their individual design staff a secret. Today this anonymity complicates the already difficult task of identifying both the designer and the manufacturer (often separate) of American Modernist furniture.

It is appropriate that the survey start with a designer who was born in America. As will become quickly evident, very few were.

Donald Deskey was one of the giants of the industrial design movement in the USA. Both his design skills and his vision were prodigious, despite – or perhaps because of – his early maverick years. Born in 1894 in Blue Earth, Minnesota, Deskey's formal education included a degree in architecture from the University of California at Berkeley, and painting instruction at the Art Students League of New York City and the Art Institute of Chicago. Yet a 1938 profile in *The New Yorker* chronicled a restless and peripatetic lifestyle, which began when he graduated from high school in 1912, taking any number of menial and office jobs along the way. It almost appears that his final choice of career was accidental. "The mystery is that this particular man should ever have designed anything at all, for until he was nearly thirty, Deskey's connection with art was either that of an amateur or of an advertising man, and the future he looked forward to was that of a sound and energetic American man of business."[25]

Two trips to France helped Deskey to narrow his focus on interior design. He enrolled at the Ecole de la Grande Chaumière in Paris, and in 1925 visited the Exposition Internationale, an event which triggered his decision to return to the USA:

1926 was a propitious year for a decorative artist and industrial designer aware of ideas current in Europe and full of enthusiasm to return to America. Joseph Urban and Paul Frankl had shown their designs; commerce was going in for art; and a boom time was coming. Deskey's first success was with screens; Frankl ordered some from him; one appeared in the background of a window at Saks-Fifth Avenue; presently, Deskey designed for Franklin Simon the first complete modern windows, using corrugated and galvanized iron, copper, and brass. In 1927 he did the cork-and-metal windows at Saks, he designed an apartment, one room of which had cork walls, copper ceiling, linoleum floor, pigskin chairs, and metal trim; the living-room had walls of transite and aluminum; the hall was of stainless steel and vitrolite. These were the first rooms done entirely in metal and industrial materials in America; six years later, they are still being photographed as examples of modern design.[26]

In 1927 Deskey formed an association with Phillip Vollmer. The pair opened a studio, Deskey-Vollmer, Inc., at 114 E. 32nd Street, New York, which remained in operation until the early 1930s. Initial commissions were received from wealthy private clients, such as Adam Gimbel, President of Saks-Fifth Avenue; Helena Rubinstein; Abby Aldrich Rockefeller, for whom Deskey designed a modern print gallery and boudoir; and John D. Rockefeller, Jr.: a picture gallery, ceramic room, and print room. In the early 1930s, as the Depression began to bite, Deskey switched his attention to the large manufacturers, such as the Ypsilanti Furniture Company, designing a wide range of furniture, textiles, and rugs for mass production. The Donald Deskey archives at the Cooper-Hewitt Museum indicate that over 400 pieces of his furniture designs were put into production in the period 1930-34.

Deskey's "room for a man" at the 1928 American Designers' Gallery drew characteristic praise from a contemporary critic for its pioneering new materials, referred to above, "a beautiful room with . . . a metal table with vitrolite top, and curious, exceedingly interesting cork walls in shades of brown. The ceiling of aluminum and the little alcove recessed in brilliant tones."[27] Other materials incorporated by Deskey in his interiors showed his conversance with the most recent discoveries: Bakelite, Formica, Fabrikoid, parchment, chromium-plated brass, spun and brushed aluminum, and transite, an asbestos factory siding material which Deskey applied to movable partitions. Deskey's use, in 1931, of aluminum foil wallpapers for the men's smoking lounge on the second mezzanine in Radio City Music Hall showed his continuing preoccupation with modern materials for modern interiors. His selection of a material frequently determined its function in the general market place for years to come.

In 1930 Deskey gave renewed attention to a line of modern furniture for small rooms (and small incomes). One model, a black lacquered wood-and-glass sideboard with ground glass inserts for lighting, received such acclaim that he later adapted it for the sideboard in the apartment above Radio City Music Hall, completed in 1932 for "Mr. Roxy" himself (S.L. Rothafel). The apartment survives intact today as a masterpiece of the period, an indisputable monument to Deskey's talents.[28]

The 1938 New Yorker article included an interesting insight into how Deskey's designs were viewed some years later,

The distinction of Deskey's furniture is simple: the basic design is good (he does all the designing, including detail, himself); there are no excrescences; and the pieces are individually striking without being startling. I have seen people come into a room he has designed and, liking it, feel thoroughly at home, discovering after a quarter of an hour that the design is modern; I know people who have lived in rooms he has designed without ever tiring of the contours and colors. He has made mistakes both in design and in color; but this was to be expected in a new medium. Generally, he designs for a harmonious whole and not for shock, and chooses lively tints rather than bright colors.[29]

Today, Deskey's interiors are as fundamentally modern as they were at the time of their creation.

To *Paul Theodore Frankl* goes the honor of being America's first Modernist in the decorative arts. He was born in Vienna in October 1886 to a Hungarian father and an Austrian mother. After studying architecture at the Technische Hochschule in his native city for one year, he transferred to the engineering faculty at the University of Berlin. Military service interrupted his studies, and Frankl finally completed his diploma in architectural engineering in Berlin in 1911. A brief apprenticeship and stint in Copenhagen followed, before Frankl set off for the New World in 1914. His first commission, a beauty parlor in the Modernist idiom, was for a Mme. Titus, later known professionally as Helena Rubinstein.[30]

Listing himself as an architect, Frankl set up business in New York. In 1922 he

Opposite, left

Kem Weber side table for Mr. and Mrs. John Bissinger, San Francisco 1928-29; mirror, burl walnut, glass, silvered and painted wood, chromium-plated metal, maple, and cedar, with metal tag KEM WEBER, 75⅜in. (191.4cm) high, c. 1929. Illustrated in *At Home in Manhattan*, Yale University Art Gallery, exhibition catalogue, 1983, p. 72, #50 (collection George Waterman III)

Opposite, right

Kem Weber desk and chair for Mr. & Mrs. John Bissinger, San Francisco, 1928-29; bird's eye maple, sage gray-green lacquer and silver leaf drawer handles, the leather writing surface decorated with a painted silver abstract design. Illustrated in *Form and Re-Form*, Paul T. Frankl, Harper and Bros., New York, 1930; and *Creative Art*, Vol. 7, 1930, p. 251 (collection Denis Gallion and Daniel Morris)

Opposite, below

Frank Lloyd Wright desk and chair commissioned by Herbert Fisk Johnson for the S. C. Johnson & Son Administration Building, Racine, Wisconsin, executed by Steelcase, unsigned, enameled steel, walnut and brass-plated metal, 33½in. (85.1cm) high, c. 1937. Illustrated in *The Decorative Designs of Frank Lloyd Wright*, David Hanks, E. P. Dutton, New York, 1979, pp. 147, 149-51; and *A Century of Chair Design*, Frank Russell, Rizzoli, New York, 1980, p. 51 (photo Christie's, New York)

Right

Winold Reiss detail of table top; part of the furnishings commissioned for the Longchamps Restaurant, Broadway, New York; Formica inlaid with anodized aluminum, 1930s (collection Alan Moss, Ltd.)

Below

Ruth Reeves tubular steel day-bed executed by the Greenpoint Metal Bed Company and exhibited at the 1928 exhibition of the American Designers' Gallery, 74½in. (189.2cm) long. Illustrated in *New York Sun*, November 9, 1928; *The Metal Arts*, November 1928-December 1929, p. 82; *Good Furniture Magazine*, January 1929, p. 43; and *Arts and Decoration*, January 1930, p. 53 (collection the Richmond Museum of Fine Arts, gift of Sydney and Frances Lewis)

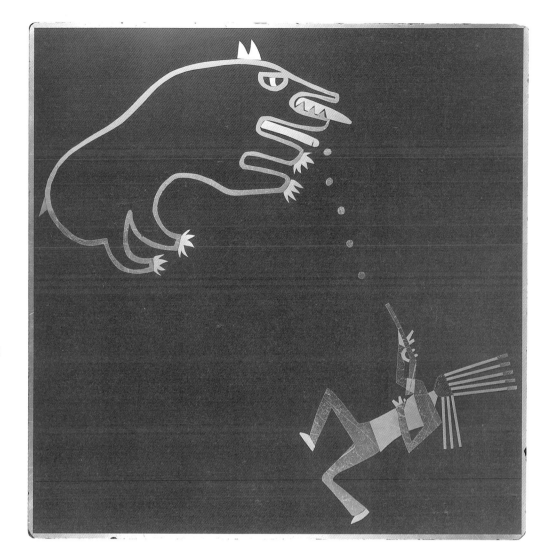

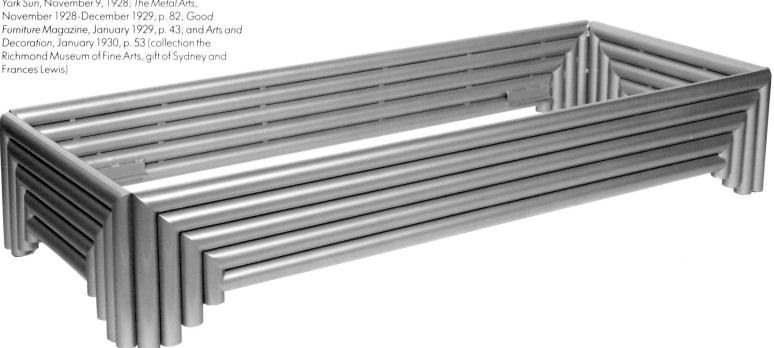

opened a gallery at 4 E. 48th Street, offering a mix of his own furniture and imported wallpaper and fabrics.

Frankl assumed the role of Modernism's most ardent crusader and publicist. Five works bear testament to his firm commitment across a broad front of the decorative arts: *New Dimensions, Form and Re-Form, Machine Age Leisure, Spaces for Living,* and *Survey of American Textiles.* Numerous magazine articles repeated the message, in addition to an absorbing unpublished auto-biography.[31] His writings were didactic: Modernism championed repeatedly against history's gilded atrocities.

Frankl designed a quiet blend of contemporary furnishings until the mid-1920s. It was only with the introduction of his skyscraper furniture, discussed earlier, in 1926/27, that he drew the attention of the international press.[32] His other furniture at the time, similarly in wood with bright lacquered accents and mirrored glass tops, vied for attention. His interior settings, entitled "The Livable House Trans-formed," at Abraham & Straus in Brooklyn in 1927, contributed greatly to the impetus of the department store exhibits in Manhattan the following year.[33] In-cluded in Brooklyn was Frankl's "puzzle" desk, in vibrant colors with a complex arrangement of silver-leaf drawers and pulls. It is regarded now as one of the most dynamic creations of the period.[34]

In the early 1930s Frankl turned to metal furnishings. His tubular chromed chairs and consoles, while meeting the strict standards of functionalism which he espoused, lacked the charm and individuality of his earlier wood pieces.

A native New Yorker, *Eugene Schoen* received a degree in architecture from Columbia University in 1901. Following a European tour, during which he visited Josef Hoffmann and Otto Wagner in Vienna, Schoen established his architectural practice in New York in 1905. Sympathetic to the Modernist movement long before it was popularized, he was inspired further by the Exposition Internationale in 1925 to set up his own interior decorating business at 115 E. 60th Street, New York, where he remained until the reversals of the Depression forced a move to 43 W. 39th Street.[35] His timing was fortunate: by the late 1920s, when Modernism made its initial forays into the American home, Schoen was perfectly placed to capitalize on its advances. He was even able to display complete room settings in

Below, left

Eugene Schoen settee/love seat manufactured by S. Karpen & Bros., 1929. Illustrated in *House Beautiful,* February 1929, p. 154; and *The Architectural Record,* April 1935, p. 228 (photo Alan Moss, Ltd.)

Below, center

Eugene Schoen woman's writing desk manufactured by Schmieg, Hungate, & Kotzian. Displayed in the "Art in Industry" 1928 exhibition at R. H. Macy's, New York. Illustrated in *The Arts,* June 1928, p. 376; and *Good Furniture Magazine,* September 1928, p. 129 (photo Alan Moss, Ltd.)

Below, right

Eugene Schoen armchair; maple and black lacquer or cherry stained black, manufactured by Schmieg, Hungate & Kotzian, 1930. Illustrated in *Form and Re-Form,* Paul T. Frankl, Harper & Bros., New York, 1930, p. 92; and *Decorative Art,* The Studio Yearbook, 1930, p. 148 (photo Alan Moss, Ltd.)

his gallery in 1928, when most of his colleagues were competing for space in department store exhibitions.[36]

Schoen's position in the American Modernist furniture movement is enigmatic. Comprehending fully the movement's philosophies concerning functionalism, the machine, and mass-production, he clung steadfastly, nevertheless, to the concept of "no duplication." As Nellie Sanford noted in 1928, "As each piece is individually made, and must differ from every other in some way, it may be seen that he has voluntarily restricted the scope of his work. Volume, and commercial furniture are evidently outside his present scheme of things. Restricting his work to the demands of those who must have unique pieces, necessarily eliminates him as a commercial factor and places him among the specialists."[37] Notwithstanding, Schoen managed a unique blend of the old and new. His designs and choice of veneers drew their inspiration directly from Europe, yet the combination produced a restraint and grace which American critics were quick to call their own.[38] "Schoen's development seems to be along the path of refinement," Sanford explained. "His taste in the use of woods, his ornamental details and suavity of lines, are impeccable, and his elegance is derived from the best of the modern French school. He is a little addicted to the use of lacquers, metals, or synthetic materials, but he is to my mind without a peer in our country in matching beautiful grains and rare veneers." No other adherent of the American modern school, working in the European aesthetic and with its materials, was permitted such latitude.

Schoen's furniture incorporates traces of both French and German influences. Much of his seat furniture rests on saber-shaped legs which have an undisguised *Directoire* inspiration; and some are unashamedly Ruhlmann. Others have the more austere line and understated decoration of the German and Austrian schools. One set of dining chairs, in particular, included tiered, fan-shaped backs derived directly from Biedermeier prototypes.[39] Meticulous attention was paid to the quality of the cabinetry, executed to his designs by both S. Karpen & Bros., and Schmieg, Hungate, & Kotzian. His preferred veneers included rosewood, Macassar ebony, Brazilian walnut, maple, cherry, and lemonwood, often with delicate silver trim.[40] Silk upholstery, both flowered and striped, lent refinement to his pieces.

A little-known Schoen commission was the RKO Center Theater in Rockefeller Center, which opened in 1933. Considerably smaller than its illustrious neighbor, the Radio City Music Hall, this theater incorporated a characteristic Schoen blend of warmth, vitality, and color harmony. The subdued ambience was preferred by many to the extravaganza in the next block.[41]

Born in Berlin in 1889, *Karl Emanuel Martin (Kem) Weber* was apprenticed in 1904 to Eduard Schultz, Potsdam's royal cabinetmaker. On obtaining his journeyman diploma, he studied under Bruno Paul, Director of the Kunstgewerbeschule in his native city from 1908 to 1910.[42] On going to San Francisco in 1914 to assist in the architectural work on the German pavilion at the Panama-Pacific Exposition, Weber was trapped when war was declared. Denied permission to return to Germany, he tried to earn a living as an interior designer. When this failed

Opposite, top left

Donald Deskey table; chromium-plated steel and Vitrolite, 15in. (38.1cm) high, c. 1928. A similar model, without the X-shaped stretchers, is illustrated in *House Beautiful*, February 1929, p. 153 (collection Geoffrey N. Bradfield)

Opposite, center left

Donald Deskey adjustable table; aluminium and Bakelite, 18in. (45.7cm) high, c. 1930 (collection Geoffrey N. Bradfield)

Opposite, top right

Donald Deskey 3-panel screen commissioned by Mr. and Mrs. Glendon Allvine for their home in Long Beach, Long Island, 1929, oil paint and metal leaf on canvas, signed *Deskey-Vollmer*, 77¾ x 60in. (197.5 x 152.4cm). Illustrated in *Creative Art*, October 1931, p. 323; and *The Folding Image*, exhibition catalogue, Yale Art Gallery and The National Gallery of Art, 1984, p. 245 (collection The Sydney and Frances Lewis Foundation, Richmond Museum of Art)

Opposite, below left

Donald Deskey lounge furniture. The armchair in aluminum manufactured by the Ypsilanti Reed Furniture Company, illustrated in *Good Furniture and Decoration*, February 1931, p.97 (collection John P. Axelrod)

Opposite, below right

Donald Deskey bedroom furniture; lacquer, aluminum and brushed chrome, c. 1929-30. The chest-of-drawers illustrated in *The American Architect*, November 1930, p. 40; the chair illustrated in *The American Architect*, November 1930, p. 41, and *House & Garden*, July 1929, p. 71; the table lamp illustrated in *House & Garden*, July 1929, p. 70 (collection Alan Moss, Ltd.)

Right, above

Donald Deskey man's smoking room exhibited at the American Designer's Gallery exhibition, New York, 1928; steel, pigskin, aluminum, and glass with cork walls. The furniture manufactured by S. Karpen & Bros. Illustrated in *House Beautiful*, February 1930, p. 165; *Arts and Decoration*, February 1929, p. 72; and *The American Architect*, December 5, 1928, p. 754, and November 1930, p. 41. The table lamp and ashstand are further illustrated in *House Beautiful*, February 1929, p. 153

Right

Donald Deskey group of furniture for Deskey-Vollmer, c. 1928

Far right

Donald Deskey seat and *torchère*; aluminum, Radio City Music Hall, Rockefeller Center, c.1933

(anti-German feelings were running high), he attempted a variety of jobs, such as lumberjacking, chicken farming and florist's assistant. After the Armistice he opened a studio in Santa Barbara, and three years later moved to Los Angeles, where he joined the design studio at Barker Bros. as a draftsman. Within a year he was promoted to Art Director. A European trip in 1925/26, during which he visited the Exposition Internationale, crystallized his determination to commit himself fully to modern design on his return. In 1927 he opened his own design studio in Hollywood, listing himself as an industrial designer. Within a year his career was fully launched.[43] He was one of only three Americans invited to participate in Macy's first International Exposition of Arts & Trades. His "6 rooms in 3" exhibit was an example of the continuing search for an answer to inner-city living.

Weber's contribution to the American Modernist movement was remarkable. His stated ambition was "to make the practical more beautiful and the beautiful more practical." To this end, he wrote numerous articles and lectured in his spare time.[44] Not only was he virtually the only decorative arts designer to raise the Modernist banner on the West Coast (although he considered as friends and kindred spirits the architects R.M. Schindler, Richard Neutra, and Frank Lloyd Wright), but his style was distinctly his own. Although his early designs showed a flamboyant, though informal, Parisian influence identified by contemporary critics as "zigzag moderne", Weber's work in the 1930s settled into a mature stream-lined style based on horizontal, rather than vertical, planes. He preferred wood to metal, using a mixture of maple, birch, and, later, plywood. These were often given a lacquered finish in sage-green (a favorite Weber color), yellow, orchid, rose, or blue-gray. Accents were in gold or silver leaf, or black.

In 1930 Weber introduced a concept for machine production that caused a great stir in the manufacturing industry, even threatening to revolutionize it. Announcing that until that moment he had never really created furniture, Weber introduced his *Bentlock* line to an astonished press.[45] The name evolved from his

Below, left
Kem Weber sketch of furniture for Barker Brothers, Los Angeles, c. 1926-27. Illustrated in *Kem Weber, the Moderne in Southern California 1920-41*, exhibition catalogue, University of California, Santa Barbara, 11 February-23 March 1969, p. 58, #16 (photo the University Art Museum, University of California, Santa Barbara)

Below, center
Kem Weber sketch of a public dining room for Barker Brothers, Los Angeles, c. 1926-27. Illustrated in *Kem Weber, the Moderne in Southern California 1920-41*, exhibition catalogue, University of California, Santa Barbara, 11 February-23 March 1969, p. 58, #15 (photo the University Art Museum, University of California, Santa Barbara)

Below, right
Kem Weber sketch of metal tubular furniture for the Lloyd Manufacturing Company, Menominee, Michigan, 1934. A Weber interior, with almost identical furnishings, is illustrated in *A History of American Furniture*, Marta K. Sironen, The Towse Publishing Company, 1936, p. 141 (photo the University Art Museum, University of California, Santa Barbara)

method for eliminating the traditional cabinetmaker's morticed and doweled joint in furniture assembly. In its place, Weber proposed using a continuous strip of hickory reinforced at the curved angles with an inserted oval section, i.e. plug, of wood. The latter, for contrasting aesthetic purposes, would be dark, preferably *tanguile*, a wood indigenous to the Philippines. A critic explained the logic behind the invention:

The great strength of bent hickory has been made use of, thus doing away with the ordinary wood joints in a most ingenious and novel fashion. Instead of the usual joint of some kind at a right-angle corner, as in the rails of a chair, the wooden member is thinned down to about three sixteenths of an inch, and then bent after steaming. The hollowed-out portion has been given the shape of an ellipse, and into each of these cavities fits a shaped upper part of a chair leg. The result is great strength of construction, and incidentally very sightly and practical rounded corners.[46]

Extending the *Bentlock* principle, Weber simultaneously introduced his proposals for standardizing furniture mass production.[47] A few interchangeable standard units would provide 125 different pieces of furniture. *Bentlock*, produced by the Higgins Manufacturing Co. in Oakland, California, appears now to have been a short-lived wonder. Weber's design for an airplane chair for the Airline Chair Co., Los Angeles, four years later, remains the most striking interpretation of the streamline ethic to emerge in the USA.[48]

A relatively late starter – he established his design office in 1929, after the spate of New York exhibitions in that and the preceding year – *Gilbert Rohde* (see p. 75) began to exert considerable influence as an industrial designer in the early 1930s. He rushed to catch up, exhibiting at the 1931 AUDAC exhibition while courting Grand Rapids manufacturers with plans for production-line furniture.[49]

In 1934, a landmark year for him, Rohde's reputation as a leading designer was sealed, and at the same time he set his primary goal as the manufacture of quality contemporary furniture for the mass market. The Herman Miller Furniture Co. and the Troy Sunshade Co. both published catalogues which showed a wide range of tubular chromed pieces for indoor and outdoor use.[50] In the same year, Rohde created "A Music Room Corner" for the Exhibition of Contemporary American Industrial Art at the Metropolitan Museum of Art.[51] The installation, though typical of much of his work at the time, met with a mixed response. One critic in particular took exception to the Steinway piano: "The piano case is fine. So are the legs. The combination is terrible – as it will continue to be until someone redesigns the piano in terms of twentieth century living, and modern music."[52] The attack seems unwarranted, especially as Lee Simonson's example at the Newark Museum five years earlier, considerably more provocative in its use of metal strut supports, had been enthusiastically received.

Like other contemporary industrial designers, especially Russel Wright, Rohde thought that the solution to the cramped modern home was combination, or sectional, units of furniture. One creation, his *Living-Sleeping-Dining* group, included multipurpose pieces for use in any room in the house. Another innovation was a bentwood side chair, manufactured by what Rohde described as an "automobile type of assembly." Produced with slight variations by three

Below

Kem Weber armchair; mahogany, manufactured by S. Karpen & Co. Illustrated in *Good Furniture Magazine*, May 1927, p. 181

companies – the Kroehler Manufacturing Co., the Herman Miller Furniture Co., and the Troy Sunshade Co. – the model required a mere eight bolts and a wrench to be put together.[53] The resulting chair was "light, springy, virtually unbreakable, eminently suited for straight-line mass production, and cheap."[54]

Contemporary magazines bear witness to Rohde's indefatigable pursuit of the machine aesthetic. Every aspect of interior design was analyzed with microscopic fervor, which enabled him to convince furniture manufacturers to re-model existing lines at the depths of the Depression. No other designer carried such authority in Grand Rapids.

A critic in 1935 provided an assessment of Rohde's place within the Modernist movement which largely reflects our view of him today: "Mr. Rohde is, in certain important ways, a middle grounder. If you would see what we mean, set on one side of him Frederick Kiesler, whose integrity is so incorruptible that he has been known to make eleven models in the effort properly to design an ash receiver. On the other side of Rohde set Donald Deskey, to whom modernism has been one grand sweet profitable song."[55]

Highly respected by her colleagues for her boundless talents and energies, *Ilonka Karasz* turned her hand as gamely to furniture design as to textiles, silverware, magazine illustrations, etc. Her enthusiasm proved infectious; her entries in the American Designers' Gallery and AUDAC exhibitions received favorable reviews, even when she was judged to have overstepped the bounds of good taste. One critic, for example, in preferring an interior she showed at the 1929 American Designers' Gallery to those of Hoffmann, Reiss, and Weber, wrote that Karasz was "the most individual and original of the four, and by far the boldest in conception. Yet occasionally one deplores an over-vigorous statement in her pieces and a heaviness due to too great solidity of the materials in which she works."[56] The same article illustrated the faulty interior, reputedly the first Modernist child's nursery in the United States![57] The following year Karasz exhibited a dining room in bird's eye maple, the angled plank chairbacks extending to the floor in a manner reminiscent of Frank Lloyd Wright prototypes twenty years earlier.[58] Another chair, with stepped architectural back in walnut with black lacquered trim, paid tribute to Frankl's skyscraper theme.[59]

Joseph Urban's influence on all aspects of the decorative arts in America was monolithic. A generation older than most of the aspiring Modernists discussed here, he emerged as a *pater familias* to the group, lending his name and flare to many of the projects which helped to establish the new movement. Among his manifold talents was a range of furnishings which varied little in inspiration or style from those he had exhibited at the Hagenbund in Vienna at the turn of the century. As Director of the short-lived Wiener Werkstätte in America Gallery established at 581 Fifth Avenue, New York, in 1921/22, Urban displayed a range of furniture typical of his style: theatrical, young, and exuberant. A noted success was his lady's bedroom in black mirrored glass at the 1928 American Designers' Gallery.[60] Less characteristic and less successful was his double bedroom at the group's second exhibition the following year.[61]

A substantial amount of Urban's furniture has remained unidentified. His archives at Columbia University, New York, reveal a wide range of furnishings for hotels and restaurants in the Midwest and New York. Other pieces, manufactured by the Mallin Furniture Company, show the designer's predilection for contrasting veneers and eye-catching applications of mother-of-pearl. None of these has reappeared on the market.

Jules Bouy is one of the most elusive furniture designers of the period. Of his occasional Modernist pieces which reach the marketplace today, none is disappointing. Novel streamlined forms are complemented by subtle color shadings, sometimes as many as five in juxtaposition.[62] It appears that Bouy, in addition to his work for Alavoine & Co., and Ferrobrandt (see Chapter 6), earned his living primarily as an interior decorator. He established his decorating firm, Bouy, Inc., in New York in 1928, providing clients with a wide range of period room-settings, such as Oriental and Louis XVI. When there were opportunities to show his penchant for the Modernist idiom, his work was full of Gallic flare. Unfortunately, like his Parisian designer/decorator counterparts, André Groult and Marcel Coard, he seems to have been called on mainly for traditional interiors. Two contemporary magazines show his attempts to introduce restrained Modernism into rooms housing collections of antique works of art.[63]

Wolfgang Hoffmann, born in 1900, was the son of Josef Hoffmann, the celebrated architect and leading spirit of the Modernist decorative arts movement which emerged in Vienna at the turn of the century. Wolfgang spent eight years at the Realschule, followed by three more at a special architectural college. From there he attended the Vienna Kunstgewerbeschule. On graduating, he worked briefly for local architects, including his father, before emigrating to the United States in December 1925.[64] His thorough grounding in both architecture and the decorative arts placed him in the vanguard of the New York Modernist movement. He opened his own studio around 1927, designing a wide range of interiors – wood and metal furnishings, rugs, pewterware, linens, etc. – in collaboration with Pola, his Polish-born wife. Their marriage and business partnership were both dissolved in the 1930s.

Hoffmann participated in all of the important New York exhibitions in the late 1920s.[65] No distinct style is evident beyond a rigid adherence to functionalism. His furniture, such as that for a Chicago executive's office and a New York doctor's waiting room, in African walnut and rosewood, was rather bland.[66] Only occasionally, in the angularity of a chair back or arm, does the viewer sense the dynamic Wiener Werkstätte spirit on which Hoffmann was nurtured.[67] One of his specialties was combination furniture for small city apartments. Within the partnership, Pola appears to have been responsible for the textile designs and the execution of all pieces.[68]

Walter von Nessen specialized in small metal furniture – ash-stands, side tables, combination table/bookcases – and light fixtures (see Chapter 4).[69] Utility of line and unadorned surfaces characterize his work. His preferred materials were

chromium and Formica. Examples illustrated in a 1930 firm's catalogue show his powerful interpretation of the Modernist idiom. The whereabouts of several of the more important models are unknown today.

Like Von Nessen, *Walter Kantack* produced a wide range of modern metal furniture. Numerous examples, including those for the decorating firm of French & Co., are illustrated in Kantack's magazine, *The Kaleidoscope*.[70]

Born in Geneva, Switzerland, *William Lescaze* attended college in his native city before studying architecture for four years under Karl Moser at the Technische Hochschule in Zürich. After graduating, Lescaze worked briefly in Europe – including a spell in Paris with Henri Sauvage, the first French architect to employ the setback theme – before emigrating to America in 1920.[71] In 1929 he formed a partnership with George Howe of Philadelphia. One of their first commissions, the Philadelphia Savings Fund Society Building, drew wide attention at the time as an early American example of the International Style.

Lescaze was an uncompromising Modernist; ornamentation was taboo.[72] His furniture was rigorously functional, more comfortable in appearance than that of Le Corbusier, Oud, or Mies van der Rohe, but spartan by American standards.[73] Wherever feasible, appliances, such as radios and photographs, were built into walls. Seat furniture was designed in both metal and wood with padded upholstery.

Lescaze's best-known interior, which he worked at in collaboration with Ilonka Karasz, was the penthouse apartment shown at the 1928 R. H. Macy's exhibition. Another notable interior was his smoking room for the Frederick Loeser department store in Brooklyn. Today his designs are indistinguishable from those of a host of other 1930s Modernists.[74]

Dutch-born *Herman Rosse* studied at Delft University, the Royal College of Art in South Kensington, and Stanford University, California, before establishing himself as an architect and decorator in Holland. He returned to the United States as the official decorator for the Netherlands section at the Panama-Pacific Exposition in 1915, and at that time decided to stay. From 1918 to 1923 he was head of the Department of Decorative Design at the Art Institute of Chicago, devoting much of his time to theater set design. His versatile talent soon led him to book-, textile-, and interior-design commissions.[75] The last-mentioned included the creation of a series of furniture models, examples of which he showed at the 1928 and 1929 American Designers' Gallery exhibitions. His 1928 entry, a dining room entirely in Monel metal and chromium-plated steel, was the hit of the show.[76] Positioned as it was, near Urban's spectacular "Repose" dressing room in black mirrored glass, this was a signal success. Other Rosse furniture, in wood, was considerably less striking, some of it even undistinguished.[77]

One of the first proponents of the Modernist movement in America, *Winold Reiss* was the founder in 1915 of *The Modern Art Collector*, the first magazine of its type in America. German-born, Reiss studied at the Kunstgewerbeschule and Royal

Academy in Munich before he emigrated to the USA in 1913. An artist by profession, he developed a reputation for his paintings of American Indians, especially the Blackfoot tribe. Furniture commissions he undertook included restaurant and hotel interiors on Long Island (the Crillon, Elysée, and Esplanade), Manhattan (Longchamps Restaurant and the Ritz-Carlton Hotel), and Chicago (the South Sea Island Ballroom in Sherman House, and the Tavern Club). In the late 1920s Reiss described himself as an "interior architect." He preferred wood to metal, and his "Young Girl's Bedroom" at the 1928 American Designers' Gallery was noteworthy for its warm blend of yellow and silver tones,[78] a product of his training as a painter. His interiors for the Tavern Club in Chicago the following year comprised a selection of furnishings saved from total lack of character only by the colorful checkered fabrics of his wife, Henriette Reiss.[79]

Joseph Sinel, a versatile industrial designer (see Chapter 15), designed several interiors in which a strong architectural line predominated. His conference table and chairs, the latter positioned when not in use in a neat line beneath the rectangular table top to form a box-like structure, was an ingenious response to the problem of limited space.[80]

The youngest of the new industrial designers – 23 years old when he was first drawn to the decorative arts in 1927 – *Russel Wright* applied the same concern for construction to his furniture as to all aspects of his design business: pewter- and silverware, brushed aluminum, ceramics, wallpapers, fabrics, floor coverings,

Right

Russel Wright end-table manufactured by the Heywood-Wakefield Company, c. 1934. A similar model is illustrated in *Decorative Art 1935*, Yearbook of The Studio, 1935, p. 41; and *Arts and Decoration*, September 1934, p. 53 (collection John Loring)

etc.[81] Among his long list of practical innovations in the 1930s was his *Flexible Modern* line of furniture for Heywood-Wakefield, one of several furniture manufacturers who retained him.[82] Wright's importance lay in his formulae for dealing with the shortage of space facing the city-dweller. His furniture models were modular.[83] Sofas were comprised of sectional units that could be positioned in any number of ways to fit into awkwardly shaped spaces. As one critic noted of a suite of furniture which Wright designed for R. H. Macy's in 1935,

You'll find any number of practical ideas incorporated in the pieces. For instance, the sleek-looking Morris chair has all the old-fashioned virtues of the old-time Morris chair, with the seat and back capable of being adjusted in three ways. Then the sectional bookcase shown in the living room . . . is enormously versatile. Clamp three sections together and you have a bookcase that reaches to the ceiling. Unclamp one section and use it as an end table. Other usable pieces are a modern gate-leg table that fits compactly against the wall and becomes a console, a small square coffee table and a secretary-bookcase divided in the center by an open niche for books, the top part a desk, the lower section a storage chest for magazines.[84]

Wright's style is difficult to classify. His furniture, as in all his designs, was largely unembellished, its flat planes conveying the functionalist message. Later designs in metal were correspondingly nondescript. Only his "pony skin" chair, which he designed in 1932 for his personal use, incorporates in its armrests an organic form reminiscent of the German *Jugendstil*, particularly the work of Richard Riemerschmid.

The stage set and industrial designer, *Norman Bel Geddes* (see Chapter 15), was commissioned in 1929 to design a range of bedroom furniture for the Simmons Company.[85] Manufactured in black-painted steel with chromium trim and vermilion accents, the suite was later offered also in green, blue and maroon. In discussing the set's unmistakable metallic look, Bel Geddes drew attention to an error prevalent among furniture designers at the time,

It has been common practice to produce metal furniture that simulated wood in appearance. This not only involves needless expense but is also poor sales psychology, bringing about an undesirable reaction when touch discloses that the furniture is of metal. Materials should be permitted to be themselves, honestly and openly, in order that the best effects be obtained.[86]

The number of examples of the Simmons suite that have survived indicates that its success was substantial.

Herbert Lippmann was another architect to turn his hand on occasion to modern furniture design. Born in 1889, he received his formal education at Columbia University in New York. His pieces show light traces of French Art Deco inspiration, not only in their angular forms, but in the choice of veneers – walnut, amaranth, and satinwood – used in arresting patterns, such as that of the Manhattan skyline inlaid on the sides of an armchair exhibited at Yale University in 1983.[87]

Less well known was *Robert Heller*, a designer in New York, who produced a range of simple, functional furniture in woods such as ebony and Brazilian

Opposite, left

Kantack & Co. in collaboration with Ely Jacques Kahn jardinière with illuminated glass panel for the Alfred E. Rose Gallery, New York; etched glass, chromium-plated metal, and marble, unsigned, 59in. (149.9cm) high. Illustrated in *House Beautiful*, February 1931, p. 198; *House & Garden*, August 1930, p. 43; and *The American Architect*, February 1930, pp. 44-45 (photo Alan Moss, Ltd.)

Opposite, right

Company of Mastercraftsmen cabinet; thuyawood and mahogany with ivory trim and ebony and satinwood veneers, 53in. (134.6cm) high, 1920s (photo The Metropolitan Museum of Art, purchase, Theodore R. Gamble, Jr., gift in honor of his mother, Mrs. Theodore Robert Gamble, 1980)

rosewood upholstered in henna rep.[88] Heller retained one important client, Ely Jacques Kahn, and manufactured Kahn's furniture designs for him.

Robert Locher, a stage set designer by profession (his commissions included theater work for Paul Poiret in Paris and C.B. Cochran in London), turned his skills to interior design in the 1920s. By 1929 his philosophy on twentieth-century taste was sufficiently respected for the magazine *House and Garden* to invite him to express his thoughts in one of its articles on Modernist interiors.[89]

Locher's entrance hall at the 1928 American Designers' Gallery exhibition generated wide interest and acclaim. The furniture, in maple with leather upholstery and glass tops, was starkly geometric and provided the exhibition viewer upon arrival with a rich taste of what lay ahead.[90] Within two years Locher had switched to chromium-plated metal, his sleekly pared-down designs for the John Wanamaker department stores resembling much of Deskey's work at the time.[91]

It was inevitable that the industrial designer, *Walter Dorwin Teague*, would at some point turn his attention to furniture, as he redesigned virtually everything from cameras to automobiles (see Chapter 15). The furniture which he designed in 1933 for his own studio at 210 Madison Avenue, New York, embodied a marriage of functionalism and sharp color contrasts – sleek tubular aluminum furniture with vermilion leather upholstery against a background of polished black and flat white walls.[92] In the same year Teague was commissioned to design the Executive Lounge in the Ford Building at the Century of Progress Exposition in Chicago. For this, he retained the same color scheme of black and white, enhanced now with gold wall trimmings and light fixtures.[93]

By the mid-1930s there was an army of furniture designers (architects, interior designers, and decorators), many of whom created a work or two of such surpassing quality that one must ask today what other works of theirs have gone unrecorded. One such was *Lee Simonson*, who designed a piano in white holly accented with blue turquoise lacquer, for Hardman, Peck, & Co.[94] Entitled *Death of a Simile*, its architectural setback case and flaring metal rod supports startled viewers at the Newark Museum where it was exhibited in 1929. Simonson's other furniture is largely undistinguished, as much of it was built-in. His leadership in the Modernist movement won him the job of coordinating the 1928 exhibition at R.H. Macy's.

Edward Steichen was also commissioned by Hardman, Peck, & Co. to design pianos "to meet the modernist tendencies in music." His models, *Vers Libre* and *Lunar Moth*, were smaller and more colorful than Simonson's. One of them in gray-green and silver, resting on slender tapering feet, incorporated a mirrored panel above the keyboard to reflect the player's hands.[95]

Another to receive quiet, but repeated, praise for his furniture was *Alexander Kachinsky*. Born in Kharkov, Russia, in 1888, Kachinsky studied at the St. Petersburg Central School of Decorative Art, and graduated in 1909. Two years later he went to Paris, where he studied painting with Maurice Denis. Arriving in the United States in 1924, he concentrated increasingly on industrial design and teaching, the latter at the School of Contemporary Arts and Crafts in New York.[96] His furniture designs, mainly in woods such as maple and oak, had a simple elegance, but lacked individuality. Kachinsky was commissioned to design several complete interiors, including carpets and lamps, for the decorator Harriet E. Brewer, of New York. He displayed furnishings also at the 1930 AUDAC exhibition.[97]

Victor Proetz was born in St. Louis, Missouri, in 1897.[98] On graduating from the Soldan High School, he enrolled at the Art Institute of Chicago to study painting and design, a program disrupted by his mobilization during World War I. Following the Armistice, he entered the School of Architecture of the Illinois Institute of Technology, from which he graduated in 1923. The following year he returned to St. Louis, where he formed a partnership with Ralph Cole Hall. The firm undertook numerous architectural commissions, Proetz broadening his repertoire in the mid-1930s with over 2,000 designs for furniture, textiles, light fixtures, ceramics, glass, etc. In 1943 he accepted Lord & Taylor's invitation to become Director of their Interior Decorating Department.

Proetz's conservative furniture designs show his traditional roots. "Restauration" (1814-18), Charles X, and Biedermeier influences are evident in a range of neat, modern wood furniture, their understated contours often heightened with light floral marquetry in contrasting veneers. There are several typical examples in the collection of the St. Louis Art Museum.

John Vassos, an industrial designer known for his book illustrations, shared Lescaze's philosophy of stark functionalism. As he explained, "there can be no compromise – no halfway adherence to the principles of modern art, but rather that the artist-designer who feels himself drawn to the credos of modernism should give himself over whole-heartedly to work in modern materials."[99] His furniture, extremely simple yet comfortably upholstered, incorporated such novelties as Fabrikoid, cork, and leatherette. One interior – an office-studio for a client on the 52nd floor of the Chrysler Building – shows a complex functional grouping of furniture, much of it built-in.[100]

Right

*Robert S. Degolyer and Charles L. Morgan
(architects)* lounge, Powhatan apartments, 4950
South Chicago Beach Drive at East 50th Street,
Chicago, 1929 (photo Hedrich-Blessing)

The ubiquitous *Henry Varnum Poor* was one of two noted artist-designers to try their hand at Modernist furniture production. Neither saw the incongruity of exhibiting hand-crafted pieces alongside the chromium-plated creations of Deskey and others at exhibitions staged, largely, to promote the machine and mass production.

Working in tulipwood, Poor executed by hand his furniture designs for an apartment owned by Donald Friede.[101] Earlier examples, with a strong Arts and Crafts simplicity, were exhibited at the American Designers' Gallery in 1929.[102] The pieces were simple in the extreme — flat planes of wood placed perpendicularly — and, ironically, far better suited to machine production. Decoration was provided by "the rhythmic markings of the circular saw, the use of lead striping, and the decorative highlights formed by exposed brass screws."[103]

The other artisan, *Wharton Esherick*, produced a considerably more interesting and avant-garde selection of hand-crafted furniture. The bold, kinetic forms of his sculpture were echoed in several pieces, especially a desk which he designed for a client in 1931. In contrasting walnut and padouk with inlaid ebony banding, the piece was cubist-inspired with a sharp, conical superstructure. Other examples, now in the Wharton Esherick Museum in Paoli, Pennsylvania, show more of a *Jugendstil* influence.

FURNITURE MANUFACTURERS

American furniture manufacturers maintained a blanket anonymity in the 1920s, as they had more or less throughout the previous hundred years. Actually there was little about which to boast. American furniture remained rooted in the past, as noted earlier, its production based on a slavish derivation of early styles. At the end of World War I the manufacturer had no reason to anticipate change, either within the industry or from outside. His control of the furniture market remained almost total: period revival styles were fed to the department stores which, in turn, persuaded their customers of the suitability of each for the season at hand. If, as everyone believed, the world's great furniture styles had already evolved, there remained now only the secondary role of recycling them periodically.

Furniture manufacturing communities sprang up in rural America, especially in Michigan, which had been populated in the nineteenth century by a large number of North Europeans, many from cabinet-making families. Grand Rapids became the nation's unlikely furniture hub, its function similar to that of the Faubourg St. Antoine in the northern *arrondissements* of Paris.

The Secretary of Commerce, Herbert Hoover, invited the furniture industry to send a number of delegates to the 1925 Exposition Internationale. Their subsequent report justified the complacency felt by the American manufacturers: Modernist furniture was bogus, its appeal ephemeral. An editorial in *Good Furniture*

Below

Warren McArthur table; aluminum with black Formica top, c. 1930, 30½in. (77.5cm) high (collection Catherine C. Kurland, photo Richard P. Goodbody)

Magazine two years later summarized the industry's attitude to the contemporary movement,

An out-and-out application of European modernistic theories in American furniture seems out of the question. American taste is too conservative to tempt our furniture manufacturers to discard historic precedent in favor of the unknown trail of the modernistic. All European attempts so far made to create furniture strictly of the present, with no allegiance to historic precedence, involve effects possible only by costly labor processes that do not lend themselves to quantity production.[104]

The article was careful, however, not to discount the new movement entirely as the American public's response to the initial department store exhibitions of European Modernist furnishings could not sensibly be ignored. A lame apology was offered in order to explain the American furniture designers' reluctance to follow American architects into the twentieth century. "The furnishings industries always trail architectural progress anywhere from ten to twenty years. This has always been so and it is not to the discredit of furniture and textile producers and the makers of other decorative furnishings to mention the fact."[105] A full ten years later, in her book *A History of American Furniture*, Marta K. Sironen found it necessary to rebuke furniture manufacturers for their persistent myopia.

They, of all people, should realize that retail buyers are becoming better informed each day and do not want that over-decorated and over-carved furniture. They won't buy it. Price is no longer the chief object. . . . People want furniture that they can be happy with, furniture that makes their lives easier, not more difficult.

You may as well try to blot out the sun as to suppress or discourage modern art in America. Every new convert becomes possessed with its unlimited possibilities and worships at its shrine. The time is not far off when factories will have to shut down unless they forget all this rubbish that they have been grinding out by the mile and start all over again, studying the simple mass, using carving, moldings and decorations only as the last resort, and allowing the wood, the glorious creation of Nature, to reveal its hidden treasures.[106]

The battle which confronted the traditional furniture industry in 1930 was waged simultaneously on two fronts: the one, within the industry itself, was between the machine and the cabinet-maker, and the other was against a common outside aggressor, metal. The cause of both can be traced to the Depression. As the economy plummeted, sales began to shrink, and new techniques had to be developed to pare down production costs. First to go, within the industry, were the more embellished period styles, especially Louis Quinze, which incorporated elaborate hand-crafted Rocaille detailing, acanthus sprays, and caryatids. As costly carved decoration was proscribed, this left a void suited admirably to the machine:

The indefatigable carver no longer is asked to labor for days with hand tools to fashion an ornament for an *escritoire*, a buffet or a ponderous bedstead. In the first place, the ornament is not desired; in the second place, the machine can grind, stamp, mold or turn an ornament with more precision than any craftsman working with tools. The machine can plane, mortise and join pieces together more perfectly than any human hand. No worker, however skilful, can compete with the machine in the making of veneers, nor can he give us the perfect matching of grains which the mechanically operated knives turn out for our use.[107]

Below

Harry's New York Bar, Chicago (Eckander & Brandt, architects) furniture designed by Harry Lund and manufactured by Warren McArthur, the mural by Hanns R. Teichert. Illustrated in *Architectural Forum*, November 1935, p. 471 (photo Hedrich-Blessing)

The introduction of the machine into wood furniture manufacture eased the path of Modernism considerably, although Grand Rapids deployed every sleight-of-hand possible to delay the inevitable. Sironen explains,

By 1930 a financial crash had occurred and manufacturers were giving more attention to financing their factories during what promised to be a long drawn out depression, than to furniture styles. Directoire – the eighteenth century French style – appeared in New York and slowly advanced to the commercial furniture centers of the Middle West. These patterns appealed to the manufacturer and dealer more than did the unstable Moderne, or Modernistic, as everyone was now calling it, and almost every manufacturer accepted Directoire as a substitute for the Modernistic.[108]

One line of furniture, introduced as a further deviant tactic, had the reverse effect of hastening the course of Modernism. Described as "adapted from Directoire, which in turn was adapted from French Empire, which originally was based upon the Greco-Roman Arts,"[109] the edition was later analyzed as the greatest commercial blunder in Grand Rapids history. Transgressions such as these were noted at the time by Richard Bach, Director of the Metropolitan Museum of Art, who saw clearly how counter-productive was the manufacturers' grip on the market: "Industry has been guilty of many misdemeanors against the good name of design. It has played down to the mass; it has foisted endless near-duplicates upon design-hungry consumers, who have had to buy below their level of taste."[110]

In Grand Rapids, wood manufacturers soldiered on, at least six introducing a selection of Modernist lines into their standard repertoire – the Johnson-Handley-Johnson Co.;[111] Berkey & Gay;[112] the Johnson Furniture Co.; the Imperial Furniture Co.;[113] the Grand Rapids Chair Co.; and the Wilhelm Furniture Co. The Johnson-Handley-Johnson Co., in particular, weathered the Depression in part through its liaison with a New York retailer of French-inspired Modernist furniture, Dynamique Creations.[114]

Beyond Michigan, Heywood-Wakefield in Boston promoted modern furniture to make "the smallest apartment livable, dinable, sleepable."[115] Offered were furniture designs by Gilbert Rohde and Russel Wright in a combination of walnut and maple veneers. In Chicago, S. Karpen & Bros. (Teague, Schoen, Karasz, Deskey, and Weber), the Simmons Co. (Geddes),[116] and the Kroehler Manufacturing Co. (Root) followed suit. In New York City, Schmieg, Hungate & Kotzian,[117] and the Mallin Furniture Co.[118] manufactured contemporary furniture for Deskey, Schoen, and Urban, among others. Several department stores, especially Barker Bros. in Los Angeles and W. & J. Sloane in New York, copied their Parisian counterparts, Galeries Lafayette and Au Bon Marché, in the establishment of their own furniture-making studios.[119]

The battle within the wood furniture industry diverted attention from the real confrontation, that between wood and metal. For this Grand Rapids had no answer – or stomach. Not only would the introduction of metal necessitate complete retooling (in itself an issue of financial insurmountability) but its use was predicated on totally foreign principles of design, principles developed, in fact, to render wood obsolete. In short, everything fundamental in two millennia of furniture-making would have to be scrapped.

Right

The Northwestern Terra Cotta Company glazed ceramic pedestal designed by Fernand Moreau, c. 1925 (collection Denis Gallion and Daniel Morris)

For the wood manufacturers who attempted the transition to metal, a need which accelerated in the early 1930s as the price of metal dropped below that of wood, outside expertise had to be sought. This came in the eager form of industrial designers who were in the process of establishing themselves as a *bona fide* profession.

In practice, most furniture designers worked in both disciplines until the mid-1930s. Many householders remained reticent about metal, its stark asceticism seeming to be best suited to far-off Dessau or American hospital wards and dentists' waiting rooms. Gilbert Rohde, more than anyone else, showed how designers could alternate between wood and metal with apparent impunity. His 1930s furniture designs were executed by at least three wood manufacturers – Heywood-Wakefield, Thonet Bros., and Kroehler – and four metal furniture firms – Herman Miller, Troy Sunshade,[120] John Widdicomb,[121] and the Mutual Sunset Co.

The foremost Modernist metal furniture manufacturers of the period were the Herman Miller Furniture Co., in Zeeland, Michigan; the Troy Sunshade Co., in Troy, Ohio; the Howell Co.,[122] in Geneva, Illinois; and Warren McArthur, in New York.[123] Smaller metal studios included Deskey-Vollmer, Inc., Kantack & Co., and Robert Heller, Inc., all in New York.[124]

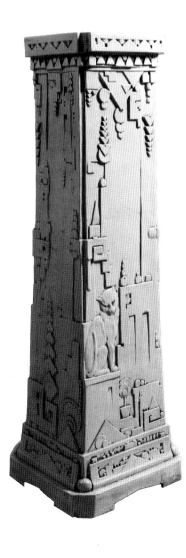

Today it is a brave historian indeed who would try to distinguish among the products of these manufacturers. As in the chromium-plated furnishings of the members of the Union des Artistes Modernes (U.A.M.) in Paris at the same time, the cross-fertilization of ideas was rampant. In some cases different models are indistinguishable, even when compared in contemporary photographs. Only a subtle difference in the contours of a chair back, or the placement of rivets, distinguishes some models by the Troy Sunshade Co. from those of the Howell Co. Identification is further complicated by the fact that this type of mass-produced furniture was invariably unsigned except for an adhesive label, which, through the years, has often been worn off.

A curious development in furniture of the 1930s was a range of sun parlor and patio seat furniture in wicker and related cane fibers, reviving a popular Victorian style. Paul Frankl was one of its innovators, who visited Japan and the Philippines to study at first-hand its techniques.[125] In 1929 he designed a line of reed furniture for the Ficks Reed Furniture Co. The following year, the Ypsilanti Reed Furniture Co. in Ionia, Michigan,[126] and the Heywood-Wakefield Co. exhibited separately a series of stick reed, woven fiber, and rattan furnishings at the Chicago Furniture Mart.[127] The angular corners and armrests on chairs and settees, in keeping with the functionalist creed of Modernism, were foreign to the natural contours of the wicker, stressing its incongruity for this type of furniture. The material's innate qualities of strength and line were better served by the traditional voluted bent-wood forms of Michael Thonet. Nevertheless, designers took the medium seriously. Deskey, in particular, designed a wide range of wicker pieces throughout the 1930s.[128]

Left, top

Joseph Urban dining-room table, model #1126U, manufactured by the Mallin Furniture Company, 1920-25 (photo Butler Library, Columbia University)

left, center

Joseph Urban center table, model #1125U, manufactured by the Mallin Furniture Company, 1920-25 (photo Butler Library, Columbia University)

Below, left

Joseph Urban lounge for the Gibson Hotel, Cincinnati (demolished 1974), 1928

Below, right

Joseph Urban lounge for the Central Park Casino, New York (demolished 1936), 1929 (photo Butler Library, Columbia University)

Right

Joseph Urban pair of armchairs and table; lacquered wood, mother-of-pearl, and airbrushed cotton and silk, the models displayed in the entrance rotunda of the New York Galleries of the Wiener Werkstätte of America, 42½in. (107.9cm) height of armchairs, c. 1921. Illustrated in *Good Furniture and Decoration*, August 1922, p. 99; *House and Garden*, September 1922, p.35; *Architectural Record*, 1923, p. 269; and *Architecture*, May 1934, p. 256 (collection George Watermann III, photo de Lorenzo Gallery)

Right

Walter von Nessen desk in birch with silver leaf trim commissioned by Mr. and Mrs. Glendon Allvine for their home in Long Beach, Long Island, c. 1929, 29¾in. (75.6cm) high, 71¾in. (182.2cm) wide. Illustrated in *Arts and Decoration*, January 1930, p. 53 (photo de Lorenzo Gallery)

⦀ LIGHTING AND CLOCKS ⦀

LIGHTING

The 1920s philosophy on domestic lighting gave the medium a new standing within the decorative arts. As one critic noted, "Modern lighting has changed its status. From being the 'last but not least' item on the decorative budget, it has become the preface to decoration. On it will depend the arrangement of your furniture, the compromise your color scheme will have to make with natural and artificial light, and possibly the dual role your most comfortable living room couch will assume if your lighting scheme is as versatile as your wardrobe."[1] During the period between 1890 and 1914, designers had concentrated on turning lamps into *objets d'art*. The fixture's primary function — to provide the required amount of light for the specific situation — had become obscured in the preoccupation with making the lamp itself beautiful. To the 1920s purist, such non-functionalism was a symptom of the whole Art Nouveau malaise, and one to which he himself would certainly not fall prey. For him, a light fixture had a specific and vital part to play in an interior: it must meet, in each instance, the requirements of visibility and ambience. Its design elements must, therefore, be subordinate to its lighting function.

The Belle Epoque *art* of lighting thus gave way to the 1920s *science* of lighting. Lamps became simply vehicles for light. The critic George B. Hotchkiss explained in 1930: "Today the tendency is to think of illumination rather than of fixtures. Certainly, the suitability of the light furnished for each purpose is of much greater importance than the fixture involved."[2] From this it was logically argued that if a lamp's *raison d'être* was solely to project the light and concentrate the attention of the inhabitants of a room *away from* itself, it would cease to be a distinct element of the interior design of that room. Lamp exponents were, in theory at least, faced with a choice: either to make their models as quietly functional and unostentatious as possible, or to eliminate them entirely and find other ways of illuminating the objects that were to be viewed: the walls, ceilings, and even the furniture. Why most Modernist lamps continued, however, to contain a measure of ornamentation was because neither alternative was found in practice to be satisfactory. Lamps were still needed to provide localized illumination for reading, for example, so most exponents refused to take their design to the extremes of ascetic logic

Above

Walter von Nessen sketch of a chandelier for the Miller Lamp Company; chalk and pencil on paper, unsigned, 16 x 10in. (40.6 x 25.4cm), c. 1930 (collection Alan Moss, Ltd.)

Above, right

Walter von Nessen sketch of a chandelier for the Miller Lamp Company; chalk and pencil on paper, signed l/l D.515 DIA. 20", 16 x 10in. (40.6 x 25.4cm), c. 1930 (collection Alan Moss, Ltd.)

Right

Walter von Nessen table lamp, chromium-plated metal, c. 1928. Illustrated in *The Metal Arts*, November 1928-December 1929, p. 43; and *Good Furniture and Decoration*, May 1931, p. 268

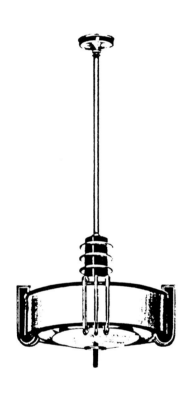

to which, say, the Frenchman Jacques Adnet, with his exposed, naked tubes, took his. When circumstances called for the use of a visible fixture, then the fixture would be worth looking at; and although its appeal was less spontaneous than that of its Art Nouveau predecessor, it was aesthetically more subtle. The shape of light fixtures also changed continually as advances on Edison's incandescent bulb were introduced throughout the 1920s. By 1931, Eugene Clute could write: "Modern light sources bear little, if any, resemblance to the lighting fixtures of even a few years ago, because they are designed for electric light, rather than being mere adaptations of designs originally intended for lighting by candles or gas."[3]

So the 1920s lamp survived as a decorative object, while its ability to meet various illumination needs was continually extended. The French led the way. Avant-garde designs were introduced by Jean Perzel in the years immediately following World War I, after which Modernist models flooded the annual Salons. Several of these, such as Chareau's sliced alabaster lamps and Desny's ingenious metal desk lamps, have already entered the realm of design classics. Illumination was suddenly the most challenging aspect of interior design, its every feature measured and analyzed. The science of photometry, for long a bona fide discipline that had been considered largely theoretical and therefore impractical for anything other than laboratory purposes, took on a new, greatly enhanced, status. Photometric units such as footcandles, lumens, lux, and intensity were measured. So were angles of reflection. So, too, were the coefficients of the transmission of light. Even the size of retinal images was recorded. This preoccupation with photometry created, in turn, a new vocation: that of the lighting, or illumination, engineer. The need to define, from an optical viewpoint, the brilliance of the surface to be lit, the distribution and accentuation of shadows, which color (if any) to use, and the position, number, and power of the light sources, called for a specialist technician – one to whom both the architect and the interior decorator could turn. The lighting engineer could apply, in each new setting, the necessary physiological, psychological, and artistic considerations.[4]

In the USA, the issues of lighting were taken no less seriously than across the Atlantic, and its progress was logged in reviews such as *The Illuminating Engineering Society*. Initially, light could be direct or indirect, that is, localized or diffused, but soon customers were advised that there were no fewer than *five* distinct types of illumination from which to choose – direct, indirect, semi-indirect, direct-indirect, and "mixed" (the last-mentioned was apparently indefinable, at least to the critics who reviewed the medium's progress).[5] The design engineer kept pace, introducing louvers, slats, and universal joints to ensure that his models could bend, diffuse, or absorb the light rays, as required. Lighting was now by design, not accident.

Walter von Nessen emerged as the premier Modernist lamp designer in the United States. Born in Germany in 1889, he trained in Berlin with Bruno Paul. Early commissions included that city's subway stations and, during a sojourn in Stockholm from 1919 to 1923, furniture for Swedish clients. In 1923 he emigrated to America and some time later established the Nessen Studio at 151 East 38th Street, New York.[6]

Right

Kurt Versen table lamp with flip-top shade; brass and chromium-plated metal. A similar model is illustrated in *Arts and Decoration*, November 1934, p. 18 (collection Alan Moss, Ltd.)

Opposite

Walter von Nessen table lamp; aluminum, glass, and Bakelite, unsigned, 19½in. (49.5cm) high. A similar model is illustrated in *Good Furniture and Decoration*, September 1930, p. 167 (collection George Waterman III)

Right

C.J. Weinstein chandelier; etched crystal and metal, c. 1931. Illustrated in *Interior Architecture and Decoration*, August 1931, p. 89 (photo Christie's, New York)

Far left

Jules Bouy piano lamp, steel, 1930s, 24½in.
(62.2cm) high (collection The Metropolitan Museum
of Art, gift of Juliette B. Castle and Mrs. Paul
Dahlstrom, 1968)

Left

Frankart, Inc. "Spirit of Modernism"; table lamp,
"skyscraper" design, cast metal with parchment
shade (replaced), model #L215, 20in. (50.8cm) high.
Illustrated in *Frankart Inc.*, firm's catalogue, 1930, p.
34 (collection Mark Feldman)

Below

Donald Deskey table lamp, brushed aluminum and
glass, exhibited in Deskey's Man's Room at the 1928
American Designers' Gallery, New York, 12¼in.
(31cm) high. Illustrated in *The American Architect*,
December 5, 1928, p. 754; *House Beautiful*, February
1929, p. 153; *House and Garden*, July 1929, p. 81;
and *Form & Reform*, Paul T. Frankl, Harper & Bros.,
New York, 1930, p. 90 (collection Miles J. Lourie)

Von Nessen designed and produced a wide range of contemporary metal furniture and light fixtures, principally for architects and interior designers. In 1930, by which time most businesses were retrenching, Von Nessen expanded to service orders from the retail trade. His lamps, especially, drew praise for their brazen modernity, both in form and in choice of bright metallic finishes. Geometric shades in frosted glass or parchment were housed on chromium-plated metal, brass, or brushed aluminum.[7] Decorative accents were provided by Formica, Bakelite, or rubber discs or trim. To accommodate both direct and indirect lighting requirements, shades could tilt, rotate, or upend themselves. A particularly successful concept reached fruition in his "Lighthouse" table lamp models, which consisted of two sections that could be lit together or separately.[8] Another Von Nessen innovation — to eliminate glare — was embodied in a stepped apron on conical lampshades which allowed the light to escape downwards through the slats. Both functional and aesthetic, Von Nessen's lamps, with their bold linear contours, matched those of his most progressive European counterparts. A series of porcelain wall sconces for the Efcolite Corporation in 1933 was uncharacteristic and unsuccessful.

Donald Deskey showed his versatility in several lamp designs which rivaled Von Nessen's in ingenuity. Deskey's lamp bases, in particular, were startlingly abstract. One — a spiraling coil in chromium-plated brass — led the eye to the above light.[9] Another, in aluminum, contained a series of square horizontal ribs that recalls contemporary International Style architecture. A further example, with a serrated front inset with rectangles of frosted glass, appears to have taken its inspiration from the work of Jean Perzel in Paris.

Deskey's 1931 commission to decorate the Roxy Rothafel apartment above the Radio City Music Hall provided a rare opportunity to design an ultramodern *ensemble* without cost constraints. The light fixtures — table, floor, and wall models — in the apartment's living room and dining room play a dominant role in the simple, yet opulent, ambience requested by Rothafel. In brushed aluminum and black Bakelite, they provide sharp, yet gracious, color accents against the rooms' soaring, paneled cherrywood walls and chestnut carpet.[10]

Nobody in America expounded the philosophy of modern lighting more vigorously than *Walter Kantack*. Every issue of his firm's magazine, *The Kaleidoscope*, carried his message on the tenets of new domestic lighting; its nuances, abuses, and potential. Kantack's lamps matched his concepts: they were crisply angular, bright, and functional. Curiously for such an ardent Modernist, Kantack stopped short of those who drew their inspiration from contemporary architecture: "I don't believe there is any relationship between a skyscraper and a lighting fixture, a skyscraper and a bookcase, or a writing desk. I believe that such terms and such associations will very soon be just remembrances of the early approaches to this problem."[11]

Others to turn their creative talents partially to the challenges of modern lighting — as part of the overall concept of interior design, rather than as a specialist venture — were Eugene Schoen, Gilbert Rohde, Ilonka Karasz, Robert E. Locher, Lurelle Guild, Wolfgang and Pola Hoffmann, and Elsie de Wolfe. There was ample room within the Modernist vernacular for fresh designs, and many were forthcoming.

In the vanguard of Modernist lighting designers, Kurt Versen created a range of table and floor models with polished chrome mounts. Shades were in opalescent glass, cellophane, Bakelite, lumerith or, his favorite, woven toyo paper.[12] Versen's best-known models incorporate hinged shades which flip upwards to provide both direct and indirect illumination.

Below

Kem Weber table lamp for the Miller Lamp Company; chromium-plated metal, c. 1930 (collection Alan Moss, Ltd.)

Opposite, left

Kem Weber digital clock for Lawson Time Inc.; brass, chromium-plated metal, and glass, 13in. long, c. 1933 (collection John P. Axelrod)

Opposite, right

Kem Weber sketch of a digital clock for Lawson Time Inc., 1934 (photo the University Art Museum, University of California, Santa Barbara)

Opposite, below

Kem Weber digital clock for Lawson Time Inc.; brass and copper, signed LAWSON ELECTRIC CLOCK 60 *cyc. style No 304* LAWSON TIME INC. *Pasadena Calif*, 3½in. (8.9cm) high, c. 1933 (collection John P. Axelrod)

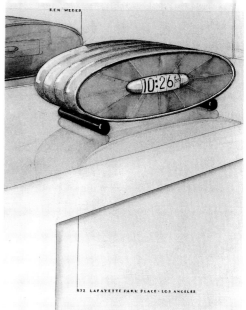

Other noted individual metal craftsmen and small studios turned their hand to contemporary lamp design: for example, John Salterini and the Lansha Studios, both of whom produced wrought-iron fixtures with frosted glass shades;[13] and Paul A. Lobel, who alternated between wrought iron and copper.

Several commercial lighting manufacturers earned recognition for up-to-date fixtures: for example, E. F. Caldwell & Co., who provided monumental fixtures such as those in the Fisher Building, Detroit (Albert Kahn, architect),[14] and the Starrett Netherland Plaza, Cincinnati (Walter W. Ahlschlager, architect); the Sterling Bronze Company, for similar architectural commissions; and Cox, Nostrand & Gunnison, who manufactured most of Joseph Urban's chandeliers, such as those in the Central Park Casino, New York.[15]

The department stores carried lighting's revolution to the market place in their exhibitions of modern interiors. Prominent in New York were B. Altman, Abraham & Straus, R. H. Macy's, Lord & Taylor, John Wanamaker, the Park Avenue Galleries, Frederick Loeser & Co.,[16] and James McCreery & Co., all of whom presented specialized lighting exhibitions between 1927 and 1931. Examples of contemporary European light fixtures were also included in the Contempora show in 1929. Several striking models were conceived by designers who are today unknown: for example, Bernard Fischer; L. L. Schacht, whose repertoire included "Skyscraper" torchères and "Chimney" table lamps,[17] and Alexander Kachinsky.[18] Among glass craftsmen, Maurice Heaton received numerous commissions for ceiling fixtures and wall sconces, his style varying from Rococo-inspired floral models to austere architectural pieces consisting of overlapping panels of painted glass.[19]

An air of questionable French levity was brought to American domestic lighting by Arthur von Frankenberg, who produced a wide range of small light fixtures — boudoir lamps, nightlights, and illuminated *bibelots* — which were marketed through his firm, Frankart, Inc., at 225 Fifth Avenue, New York. A 1930/31 catalog shows a repetitious selection of stylized "Jazz Age" nudes, often in pairs, clasping cylindrical or spherical globes. Inexpensively cast in spelter, Britannia metal, or aluminum with etched glass, parchment, or pleated shades, the models take their inspiration from those by Etling, Le Verrier, and Robj in Paris five years earlier. A matching selection of clocks, ashtrays, and bookends complemented the lamps.

CLOCKS

By 1929 clockcases were smart and crisply angular. On the dial, serifs disappeared from the numerals, which were often italicized, apparently to make it easier for the contemporary man of action to tell the time as he hurried by. The traditional richly grained wood clockcase — cherry or mahogany — was gradually phased out, and replaced by chromium-plated metal enhanced with enameled trim. By the mid-1930s, the numerals themselves were deemed redundant, and the hours were identified by sharp painted or incised lines or chromium-plated balls screwed into the clock face. In 1933 Gilbert Rohde eliminated the clockcase entirely by mounting the mechanism and dial on a chrome

Above

Unidentified designer table lamp offered by Altman & Co., New York; red, black, and white geometric decoration. Illustrated in *Good Furniture Magazine,* #31, 1928, p. 353

Below

The Sterling Bronze Company wall sconce; bronze and glass, for the Fox Theater, Washington, D.C. Illustrated in *The Metal Arts,* November 1928-December 1929, p. 127

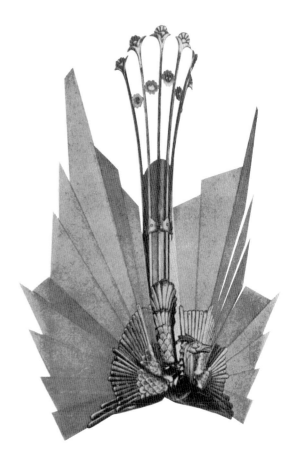

diagonal bar. This both pared down production costs and exemplified "the directness and simplicity of modern design and emphasizes the natural beauty of the materials." The revolution worked its way, finally, into the clock's mechanism: the "tick-tock" of yesteryear gave way to a rhythmic, pulse-like beat; to mark the hour, the old sonorous chime was replaced by a strident note. Even the prestigious clock-making firm of Seth Thomas, in New England, found it necessary to forgo their Colonial-style traditionalism to experiment with the "chic" new look. Henry Dreyfuss was retained to design a series of Modernist desk and mantel clocks. Included were models with veneered hardwood cases, silver dials, and gunmetal hands, the hours identified by black dots.

Gilbert Rohde emerged as the period's foremost clock designer, an honor he would certainly have seen as incidental, and secondary, to his role as a furniture designer. Rohde's contribution to the American Modernist design movement was relatively brief, beginning in 1929 and continuing to World War II. Information on his upbringing is sketchy: he was born to Prussian immigrants, Max and Mathilda Rohde, in New York on June 1, 1894. He attended high school in the Bronx, an early interest in mechanics and woodworking later proving influential in his designs for mass-production furniture. On graduating in 1913, he held a variety of jobs into the early 1920s. In 1923 he was employed by the Abraham & Straus department store as a furniture illustrator. There he met Gladys Vorsanger, another employee, who quickly had a profound effect on his career, both as his good counsel and, from July 1927, as his wife.[20]

A European tour in 1927 sharpened Rohde's awareness of contemporary French and German design, preparing him well for the stampede to Modernism which the New York department store exhibitions precipitated the following year but in which he was not ready to participate. In the late 1920s Rohde worked primarily on a custom basis, but, increasingly in the 1930s, this represented a diminishing part of his output. His time and energy were invested more and more in the design of mass-production furnishings for a broad consumer market. A major contract was forthcoming. The Heywood-Wakefield Company of Gardner, Massachusetts, commissioned an extensive line of indoor and outdoor furniture in 1930, on which Rohde later produced variations for the Koehler Manufacturing Company and the Herman Miller Furniture Company. By 1933 Rohde's reputation was sufficiently established for him to be issued an invitation to design interiors in the "Design for Living" house at the Century of Progress Fair in Chicago. Further regional fairs and department store participation followed, culminating in his design for the Administration Center at the 1936 Texas Centennial exposition. World War II reduced his market cruelly as many of the nation's manufacturing concerns diverted their production lines to wartime needs. For Rohde, ten years of pioneering design, under the most adverse economic conditions, came to an abrupt end. He died shortly after, on June 16, 1944.[21] Predictably, many of his achievements were forgotten in the postwar euphoria of the late 1940s.

Rohde's clock designs stand out from those of his contemporaries through their interpretation of modern forms and materials. In particular, his model mounted on a chrome diagonal bar, mentioned above, caught exactly the period's dual

Below

Paul Theodore Frankl "Telechron"; mantel clock designed for the Warren Telechron Company, polished and brush-burnished silver, 7¾in. (19.7cm) high, 1928/29. Illustrated in *House Beautiful*, February 1929, p. 153; *House and Garden*, March 1929, p. 100; *Vogue*, March 16, 1929, p. 98; and *House and Garden*, July 1929, p. 8 (collection Geoffrey N. Bradfield, photo Richard P. Goodbody)

Opposite, above

Bullocks Wilshire wall clock, sportswear department, probably designed by Gjuro Stojano, c. 1929 (photo Randall Michelson)

Opposite, below

Gilbert Rohde two mantel clocks for the Herman Miller Clock Company. *Left*: walnut and chromium-plated metal, signed *Mfd under Pats.* with patent numbers, 5½in. (13.9cm) high, c. 1933. *Right*: brushed chromium-plated metal and peach-tinted mirror, c. 1933. Similar models are illustrated in *House Beautiful*, November 1933, p. 219; and *Decorative Art 1936, Yearbook of The Studio, 1936*, unpaginated (collection Inglett-Watson)

goal of economy and elegance. Most of Rohde's clocks were designed for the Herman Miller Clock Company, a short-lived independent subsidiary of the Herman Miller Furniture Company, which filed for bankruptcy in the late 1930s. Other examples incorporated black glass dials on brushed aluminum stands.[22] In place of the glass, the customer could select Formica, Micarta, or pearl celluloid, all trendy new materials.[23]

Paul T. Frankl was another prominent designer who produced Modernist clocks. His "Telechron" model was introduced in 1929 as "the ultra-modern clock, appropriately dressed in the art moderne, the new mode of decoration so sharply expressive of our swiftly moving age. . . . For rooms decorated in the modern manner, what could be more appropriate? Its daring originality inspired admiration – its perfect balance of form and tone satisfies the most exacting devotee of the new mode."[24] Today the model appears distinctly subdued in comparison with the skyscraper and theatrical furniture which Frankl designed at the time.

By 1930 the department store led the way: R. H. Macy's, Stern's, Ross Pennell, B. Altman, and Abercrombie & Fitch[25] were offering a selection of electrified clocks, costing between $5 and $22, in which "precision and simplicity and beauty [are] the new watchwords." Chrome and mirrored glass, the latter often with a sapphire blue or peach tint, proved most fashionable. The clock's function was sometimes forgotten in the race to make it conform to the furniture amidst which it would be positioned.

The advent of the digital clock provided designers with a freedom similar to that afforded the 1900 lamp designer when Edison's electric bulb rendered fuel canisters obsolete. Kem Weber was one of the first Modernists to comprehend, and to seize, the new freedoms for clock designers. The traditional dial (circular or square) yielded to two small windows for the hour and minutes, allowing the clockcase to be of any preferred form. Weber's digital clocks for Lawson Clocks of Los Angeles, introduced in 1933, showed how successfully he grasped this new freedom. The models were revolutionary: their sleek, kinetic contours and unadorned surfaces captured exactly the message of the "Machine Age" exhibition staged in the same year at the Museum of Modern Art in New York.

Above

Gilbert Rohde clock for the Herman Miller Clock Company, chromium-plated metal and etched glass, 11¼in. (38.6cm) high, 1933. Illustrated in *Arts and Decoration*, September 1934, p. 55; *Fortune*, November 1935, p. 97; *Design*, December 1936/37, p. 14; and *Arts Magazine*, October 1981, p. 106

Left

Gilbert Rohde clock for the Herman Miller Clock Company, aluminum and black lacquer, signed *Herman Miller*, 3½in. (8.9cm) high (collection Denis Gallion and Daniel Morris)

T he American silversmith in the 1920s kept a low profile. His market was safe and conservative, its tastes built on proven traditional styles such as Rococo (Louis XV), "Old English" (Adam and Georgian), American Colonial, Victorian, and Art Nouveau. Period-revival styles alternated, the introduction of each carefully monitored to maintain a quiet but vigorous market. If Gorham's florid *martelé* pattern is dismissed as an international, rather than national, Victorian style, then the 1920s American silversmith had only the Colonial style to call his own. The latter enjoyed a revival prior to World War I which provided a welcome end to the shell and scroll Rococo pattern of the 1890s and the sinuosities of Art Nouveau. The renewed popularity of the Colonial style helped greatly to ease the transition to the Modernist style.

Although the work of the foremost 1920s European silversmiths was exhibited in the USA, its influence was less than that of other disciplines. Jean Puiforcat's powerful geometric forms, shown together with the rather more restrained examples of his French colleague, Boin-Taburet, and those of the two giant silver manufacturers, Cardeilhac and Christofle, in the 1926 exhibition at the Metropolitan Museum of Art, drew a polite, but quizzical, response. Puiforcat participated again in 1928 at Lord & Taylor's, this time with another Frenchman, Maurice Daurat. Again, his forceful angularity was seen as specifically French, too avantgarde for the local market. Americans identified more readily with Jensen's lingering Art Nouveau style and the fluted bowls of the Austrians, Josef Hoffmann and Dagobert Peche, whose silverware could be seen at the Wiener Werkstätte in America Gallery at 581 Fifth Avenue, New York, in June 1922.

What emerged in the USA was a "Modern Classic" style, a marriage of the new and old: dignified, understated, rational, safe rather than bold. Elaborate decoration was seen as exaggerated and meaningless. Simplicity accentuated the material's intrinsic beauty. As one critic explained:

Apparently there has been far less of the freakish phase of applied modernism in our silverware than in any other field of design. This, perhaps, has been due to the fact that silverware is one of the most conservative of furnishings, changing its design only after the more ephemeral accessories of home decoration have felt the influence of new fashions. Also, the fact that the bona-fide designer of silverware has not lost his head in this mad scramble for newness, but has wisely chosen a middle course.[1]

Below

Erik Magnussen covered chalice designed for the Gorham Manufacturing Company; silver and amethyst, impressed artist's initials and firm's hallmarks, 74 STERLING GORHAM, 6in. (15.2cm) high, c. 1928. Illustrated in *Vogue*, July 1, 1928, p. 94 (collection The Newark Museum)

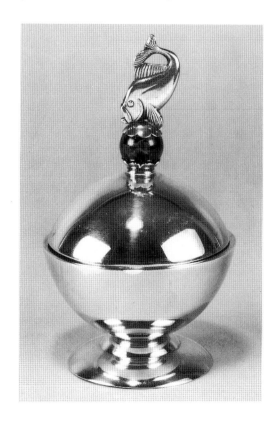

Below

Erik Magnussen "The Lights and Shadows of Manhattan"; coffee service designed for the Gorham Manufacturing Company, burnished silver with gold and oxidized gray panels, 9½in. (24.1cm) height of coffee pot, 1927, all impressed *Gorham,* with conjoined EM, a lion, anchor, G, 28/sterling, and inscribed DESIGNED AND EXECUTED BY ERIK MAGNUSSEN 1927. Illustrated in *The Jewellers' Circular,* 23 February 1928, p. 101; *Arts and Decoration,* April 1928, p. 52; and *At Home in Manhattan,* Yale University Art Gallery, exhibition catalogue, 1983, p. 47, #3 (collection Charles H. Carpenter, Jr.)

Opposite

Erik Magnussen tazza designed for the Gorham Manufacturing Company; silver and ivory, impressed hallmarks and GORHAM STERLING YFS, 12¼in. (31.1cm) high (collection The Art Institute of Chicago, gift of the Antiquarian Society)

This understated style provided the American silversmith with a further advantage: his designs fitted without discordance into both traditional settings *and* those of the most ardent iconoclast.

The progress of Modernism was therefore cautious and piecemeal. One of the more dramatic changes in design was provided by Eliel Saarinen in the flatware service which he displayed in his dining room at the 1929 exhibition "The Architect and the Industrial Arts" at the Metropolitan Museum of Art. Executed by the International Silver Company, the service incorporated an architectural setback imagery on the attenuated handles. More radical, however, was the introduction of an unusually long handle in proportion to the knife blade. This allowed the index finger to apply cutting pressure to the handle rather than the top edge of the blade.[2] By 1937 the concept had been refined: the elongated handles were further extended, their blades and bowls reduced and sharply squared off.

Danish-born *Erik Magnussen* grew up in the same artistic circle as Gustav Jensen, whose distinct floral and beaded style is evident in much of Magnussen's work. Magnussen closed his Copenhagen workshop in 1925, joining the Gorham Manufacturing Company in Providence, Rhode Island, to spearhead that firm's drive to develop modern alternatives to its repertoire of period-revival wares. The liaison was productive, but short-lived. The designer left in 1929 to join August Dingeldein & Son of Hanau and Idar, Germany, which had a retail outlet in New York City.

Magnussen created a range of restrained Modernist silverware for Gorham. His Danish heritage is evident in the classical formality of designs enhanced with Jensen-like scrolled floral accents, and reeded ivory stems and finials. Magnussen deviated only occasionally from this formula in a few sharply angular tea services and vases which recall Marianne Brandt's contemporary silver designs at the Bauhaus, and particularly in one coffee service, whose bold, borrowed theme stirred passionate sentiments at the time and continues to provoke controversy. The visceral response generated today by Magnussen's "The Lights and Shadows of Manhattan" was matched at the time of its creation. Its triangular panels of burnished silver with gilded and oxidized facets evoked the kaleidoscopic effects of sunlight and shade on the 1920s American skyline. Opinions were sharply divided. Proponents claimed that modern silver design should reflect contemporary advancement in other disciplines, especially architecture, in which America led the field. As the critic Elizabeth Lounsberg wrote,

The most important manifestation of the new industrial art is to reproduce in design, boldly and almost literally, the peculiar physical influences of the age, particularly as they are represented in our great modern cities. Thus, in his modernistic designs in sterling silver, Eric Magnussen of the Gorham Co. has attempted to reflect lights and shadows of a skyscraper city, rather exactly, in both color and form. . . . In this new design of the sterling silver coffee service a strong response to the spirit of modern America is exhibited. As applied to sterling, this spirit takes the form of sharp angles and sharp variations of light and shade, which are clearly the product of those phenomena found in our skyscraper civilization.[3]

The coffee service generated a far different sentiment in other critics. C. Adolph Glassgold, for example, made no secret of his outrage:

Below

William Spratling pitcher; silver and ebony, impressed SPRATLING MADE IN MEXICO STERLING, with conjoined WS initials, 6⅞in. (17.5cm) high (collection Denis Gallion and Daniel Morris)

I came upon a display of modern American silverware on Fifth Avenue the other day which was both painful and funny. It was funny because the manufacturer had obviously gritted his teeth and said to the designer: "Go as far as you like!" It was painful because the designer had applied a cubistic technique to surfaces that, in the sheer nature of things, cannot be treated cubistically; and because, instead of deriving his design from the actual function of a tea set and a salad set, he had sought to derive it, the advertisement placard said, from the skyscrapers of New York! Our skyscraper worship has produced some pretty sad results; but I think this cubistic claptrap in silver is about the worst I have seen.[4]

Glassgold's scorn went largely unheeded in 1928 as several commercial imitations of Magnussen's service quickly found their way on to the market. Bernard Rice's Sons introduced two nickel-plated Apollo "Skyscraper" tea and coffee service models, one in which the rectangular vessels were surmounted by architectural setback tops flanked by handles carved as smokestacks; the other with triangular planes.[5] The Middletown Silver Company introduced a modified version of Magnussen's prototype with paneled cubistic bodies.

By 1930 the experiment was judged specious and outmoded. One expert wrote, "At last we seem to have awakened to the fact that skyscraper architecture belongs to city buildings and not to table silver, a fact that should remind one that it is useless for an object to attempt to borrow beauty from something foreign to itself and its use. Modern art lends itself very well to certain things, yet not at all to others."[6] In retrospect, one is grateful that Magnussen was afforded the commission – one so uncharacteristic of his restrained, standard work – which he appears to have undertaken in order to placate or perhaps to ridicule the ultra-Modernist fringe. Included with the service was a matching trapezoidal tray (its whereabouts now unrecorded) and a salad set.[7]

No silversmith's work of this period excites wider enthusiasm today than that of *Peter Müller-Munk*. Born in Germany in 1904, Müller-Munk studied at the University of Berlin before enrolling in the city's Kunstgewerbeschule. A series of European commissions and exhibitions followed, culminating in the artist's independent participation at the 1925 Exposition Internationale in Paris, at which Germany was not formally represented. He moved the following year to New York, where he worked briefly for Tiffany & Co. before establishing his own studio in 1927.

In America, Müller-Munk designed and crafted a range of elegant silverware for private clients, while participating in the 1928 R.H. Macy's exhibition and the "Modern American Design in Metal Show" at the Newark Museum the following year. In the mid-1930s, after the Depression had taken its deep toll of the market for custom-made silver, Müller-Munk accepted an Associate Professorship at Carnegie Institute in Pittsburgh. He later founded the industrial design firm which bears his name to this day.

Müller-Munk's importance lay in his ability to embrace the modern idiom within the confines of traditionalism, the latter a well-entrenched discipline instilled by his Teutonic upbringing. Neoclassicism predominates, its forms elongated to provide greater vertical emphasis and modernity. Most of his silverware – tea sets, candlesticks, bowls, boudoir sets, loving cups, etc. – retains simple, well-defined contours and lightly ornamented surfaces. Only in one commission did

Below

William Spratling cup and cake server; silver and silver with ebony, both with impressed hallmarks and *William Spratling Taxco Mexico*, 3⅜in. (8.6cm) height of cup, 9¼in. (23.5cm) length of cake server, probably 1930s (collection Mitchell Wolfson, Jr., Miami-Dade Community College)

Above, left

Towle Manufacturing Company coffee service; silver and plastic, signed PATENTED – May 21, 1929 – by TOWLE T STERLING 55290, 8½in. (21.6cm) high, 1929 (collection Geoffrey N. Bradfield)

Left

Kem Weber (attributed to) tea and coffee service designed for Porter Blanchard; silver, all impressed PORTER BLANCHARD SILVER HANDMADE, 10½in. (26.7cm) height of coffee pot (collection Mitchell Wolfson, Jr., Miami-Dade Community College)

Below, left

Kem Weber coffee pot; silver-plated metal and rosewood, impressed TODAY *Kem Weber E.P. -N.S. BEI*, with encircled D and hallmarks, 10½in. (26.7cm) high, c. 1930 (collection Alan Moss, Ltd.)

Below, right

Bernard Rice's Sons, Inc. water pitcher; Apollo "skyscraper" design, nickel silver-plate, impressed SKYSCRAPER DES. PAT. PENDING APOLLO E.P.N.S. MADE IN U.S.A. BY BERNARD RICE'S SONS INC. 5258, 9¾in. (24.8cm) high, c. 1928. A matching tea and coffee service is illustrated in *The Jewellers' Circular,* 31 May 1928, p. 14; and *Vogue,* June 1, 1928, p. 116 (collection Alan Moss, Ltd.)

Müller-Munk appear to bend convention: in the tea and coffee service at the Metropolitan Museum of Art. Its tusk-like ivory handles combine Chinese traditionalism and the exuberance of Rembrandt Bugatti's exotic animal tea services several years earlier in Paris.

Müller-Munk was not awed by the threat of the encroaching machine. In acknowledging the latter's potential for mass production, he stressed its decorative limitations against those of the traditional silversmith: "In keeping alive the craft of the hand-worker, I am not afraid of the machine's rivalry. The pieces which leave my hands should have the virtues of the slow and calculating process of design and execution with which they grew. On the other side, the factory product should reflect the exactness and mathematical economy of the machine that created it."[8] Sadly, the Depression's impact on the individual silversmith prevented Müller-Munk from engaging the machine in fair battle.

For a large commercial enterprise whose reputation had been built on period-revival wares, the International Silver Company made a surprisingly spirited contribution to the modern movement. Incorporated in 1898 in Meriden, Connecticut, the company produced in the 1920s a wide range of hollow- and flatware in silver, silver plate, and pewter, the last two through divisions such as the Wilcox Silver Plate Co. and Simpson, Hall, Miller & Co. The key to the firm's success was its decision to retain outside designers to provide up-to-the-minute designs, a step from which most large firms have, by tradition, shied away. In the late 1920s, Gilbert Rohde and Gene Theobald propelled the firm smartly into avant-gardism with a series of three-piece tea services – pot, creamer, and sugar – designed as architectural units housed on a conforming tray. Although clearly "machine-made," the prototypes had to be finished by hand.

The transition from hand-crafted to machine-made silverware presented engineering problems unforeseen by the industrial designer. Contrary to expectations, straight, angular forms did not at first lend themselves readily to machine production, with the result that the first batch of sparkling machined pieces were, paradoxically, hand-wrought. The absurdity of this situation was explained in an article in *Creative Art*: "For the simplicity of the rectangular form is really deceptive: the sharp corners must be skilfully soldered together out of separate pieces, and the plain faces must be handled with much care to keep them smooth. This design reminds the writer of hours spent in a small "studio" shop trying by disparate handicraft to produce metal work that might look direct enough to have been inspired by a machine, and clean enough to have been made by one – in modernism's name!"[9] Silver's standard mechanical processes – spinning and die-stamping – could not easily create perpendicular forms. The Rohde and Theobald tea services represent a milestone in American silver design, one that took it beyond Puiforcat's Cubism to the advent of mass-produced industrial design.

In 1928 Alfred G. Kintz introduced his popular "Spirit of Today" line. Included were "Northern Lights," a pattern inspired by the darting lights of the aurora-borealis, "Tropical Sunrise," and "Ebb Tide."[10] More conventional than the tea services by Rohde and Theobald, the "Spirit of Today" series incorporated broad, unornamented surfaces within decorative borders which gave emphasis to contrasts of light and shade.

Above

Eliel Saarinen urn and tray manufactured by the International Silver Company, silver, 14¼in. (36.2cm) height of urn, 18in. (45.7cm) diameter of tray, 1934. Illustrated in *Arts and Decoration*, December 1934, p. 21, exhibited at the Industrial Art Show, the Metropolitan Museum of Art, 1934 (collection Cranbrook Academy of Art/Museum)

Below

Two medallions: left: Norman Bel Geddes, designed for the General Motors 25th Anniversary, silver-plated bronze, 2¹⁵⁄₁₆in. (7.5cm) diameter, 1933 *right: Artist unidentified*, designed for the National Broadcasting Co.'s 10th Anniversary, silver-plated bronze, 2¹⁵⁄₁₆in. (7.5cm) diameter, 1936 (collection Mitchell Wolfson, Jr., Miami-Dade Community College)

Below

Norman Bel Geddes "Skyscraper" cocktail service with "Manhattan" serving tray, manufactured by the Revere Brass and Copper Company; chromium-plated metal, 12¾in. (32.4cm) height of cocktail shaker, 15⅛in. (38.4cm) length of tray (collection The Brooklyn Museum, gift of Paul F. Walter)

Above, left

Henry Dreyfuss thermos bottle and tray, enameled and chromium-plated metal and glass, 6in. (15.2cm) height of jug, 9¼in. (23.5cm) length of tray, impressed *The American Thermos Bottle Co Norwich Conn USA The Only THERMOS Reg. U.S. Pat. Office No 539 Vacuum Bottle Henry Dreyfuss*, c. 1935. Illustrated in *Streamline Design: How The Future Was*, exhibition catalogue, The Queens Museum, 28 January-6 May, 1984, #8 (collection Château Dufresne, Musée des Arts Décoratifs de Montréal, the Liliane Stewart Collection)

Above, right

James Mont coffee service; chromium-plated metal and painted wood, all impressed JAMES MONT 103, 7½in. (19.1cm) height of coffee pot, probably 1930s (collection Inglett-Watson)

Below

Norman Bel Geddes "Soda King" syphon bottle; chromium-plated metal, red enamel, and brass, impressed PAT. 20535 OTHERS PEND. SODA KING SYPHON MADE IN USA and WALTER KIDDE SALES CO. INC. BLOOMFIELD N.J. DESIGNER NORMAN BEL GEDDES, 9¾in. (24.8cm) high, c. 1935. Illustrated in *Streamline Design: How The Future Was*, exhibition catalogue, Queens Museum, 28 January-6 May, 1984, #69 (collection Château Dufresne, Musée des Arts Décoratifs de Montréal)

Top, left

Wallace Brothers water pitcher with incised "Sun-Ray" motif; silver-plated brass, impressed B.M. MTS *Made in U.S.A.* W.B. MFG. CO. 3806, 8⅝in. (21.9cm) high, c. 1925 (collection Mitchell Wolfson, Jr., Miami-Dade Community College)

Top, right

Otar inkwell; copper and brass, impressed OTAR U.S.A. *Pat. Pend.,* 4½in. (11.4cm) high, c. 1928. Illustrated in *Brave New Worlds: America's Futurist Vision,* exhibition catalogue, The Mitchell Wolfson, Jr., Collection of Decorative and Propaganda Arts, 1984, p. 29, no. 250 (collection Mitchell Wolfson, Jr., Miami-Dade Community College)

Center

Gilbert Rohde tea service designed for the International Silver Company and manufactured by the Wilcox Plate Company, c. 1928. Silver-plated pewter and ebonized wood, all impressed *Pewter by Wilcox P25* with serial numbers, 2¾in. (6.9cm) height of teapot, 7¾in. (19.7cm) diameter of tray. Illustrated in *House and Garden,* May 1929, p. 149; and *Vogue,* May 11, 1929, p. 71 (collection Miles J. Lourie)

Bottom

Edward F. Caldwell & Co. desk set; silver, enamel, ivory, plastic, and leather, 6¼ in. (15.9cm) height of cigarette box, 19¹⁄₁₆in. (48.4cm) width of blotter, c. 1931. Illustrated in *The American Magazine of Art,* April 1932, p. 273; and *At Home in Manhattan,* Yale University Art Gallery, exhibition catalogue, 1983, p. 29, #10. A variation of the cigarette box, exhibited at the Industrial Art Exhibition at the Metropolitan Museum of Art, 1931, is illustrated in *Metalcraft,* October 1931, p. 144 (collection Albert Nesle, photo Charles Uht)

Below

International Silver Company "Diament"; tea service designed by Gene Theobald and manufactured by the Wilcox Silver Plate Company, silver-plated nickel silver and Bakelite, impressed WILCOX S.P. CO. EPNS INTERNATIONAL S. CO., 13¼in. (33.7cm) diameter of tray, 7¾in. (19.7cm) height of teapot, c. 1928. Illustrated in *Creative Art*, December 1928, p. I, and January 1929, p. xxii; *Vogue*, May 11, 1929, p. 71; and *House & Garden*, May 1929, p. 149 (collection John P. Axelrod)

Right

International Silver Company "Northern Lights" bowl from "Spirit of Today" series, designed by Alfred G. Kintz for Simpson, Hall, Miller & Co., a division of the International Silver Company, silver, 11¹¹⁄₁₆in. (29.7cm) diameter, impressed INTERNATIONAL with a plumed knight's helmet over a shield enclosing S, D105A, c. 1928. Illustrated in *House and Garden*, September 1928, p. 87; *The Jewellers' Circular*, 10 January 1929, p. 30, and 21 February 1929, p. 109; and *Vogue*, July 1, 1928, p. 59 (collection Geoffrey N. Bradfield)

Left

Ilonka Karasz coffee and tea service; electro-plated nickel silver, 7in. (17.8cm) height of coffee pot. Exhibited at the American Designer's Gallery, New York, 1928. Illustrated in *Creative Art*, Vol. 3, 1928, p. xviii; *The American Architect*, December 5, 1928, p. 751, and *House Beautiful*, February 1929, p. 153 (collection The Metropolitan Museum of Art, Purchase, Theodore R. Gamble, Jr. Gift, in honor of his mother, Mrs. Theodore Robert Gamble, 1979 (1979.219.1ab-4ab)

Other distinguished designers were retained by the firm in the 1930s, including Fred Stark, whose "Continental" flatware pattern was well received; Lurelle Guild, for a range of silver-plated hollow-ware, including a wine cooler and cocktail shaker with enameled detailing; Paul A. Lobel, for a characteristically sleek cocktail shaker; and Donald Deskey, for several significant designs.[11] Other established silver manufacturers likewise drew on the talents of top designers. For example, Rogers, Lunt, & Bowlen, whose origins can be traced to Newburyport in the 1880s, commissioned Robert E. Locher to design a range of Modernist silverware. His "Modern Classic" flatware service, with stepped, articulated handles, was introduced in 1934. In Taunton, Massachusetts, Reed & Barton introduced a crisp selection of ribbed and fluted contemporary pieces,[12] while in Philadelphia, J. E. Caldwell & Co. took a more cautious approach "to blend agreeably with any style of interior decoration."

Tiffany & Co.'s reluctance to pursue the modern aesthetic in its jewelry was echoed in its policy with regard to silverware. The firm's tradition of quiet and elegant restraint – demonstrated in a range of period-revival tableware and toiletry accessories was the proven choice of its patrician New England clientele throughout the 1920s. Only in the 1930s did it begin to promote Modernist silver, although one of its first ultra-modern designs – a faceted trophy weighing 150 ounces designed for the 1933 Century of Progress Exposition in Chicago – was made not in silver but in platinum and crystal.[13]

By 1937 examples of Tiffany's Modernist silver were more common, the company receiving enthusiastic press coverage for its entries in the "Contemporary American Design" exhibition at the Metropolitan Museum of Art. Included were several pieces designed and hand-wrought by the Dane, Peer Smed, who alternated between a lightly decorated Scandinavian-inspired style and that of a sheer, rectangular German functionalism.[14] In the same year the firm celebrated its centenary with the introduction of its "Century Pattern" flatware. By 1939 the

Below

Reed & Barton tureen, silver-plate, 13½in. (34.2cm) long, impressed REED & BARTON 1610 E.P.N.S., with trumpet and hallmarks (collection Denis Gallion and Daniel Morris)

earlier hesitancy was forgotten; Tiffany's Modernist silver display in the House of Jewels at the World's Fair surpassed those of its nearest competitors.

The battle between hand- and machine-made silver, referred to above, was abruptly set aside in 1930 by a formidable new adversary: a range of inexpensive, plated metal alternatives. Silver's elitist status was suddenly vulnerable, its costliness the target for designers of mass-produced metal home accessories, who offered a cheap range of duplicate metalwares. The challenge was made considerably easier by the deteriorating economy. Emphasis was placed on "stock" patterns: if a unique hand-wrought silver piece was out of reach – if one's pocket had to govern one's taste – it was preferable to acquire *some* distinctive pieces created by eminent designers, even if they were mass-produced, than to have nothing at all. "There is something in the idea of having copies of a few really good designs at prices that make it possible for many people to enjoy them."[15]

Metal's toll on silver was tremendous in the 1930s. Not only could the bright sheen of chrome and nickel compete with that of silver, but its rather garish glitter provided a semblance of opulence to the average homeowner in search of self-reinforcement. One firm, in particular, was successful in challenging silver's sovereignty: the Chase Brass & Copper Company.

Founded in Waterbury, Connecticut, in 1876, the Chase Brass & Copper Company manufactured industrial metalware such as wires, pipes, and electrical tubing. In the late 1920s the firm saw the opportunity to diversify into the domestic field, and in 1930 introduced a line of chromium-plated household products – not only kitchen utensils, but tableware, cocktail accessories, and dressing table

Below, left

Tiffany & Co. coffee service exhibited in The House of Jewels at the 1939 World's Fair, comprising a coffee pot, sugar bowl, cream pitcher, and tray; silver and black fiber, 9¾in. (24.8cm) height of coffee pot, 13in. (33cm) diameter of tray (photo Tiffany & Co.)

Below, right

Tiffany & Co. cocktail service exhibited in The House of Jewels at the 1939 World's Fair, comprising a mixer, 8 cups, and a tray; silver and cabochon emeralds, 14in. (35.6cm) height of mixer, 21⅞in. (55.6cm) length of tray (photo Tiffany & Co.)

Peter Müller-Munk coffee service; silver, gold, and ebony, all marked with encircled P, STERLING SILVER 925 1000, 7¼in. (18.4cm) height of coffee pot. Illustrated in *At Home in Manhattan*, Yale University Art Gallery, exhibition catalogue, 1983, p. 28, #9 (private collection, photo E. Irving Blomstrann)

Peter Müller-Munk tea and coffee service; silver and ivory, 10in. (25.4cm) height of kettle, 24¾in. (62.9cm) length of tray, impressed Ⓟ PETER MULLER-MUNK HANDWROUGHT STERLING SILVER 925/1000 STERLING, c. 1931. Illustrated in *Town and Country*, January 15, 1932, pp. 46-7 (collection The Metropolitan Museum of Art, gift of Mr. & Mrs. Herbert J. Isenburger, 1978)

Right

Peter Müller-Munk memorandum pad holder; silver, impressed PETER MÜLLER-MUNK, HANDWROUGHT STERLING SILVER 925/1000 with encircled P, 7¼in. (18.4cm) long (collection Miles J. Lourie)

Far right

Peter Müller-Munk "Normandie" pitcher manufactured by the Revere Copper and Brass Company, model #723, chromium-plated metal, impressed *Revere Rome N.Y.*, 12in. (30.5cm) high, c. 1936 (collection The Brooklyn Museum, H. Randolph Lever Fund)

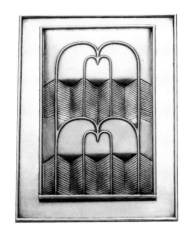

Below

Walter von Nessen "Diplomat" coffee set, model #17029 (pot, sugar, and creamer) and model #17030 (tray), designed for the Chase Brass & Copper Company, chromium-plated copper and plastic, the creamer impressed CHASE U.S.A., with firm's centaur logo, 8in. (20.3cm) height of coffee pot, 10in. (25.4cm) diameter of tray. Illustrated in *Interior Architecture & Decoration*, December 1931, p. 274 (collection John P. Axelrod)

Below, right

Walter von Nessen sketch of a covered punch bowl and cup in glass, chrome, and erinoid plastic; signed l/l FULL SIZE and l/r *Walter von Nessen Sep 12, 1935*, chalk and gouache on colored paper with applied silver cardboard cut-outs, 13 x 21in. (33 x 53.3cm). Illustrated in *Connoisseur*, January 1979, p. 49 (collection Alan Moss, Ltd.)

Below

Walter von Nessen sketch of a compact; pencil, and gouache on paper, signed l/r *Walter von Nessen May 10, 1935*, 8¼ x 10¾in. (20.9 x 27.3cm) (collection Alan Moss, Ltd.)

Below, right

Walter von Nessen sketch of a coffee pot; signed and dated l/r *Walter von Nessen Sep 12, 1935*, and l/l FULL SIZE, chalk and gouache on colored paper with applied silver cardboard cut-outs, 20⅞ x 13in. (53 x 33cm) (collection Alan Moss, Ltd.)

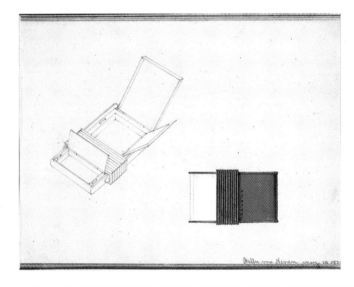

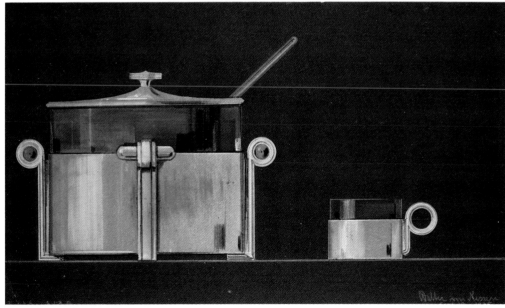

toiletry pieces. The timing was propitious: in the collapsing economy, chromium was an affordable alternative to silver. To assist it in its new departure, the firm hired designers such as Walter von Nessen, Gilbert Rohde, the Gerths (a husband and wife team), Russel Wright, Lurelle Guild, Rockwell Kent, Charles Arcularius, and Dr. Reimann, who was Director of the Reimann-Schuker School in Berlin.[16]

The firm deserves credit for several outstanding Modernist designs. Its cocktail and smoking accessories, in particular, were functional, chic, and crisply machined, the last an important promotional ploy in the pursuit of the Modernist market. Noteworthy were the "Smokestack" and "Cube" cigarette boxes; the pancake and corn set designed by Russel Wright; and after-dinner coffee services and martini mixers by Von Nessen. Rockwell's contribution, trumpeted in the firm's literature, appears to have been limited to a medallion of Bacchus applied to a wine cooler.

A small range of kitsch accessories – "Colonel" and "Colonel's Lady" nightlights and "Pelican" ash receivers – considerably weakened the firm's claim "to produce machine-made articles in quantity, at reasonable price, which will yet satisfy a high aesthetic standard."[17]

By 1934 Chase had gained sufficient respectability to persuade Emily Post to lend her influential name to the promotion of a new line of buffet serving pieces. She explained the timeliness of the firm's new line:

The present enthusiasm for every variety of buffet party would seem to be at least one happy result of the Depression, which, in shortening the purses of all of us, has brought appreciation of the simpler hospitalities. But whatever the cause, it is certainly true that among the nicest parties possible to give, the buffet luncheon, dinner or supper is far and away the most popular and smart. . . . Chase has designed an entirely new line of chromium articles. They are modern in feeling and yet harmonious with the knives, forks, plates, furniture and setting of the average home. Chromium that doesn't need polishing. Chromium that is moderate in price. Chromium that is new, smart and popular."[18]

To evoke further the sophisticated lifestyle with which it aligned itself, Chase introduced product names such as "Aristocrat" (an ashtray), and "Cosmopolitan" and "Connoisseur" (cigarette boxes). Smoking was, of course, highly fashionable among the young jazz set at the time, and the Chase catalogue shows that the firm produced an inordinate number of smoking accessories to meet the demand.

Below

Chase Brass and Copper Company candlestick designed by A. Reimann; copper, 6in. (15.2cm) high, c. 1931. Illustrated in *Creative Art*, Vol. 9, 1931, p. 479 (collection the Metropolitan Museum of Art, the Chase Foundation, Inc., and Edgar Kaufmann Gifts, 1976)

The initial inspiration for America's Modernist metalware came from the work produced by contemporary French ironsmiths: Brandt, Subes, Kiss, Piquet, Poillerat, and a host of now unsung *ferronniers*. Of these, Edgar Brandt demands special mention.

By 1920 Brandt had emerged from the shadow of the master nineteenth-century ironsmith, Emile Robert, to whom the credit for the French revival in metalware is due. Brandt surpassed his predecessor in both design and technique. The apparent ease with which he transformed iron's unyielding mass into the most ephemeral spray of summer flowers belied the metal's innate lack of malleability. He succeeded in taming iron, making it at once robust and plastic, bold and sinewy.

In the United States, Brandt's achievements, illustrated and documented in art reviews since the Art Nouveau era, became reality when he was commissioned to design and execute the metal elements for the Cheney Brothers building on the south-east corner of Madison Avenue and 34th Street, New York City.

The opening of the Cheney textile store (or silk emporium, as it was often referred to at the time) took place on October 14, 1925, at the moment when the curtain was being drawn on the Exposition Internationale in Paris. The American press understood fully the importance of Brandt's achievement: "The Cheney Building is the first building in this, or any other country, which Brandt has worked out as a complete unit in accordance with his own personal concept of modern design."[1] The Madison Avenue entrance created the most dramatic impact, its giant iron doors wrought with stylized palm fronds and florettes beneath a classic art moderne stepped fountain;[2] the design was an adaptation of the five-panel "Oasis" screen which Brandt had exhibited both at the 1924 Salon d'Automne and in his gallery at the 1925 Exposition Internationale.[3] Further delights awaited the customer on entering; most particularly, a series of fanciful wrought-iron "trees" on which the samples of silk were displayed.[4]

The Cheney commission, executed by Brandt in his Paris atelier, brought incalculable respectability to the Modernist movement in American architecture, then still in its infancy, and spawned a host of local imitations. In trade journal advertisements, the palm frond and fountain motifs, in repeat patterns, were offered by foundries and terracotta companies as spandrel and cornice decoration.

Left

Rose Iron Works screen designed by Paul Feher; wrought iron with aluminum and brass plate applications, impressed *Rose Iron Works Cleveland Ohio*, 62½in. (158.7cm) high. Exhibited at the 3rd International Exhibition of Contemporary Industrial Art, 1930-31, item #410. Illustrated in *Arts and Decoration*, January 1931, p. 58 (photo Severance Hall, Cleveland)

Below

Rose Iron Works console table; cadmium-plated iron and plate glass, 37in. (94cm) high, c. 1930 (photo Severance Hall, Cleveland)

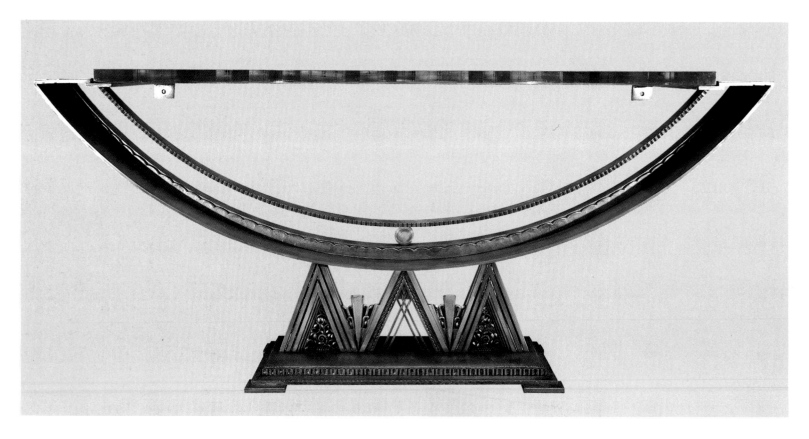

Further Brandt commissions followed quickly. The enthusiasm of one New York client, Miss A. Miles Carpenter, even ran to a novel set of window drapes made of wrought iron rather than fabric, complete with scalloped drapes, curtain ties, and bow-knots.[5]

In 1925 Brandt opened a branch office, Ferrobrandt, at 247 Park Avenue, New York, to service American customers. Its timing was auspicious, not only coinciding with the Exposition Internationale in Paris, but also preparing the way for Brandt's participation in the Exhibition of French Decorative Art at the Metropolitan Museum of Art the following year, and in the Lord & Taylor and R. H. Macy's exhibitions in 1928. Brandt's most expensive work, "L'Age d'Or," a monumental extravaganza in wrought iron with gilt-bronze applications, was shipped from Paris in July 1925 for exhibition in Ferrobrandt's booth at the International Exposition of Architectural and Allied Arts at the Grand Central Palace, New York.[6] For reasons that are not recorded, the firm appears to have closed within three years, though Brandt continued to furnish architectural elements for American buildings – grilles, gates, and furnishings – from Paris.

By 1930 the presence of metal in the American home could no longer be ignored and its progress matched that of European metal three to five years earlier. The Chase Brass & Copper Company, in a 1951 booklet, traced the metal industry's inroads into the decorative arts in the early 1930s: "A business enterprise dealing in raw materials first sees its products absorbed in strictly utilitarian operations. Metals at one time seemed relegated to this purpose. The engineering field alone in this mighty machine age could be depended upon to take care of all metal production. It was evidently not so. Metal, via architecture, entered the home, and having ingratiated itself as an acceptable material for furniture, is now an important decorative medium. This has been accomplished by what can truly be designated as art in industry."[7]

The American architect and designer were faced with what seemed like a new metal virtually every day, a bewildering array made increasingly complex by the large number of manufacturers and the range of alloys which each produced. An alloy offered by one foundry might be identical to that of another, but each carried its own brand name, further clouding the issue. Considerations of cost, color, tensile strength, durability, and beauty had to be made in each instance. In addition, certain metals required periodic cleaning and polishing to prevent tarnishing – an important factor in the choice of a metal for an inaccessible chandelier or architectural element. Although atmospheric weathering helped to enrich the patina on copper alloys, the dull lead-gray film which formed on the surface of nickel-copper, for example, was most unappealing.

To match an object to its preferred alloy was therefore a difficult task, requiring close collaboration between designer and metallurgist. Even when the choice had been narrowed in theory to a single alloy, there remained the question of whether its components would preclude its use for the job at hand. This, known as a metal's "workability" or degree of ductility, allowed for some alloys to be formed in one way, but not in another. "Monel" metal, for example, could be molded, drawn, rolled, stamped, forged, or machined, but could not be die-cast or extruded. If the shape of an item required its manufacture by spinning, another,

Below

Lee Schoen design of an iron door for Eugene Schoen, Inc.; pencil on tissue, signed l/r *Drawn by Lee Schoen*, 27⅛ x 17¾in. (68.9 x 45.1cm) , c. 1927 (collection Alan Moss, Ltd.)

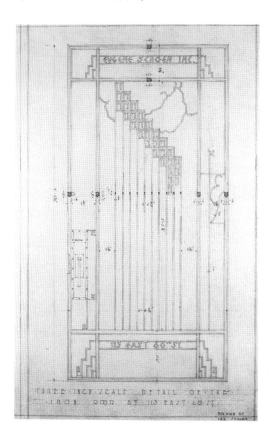

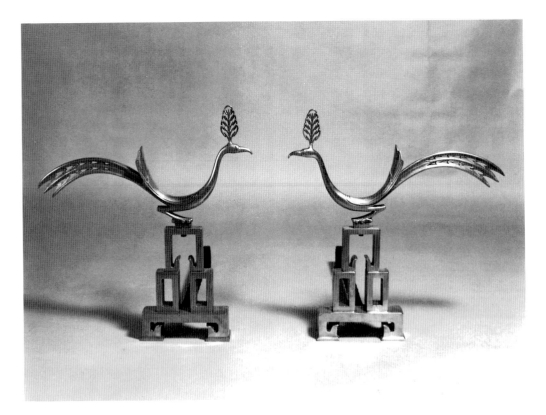

Eliel Saarinen bronze andirons; designed for the Saarinen house, Cranbrook, executed by the Sterling Bronze Co., 22⅜in. (56.8cm) high. Shown at the Exhibition of the Architectural League of New York, 1929. Illustrated in *The Metal Arts*, November 1928-December 1929, p. 224; and *Design in America: The Cranbrook Vision 1925-1950*, The Detroit Institute of Arts and the Metropolitan Museum of Art, exhibition catalogue, 1983, p. 161 (collection Cranbrook Academy of Art/Museum)

more suitable, metal would have to be used.[8]

The American Modernist movement settled on a group of five "white metals" for both its architectural and interior needs. These included aluminum, chrome steel, chrome nickel steel, "Monel" metal, and nickel-silver. In brief, their characteristics were as follows:

Aluminum had been associated with the household pot and pan since its first use in the late nineteenth century. From this humble obscurity it emerged to head the field of Modernist materials. It was light, strong, impervious to corrosion, and relatively inexpensive. Furthermore, its bright, natural finish was visually attractive, especially when used as a color note for upholstery fabrics and curtain drapes. Aluminum tubing was widely used for machine-made furniture by designers such as Warren McArthur, Eugene Schoen, and Kantack & Co.

Chrome steel was produced by a large number of firms, with only minor differences among the brands. Its great strength and high resistance to corrosion made it ideal for industrial usage, such as kitchenware. Marring its suitability for architectural decoration was the need for regular cleaning to maintain its surface luster. *Chrome nickel steel* was similar to chrome steel, but required virtually no maintenance, the added nickel content making it weather resistant (and more costly).

"Monel" metal was the brand name for a nickel-copper alloy, produced by the International Copper Company, which became a fashionable alternative to aluminum.[9] Its hardness made it ideal for machine production, in which the design could be stamped out. "Monel" was widely used for decorative trim, elevator doors, radiator covers, and balustrades, its silvery, mirrored surface resembling that of platinum. The fifth alloy in general use was *nickel-silver*, another hard metal which required cleaning. It resembled "Monel," but had a slightly yellowish cast.

The newly enhanced status of metal in interior decoration in the late 1920s was established, in part, by several New York exhibitions. Its greatest success was achieved in a single *ensemble*, that of Herman Rosse's all-metal dining room at the inaugural American Designers' Gallery exhibition in 1928. Suddenly gone was Brandt's ornamentation, to be replaced by the starkness promoted by the German Werkbund and the Bauhaus. Comprised of furniture and wall-paneling in "Monel" metal and chromium plated steel, the room was hailed as "the most revolutionary example of contemporary art that has yet been seen in this country."[10] Rosse's *ensemble* captured the critics' attention only momentarily. Other metal interiors were soon forthcoming, most notably at the 1929 exhibition of "The Architect and the Industrial Arts" at the Metropolitan Museum of Art and, in the same year, the exhibition of "Modern American Design in Metal" at the Newark Museum in New Jersey.

The nine architects in the Metropolitan Museum of Art exhibition took as their credo the promotion of metal within the modern interior. Furniture had to show in its form the characteristics of metal, rather than of wood. It was not surprising, considering the accumulated talents of the participants, that the groundwork was well laid for the American metal furniture industry: "The amount of metal work in the interior treatments shown in the Exhibition of Contemporary Design now being held at the Metropolitan Museum of Art is one of the strongest proofs that the present increase in the use of ornamental metal work is but the beginning of an astonishing development."[11]

At Newark, thirty designers and architects contributed a series of metal room settings. Works by Ely Jacques Kahn, William Lescaze, Kem Weber, and Alexander Archipenko were included. Noteworthy was the selection of aluminum seat furniture by Von Nessen, and Formica-topped metal tables by Frankl and Deskey. Pride of place, however, was reserved for Lee Simonson's stepped grand piano, its tapering metal supports reminiscent of the Modernist prototype in glass and metal by Pierre Legrain some years earlier in Paris.[12]

After a further, and final, museum show in 1930/31, which placed special emphasis on metal furnishings, metal's legitimacy was assured, and the corresponding need for its promotion waned. The Third International Exhibition of Contemporary Industrial Art, staged by the American Federation of the Arts at the Metropolitan Museum of Art, was shared by two seemingly unrelated media. Entitled "Decorative Metalwork and Cotton Textiles," the metal section, in particular, yielded a bounty of exquisite contemporary designs.[13] In addition to works by seasoned Modernists such as Pola and Wolfgang Hoffmann, Reiss, Von Nessen, Schoen, and Deskey, there was a crop of fresh pieces, including a screen by Paul Feher for the Rose Iron Works, Cleveland, its execution of surpassing quality for an American ironsmithery. Paul A. Lobel's screens and the chic, angular accessories shown by the Chase Brass & Copper Company, and Edward F. Caldwell & Co., also drew praise.

Only one metalworker in the United States could match Brandt's technical virtuosity, the German-born *Oscar Bach*. By the age of 20, Bach had established his reputation with the commission to design all the metal work in Berlin City Hall. Success followed success until, in 1914, he left for the United States, opening a studio at 511 W. 42nd Street, New York.[14] A thorough training in European art enabled Bach to create works of different periods and styles with equal proficiency. Liturgical commissions, especially, provided a steady source of income, as, increasingly in the 1920s, did both architectural and domestic work.

Bach's participation in the Modernist movement was substantial, both in the numerous items which he designed and executed himself – for example, the chrome nickel steel furniture for Raymond Hood's office in the Daily News Building, New York,[15] – and in those which he made to others' designs. These included, most importantly, interior metalware in the Chrysler and Empire State Buildings, and four monumental plaques by Hildreth Meiere for the façade of the Radio City Music Hall. Three of these, 18 feet (5.5 meters) in diameter, and depicting the spirits of song, dance, and drama, were for the exterior of the Music Hall. The fourth, 42 by 24 feet (12.8 x 7.3 meters), was positioned over the entrance. The plaques allowed Bach to give full play to his technical prowess: enameled and *repoussé* copper, bronze, aluminum, and chrome nickel steel components were soldered or riveted together, each chosen to provide a specific textural or contrasting color effect.[16] For the interior of the Music Hall, Bach created steel overdoor ornamentation and bronze panels inlaid with black Bakelite.

Walter Kantack emerged as a foremost manufacturer of metalware in the modern idiom. Situated at 238-240 E. 40th Street, New York, he came to prominence partly through his association with the decorating firm, French & Co.,[17] and architects such as Buchman & Kahn and Voorhees, Gmelin, & Walker, for whom he provided a wide range of metal furnishings and decorative accessories, such as grilles, mirrors, and tables in sheet and cast aluminum. The tables, in particular, showed a high degree of complexity and artisanship, their polished cast aluminum frames applied with teak and ebony veneers to set off the metal's bright sheen.[18]

Other important commissions included the metalware for Mr. A. V. Davis' yacht, "Elda," in which a pair of pierced aluminum grilles of seagulls caught the interior's contemporary theme.[19] Another opportunity was provided by the commission to decorate the Irving Trust Company's offices in New York for Voorhees, Gmelin, & Walker. At the 1929 Exhibition of Industrial Art at the Metropolitan Museum of Art, Kantack collaborated with Ely Jacques Kahn and also with the sculptor Edmond R. Amateis, for whom he executed a large urn decorated in bas-relief with a band of giraffes, for display in the backyard garden presented by Ely Jacques Kahn.[20]

Below

Unidentified designer chromium-plated frieze, St. George's Hotel, Brooklyn (Schlanger & Ehrenrich, architects), 7 ft (21m) long, probably 1930s

Right

Wilhelm Hunt Diederich "Fox and Hounds" fire-
screen; wrought iron and wire mesh, *unsigned*, 44in.
(111.8cm) high, late 1920s (collection de Lorenzo
Gallery)

Right

Jules Bouy mantelpiece designed for Ferrobrandt,
Inc.; wrought iron and shellac, 77¾in. (197.5cm)
high, c. 1930. Illustrated in *Talk of the Town*, 6 April,
1930, p. 19; and *At Home in Manhattan*, Yale
University Art Museum, exhibition catalogue, 1983,
p. 75 (collection The Metropolitan Museum of Art, gift
of Juliette B. Castle and Mrs. Paul Dahlstrom, 1968)

From 1928 to 1933 Kantack & Co. published *Kaleidoscope*, a quarterly magazine in which the firm's philosophies and recent works were reviewed. Included were numerous articles by Walter Kantack, outlining his doctrine on modern lighting. Lighting was clearly Kantack's principal fascination. Lengthy dissertations were given on the union of metal and glass, and the related soft interplay of light, both direct and indirect. Examples of the firm's modern fixtures, such as those in polished aluminum for the Center Theater in Rockefeller Center[21] and the Joslyn Memorial in Omaha, Nebraska, accompanied the text. The lamps included etched glass panels provided by the Corning Glass Works.

Jules Bouy is one of the more tantalizing figures of the American Modernist movement. Little information is available on his work in the 1925 to 1935 years, a period in which he created several arrestingly beautiful metal pieces. French-born, Bouy moved to the United States in 1913 after a stay in Belgium. In the mid-1920s his time was divided between the production of period furnishings for Alavoine & Co., and the management of Brandt's New York office, Ferrobrandt. It was while he was with Ferrobrandt, presumably, that Bouy developed his distinctive Modernist style. A series of metal table lamps and tables incorporated skyscraper columns which matched developments in contemporary New York architecture.[22] His wrought-iron mantelpiece with its powerful depiction of the spire on the Chrysler Building, further shows his commitment to the new aesthetic.

Born to the Hungarian gentry, *Wilhelm Hunt Diederich* emigrated to the United States at the age of 15, "an untamed spirit, wild, romantic, full of enthusiasm." He settled in Boston, the home of his grandfather, William Morris Hunt, a noted local artist. During a restless adolescence he moved back and forth to ranches in Wyoming and Arizona, before enrolment at the Pennsylvania Academy of Art.[23]

Diederich brought a vivacious personality to his work in several disciplines, especially metalware, ceramics, and printed fabrics. Of these, metalware held pride of place. The artist's lifelong love of animals manifested itself in his work. "Animals are part of art themselves, they possess such glorious rhythm and spontaneity," he wrote,[24] and his bestiary included coursing greyhounds, prancing stallions, bulls, and ibexes.[25] A favorite theme was "The Fox Hunt," repeated in firescreens, stair railings, and *torchères*.

It is hard to conceive of a more delightful medium of expression for Diederich than wrought iron. His animals – elongated, highly stylized, playful, or locked in violent motion – were portrayed marvelously in handwrought metal, the effect heightened when seen in silhouette.

Paul A. Lobel was another artisan to ally himself with the contemporary movement in the decorative arts. He designed and executed a group of small household accouterments – andirons, screens, doorsteps, etc. – at his New York studio, Lobel-Uris, Inc. These, in rolled steel and brass, retain a distinct ultramodern charm, their light tubular frames tracing the silhouettes of birds and animals.[26]

An ironsmith of merit, although the paucity of his works on today's market seems to suggest a modest output, *John B. Salterini* headed a small team of artisans at his studio on West 23rd Street, New York. Salterini produced an inspired selection of Modernist furnishings, especially light fixtures, in wrought iron accented with enamels of inlays of other metals.[27]

Below

Kantack & Co. furniture for the Officers' lounge of the Irving Trust Co. (Voorhees, Gmelin, & Walker, architects); bronze and aluminum, the woven wallpaper fabric depicting a recurring Indian war bonnet motif)

Obscure foundries achieved passing fame, particularly in the New York boroughs, where many of the commissions for decorative metalware, both architectural and household, were awarded; for example, Renner & Maras, Stern & Matzner, Sexauer & Lemke,[28] in Long Island City; and Lansha Studios, E. Fechner & Co., the Sterling Bronze Co., the Metal Door & Trim Co., Wm. H. Jackson & Co., and the General Bronze Corporation, in Manhattan. For five industrious years, firms such as these churned out metal fixtures of remarkable quality. By the end of 1931, however, when most of the grandiose Modernist façades and lobbies of America's pre-Crash architectural boom had been built, production fell precipitously as the need for decorative elements was suddenly seen to be obsolete.

Largely forgotten since America's Colonial days, pewter recaptured the limelight briefly in the late 1920s thanks to Pola and Wolfgang Hoffmann, who chose the alloy for a distinctive series of Constructivist-style desk accessories – pentrays, cigarette holders, etc. The inspiration for these small objects was probably Rena Rosenthal, who imported pewter items by George van Anda and Martinus Andersen for her New York gallery. Another to select pewter, if only momentarily, was Walter Dorwin Teague, who designed a range of bowls and candelabra for Marshall Field in Chicago. Not only was pewter too soft for most manufacturing purposes, but also its dull gunmetal color could not compete with the fashionable gleaming metals of the 1930s.

Right

E.H. Faile (architect) duplicate panel to that installed above the entrance of the Goelet Building, 608 Fifth Avenue, New York, 1930, polychromed cast aluminum. Illustrated in *Metalcraft*, December 1931, p. 232 (photo Sotheby's, New York, courtesy of Catherine C. Kurland)

≡ CERAMICS

American ceramics underwent a dramatic revolution between the two World Wars, in a battle waged on the two fronts of technique and style. Like related disciplines in the applied arts (especially glass), the ceramics industry – consisting of both commercial potteries and individual art potters – had passed through the pre-1914 years unceremoniously and without character. The public's need for domestic pottery – principally tableware – was met by a range of molded and lightly painted functional objects, their shapes and decoration rehashed on occasion to provide slight variety. Matters remained largely unchanged until the late 1920s, when a series of events created an infusion of ideas unparalleled in the history of the medium.

Curiously, neither the cause nor the effect of this most fertile period in American ceramics has been analyzed until very recently.[1] The reasons for this are twofold. Firstly, the development of postwar ceramics was – to American eyes – in the hands of German designers, and the anti-German mood in the United States following World War II brought with it a reluctance to credit anything German. Secondly, there was a re-emergence in the same 1950s period of the belief that the traditional vessel (vase or bowl), rather than ceramic sculpture, was the medium's proper vehicle.

In fact, in the ceramic context, the postwar anti-German feeling was misplaced. Not only was the influence which inspired Americans Viennese rather than German, but its very appeal lay in the Austrians' rejection of all traditional European influences (the new style was appropriately called the Secession). The Viennese style, formulated in the first decade of this century in the work of Josef Hoffmann and his Wiener Werkstätte, came after World War I as a blast of fresh air to the American potter in search of a renaissance of his own.

By chance, the impact was felt most forcefully in Cleveland, where a Viennese designer, Julius Mihalik, brought its message to a class of eager young students at the Institute of Art. This happy accident in time and place changed the course of American ceramics for the next twenty years. At Mihalik's suggestion, Viktor Schreckengost, Russell Barnett Aitken, and Edward Winter, among others, made artistic pilgrimages to Vienna to witness first-hand the work of Michael Powolny, Vally Wieselthier, and other leading Wiener Werkstätte designers.[2]

The young Americans saw in the Secession style an unprecedented freshness and irreverence which echoed their own sense of rebellion. Wieselthier's roughly hand-molded ceramic figures epitomized the new disregard for traditional ceramic techniques. Imperfections in the clay were left untouched, uneven glazes allowed to drip unceremoniously. An object's impact lay in its spontaneity, not in its technical mastery. The new message was neither didactic nor morally elevating; it was, above all, wholesome. The new artist's tools were wit and vitality. These last would prove the most effective antidote to the lengthening shadow cast by the 1929 Crash. Although few of these ceramic artists, either in Vienna or in Cleveland, laid claim to ardent intellectualism, their new gaiety of expression was in no way intended to be superficial.

By the late 1920s the young Clevelanders had already been exposed to the numerous figurines which Guy Cowan used to decorate his commercial pottery. Now they returned from Vienna certain that the medium was best served by sculpture, rather than the vessel. This philosophy, coincidentally, elevated ceramics from the applied to the fine arts, bringing it wider public exposure and appreciation. In 1932, Edna Maria Clark reviewed Cowan's part in this breakthrough:

It was the work from the Cowan studio which first caused the art authorities to recognize ceramic sculpture as a true form of artistic expression; a precedent of long standing was broken when the Pennsylvania Academy of Fine Arts in 1928 invited an exhibition of Cowan pottery. Up to this time pottery and figures made of clay had occupied a secondary position in relation to the works of sculptors, whose media are marble or bronze.[3]

If marble and bronze were materials more suited to the heroic mode, nobody in Cleveland seemed either to notice or to care.

Beyond northern Ohio, the traditional world of decorated ceramic vessels remained largely unchanged. The Victorian painterly approach, developed into a cottage industry by pottery clubs in Cincinnati and elsewhere in the 1890s, prevailed in most industrial potteries. Decoration was eclectic, a mélange of

Left

Cowan Pottery group of artists, c. 1931. *Kneeling:* Waylande Gregory, Thelma Frazier Winter, R. Guy Cowan. *Standing:* Paul Bogatay, José Martin, Raoul Josett (photo Victoria Peltz)

Right

Cowan Pottery retouching figures as they were taken from the mold, c. 1929 (photo Victoria Peltz)

nineteenth-century, Oriental, Art Nouveau, Arts and Crafts, and French Modernist themes interchanged by most potteries seemingly at random.

The attention paid to the technical side of the craft was more intense and directed. The merits of underglaze slip decoration and sgraffito decoration were analyzed *ad infinitum*, as were those of high v. low temperature firing. Much valuable advice was made available to the artist potter by Adelaide Alsop Robineau in her monthly magazine, *Keramic Studio*, and in a host of other trade journals.

Cleveland's influence on ceramics can be traced, in part, to the series of annual exhibitions and competitions staged there between the Wars. William M. Milliken's appointment as Curator of Decorative Arts at the Cleveland Museum in 1919 provided an auspicious start. Among his responsibilities was the organization of a yearly exhibition to feature the work of local artists. Inaugurated in the year of his appointment, the Cleveland Exhibition of Artists and Craftsmen became an annual event known subsequently as the "May Show." In 1924 a special category was introduced for pottery and, in 1927, a further one for ceramic sculpture.[4]

The 1926 exhibition at New York's Metropolitan Museum of Art of objects from the 1925 Exposition Internationale introduced Americans to contemporary European ceramics, mostly French. Included were works by studio potters such as René Buthaud, Emile Decoeur, Auguste Delaherche, Emile Lenoble, and Jean Mayodon, in addition to examples from major manufacturers such as Sèvres, Haviland, and Longwy.[5]

American ceramics came of age two years later, in 1928, when four New York exhibitions provided the vast stage on which local ceramics would be pitted against those of Europe's finest artisans. The most important of these shows was the International Ceramic Exhibition, organized by the American Federation of the Arts, which opened its American tour at the Metropolitan Museum of Art in October, before continuing to seven other cities. Eight countries were represented. In retrospect, the sheer number of top names in the list of participants is impressive: Emile Decoeur and Emile Lenoble (France); W.B. Dalton and the Pilkington Tile and Pottery Company (England); Bing & Grondahl and the Royal Porcelain Manufactory of Copenhagen (Denmark); Max Läuger (Germany); Vally Wieselthier and Susi Singer (Austria); and Adelaide Alsop Robineau, Henry Varnum Poor, Carl Walters, Dorothy Warren O'Hara, Charles F. Binns, and Leon V. Solon (United States).[6] Analysis of the press coverage accompanying the exhibition shows that, although Europe was ahead, America's ex-Europeans were quickly catching up.

Three other exhibitions in which ceramics were included helped the critics to evaluate the progress of American potters: those at R. H. Macy's, Lord & Taylor, and the American Designers' Gallery. European and local potters exhibited in both department store shows,[7] but entry to the American Designers' Gallery was reserved for Americans only. At the last-mentioned it was Henry Varnum Poor's tiled ceramic bathroom, fired by Thomas Maddocks Sons, which won unanimous praise as the show's masterpiece. One ecstatic critic interpreted it as "the evident love, respect, and humility of a worker before his material."[8]

Right

Russell Barnett Aitken "Trojan Plaque"; signed and dated *Russell B. Aitken 1932*, 18½in. (47cm) diameter. Displayed at the Fourteenth Annual Exhibition of Work by Cleveland Artists and Craftsmen, 27 April-5 June, 1932, Cleveland Museum of Art (collection Cowan Pottery Museum, photo Larry L. Peltz)

Another selection of ceramics appeared in 1929 in the American Designers' Gallery's second, and final, exhibition. Included were a luncheon set and plaques by Poor, a terracotta group by William Zorach, and faience sculptures by America's newest immigrant, Vally Wieselthier. In 1931 a further show, entitled Contemporary American Ceramics, was held in New York at W. & J. Sloane on Fifth Avenue. Entrants included Arthur E. Baggs, Paul Bogatay, Guy Cowan, Viktor Schreckengost, Maija Grotell, and the ubiquitous Poor.[9]

The center of gravity of the modern ceramics movement shifted in the 1930s to northern New York state. In 1931 the Syracuse Museum of Arts (now the Everson Museum of Art) established itself as a major influence in the field with the introduction of the first of its celebrated annual shows, the Robineau Memorial Ceramic Exhibition.[10] One key to the Museum's success was its neutrality in the ceramic sculpture v. vessels dispute. Its philosophy was that all ceramics – whatever the individual artist's preferred form of expression – should be promoted as a unified art rather than as a fractured craft. Another factor in its favor was its location, more or less midway between Cleveland and New York, which made it both neutral and mutually convenient. The success of the inaugural 1931 show – limited to New York State entrants – led the following year to its expansion into a national show.[11]

The Syracuse exhibition afforded numerous Ohio and New York potters nationwide prominence throughout the 1930s. Among the regular participants were Carlton Atherton, Russell Barnett Aitken, William Hentschel, Viktor Schreckengost, Arthur E. Baggs, and Paul Bogatay.

The success of the Syracuse Museum's annual show can be measured by the fact that in 1936 it was renamed the Fifth National Ceramic Exhibition (Robineau's name now reduced to parenthesis beneath the title). In celebration, 135 pieces by living American potters were selected for a two-part traveling exhibition, initially within the USA and then to four Scandinavian museums. The Scandinavian exhibition, the first by American potters overseas, generated an article in *Fortune* magazine which provides an interesting chronicle of the way in which ceramics was perceived by the American public at the time. After a brief description of the medium, in which the writer found that American ceramics "lacked even a high point from which to decline," he wrote enthusiastically of some of the items included in the Scandinavian tour, and of the potential they engendered: "The Transatlantic journey of the Syracuse show does not mean that American ceramic art has suddenly taken an equal place with that of other countries in their great periods. But it is being permitted to appear on the same stage."[12]

None of America's foremost Art Nouveau potteries made an enthusiastic or successful transition to 1920s Modernism. Even the Rookwood Pottery Company, a monolith of the pre-1914 era, failed to align itself with the move towards ceramic sculpture between the Wars. The firm's focus remained firmly on the vessel as the medium's traditional, and therefore proven, vehicle. This policy, it must be noted, was forged of economic necessity. It was risky for a large firm to embrace a new style – the costs of experimentation and marketing, not to mention public caprice – were enough to deter Rookwood from making a full commitment to anything new. The firm did, however, encourage its individual decorators to

pursue the new vogue, both through a study of the top French exponents
(especially Decoeur) and through research in its extensive library.[13] Fine Modernist examples were created, but Rookwood's goal in the 1920s and '30s was
primarily to survive. This it did, only precariously, and in 1939 the firm filed for
bankruptcy.

Not only did the shapes of Rookwood's vessels remain basically Neoclassical,
but most of its 1920s decoration appears as a diluted, if not exhausted, variant of
its earlier, dynamic aesthetic. In addition, the majority of the items produced were
unsigned, a telling change from the proud 1900-1910 era when the artist's initials
were as fundamental to a vase's creation as its appealing floral or landscape
decoration.

Several decorators did, however, master the newest design challenge from
Paris, especially William Hentschel, Jens Jensen, Edward T. Hurley, Sara Sax,
Harriet E. Wilcox, and Elizabeth Barrett. Hentschel and Jensen, in particular,
adopted the modern French style with an ease and immediacy which belied their
employment by a Cincinnati-based pottery. Attention was also paid to the creation of new glazes: six at least were introduced in the 1920s: Tiger's Eye (a
variation on an earlier glaze with the same name), Flambé, Oxblood, Jewel
Porcelain, Wax Mat, and the so-called Water Color.[14]

Most other pottery studios and individual artist potters who had come to prominence at the turn of the century in America — for example, Fulper, Grueby,
Newcomb, Roseville, Van Briggle, Weller, Pewabic, Lenox, and Dedham — continued to produce a largely predictable, lightly decorated range of tableware
and accessories. Several of these disappeared quietly between 1900 and World

War I – Grueby, for example, closed its doors in 1910 – while others continued to service the department store market, apparently oblivious to the rejuvenation underway in northern Ohio and New York.

Isolated examples of modern design indicate that matters might have been otherwise. Roseville, for example, interrupted its annual production of coarsely decorated commercial fares to introduce, in 1924, its "Futura" pattern and, in the late 1930s, "Moderne" – two up-to-the-minute designs introduced, curiously, fifteen years apart.[15] Futura's stepped streamlined shapes in fact seem to have predated by four or five years the New York skyscrapers whose contours they appeared to echo.

Two large pottery manufacturers – the American Encaustic Tiling Company in New York, and the Enfield Pottery and Tile Works in Pennsylvania – showed what industrial firms with a little imagination might have achieved. Both drew on out-side designers – for example, Paul P. Cret (by Enfield) and Leon V. Solon and Augustine Lazo (by the American Encaustic Tiling Co.) – to produce a charming selection of glazed faience tiles in the Modernist idiom.[16] Demand for these was both domestic and industrial, the latter a potential goldmine for any alert potter in the 1920s. Architectural decoration offered boundless opportunities for decorative ceramics in America.

No analysis of twentieth-century American ceramics – even one on the modern style which came to bloom in the last few years of her life and which touched only marginally on her work – is complete without a reference to the country's single virtuoso artist, *Adelaide Alsop Robineau*. Robineau was the potter's compleat potter, her "taste and technique magnificently fused."[17] Her achievements matched anything by Europe's finest potters. This instilled in her fellow American ceramicists the hope, if not the expectation, that they could do as well.

Reginald Guy Cowan provided, through the Cowan Pottery, the forum, however momentary and fragile, for a dozen of America's most gifted young ceramicists. For ten years – from 1921 until the firm went into receivership in late 1930 – the Cowan Pottery was at the forefront of modern American ceramic design. Part of its success lay, as already mentioned, in Cowan's emphasis on pottery as sculpture.

Cowan was born in East Liverpool, Ohio, to a family of potters. Early practical and formal training led to the establishment of his own pottery on Nicholson Avenue in Lakewood, Cleveland, from where he moved, when the local gas well ran dry, to Rocky River, west of the city. In the early 1920s the Cowan Pottery Studio began commercial production and distribution. Some 1,200 national out-lets were established, including Marshall Field in Chicago, Wanamaker's in Philadelphia, and Ovington in New York.[18] On offer was a wide range of desk-top items – comports, figurines, vases, bookends – in bright lustered glazes, the most characteristic of which was a vibrant marigold color.

Commercial success came from Cowan's early adoption of the modernistic style. Vessels were angular, figurines likewise stylistically *à la mode*. The public responded eagerly to both the designs and the prices. From 1925 many well-known artists were affiliated with the Cowan Pottery, most notably Russell B. Aitken, Arthur E. Baggs, Paul Bogatay, Edris Eckhardt, Waylande Gregory, A. Drexel Jacobson, Margaret Postgate, Viktor Schreckengost, Elsa V. Shaw, Thelma Frazier and Edward Winter. Baggs and Cowan, with Richard O. Hummel, acted as the chemists, producing all the firm's glazes.[19] Many of these young talents were given free rein, and the resulting flow of stylish flower bowls, figurines, ivy jars, centerpieces, etc., perpetuated the pottery's earlier commercial success. If many of these are seen today as trivial, it should be remembered that the customers for whom they were intended were neither wealthy nor sophisticated. Like the wares of their counterparts in Europe – Goldscheider and Etling, for example – they were inexpensively made, often in a single glaze. The designs of several, however, such as Margaret Postgate's "Push-Pull" elephant bookends, transcend their modest budget.

In 1929 financial difficulties developed as the delicate balance between art pottery and commercial production began to erode. Quality fell as the Depression began to affect the volume of sales, and one particularly unpopular line of flower containers ("Lakeware") contributed greatly to the firm's loss of revenue. An attempted reorganization failed, and the Pottery went into receivership in December 1930. Ironically, some of the firm's most original pieces were created during this brief interim when closure was imminent.[20]

Cowan's major contribution to American ceramics was over, yet in a mere ten years he had steered it, and his young staff, away from the stuffy traditionalism inherent in Ohio's potteries and into the twentieth century.

Kansas-born *Waylande de Santis Gregory* undertook several architectural commissions before joining the Cowan Pottery in 1928, where he remained until its demise. His output in this period was stupendous; his sharply angular fashion-

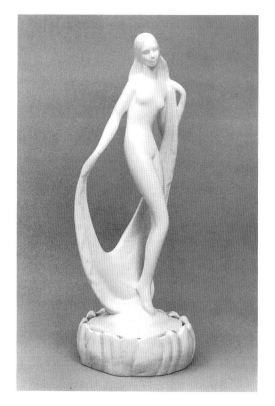

Far left

Waylande Gregory "Persephone," white glazed figurine for Cowan Pottery, 15in. (38cm) high, c. 1930 (collection Cowan Pottery Museum, photo Larry L. Peltz)

Left

Waylande Gregory "Boy and Fawn," glazed pottery for Cowan Pottery, 16½in. (42cm) high, c. 1929 (collection Cowan Pottery Museum, photo Larry L. Peltz)

able designs for pottery tableware pieces, in particular, won him numerous awards at the annual Cleveland Museum "May Shows" and contributed to the commercial success of his employer. His flower frogs, bookends, and – a singular Gregory success – Modernist "figure-in-a-bowl" centerpieces in gray, silver, and black glazes made his influence at the pottery second only to that of Cowan himself.

In the fall of 1931 Gregory moved from Rocky River to the Cranbrook Academy of Art, where he became an artist-in-residence with his own studio and kiln. No longer bound to designs which had to be adapted to a mold for commercial reproduction, he concentrated on technical innovation and, increasingly, on large-scale architectural ceramic sculpture. One of his inventions was a honeycomb technique of construction for oversized terracotta pieces. By the mid-1930s his work had lost its earlier art moderne stylization and his figures had become full-bodied and more naturalistic, similar to those of his Cranbrook colleague, Carl Milles. The decade was highlighted for Gregory by two important commissions for the 1939 New York World's Fair: *The Fountain of the Atom* and *American Imports and Exports*, the latter for General Motors.[21]

Many critics have recognized Gregory as the most gifted ceramicist of the period, and there is no doubt that his innate affinity for clay was boundless. Yet life was less kind: a series of professional and personal mishaps, accelerating in gravity as he grew older, eroded his talent.

Like Guy Cowan, *Viktor Schreckengost* was born into a family of Ohio potters. In 1924 he left Sebring to study at the Cleveland School of Art, spending his free time playing the saxophone and clarinet in "any band that would have him."[22] (Schreckengost's love of jazz has remained an important influence on his work as a ceramicist.) At Cleveland, one of his art instructors was the Viennese designer,

Right

Viktor Schreckengost "The Hunt"; punch bowl and plates for Cowan Pottery, underglaze decoration on white porcelain, 1931. Punch bowl 12in. (30.5cm) high, 16in. (40.6cm) diameter, plates 11½in. (29.2cm) diameter. The fox was painted on the bottom of the bowl's interior so that it is only visible when all the punch has been drunk. Illustrated in *Viktor Schreckengost*, retrospective exhibition catalogue, Cleveland Institute of Art, 14 March-3 April, 1976, inside cover (collection Viktor Schreckengost, photo Cleveland Institute of Art)

Julius Mihalik, whose influence on Schreckengost's generation of students has already been noted. The young artist's appreciation of the Viennese school was enhanced by the traveling International Ceramic Exhibition which opened at the Cleveland Museum of Art in 1929. Included was a collection of ceramic sculpture by Michael Powolny, in which Schreckengost found the freshness and vitality lacking in the formal pottery being produced in the USA. His application for the modest Page scholarship was accepted and, on the completion of his studies, he left to study under Powolny at the Kunstgewerbeschule in Vienna. The bustling gaiety of the Austrian capital, with its nightly cycle of cabaret and café entertainments, provided Schreckengost with the inspiration that helped him to revitalize the moribund Ohio pottery industry on his return. Reinstalled in Cleveland in 1930, he divided his week between teaching at the Institute of Art (where he still lectures, fifty-five years later), and working with the small group of artist-designers retained by Cowan in his last-ditch stand against bankruptcy.

Schreckengost's own recollection serves best to trace the events leading to the creation of his "Jazz Bowl," a period masterpiece which captured the dazzling mood of the early 1930s in a montage of skyscrapers, musical notes, cocktail glasses, gas lamps, and champagne bubbles:

I think it was my first week at the studio when Guy handed me this letter from a New York Gallery. They had a customer – "a lady in Albany" is all they said – who wanted a punch bowl "New Yorkish" in effect. New Yorkish! Now, that really piqued my interest and I imagined what the city meant to me. I always felt New York was most exciting at night, when it had a funny blue light over everything and great jazz bands were playing everywhere, Ozzie Nelson, Cab Calloway.

I thought back to a magical night when a friend and I went to see Calloway at the Cotton Club. My friend had only just arrived in New York from Vienna and he just flipped; he fell in love with the city, the jazz, the Cotton Club – everything. As I remembered that night, I knew I had to get it all on the bowl.

From the gallery came word that the "Jazz Bowl" as it has since become known, was a very big hit. This time they telephoned to say that the lady in Albany wanted two more just like it. "She wants one for Hyde Park," they said. That was our first clue that the customer was Eleanor Roosevelt. The other one was for the White House. According to the gallery, she was sure her husband – FDR was then governor of New York – would be there before too long.[23]

The "Jazz Bowl" was one of the last items put into production by the Cowan Pottery. A total of fifty, each a slight variation on the Roosevelt original, with carved sgraffito decoration in black slip over the white body with an Egyptian blue-green transparent overglaze, were sold through galleries and department stores at a suggested retail price of $50. The whereabouts of almost all of these are today unknown.

Schreckengost's impact on 1930s American ceramics extends beyond this short summary of his formative years. His entries at both the Cleveland "May Shows" and the National Ceramic Exhibitions drew repeated acclaim and awards. His designs, inspired always by his Austrian sojourn, were often bold and colorful, even exuberant. A touch of humour plays over everything he made. Two sets of dinnerware plates depicting, respectively, baseball and polo players,

Above

Henry Varnum Poor ceramic plate; underglaze decoration on white slip clay, c. 1923, signed H.V.P., impressed twice with Crowhouse kiln mark, 8in. (20.3cm) diameter. Illustrated in *At Home in Manhattan*, exhibition catalogue, Yale University Art Gallery, 1983, p. 55, #35 (collection Martin Eidelberg, photo Charles Uht)

Below

Adelaide Alsop Robineau "The Urn of Dreams"; porcelain vase, incised and glazed decoration, 1921, impressed with conjoined artist's monogram within a circle, I, THE URN OF DREAMS, and 1921, 10⅜in. (26.4cm) high (Museum of Art, Carnegie Institute, gift of Dana Robineau Kelley and family)

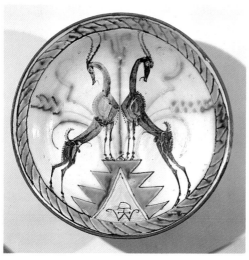

Above

Henry Varnum Poor ceramic plate; underglaze decoration on white slip clay, c. 1930, signed *H.V.P.* with impressed Crowhouse kiln mark, 8½in. (21.6cm) diameter. Illustrated in *Design*, Vol. 32, 1930-31, p. 214, and February 1934, p. 7; and *Henry Varnum Poor 1887-1970*, traveling exhibition catalogue, Pennsylvania State University Museum of Art, 1983, p. 40, #104 (collection Martin Eidelberg)

Right

Carl Walters walrus; lead-glazed earthenware, 1933, 7in. (17.8cm) high (collection National Museum of American Art, Smithsonian Institution, gift of IBM Corporation)

Below, right

Carl Walters pig; lead-glazed earthenware, 1930. Incised WALTERS 1930 with a circle in a square and a horse's head in profile, 8⅛in. (20.6cm) high. Illustrated in *Design*, June 1932, p. 56; and *At Home in Manhattan*, exhibition catalogue, Yale University Art Gallery, 1983, p. 60, #43 (photo Sotheby's, New York)

Below

Adelaide Alsop Robineau "Fox and Grapes"; incised and glazed porcelain covered jar. Signed AR within a circle, *1922*, and 4, 7¼in. (18.4cm) high (collection Jordan-Volpe Gallery)

Above

Wilhelm Hunt Diederich ceramic plate; painted signature *Hunt Diederich*, 10½in. (26.7cm) diameter (collection Inglett-Watson)

Above

Wilhelm Hunt Diederich bowl; lead-glazed earthenware, c. 1925, 15¾in. (40cm) diameter. Signed with artist's conjoined monogram (collection Martin Eidelberg)

provide an example of this ability to inject a much-needed degree of levity into the
American home,[24] as do his Hunt punchbowl and matching plates. Another
1930s creation, a set of sculpted figurines of Danish circus performers, was sheer
comedy.[25] A different side of the artist is seen in two satirical groups inspired by a
return trip he made to Europe in 1937 during which he became aware of the
specter of Fascism. These, "The Dictator" (1939) and "Apocalypse '42" (1942),
depict the Axis leaders and their intentions with a clarity that leads today's viewer
to question why others did not see matters similarly.[26]

Vally Wieselthier brought an unprecedented vitality and spontaneity to American
ceramics. Her colorful and carefree style, nurtured under Josef Hoffmann at the
Viennese Kunstgewerbeschule and then at the Wiener Werkstätte (which she left
in 1922), came to fruition at the 1925 Exposition Internationale. Two years later,
after a series of financial reversals, she returned to head the Wiener Werkstätte's
two ceramic departments. In October 1928, she accompanied the president of
the workshops on a trip to the USA, intending to stay in New York for six weeks,
partly, no doubt, to judge the response to her exhibits in the International Ceramic
Exhibition and the American Designers' Gallery. Eighteen months later Wieselthier returned briefly to Vienna, before settling permanently in the United States in
1929.[27]

Her impact on American ceramics, and especially on its Cleveland exponents,
cannot be overstated. Her modeled figures – playful, joyous, whimsical, vividly
colorful yet chic and sophisticated – provided the inspiration for those who
sought to escape the restrictive formality of the local craft. Her technique, likewise
unconventional, added to the charm: items were hand-formed, their separate
elements roughly joined. Inconsistencies and fingerprints were unconcealed

beneath an irregular glaze applied at a low temperature in a first firing. Bright accents of color – vermilion, cobalt, green, etc. – followed in the second trip to the kiln. The result was spontaneous, yet highly decorative. Lucian Bernhard has provided an eloquent summary of the appeal of Wieselthier's work:

Nature and the work of the man are contrasts – but when these combine, it results in a charming and spicy tension. Such is the work of Vally Wieselthier. Her art is playing and playful. It is an art originating in her joy of life, expressing a riotous combination of devilry and bubbling beautiful ideas. Her figures are jolly and happy in their droll garb, naive in their fresh color and in their utter friendliness to the plants among which they are destined to live. To see her work is to be livened and refreshed.[28]

Wieselthier created a wide selection of ceramic figures, masks, tableware items, mannikins, and busts, examples of which were shown by both Contempora and AUDAC, in addition to the National Ceramic Exhibitions.[29]

Two ceramicists, *Henry Varnum Poor* and *Carl Walters*, stand apart from those discussed above in their technique and interpretation of the modern style. Both came to the medium from a formal training in painting and both brought with them the fundamentals of that background. Poor was drawn to ceramics largely by expediency: he was unable to earn a living as an artist. The commercial failure of his first one-man exhibition of paintings at the Kevorkian Galleries in New York in 1920 provided the impetus for change. He described later how he came to choose ceramics as an alternative medium in *A Book of Pottery, From Mud into Immortality*:

I started doing pottery for the pleasure of decorating it, of having something entirely in my control from beginning to end so that both the object and images it held would be equally mine.[30]

Picking up the fundamentals of clay preparation and glazes from the sparse body of literature available to him, Poor quickly filled in the rest by experimentation. By the winter of 1920 he had installed a homemade kick wheel in a corner of his painting studio at "Crow House," his home in New City, Rockland County, New York. Now thirty-three years old, Poor began to throw and fire his first pottery commissions. By Christmas 1921, a selection of vases was on sale in the Bel Maison Gallery at Wanamaker's in New York City.[31] In mid-1922 he concluded a business arrangement with Newman Emerson Montross, a prominent dealer in modern art, and his first one-man show at Montross's gallery, entitled "Decorated Pottery, Paintings and Drawings by Henry Varnum Poor," followed in December of that year. Poor's technique was explained in the accompanying catalogue. Very simply, the shaped bone-dry clay model was coated with a white or cream-colored slip (liquid clay). Following an initial firing, the decoration was painted on in one or more metallic oxides, usually cobalt, manganese, copper, or iron. He adhered to the same basic formula in all his work, varying it on occasion from the mid-1920s with the addition of a second brown or black slip to allow him to articulate his images with carved sgraffito definition, such as his use of cross-hatching. A final colorless or lightly tinted lead overglaze accompanied the second, and final, firing.[32]

Above, left

Rookwood urn; decorated by Edward T. Hurley, impressed firm's mark, XXVIII, *2818*, with painted artist's initials, 19in. (48.3cm) high (photo Christie's, New York)

Above, center

Rookwood vase; decorated by William E. Hentschel, impressed firm's mark, XXVII, *1918*, with incised artist's monogram, 8¾in. (22.2cm) high (photo Christie's, New York)

Above, right

Rookwood vase; decorated by Wilhelmine Rehm, 1930, impressed firm's mark, XXX, *1780*, with incised artist's initials, 6½in. (16.5cm) hiah (collection John P.

Left

Waylande Gregory three glazed ceramic figures, late 1920s/30s. *Center:* "Salome," 1929, 19in. (48.3cm) high; *right:* "Radio," porcelain figure, illustrated in *Design*, April 1935, cover illustration (photo Cleveland Institute of Art)

Right

Vally Wieselthier sculpture in lead-glazed earthenware, incised MADE IN AUSTRIA VW with the Wiener Werkstätte monogram, 17½in. (44.5cm) high, before 1929. Illustrated in *At Home in Manhattan*, exhibition catalogue, Yale University Art Gallery, 1983, p. 93, #63 (collection Muriel Karasik, photo Charles Uht)

Far right

Vally Wieselthier "Fiona" stoneware bust, signed in relief slip clay FIONA WV, 14⅜in. (36.5cm) high. (The reversed artist's initials indicate that the piece was for exhibition purposes only.) (collection Alan Moss, Ltd.)

Right

Viktor Schreckengost (obverse) punch bowl for Cowan Pottery; porcelain with graffito decoration, 1931, 11½ x 16½in. (29.2 x 41.9cm). The model illustrated in *The Cowan Potters, Inc.*, March 17, 1931, p. 2, and *Cowan Pottery Museum*, Rocky River Public Library, exhibition booklet, 1978, p. 14 (collection Cowan Pottery Museum, photo Larry L. Peltz)

Right, below

Viktor Schreckengost (reverse) punch bowl for Cowan Pottery

Poor's style of pottery decoration is difficult to define within the context of the applied arts. His work remained deeply rooted in French Modernist painting, many subjects showing a Fauvist influence. Elsewhere, Cézanne, Braque, and Gris appear to have provided the inspiration. Although Poor did introduce some abstract motifs into his pottery decoration (mainly as borders), his style in ceramics and painting did not vary greatly, though he occasionally maintained that it did. In fact, he seemed little affected by the French art moderne movement within the decorative arts until about 1927, when he created a group of faceted vessels and star-shaped *jardinières* which evoked the style. In short, he appears in retrospect to be rather a painter-on-pottery than a ceramicist *per se*. None of this would bear comment were Poor not frequently identified by contemporary critics as "the best *potter* of the time."[33] The critics were, in fact, unanimous in their praise of his ceramic decoration, finding in his choice of color and painterly concern for composition a simplicity, softness, tranquility and restraint. To others, however, must belong the honor of being the medium's foremost technicians: Binns, Robineau, Cowan, and Baggs.

Following his exhibit at the 1928 American Designers' Gallery, Poor accepted several similar architectural commissions including, in the same year, a mural entitled *Sports* for the Hotel Shelton in New York City.[34] Later commissions included an eight-tile mural, *Tennis Players and Bathers*, for the financier, Edgar A. Levy.

Carl Walters created the period's most distinctly individual style in his speckled menagerie of terracotta and pottery animal figures. Self-taught as a ceramicist — to the point that he built his own stone studio and kiln at his home in Woodstock,

New York, and whenever possible created his own glazes – Walters came to the medium relatively late, having trained and worked as a painter until he was nearly 40. Among his most notable achievements was the development of a translucent blue glaze which closely rivaled that on ancient Persian ceramics.[35]

A procession of Walters's colorful and humorous animals, including a stallion, hippopotamus, mandrill, tiger, lion, duck, and cow, delighted viewers at the annual National Ceramic Exhibitions in Syracuse.[36] Shallow bowls carried the same themes in two dimensions. His entries at the 1933/34 Century of Progress Exposition – a bull and warthog – brought wide acclaim for their "pleasing unity of basic form, surface modeling, and glaze texture."[37] Walters did not attempt to model these animals literally, preferring to provide the subject with its own distinct personality in his choice of color and surface treatment. Most of these figures were produced in small editions from the same mold, the artist cleverly disguising this fact by adding small details to the final wet clay and by glazing and decorating them differently.[38]

Wilhelm Hunt Diederich was another whose versatility afforded him movement between media. Primarily a metalworker (see Chapter 6), he became interested in ceramics around 1923 during a trip to Morocco, and he used an identical range of sporting and animal themes to decorate a selection of pottery plates. He was awarded a gold metal for his entry at the 1927 Architectural League exhibition in New York.[39]

Right

A. Drexel Jacobson "Introspection," black glazed pottery figure for Cowan Pottery, 8⅜in. (21.2cm) high, c. 1929 (collection Cowan Pottery Museum, photo Larry L. Peltz)

Above

Thelma Frazier Winter vase for Cowan Pottery; incised relief decoration, 10in. (25.4cm) high (collection Cowan Pottery Museum, photo Larry L. Peltz)

Above, right

Thelma Frazier Winter octagonal plate; signed and dated *T. Frazier 1930* with impressed Cowan underglaze mark, 13in. (33.1cm) diameter (collection Martin Eidelberg)

Below, left

William E. Hentschel sketch for a ceramic plaque; *pochoir* on paper, 1929, signed and dated, 10 x 9in. (25.4 x 22.9cm) (collection Jordan-Volpe Gallery)

Below

Elsa Vick Shaw ceramic tile; incised relief decoration, incised artist's initials, 16¼in. (41.3cm) square (collection Denis Gallion and Daniel Morris)

Right

Hall China Company five teapots in Chinese red glaze. *Top row:* Football (1938) and Airflow (1940); *bottom row:* Doughnut (1938), Automobile (1938), and Rhythm (1939); all with gilt-stenciled signature HALLS SUPERIOR QUALITY KITCHENWARE within a rectangle, and MADE IN U.S.A. (collections William Straus, Diane Petipas, and Jon Brothers)

Right

Russel Wright selection of "American Modern" dinnerware. *Top row, left to right:* teapot, water pitcher, sauce boat, and wine carafe; *bottom row, left to right:* sugar, cereal bowl, salt and pepper, cup and saucer, celery dish, and creamer. Bean brown and coral glazes, designed 1937 (collection William Straus)

Below

Roseville three "Futura" vases. *Center:* #368, 8in. (20.3cm) high; *right:* #385, 8in. (20.3cm) high (collection John P. Axelrod)

Below, right

Roseville four "Futura" vases. *From the left:* #402, 8in. (20.3cm) high; #393, 12in. (30.5cm) high; #411, 14in. (35.6cm) high; and #401, 8in. (20.3cm) high (collection John P. Axelrod)

GLASS

The standard of design in American glass between the two World Wars fell in general well short of that in other disciplines, for reasons that are not fully clear. Only twenty-five years earlier, American art glass matched that of Europe in its interpretation of, and enthusiasm for, the then prevailing "modern" style: Art Nouveau. Tiffany's inimitable creations had brought America preeminence in a revolution whose genesis can be traced to Emile Gallé's floral prototypes at the 1878 and 1889 World Expositions. Steuben, Quezal, Durand, and Kew Blas had followed Tiffany's leadership, their vibrant handblown flower-form vessels capturing precisely the turn-of-the-century's new mood and taste. Today, however, American glass of the 1925 to 1939 era appears disjointed; no clear style or direction emerges. Certainly there were occasional pieces of arresting originality, but designs were in general banal, and often "kitsch." Convention proved the norm, with glasshouses reverting to eighteenth- and nineteenth-century forms. On the relatively few occasions when Modernist design was adopted, it featured in an object's decoration, rather than in its shape.

As in Europe, the vivid, pre–World War I palette yielded to achromatism; where previously the rainbow had predominated, absence of color was now the norm, embellished, on occasion, with enameled accents. Newly named colors appeared – ice (clear glass with a touch of green), salmon, coral, topaz, wisteria – and sparingly cut or etched decoration complemented them. Intaglio decoration allowed the light to play on the crystal's surface, emphasizing its innate transparency and brilliance. Cheaper wares were molded with bas-relief decoration.

There was no lack of opportunities for the American glass designer to keep abreast of new developments in European glass. For those who missed the 1925 Exposition in Paris, the Metropolitan Museum of Art's 1926 exhibition provided a showcase of the finest of modern French glass – examples by Daum, Lalique, Goupy, Walter, Decorchemont, and the epoch's widely acclaimed *maître*, Maurice Marinot. Also shown were examples manufactured by J. and L. Lobmeyr (from designs by Josef Hoffmann and Michael Powolny) and Orrefors.[1]

The 1928 exhibitions at R. H. Macy's and Lord & Taylor increased American exposure to modern European design. Important names now added included: Navarre, Luce, Baccarat, and Rouard (French); Kosta (Swedish); Vetri Soffiati

Above

Sidney Biehler Waugh "Europa"; crystal bowl designed for the Steuben Glass Company, engraved by Joseph Libisch, 9%6in. (24.3cm) high, 1935. Illustrated in *Sidney Waugh*, American Sculptors Series 6, W. W. Norton, 1948, p. 50; and *Steuben Glass*, James S. Plaut, H. Bittner, New York, 1951, pl. 52 (collection The Cleveland Museum of Art, Dudley P. Allen Fund)

Below

Walter Dorwin Teague "Spiral" pattern candlestick; designed for the Steuben Glass Company, model T-32, catalogue No. 7486. Blown and etched glass with etched signature *Steuben*, 5⅜in. (13.7cm) high, 1932. The pattern illustrated in *The Glass of Frederick Carder*, Paul V. Gardner, Crown Publishers, 1971, p. 321 (collection The Chrysler Museum, gift of Walter P. Chrysler, Jr.)

Muranesi Venini (Italian); and the Deutsche Werkstätten A.G. (German).[2] Further examples of avant-garde European glassware were imported throughout the 1920s and early 1930s by New York galleries and department stores; for example, Rena Rosenthal (especially fluted beakers and bowls by Hoffmann), the Park Avenue Galleries (La Maison de May), Wanamaker's and Saks Fifth Avenue (both Lalique).[3] Bullocks Wilshire and Barker Bros. in Los Angeles, Marshall Field in Chicago, and Wanamaker's in Philadelphia followed suit.

What impact did the modern style have on America's premier glassmakers, in particular, on *Louis Comfort Tiffany* himself? Tiffany's monolithic influence on the American decorative arts in general, and glass in particular, at the turn of the century lessened his ability to comprehend or accept in any way the new Modernism of the 1920s. Certainly his years militated against change – in 1920 he was 72 – and he continued to oppose the new Parisian style and the gradual inroads it made into American taste until his death in 1933. Output at Tiffany studios reflected its founder's intransigence. Annual sales diminished steadily from the spectacular 1900-10 years until bankruptcy loomed in 1930. Other Art Nouveau glasshouses which had failed to adjust to the new mood became casualties in the same way. In France a host of glassworks in and around Nancy in Alsace quietly closed their doors, including the Gallé works – another Art Nouveau giant which had failed to modify its product to the new dictates of Paris. As late as 1929, Tiffany's participation in the International Exhibition of Contemporary Glass and Rugs, arranged under the auspices of the American Federation of Arts, included a selection of Favrile vases, in decoration and shape indistinguishable from those created a full quarter-century earlier. More astonishing even than the firm's selection of such items for an exposition of contemporary art in 1929 is the fact of their acceptance by the show's reviewing committee.

Another designer whose training was rooted in the nineteenth century was *Frederick Carder*. An accomplished competitor to Tiffany from 1903, when he established the Steuben Glass Company in Corning, until World War I (Steuben was absorbed by the Corning Glass Works in 1918), Carder managed the transition to 1920s taste adroitly, probably for the simple reason that he had to, lacking as he did the financial independence that Tiffany had by birth. Carder's 1920s glass was frequently an evocation of the early years – its palette often brilliantly colored and its shapes organic – but he did also produce a solid body of work in the modern style. Some of this was refreshingly innovative in a new line of techniques which incorporated cased layers applied internally with bubbles and patterning; for example, Cluthra, Cintra, Moss Agate, Silverine, and Intarsia.

Walter Dorwin Teague was retained by the Steuben Glass Company around 1932 to design a range of crystal stemware. Several elegant patterns bear testament to Teague's efforts, notably "Riviera," "Spiral," "Blue Empire," "Winston," and "St. Tropez."[4] Teague's contract was not renewed, however, when the company's new president, Arthur A. Houghton, Jr., took office in 1933. Far more rewarding for the firm was its liaison with *Sidney Biehler Waugh*, who in the 1930s designed a range of crystalware inspired by traditional – often mythological – themes. Waugh's glassware style, quite different from that of his sculpture, drew unashamedly on the style of the two Orrefors glassmasters, Simon Gate and

Left, above

Consolidated Lamp & Glass Company selection of "Ruba Rombic" tableware; cased blown glass, 1931. *Left to right*: plate (#809), pair of candlesticks (#805), jug (#812), creamer, tumbler, and bouillon (#819) (collection W. M. Schmid, Jr.)

Left

Sidney Biehler Waugh "Mariner's Bowl"; crystal designed for the Steuben Glass Company, engraved by Joseph Libisch, 15¾in. (40cm) diameter, 1935. Illustrated in *Sidney Waugh*, American Sculptors Series 6, W. W. Norton, 1948, p. 44; and *50 Years on 5th*, retrospective exhibition catalogue, Steuben Glass, New York, 1983/84, p. 10, #1 (collection the Steuben Glass Company)

Opposite

Sidney Biehler Waugh "Gazelle"; crystal bowl designed for the Steuben Glass Company, engraved by Joseph Libisch, 7in. (17.8cm) high, 1935. Illustrated in *Design*, December 1935, p. 31; *Sidney Waugh*, American Sculptors Series 6, W.W. Norton, 1948, p. 51; and *Steuben Glass*, James S. Plaut, H. Bittner, New York, 1951 pl. 49 (collection the Steuben Glass Company)

Edvard Hald, whose works had been exhibited widely in the United States from the early 1920s.[5] Elongated, highly stylized figures, crisply engraved to give the impression of bas-relief sculpture, interpreted exactly the Art Deco idiom of 1920s Europe. Issued in limited editions, these Waugh pieces quickly found their way into the foremost American museum collections.

Other glasshouses retained outside designers to boost the quality of their wares: George Sakier by Fostoria, Dorothy Thorpe by A. H. Heisey, and A. Douglas Nash (Manager at Tiffany Studios until 1929 when he established his own Corona Art Glass Company on Long Island) by Libbey in 1933. Libbey emerged in the vanguard of 1930s American commercial glass design. Several crystal stemware services bear testament; for example, Malmaison and Moonbeam. Another pattern, in this instance charming and inexpensive rather than formal, was a set of stemware designed by Fred A. Vuillemenot and entitled the Libbey Silhouette, introduced in 1933. Each of the crystal vessels – claret, sherry, sherbet, etc. – contained an opalescent white ("moonstone") or black stem molded with a different animal. Another successful 1933 design was a pair of cubist crystal bookends, a variation on the Syncopation goblet. In the struggle to attract customers, Libbey even published a booklet in 1934 entitled *Notes for an Epicure*, a guide for the aspiring hostess who could not remember her etiquette after five long years of Depression living.

The most modern American glassware of the period was the Ruba Rombic pattern introduced in 1928 by the Consolidated Lamp and Glass Company of Coraopolis, Pennsylvania. Strongly reminiscent of Erik Magnussen's "The Lights and Shadows of Manhattan" silver tea and coffee service in its sharp and irregular angularity which traced the interplay of light within New York's burgeoning skyline, the pattern derived its name from the words "Rubaic" (meaning epic or poem) and "Rombic" (meaning irregular in shape).[6] Included was a wide range of mold-blown tableware and toiletry items in smoky gray, lavender, and amber. Invariably unsigned, the model remains relatively unknown and underpriced.

Less innovative by far was the Consolidated Lamp and Glass Company's range of molded vases and lamp bases which copied, in some instances exactly, designs which had been introduced by Lalique in Paris five to seven years earlier. Most of these, in particular the models depicting pairs of love birds perched among blossoms (*Les Perruches*) and grasshoppers (*Les Sauterelles*) are usually credited to the Phoenix Glass Company in Monaca, a few miles north of Coraopolis. Both companies produced copies of Lalique patterns – for example, the pine cone, bittersweet, cockatoo, and dragonfly models so popular among Lalique collectors – in a range of two-colored cased blown glass. These often appear at antique shows today as "Lalique," their undersides inscribed with the French glassmaster's "authentic" signature.

The Phoenix Glass Company introduced a further range of French-inspired models entitled "Sculptured Glassware" in the mid-1930s. Offered in three finishes – Artware, Cameo, and Brilliante – the "Sculptured" series was virtually indistinguishable in design (but not in the quality of its manufacture, which was coarsely molded in an insipid choice of hues) from a range of glassware produced in 1920s Paris by Hunebelle, Verlys, and Etling. In 1943 the company

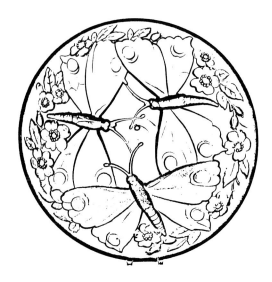

Above

Verlys of America "Les Papillons"; bowl, molded opalescent glass with relief decoration, inscribed *Verlys A & C*, 13⅝in. (34.6cm) diameter, c. 1935 (collection The Chrysler Museum, gift of Walter P. Chrysler, Jr.)

Below

Libbey Glass Company "Embassy"; pattern, model #4900, designed by Edwin W. Fuerst and Walter Dorwin Teague, 1939. Goblet, champagne, sherry, and wine, etched signatures *Libbey*, 8⅝in. (22cm) height of goblet. The model was decorated with a crest incorporating the American eagle beneath 13 stars for use in the State dining room in the Federal Building at the 1939 World's Fair (collection John P. Axelrod)

Above

Maurice Heaton plate; clear bubbly glass, green swirl pattern applied on the reverse, 13⅞in. (35.2cm) diameter, c. 1930. A similar dinnerware service is illustrated in *Design*, May 1934, p. 4 (collection The Metropolitan Museum of Art, gift of Mr. and Mrs. Niles M. Davies, Jr., 1979)

Below

Libbey Glass Company "Syncopation"; 4-ounce novelty cocktail glass, model K5-1019, 3¾in. (9.5cm) high, c. 1933. Illustrated in the Libbey-Nash catalogue, 1933, p. 9-C (collection Richard Bohl, Custer Antiques)

for this, common to several partnerships forged during the early 1930s to counter the prevailing austerity, was given with rare frankness in a later Phoenix catalogue: "There was an off and on movement of workers, information and a few molds between the two glass houses during the Thirties and Forties. Even today, when demand outstrips production facilities, a glass house may send a mold and supervisory personnel to another glass house where the order is filled, the glass trucked back, boxed and sold! As glass works are in business to make money, not glass (so to speak), movements of this nature should come as no surprise."[8] Collectors should note that liaisons such as this, common in harsh economic times, can explain the seeming duplication of design between competitors.

No discussion of American glass between the Wars can omit a reference, however brief, to "Carnival" and "Depression" glass. Carnival glass, which describes the wares awarded as prizes at country carnivals or fairs, consisted of molded pieces enhanced with an iridescent metallic surface finish inspired by that on much of Tiffany's art glass. Depression glassware describes a wide range of low-budget domestic wares produced for the general market by numerous commercial firms in the early 1930s. Today the two terms are used almost synonymously, but incorrectly, to denote low-quality wares produced by glass companies such as A. H. Heisey, Indiana, Jeannette, Anchor Hocking, Federal, Imperial, and Hazel Atlas. Most of this glass, appropriately unsigned, has slipped quickly into anonymity, although some models warrant consideration for powerful modernistic designs which belie their modest manufacturing costs; for example, the Indiana Glass Company's "Tea Room" and "Pyramid" patterns, and Anchor Hocking's "Manhattan."

Maurice Heaton stands as the one artist–craftsman of note in glass work between the World Wars. He served a lengthy apprenticeship under his father, Clement Heaton, who had worked as a stained glass artist in Switzerland before emigrating to the USA in 1910. In the late 1920s Heaton transposed on to glass a series of ultramodern geometric designs, their patterns consisting of translucent muted enamels fired on handcut sheets of clear, bubbly glass. These designs remain remarkably fresh, their execution most appealing. Eugene Schoen and Rena Rosenthal were among those who marketed Heaton's work.

ARCHITECTURAL GLASS

I f American designs for domestic art glass remained in large part unimaginative, the opportunities afforded the medium within the realm of architecture were met with alacrity. Architecture's new tools — stainless steel and reinforced concrete — provided the breakthrough, freeing large areas previously needed for structural purposes to be used for decoration. Initial doubts about

Left

Steuben Glass Company bowl; cased black and alabaster glass, 1920 (collection the Rockwell Museum)

Left, below

Steuben Glass Company selection of cased rose and alabaster glassware, 1920s. *Left to right:* Gordon pattern vase (#7441), 8⅛in. (20.6cm) high; Matzu pattern vase (#6034), 12in. (30.5cm) high; sculptural pattern vase (#6468), 9¾in. (24.8cm) high; puff box (#5074), 4¾in. (12.1cm) high (collection the Rockwell Museum)

Below, left

Steuben Glass Company vase designed by Frederick Carder; blue Aurene over Jade Yellow glass, inscribed *Aurene F. Carder,* 8¼in. (46.4cm) high, 1920s (collection the Corning Museum of Glass, Estate of Mrs. Welles, daughter of the artist, 1969)

Below, right

Steuben Glass Company "Cintra" cologne bottle; blown, cased and cut crystal, 11¼in. (28.6cm) high, c. 1928 (collection the Corning Museum of Glass)

glass's innate qualities – its fragility, tensile strength, inflammability, etc. – were quickly dispelled. Even concerns about the lack of privacy inherent in its transparency were quickly overcome by the application of molded patterns to its surface.

The appeal of glass for exterior architectural decoration was due in large part to its alliance with Edison's light bulb, which by the 1920s was an increasingly important factor in innumerable architectural projects. William van Alen's initial design for the Chrysler Building included a spire made entirely of curved glass panels lit at night from within. Why this project was abandoned is unclear. It was certainly well within the expressed ambitions of Van Alen's client, Walter Chrysler, Jr., to commission a monument that would immortalize his automobile, and, thereby, himself.

Glass roofs which were completed at the time included that of the Barbizon-Plaza Hotel at 58th Street and 6th Avenue, New York,[9] in which illuminated hollow glass bricks were employed, and the spire on the Kansas City Power and Light Building, still a landmark of arresting beauty in the Missouri night.

Most of the firms which manufactured decorative architectural glass have remained unidentified, like those which produced metal light fixtures. Two names, however, recur in contemporary literature: those of David M. Harriton, whose sand-blasted glass murals were popular in New York from the mid-1930s, and the firm of Eny Art Inc.,[10] also in New York, which produced a range of etched and illuminated glass furnishings à la Lalique.

By the late 1920s, glass had become a viable means of decorating both the interior and exterior of new buildings. It proved especially suited to movie theaters, restaurants, and cocktail lounges, where brightly lit sand-blasted glass murals depicting Jazz Age themes caught the era's gay ambiance. Exceptional examples of decorative glass appeared across the United States; for example, in the Boyd Theater, Philadelphia; the Enright Theater, East Liberty, Pittsburgh; the Diamond Bros. dress house, Columbus, Ohio; Bamberger Bros., Newark; Gimbels, New York; the Marcel Guerlain perfumery in the Waldorf-Astoria Hotel, New York; and the J. Thorpe department store, the official Lalique retailer in New York. The Wise Shoe Shop on Fifth Avenue received considerable attention for its use of illuminated glass, both inside and out: the façade, windows, valances, transoms, and signs were all decorated in the most exuberant French Modernist style. By 1933, the Union Carbide and Carbon Corporation pavilion at the Century of Progress Exposition could boast the largest glass mural in the world, a 55-foot-long colored panel engraved and lit from below.[11] In the same year the American glass industry went one better, celebrating the installation of one million square feet of glass in Rockefeller Center, much of it – such as the frieze by Lee Lawrie over the main entrance of the RCA building and Maurice Heaton's glass mural in the Women's Lounge symbolizing Amelia Earhart's transatlantic flight[12] – decorated in the modern idiom.

FABRICS

Despite sporadic contemporary criticism, American Modernist textile design appears in retrospect to have shown remarkable vitality, thanks, in large part, to the handful of women designers who applied their considerable talents to the medium.

American textile designers drew their inspiration, as in most disciplines, from Paris, and as there were in that city some of the most gifted adherents of the art moderne movement—Raoul Dufy, Paul Rodier, Hélène Henry, Benedictus, Robert Bonfils, etc. — it is not surprising that American textiles reflected much of this vibrancy. The French textile designers' participation in the 1926 exhibition at the Metropolitan Museum of Art, and at both Lord & Taylor and R. H. Macy's in 1928, provided up-to-the-minute exposure of their most recent creations. These were subsequently marketed with considerable success in New York by F. Schumacher & Co., and Cheney Brothers.[1] Both of these carried the wares of giant French textile mills and wholesalers such as Aubusson, Cornille, Richard Thibaut, Inc., and Bianchini-Férier.[2]

The early errors made by the French — errors of exuberance — were judged to have been inherited by their American counterparts. As Louise Bonney, a noted American observer and critic of the contemporary movement within the decorative arts, summarized it: "The geometrical design has had a bad start in this country, where in the infancy of the modern movement two false ideas prevailed — that anything geometrical was modern; that anything violently colored was modern. Terrible monstrosities were perpetrated in the name of geometry!"[3] A selection of Paul Poiret's fabrics, on view at the 1929 Contempora exhibition in New York, showed how narrow was considered the line between good and bad taste: "They are of the moment, high colored, excessive, smart with the impudence of privileged bad manners."[4]

Another critic, M.D.C. Crawford, went to the heart of the problem within the American textile industry — namely, that it lacked a cohesive ongoing design program.

Our textile machines are slightly different but often better than their European competitors but our designs have been polyglot in motives, lacking in character and not our own, and

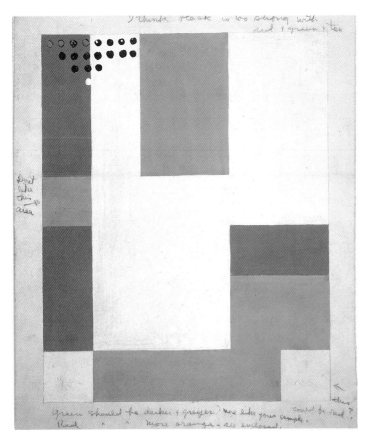

Left

Donald Deskey rug design of abstract geometric forms with dots; white, green, red, and black opaque watercolors on board, with notations in pencil, 11½ x 9½in. (29.2 x 24.1cm) (collection the Cooper-Hewitt Museum, gift of Donald Deskey, 1975-11-44)

Below, left

Donald Deskey textile design of repeat pattern of Cubist forms; green, brown, and cream opaque watercolors and graphite on board, 29¾ x 21³⁄₁₆in. (75.6 x 53.8cm). A machine-hooked rug of the same design, made by the new England Guild, is illustrated in *Creative Art*, Vol. 9, 1931, p. 42 (collection of Donald Deskey, courtesy of the Cooper-Hewitt Museum)

Below

Donald Deskey textile design of abstract geometric forms; brown, green, and gray opaque watercolors and graphite on board, 22⅛ x 17½in. (56.2 x 44.5cm) (collection the Cooper-Hewitt Museum, gift of Donald Deskey, 1975-11-32)

Below, left

Bigelow-Hartford Carpet Company (attributed to) rug, 27 x 53½in. (68.6 x 135.9cm) (collection Denis Gallion and Daniel Morris)

Below

Bigelow-Hartford Carpet Company rug; LaSalle Wiltern pattern #15364, 27 x 54in. (68.6 x 137.2cm) (collection Denis Gallion and Daniel Morris)

seldom good if our own. . . . For some reason difficult to understand, the average textile mill looks upon design as a sort of necessary evil to be had as cheaply as possible and as nearly like what their foreign competitors have already sold in this country as the conscience of the average American manufacturer will permit. I suppose this is a natural evolutionary stage. The history of decorative art shows how people borrowed from each other and modified their loans to fit their own conscience. But perhaps never in the history of the world has plagiarism been carried to so high an art as in the last generation and particularly in the textile field in the United States. This is a matter of little national pride.[5]

The reluctance of the manufacturers to take the initiative is extraordinary when measured against the speed with which they had always responded to changes in "period" styles – Federal, American and Spanish Colonial, Victorian, etc. Certainly there was ample room to increase American textile production – in 1930 John Cotton Dana, Director of the Newark Museum, reported that the USA had imported nearly $1 billion worth of fabrics in a recent year[6] – but apprehension about the "faddishness" of the new aesthetic continued to hold the manufacturers back. A comment heard repeatedly within the textile industry was, "Oh, it is just another of those King Tut things! That didn't last six months!"[7] It was therefore left to the individual American artist and designer to make the running, a challenge responded to with alacrity.

By 1930, the modern textile movement had settled into its stride, its tenet being simplicity of form and color. No finer example of this simplicity was provided than a printed linen fabric, entitled "Triptych," which was designed by Jules Bouy. Three vertical bands of a single color, shading from a deep to light tone, were juxtaposed, lending themselves perfectly to the natural folds of a curtain to emphasize its structural line.[8] Another to employ simplicity in a refreshing way was Henriette Reiss, who developed a range of "Rhythmic" patterns.[9] These were based on the theory that any rhythm from nature – music, poetry, running water, etc. – could be translated into line and color. Undulating bands, comprised of blocks of color, swirled across the fabric, often turning sharply back on themselves to create a strong sense of movement and speed.

Ruth Reeves was the *doyenne* of the American Modernist textile school, an honor accorded her both by her peers and, even more, by today's historians. Her peripatetic lifestyle – initiated, it appears, by her running away from home in California before the age of 10, and terminated by her death at the age of 72, as a handicraft adviser in the provinces in India – did not prevent the creation of a considerable body of work in all areas of textile design and general furnishings.

Curiosity was the key to Reeves's success. Her one-woman textile show at W. & J. Sloane's in 1930 showed her compulsion for experimentation.[10] Her selection of modern fabric designs was presented on thirteen different types of cotton – chintz, monk's cloth, voile, velvet, muslin, etc. – each chosen to meet a specific need within a room, such as tablecloths, curtains, wall coverings, or upholstery.

Even more impressive than her technical mastery was Reeves's ability to bring a refreshingly chic and colorful blend of Modernism to any subject, whether classical, primitive, anecdotal, figural, or abstract. All styles and themes were handled with equal ease for exhibitions both at home – for example, the American Designers' Gallery, AUDAC, the Exhibition of Metalwork and Cotton Textiles at the

Right
Edward Steichen "Moth Balls and Sugar Cubes," photographic image printed in blue, navy blue, and white on crêpe-de-chine silk, textile design for Stehli fabrics, 1927 (collection Newark Museum)

Metropolitan Museum of Art, and the National Alliance of Art and Industry at the Art Center, New York – and abroad. From the kinetic angularity of her "Electric" pattern to the softly humanistic touch of "Homage to Emily Dickinson" and the Matisse-inspired expressionism of "Figures with Still Life," Reeves achieved a multitude of effects with apparent ease.[11] Her carpet and wallpaper designs, the latter in 16 ft. (4·88 meters) repeat patterns depicting circus and music hall performers, bear further testimony of her versatility to today's visitor to the Radio City Music Hall. A trip she took to Guatemala and neighboring countries in 1934 resulted in a sharply divergent form of Modernism – abstract Mayan motifs in simulated hand-blocked patterns.[12]

Ilonka Karasz was another to bring a diverse talent and boundless energy to contemporary textile design. Perhaps more than any of her colleagues, Karasz realized the importance of the cloth itself: "My idea in design is to intensify texture by every element of the design so as to produce a richer looking fabric."[13] Paul Frankl also stressed the tactile qualities of the material: "Let us not be trapped into the error . . . of supposing that the beauty of a fabric can be judged by its design and color only. More fundamental is the quality of the weaving itself. A fabric is to be judged not by the eyes alone. It is to be felt. The quality of its weaving, the language of its texture, must come first. Design superimposed without reference to texture cannot be considered appropriate."[14]

Karasz switched from wallpaper to fabric and carpet design at will, mixing a sparkling array of shadow effects, graduated stripes, and abstract floral patterns. Her work was carried by a large number of textile mills and retailers, including Rockledge, Schwartenbach & Huber, and Ginzkey & Maffersdorf, Inc.

Martha Ryther was yet another designer who embraced modern textile design with ease. A member of the American Designers' Gallery, she produced, among a broad range of furnishings in the Modernist aesthetic, a limited number of dynamic fabrics.[15] While she was employed by H. R. Mallison & Co., she designed eight silk panels on the history of silk weaving.

Others, whose textiles captured the new spirit, included Donald Deskey, Herman Rosse, Winold Reiss, Gilbert Rohde, Pola and Wolfgang Hoffmann, John Held, Jr., Eugene Schoen, and Vally Wieselthier. Edward Steichen contributed a highly original and effective series of designs achieved by a photographic process of placing objects on a piece of photographic paper and flashing a light on them from various directions. The resulting images were transferred on to fabric in a variety of muted half-tones.[16]

American textile design underwent continual refinement, to the point where Louise Bonney could report by 1930, "We have produced some vigorous patterns which hold their own with foreign production, and many compromise designs, charming, usable, and well-planned to attract the average buyer who is still wavering. These latter are toned down by clever color gradations, variations in weave, and breaking of lines."[17]

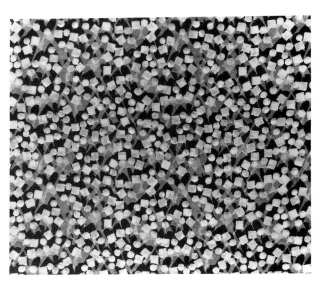

Modernist fabric designers drew primarily on geometric and abstract motifs, both of which became less and less pronounced as the movement matured. The former included, most popularly, striped designs, both vertical and diagonal, which were given subtlety by the introduction of shadow lines, a technique known

Left

Lydia Bush-Brown "Manhattan"; designed and executed by the artist, silk batik. Similar batiks are illustrated in *House and Garden*, October 1929, p. 124 (collection the Cooper-Hewitt Museum, 1974-23-6)

Below

Waite Carpet Company summer rug; pattern #73004, black design, kraft fiber, 12 x 6ft (3.7 x 1.8m) c. 1929

as *ombré* patterning, which traced the principal design in half-tones. Abstractions included the standard range of floral and animal motifs found in European fabrics, in addition to a delightful range of designs inspired by succulent desert plants – cacti and aloes – indigenous to the American Southwest.[18]

If the American textile industry lacked design creativity, no such criticism could be voiced of its technical mastery. A bewildering array of damasks, voiles, chintzes, chenilles, cretonnes, chiffons, taffetas, brocades, georgettes, brocatelles, etc. poured from its looms. Synthetic materials were also drawn into the Modernist fold, especially "Salubra," a textured and washable wallpaper fabric marketed by Frederick Blank & Co., used, among others, by Paul Frankl.[19] Another popular synthetic fabric was rayon, which by the late 1920s had shed its earlier unfortunate epithet, "artificial silk." Other coated or impregnated materials, including oilcloths and pyroxolins, were marketed under brandnames such as Permatex, Fabrikoid, and Lustersheen.

To the department stores fell the role of drawing the textile manufacturer and designer together, a function performed in earnest by W. & J. Sloane, Lord & Taylor, R. H. Macy's, and James McCreery & Co., as sales spiraled upwards.[20] The major mills that produced a range of contemporary designs were the Stehli Silk Company, Orinoka Mills, Robert McBratney, Lesher-Whitman & Co., Lehman-Connor, Stead & Miller, Dupont-Rayon, and Katzenbach & Warren. Other designers to warrant attention were M. H. Birge & Co., Nancy McClelland, and Victor Proetz.

RUGS

The American rug industry's apprehension about the Modernist movement lost it the race to pioneer contemporary carpets in the USA. By mid-1928, several critics were sufficiently disturbed to try to shame the manufacturers into participation. As N. C. Sanford noted, "Rugs and floor coverings generally are, in America, the last branch of the decorative arts to hold off from the modern movement, or to have called forth the talent of artists who are in touch with modern trends in decoration. It is rather baffling to be convinced that the United States, which is supposed to be so progressive, has, in this connection, clung to the thought that 'what was good enough for my father is good enough for me.' It is not. We are living in a new age, and the sooner the big U.S. mills scrap a lot of their old designs and fall into step with the modern movement, the better off they will be."[21]

The rug manufacturers adopted a "wait-and-see" position. The interim strategy included the plagiarism of European designs, to the extent that a curator at the Metropolitan Museum of Art, on a tour of Europe to gather Modernist carpets for exhibition purposes, faced a virtual boycott. As he explained, "This drastic action was taken by foreign manufacturers who rightly object to the copying of their artists' work 'without either remuneration or credit'."[22] Another expedient was a line of carpets which, while showing an understated modern influence, retained the use of transitional motifs, such as flowers, as a half-measure to draw adherents of the new while retaining clients with more conservative tastes.

The textile mills' hesitancy concerning the new vogue left a void which was promptly filled by the individual artist. As one critic observed,

It appears that if modern rugs are to be designed at all in America, they are going to be done by creative artists rather than designers for the big producers of floor coverings. While commercial designers continue to turn out the same old thing, there is a considerable number of artists in other lines who have turned to rug designing. We find in the list such well-known names as Thomas Benton, the mural painter; Buk and Nura Ulreich who have held successful exhibitions of their modern paintings in Paris, New York and other cities; George Biddle of Philadelphia; John Storrs, the sculptor, who works both in Paris and Chicago; Ralph Pearson, the etcher and author; the distinguished Pola Hoffmann, and many others. Most of the members of this group have turned to rug designing just to be doing something outside of their usual media of expression.[23]

Other designers to undertake rug design, if only sporadically, were Eugene Schoen, Donald Deskey, Joseph Urban, Gilbert Rohde, and Henry Varnum Poor. Others, whose talents lay in the related field of fabric design, displayed an easy affinity: Ruth Reeves, Henriette Reiss, Zoltan Hecht, and Loja Saarinen. For a short period, between 1928 and 1929, the demand for Modernist rugs at the department stores far outstripped the supply of imported rugs.

To manufacture their creations, these designers had to search out groups of obscure carpet weavers dotted around the country; in particular, the New England Guild in Portland, Maine; the Connecticut Handicraft Industry; the New-Age Workers in the Blue Ridge Mountains, North Carolina; and the Contemporary American Artists Handhooked Rugs Guild in New York.

Three specialized exhibitions helped to stimulate modern carpet design in the USA: those at the Art Center, New York, in 1928;[24] the Newark Museum, 1930;[25] and the Metropolitan Museum of Art, New York, 1931.[26] Other general furniture exhibitions, such as AUDAC and those of the American Designers' Gallery, provided further opportunities.

In the late 1920s the mills hastened to redress the situation by retaining some of the designers mentioned here, or by revamping their design departments. A contemporary critic reported on the manufacturers' resurgence: "A great factory of first importance has prepared for its current market a considerable variety of small and large rugs, as well as numerous carpets, all of modern designing. Another equally important mill, seeking modern designs, has recently given prizes in a designing contest promoted by the Art Alliance, and distributed several thousand dollars. The first prize of $1,000 and the second of $500 went to professional designers for strictly modern ideas."[27]

Fundamental issues of philosophy – whether a rug's true purpose was to dominate a room or, conversely, to provide a subtle blending between its draperies and furnishings – were put aside as the race for the market intensified. Sales of Modernist rugs at one department store were described as "almost embarrassing." Other New York stores, such as James McCreery & Co., Stern Brothers, and B. Altman's enjoyed buoyant sales, to the point where the Whitall

Below

Ruth Reeves "Manhattan"; textile for an office, designed for W. & J. Sloane, block-printed cotton glazed chintz, Osnaburg cloth, or voile, 35¼in. (87cm) wide, 52½in. (133.4cm) pattern repeat, printed in the margin *Designed by Ruth Reeves for W. & J. Sloane.* Illustrated in *Good Furniture & Decoration*, December 1930, p. 301; *W. & J. Sloane,* firm's exhibition catalogue, December 1930, cover illustration; *The American Magazine of Art,* Vol. 22, 1931, p. 31; and *At Home in Manhattan,* Yale University Art Gallery, exhibition catalogue, 1983, p 69 (collection Estate of Ruth Reeves)

Below, right

Ruth Reeves "The American Scene"; textile pattern depicting the artist's life, for W. & J. Sloane, block-printed cotton for living-room curtains or monk's cloth, 47¼in. (120cm) wide, 56in. (142.2cm) pattern repeat, 1930, printed in the margin *Designed by Ruth Reeves for W. & J. Sloane.* Illustrated in *Good Furniture & Decoration*, December 1930, p. 301; *W. & J. Sloane,* firm's exhibition catalogue, December 1930, unpaginated; and *At Home in Manhattan,* Yale University Art Gallery, exhibition catalogue, 1983, p. 98 (collection Estate of Ruth Reeves)

Below, left

Ruth Reeves "Breakfast"; table cloth, block-printed cotton, 60 x 40in. (152.4 x 101.6cm), 1931/32. Illustrated in *Form and Re-Form*, Paul T. Frankl, Harper & Bros., 1930, p. 122 (collection Estate of Ruth Reeves)

Below

Ruth Reeves "Electric"; textile design for W. & J. Sloane, hand-printed cotton, felt, or billiard cloth for upholstery for metal furniture or duo-print felt for curtains in a radio room, 74⅛ x 42⅛in. (188.3 x 107cm). Illustrated in *Good Furniture & Decoration*, December 1930, p. 303; *W. & J. Sloane*, firm's exhibition catalogue, December 1930, unpaginated; and *At Home in Manhattan*, Yale University Art Gallery, exhibition catalogue, 1983, p. 80 (collection Estate of Ruth Reeves)

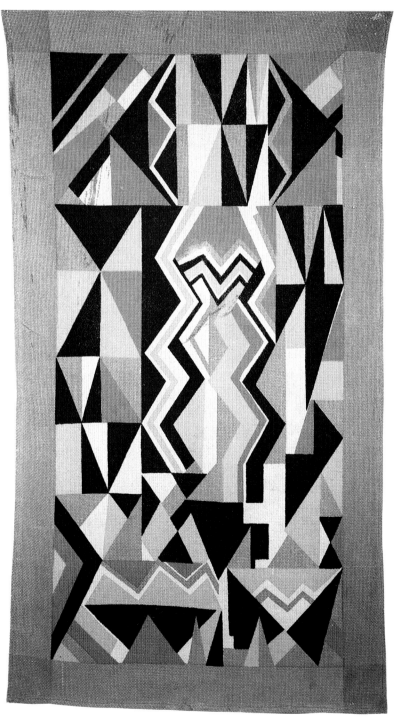

Below

Ruth Reeves "Circus," textile design for the National Silk Dyeing Company; printed in the margin *Designed for the National Silk Dyeing Co.*, executed on hopsacking or drapery fabric. Shown in the AUDAC exhibition, the Brooklyn Museum, 1931. Illustrated in *Design*, September 1931/32, p. 86, and May 1933, p. 8; and *Good Furniture and Decoration*, June 1931, p. 324

Rug Company received sixty-nine orders for one of its earliest Modernist rugs, designed for the firm by Victor de Kubinyi, from customers who were shown only the cartoon (i.e., before the model was even put into production).[28] In another instance, demand for the work of the Modernist carpet designer, James Arxer, was too large to be met by the American mill which had commissioned the design, forcing them to order its production in China.[29] By the mid-1930s the American mills had matters firmly in hand, and were able to offer a full range of contemporary machine-hooked rugs, including Saxonys, Wiltons, and Axminsters, to the department store buyers at prices which rarely exceeded $100 apiece. Proven designs were offered in subdued color combinations selected by the customer. The major textile mills associated with the mainstream modern rug movement were the Bigelow-Hartford Carpet Company; Stephen Sanford & Sons, Inc.; and the W. & J. Sloane Manufacturing Company.

The Americans' inspiration was largely French and German. Modernist French carpet design fell roughly into two schools: floral and geometric. The former included Paul Rodier, "La Martine" (Paul Poiret's cottage industry of young women), Benedictus, and the Parisian department stores Pomone and Primavera, all of whom produced a range of gay, rather feminine, floral rugs. These proved to be very effective in drawing the American homeowner across the gap between old and new; "stylized and blurred . . . with impressionistic effects of wind and water, yet [with the] appeal of a colorful garden . . . these charming color effects introduce the conventionally-minded customer to a gradual appreciation of modernistic treatments where she might recoil sharply from the more extreme animal and geometric designs."[30] More sophisticated, and therefore less immediate, in its appeal was the work of the second Parisian school, which espoused a sharply linear and abstract form of design. Led by Ivan da Silva Bruhns, these ultra-Modernist designers included Jean Lurçat, Sonia Delaunay, René Kinsbourg, Ivan Desny, Fernand Léger, and Henri Marcoussis, whose works ranged from the purely geometric to the cubist and futurist.

Modernist German carpet design was similarly geometric, but more formal. Contrasting patterns of planes and masses were combined with architectural groupings of lights and shadows in a muted palette of half-tones. Examples by Ernest Boehm, Bruno Paul, and Wilhelm Poetter were exhibited in New York, as were those by the two leading English designers, E. McKnight Kauffer and Marion V. Dorn.[31] The diversity of these European rugs provided the Americans with ample inspiration to generate their own brand of modernism.

The first American Modernist rugs were for the most part too bright, repeating the error of the French prototypes five to seven years earlier. Color combinations were criticized for being too bold and contrasting, even violent.[32] The lessons learned by the French were apparently ignored; and some retailers were so put off by the harsh color contrasts that they reverted to plain carpets as the haven to which would-be Modernists could fly until more palatable alternatives evolved.

What finally emerged was a pastiche of designs similar to those in Europe. These were largely geometric or pictorial (floral patterns were not received enthusiastically). Popular throughout the period were abstract designs consisting of either broken or enclosed squares, oblongs, and pyramids (for example, by

Above

Ilonka Karasz table cover; executed by Mariska Karasz, backgammon board design, crewel on silk grosgrain backed with cotton velvet, 39 x 37in. (99.1 x 94cm). Exhibited at the 1931 AUDAC exhibition. Illustrated in *At Home in Manhattan*, Yale University Art Gallery, exhibition catalogue, 1983, p. 42, #27 (collection Nathan George Horwitt, photo Charles Uht)

Left, above

John Held "Rhapsody"; designed for Stehli Silks, black and white printed silk, *c.* 1928 (collection the Newark Museum)

Left, below

René Clarke "Stadium"; printed silk, rust and pink on cream, *c.* 1927 (collection the Newark Museum)

Below

Frederick Suhr abstract design of warriors from the "Safari" series; designed for Belding Heminway, printed silk, *c.* 1929 (collection the Newark Museum)

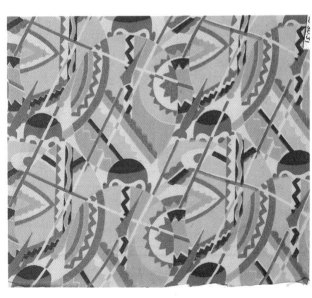

Deskey, Reiss, and Hoffmann), arcs or overlapping circles. An interesting variation was provided by the substitution of planets, half-moons, and constellations. Another eye-catching effect was achieved by a composition of industrial machine parts.

A charming innovation were the three-part rugs designed by Eugene Schoen and Thomas Benton, in which the design was continuous.[33] This allowed the three sections to be used together as a single unit, or spread out over a large floor space. Benton showed his versatility with a circular hand-hooked rug entitled "Railroads," in which a montage of locomotives and railroad tracks caught precisely the new vogue.[34]

WALL HANGINGS

The French modernist artist, Jean Lurçat, provided the inspiration for several Americans to turn their hand to tapestry design. As a critic for *Arts and Decoration* wrote, "He believes that the art of our time is moving toward the wall. Modern architecture with its clean, open planes and unadorned areas is providing the contemporary artist with blackboards for self-expression and the diversion of mankind. 'The tapestry,' says M. Lurçat, 'is a fresco, but a transportable one'."[35]

Lurçat's tapestries, displayed in American exhibitions and used by Donald Deskey and Elizabeth Hawes, were richly ornamental, their abstract figural themes providing the artist with the means to build up blocks of intense color.[36]

Lorentz Kleiser, taking Lurçat's cue, became America's pioneer Modernist tapestry artist. His early works depicted tropical forests pierced with rainbows, the spectrum's colors repeated throughout the composition.[37]

Marguerite Zorach was another American to respond to Lurçat's philosophy with a series of embroidered tapestries. As she explained, "I am first of all a painter. It was my interest in color (later in texture) and a certain spirit of adventure that led me to do a picture in wool."[38] Zorach's themes were mostly figural.

Lydia Bush-Brown was the third artisan to select wall-hangings as a preferred form of expression. Employing the traditional Javanese batik technique of building up colors on silk, Bush-Brown's compositions incorporated precise detailing and contrasting colors. She did not use the accidental "crackled" effects for which batiks are characteristically known. Her themes were fanciful and animated, the Manhattan skyline and underwater panoramas becoming popular subjects.[39] The effect was original and contemporary. In the late 1920s her work was offered by the Ehrich Galleries, New York.

ARCHITECTURE

It should be stated immediately that the subject "Art Deco architecture" does not relate to a specific style of 1920s/30s architecture *per se*, but to the distinctive style of modern ornamentation applied to new American buildings at the time. Skyscrapers such as the Chrysler and Chanin Buildings do not qualify as "Art Deco" because of their date of completion, or their distinctive terraced forms, but because of the often fanciful new decoration with which they were dressed to emphasize their modernity.

Art Deco architectural ornamentation did, however, align itself closely with the growth of the tall American building – the nation's first truly national architectural style – as a study of the latter's evolution shows.

Chicago's primacy as the innovator of the skyscraper in the closing two decades of the last century cannot be challenged. Contributing in the drive to rebuild the city after its disastrous fire in 1871 were the two great theorists of the skyscraper, Louis Sullivan (of Adler & Sullivan) and John Wellborn Root (of Burnham & Root), in addition to others such as William Holabird, Martin Roche, and, later, Frank Lloyd Wright. As engineering advances provided new possibilities for height – in particular, the introduction of steel-frame construction and the elevator[1] – Sullivan and some of his contemporaries took up a stand against the use of historical elements in the new tall building, and called for a reflection in architecture of what they took to be American impulses. In his now classic essay of 1896, "The Tall Office Building Artistically Considered," Sullivan claimed that new types of buildings required new architectural expression, i.e., decoration.[2] Several early tall buildings bear testimony to his pursuit of a new American architecture; for example, the Wainwright Building in St. Louis (1891)[3] and the Guaranty Building in Buffalo (1895).[4] To these, Sullivan applied his own distinctly luxurious, but compact, form of ornamentation.[5]

By the early 1900s, buildings in excess of ten stories were seen as "scraping the sky," the seemingly dark streets dividing such structures as "canyons." The ornamentation on these structures remained for several years firmly historical; for example, the campanile crowning the Metropolitan Life Tower in New York (1909), and Gilbert Cass's neo-Gothic Woolworth Building of 1913. In the early 1920s, however, an international event of unprecedented importance took place in Chicago which hastened a change in attitude among America's architects

Below

Hugh Ferriss study for the Maximum Mass Permitted by the 1916 New York Zoning Law, Stage 4; black crayon, stumped and varnished, 26⅜ x 19¹⁵⁄₁₆in. (67 x 50.6cm) (collection Cooper-Hewitt Museum, gift of Mrs. Hugh Ferriss, 1969-137-4)

towards the way in which twentieth-century building should be conceived.

In June, 1922, the Chicago Tribune Company announced a competition for an office building "of great height" for its new home on North Michigan Avenue. The first prize of $50,000, drawing 260 entrants from 23 countries, provided something of a World's Fair of skyscraper design. The Tribune's brief was for a tall modern building to symbolize the power and authority of the newspaper.[6]

The first prize was awarded to John M. Howells & Raymond M. Hood, of New York, for a building which, paradoxically, evoked the past, rather than the future, in its choice of Gothic ornamentation.[7] A cathedral tower, replete with pinnacles and flying buttresses, crowned a structure which, although tall, appears today as an anachronism in the heart of downtown Chicago. The jury's choice seems extraordinary, especially as the second placed entry, a soaring, tiered Modernist design by Eliel Saarinen, quickly became the prototype for the host of truly modern skyscrapers which sprang up across America within the next decade.[8]

The Tribune Tower became a rallying point for the proponents of modern American architectural ornamentation.[9] Suddenly, something about which the architectural community had been uneasy, or undecided, for years, became self-evident: for American architecture to come of age, and obtain independence, it had to rid itself of all traces of past foreign influence. In 1925, R. W. Sexton traced the problem,

For fifty years, from its earliest conception to most recent times, one might well say that the American skyscraper was not American at all. For ornamental details, architects and designers of skyscrapers seemed content to adapt (as we say, to avoid plagiarism, but we mean actually to apply) forms and motifs of old European styles and periods without regard to materials or structure, to say nothing of habits and customs, climate or tradition. In spite, then, of certain features which would seem to stamp it as purely American, the skyscraper, adorned and embellished with ornament of European origin, lost whatever individuality it possessed, and in our big cities Classic, Renaissance, Italian, and even Adam skyscrapers vied with one another for prominence. In attempting to adapt forms and details peculiar to European conditions of the sixteenth and seventeenth centuries to a structural mass characteristic of America of the twentieth century, progress in the new architecture was delayed.[10]

Paul Philippe Cret provided an eloquent summary of the problem some years later: "We were still living in the 'Age of Innocence,' blessedly ignorant of the original sin, which we have since learned consists in not being original."[11]

All at once Neoclassical entablatures, columns, flying buttresses, ogives, architraves, gargoyles and all the standard Beaux-Arts motifs were *passé*, stylistic remnants of bygone architectural eras.

If it was one matter to forgo historical influences as a means of decorating modern buildings, it was quite another to find a satisfactory substitute, especially an American one.

Ironically, American architects began by looking right back at Europe, though this time to the 1925 Exposition Internationale. As one critic noted in 1929,

We have almost always borrowed our ornament from Europe. The plan and construction of all our buildings, from houses to skyscrapers, is as distinctly American as their ornament is European. It has always been so, and the discouraging aspect of "this modernism" is that we are continuing the same practice, for while we are evolving our own forms we are

Below

Morgan, Walls, & Clements (architects) Richfield Oil Company Building, Los Angeles, glazed black and gold terracotta tiling, 1928-29 (demolished 1968). Illustrated in *The American Architect,* May 1931, p. 45; and *The Architectural Record,* June 1930, pp. 505-9 (photo Corporate Archives, Atlantic Richfield Company)

taking our ornament from the Exposition of Modern Decorative Arts in Paris or from European publications exploiting the modern movement. Why do we do this? Because the forms of our buildings are determined by factors of stern necessity – purpose, cost, and available materials; the ornament is an amenity. "They do these things better in France," and we are so frightfully rushed that no architect seems to have time to evolve original ornament. The study of original design is not taught in our architectural schools, and we have no important schools of industrial design; in consequence, we have no great decorative artists like Edgar Brandt in France or Josef Hoffmann in Germany; Connick and Yellin perhaps, but they work in ancient styles.[12]

The Zoning Law introduced in New York in 1916 (and later, with variations, in other cities), to ensure adequate light and air for the city's working populace, determined the basic shapes of future tall buildings, and inevitably had a significant influence on their need for, and type of, decoration.[13] The Law allowed, broadly, for a structure to rise straight up from the street line only to a height determined by the width of the street on which it faced. Beyond that height it had to slant backwards and hold to a line drawn from the center of the street through the predetermined limiting height at the street line. A pyramid could therefore be superimposed on top of a cube, but as pyramids were especially unsuited to windows (unless they were dormers), architects developed a series of setbacks, or terraces, which, as they stepped backwards and upwards, kept to the pyramidal, or, as it was then known, the building line. (Provisions in the Zoning Law allowed for variations: for example, a building could be carried to an unlimited, unbroken, height if constructed on only 25 percent of the plot of land.)[14]

As in traditional architecture, Modernist decoration was used as a transitional device to alert the eye to a change in the building's contour. Stepped vertical decoration was found to accentuate a skyscraper's height, horizontal decorative bands that of the rhythmic ascent of its setbacks. In addition to its exterior use in this manner, Art Deco ornamentation was concentrated principally on that part of a building seen and used most by its occupants, i.e., its entranceway – exterior grillework, doors, vestibule, and bank of elevators. Often a sumptuous combination of stone, brick, terracotta, and metal transformed an otherwise bland structure into a great source of civic pride.

Research on Art Deco architectural ornamentation makes it evident that, in a great many instances, the architect who designed the building did not himself design its decorative elements. There are countless commercial buildings, factories, and shops across the country with terracotta and bronze ornamental friezes, spandrels, and entranceways, which are identical. Contemporary architectural reviews and trade journals provide the answer to their authorship. Manufacturers such as the Northwestern Terra Cotta Company,[15] the National Terra Cotta Society,[16] and the Atlantic Terra Cotta Company,[17] advertised portfolios of Modernist designs from which the architect could select any number of stock items with which to decorate his building. The American Brass Company, among others, offered a similar service in metal, "limitless possibilities for the creation of original design by utilizing the 2313 shapes for which dies are maintained."[18] These shapes were decidedly Parisian, covering the entire grammar of contemporary French ornamentation: stylized fountains, cloud patterns, sunbursts, tightly

Below, left

Morgan, Walls, & Clements (architects) entrance, Richfield Oil Company Building, the sculpted terracotta figures by Haig Patigian representing "motive power." Illustrated in *Metalcraft*, February 1930, p. 359; *The American Architect*, May 1931, p. 44; and *The Architectural Record*, June 1930, pp. 505-9 (photo Corporate Archives, Atlantic Richfield Company)

Below, right

Morgan Walls, & Clements (architects) bronze stair door, lobby, Richfield Oil Company Building. Illustrated in *Metalcraft*, February 1930, p. 360; and *The Architectural Record*, June 1930, p. 508

packed fields of flowers, etc., which one could shuffle to create one's own "original" border.

With the marked exception of Frank Lloyd Wright, Ely Jacques Kahn, Ralph Walker, and Stiles Clements, very few architects concerned themselves directly at this level, leaving the initial selection of decorative trim to their draftsmen, for later approval. Whereas it was common practice to apply bands of color to various parts of a building – for example, along the setbacks on a skyscraper – it was the color (i.e., *any* color), rather than the decorative components themselves, which provided the definition to the passerby far below.

In the 1920s, terracotta proved the most popular material for exterior Modernist decoration, its molded surface glazed frequently with a muted palette of greens, golds, browns, and reds. Sometimes, it clothed the entire building – most dramatically in Los Angeles, on the Richfield Oil and Eastern-Columbia Buildings; in New York, the McGraw-Hill Building, and, in Detroit, the roof of Albert Kahn's Fisher Building. Alternatives, usually unglazed, were plaster and cast stone.[19]

Towards 1930, however, architects began to comprehend that new building materials – specifically, metal and glass – were more in harmony with new architecture than were traditional ones. Modern man's imagination was stirred now by the enormous tensile strength and brilliant sheen of steel, science's newest building aid. The age of metal began to phase out the terracotta and stone age in architecture, as it was doing in the decorative arts. As a critic noted in 1931,

The Empire State Building is a structure built of steel and designed in steel. The forms are a product of a twentieth century imagination – not a memory from some previous century. The design expresses the imagination of the machine age, not the spirit of the handicraft period. If not the first, this is one of the first buildings that actually belong to men of today instead of to men of the past. Most of our so-called modern structures have been hand-me-downs, remodeled for our generation, but not made to our measure or cut to our taste.[20]

Later in the editorial came a now common plea, "We must cease to be copyists of the past, and must recognize that the society that these ancient forms adequately served has now passed away, that our duty is to develop equally effective and appropriate expressions of our own social order."[21]

At the same time that the American architect was searching for a national modern decorative style, he came under sharp attack from the ultramodernist school, known as the Internationalists. For them, *all* ornament, whether traditional or new, was extraneous, and therefore superfluous. Its application concealed the intrinsic beauty and honesty of modern architecture's chosen materials, metal and glass. Despite the vast coverage afforded the movement's European pioneers – J. J. P. Oud, Le Corbusier, Walter Gropius, etc.[22] – few buildings were designed in the United States in the International Style outside of California, where four immigrant architects formed the movement's Western outpost, Richard Neutra, R. M. Schindler, J. R. Davidson, and Jock D. Peters.[23] The reason for this was that the American people, including its architects, if given the choice, overwhelmingly preferred decoration to none at all. In 1932, Hildreth Meiere explained why traditional decoration was such a deep-rooted, if irrational, force

Below

Stiles O. Clements (Morgan, Walls, & Clements, architects) W. P. Story Building and Parking Garage, medallion on garage entrance gates, West 6th Street at 610 S. Broadway, Los Angeles, 1934 (photo Library of Congress, Washington, D.C.)

in America, and why, therefore, the road ahead for the Internationalists would be so tough:

Decoration is that which gives color or texture, scale or pattern or interest, which is used, whether functionally or not, because it gives pleasure or expression. An architect instinctively employs it because he is an artist who designs for aesthetic enjoyment as well as a builder who must build adequately for physical needs. . . . To choose a certain brick for a wall, is to choose decoration; to design a terrazzo floor, is to start ornamenting. The extreme Left Wing Modernists have confused decoration with historic ornament, and I feel that in disclaiming all interest in decoration or ornament they are taking an attitude that they will eventually abandon. Human nature demands interest and relief from barrenness by some sort of enrichment. Even the most modern architects must deal somehow with their plain surfaces and that, under my definition, brings them to decoration in spite of themselves. Cornices and columns may be relegated to oblivion but windows and doors remain. How can one treat these elements without evolving some expressive form and treatment of texture and color? Granted that something new must evolve to be appropriate and right with the new conditions and tastes in architecture itself, granted that perhaps even the conception of decoration is developing from that of a generation ago, we cannot get away from its necessity – nor should we try.[24]

The Internationalists could claim one important breakthrough on the east coast, however – the Philadelphia Savings Fund Society (PSFS) Building by George Howe and William Lescaze, at the corner of Market and 12th Streets, Philadelphia, in 1932.[25] The building's crisp contour, accentuated by bands of fenestration issuing from a curved base, was devoid of surface decoration. A contemporary critic noted the city's initial surprise: "Office-bound and homeward-bound workers gaze daily at its unornamented façades, its huge areas of glass, its abrupt proportions, and wonder how such a building could have been erected by what is to them the most conservative institution in the U.S. Aristocratic Philadelphians gaze absently into its stone and steel as if it were not there. And the ever-knowing dismiss it with a shrug as a good publicity stunt put over on the unsuspecting bankers by some genius of an advertising man."[26] Today one can be readily forgiven for presuming that the PSFS is one of downtown Philadelphia's most recent structures, a fitting testimony to Howe & Lescaze's seminal design.

The adherents of the International Style made steady advances in the USA from the late 1930s, but in the 1925-30 period the country was simply not ready for such ascetic idealism. It was in a romantic mood, and wanted its buildings to reflect this.

Modernist architectural decoration gradually worked its way from 1925 into every corner of the country. New York's skyscrapers (and their ornamentation) were recreated in numerous small urban communities, to the chagrin of many, including Frank Lloyd Wright, who railed against the impracticality of placing large structures in sparsely populated areas. Regionalism played a surprisingly small part in the movement's growth; one finds the same Parisian sunbursts and chevrons on factory buildings in San Diego as those on shops and banks in northern Michigan and Seattle. The KiMo theater (Carl and Robert Boller, architects, 1926-27), in Albuquerque, New Mexico, provides a rare example of a direct regional influence, its colorful terracotta frieze fusing Pueblo and Navajo motifs on a Spanish Mission-style building.[27] Few other architects attempted to

Below

Samuel Hannaford & Sons (architects) ventilation grille, lobby, Cincinnati Times Star Building (now Burke Marketing Services), 800 Broadway, Cincinnati, 1931-33 (photo Randy Juster)

derive their Modernist decoration from local traditions. Only in southern Florida, in particular, Miami Beach, did an entire community of identifiable modern architecture emerge that set itself fully apart from New York.

The following nationwide survey of American Art Deco architectural ornamentation provides a summary of the movement's finest examples, commencing with the two largest areas of concentration, New York and California:

The New York Telephone Company was the first in New York to align itself with Modernist architectural decoration, retaining the firm of McKenzie, Voorhees, & Gmelin (later, Voorhees, Gmelin, & Walker) in 1923 to design its corporate offices on West Street, between Barclay and Vesey Streets, in lower Manhattan. Known now as the Barclay-Vesey, the building received considerable attention on its completion in 1926 for its massing and ornamentation, neither of which were thought to show any trace of historical influence.[28]

The architects' explanation of the ornamentation, applied broadly on both the exterior and interior, proved an eloquent rebuttal to the adherents of the International Style:

The function of ornament is to add texture and interest to the building which it embellishes. Its primary function is that of texture for it permits of relief from monotony; it enriches in such a manner as to soften otherwise severe surfaces; and it makes for easy transition from one material to another. Its secondary purpose is to afford a relief from the restlessness the mind cannot help but feel, if ornament is lacking. It creates a feeling of friendliness because of its interest to the passerby. In many ways, in the skyscraper it should afford to the eye a welcome rest from the gigantic power of mass and in so doing aid to bring down to a human scale, that which otherwise is too great for comfortable comprehension.[29]

To achieve the desired effect, a beige cast stone was chosen to offset the building's darker brick façade. The decoration today surprises one, not only in its quantity, but because it was considered so modern *and* American at the time. A compact design of grape vines, fruit, plants, and game covers every cornice, arch, window sill, and lintel, to "interest the majority of passersby, who, in this case, are commuters, many of whom cherish a love for their garden at home and the plant life which grows therein."[30]

Today the design appears distinctly Renaissance, its profuse application Victorian. Not surprisingly, it did not become the wellspring of a subsequent American architectural Modernist movement. McKenzie, Voorhees, & Gmelin lost a great opportunity to introduce a modern design concept based on their clients' new field of telecommunications. The terrazzo mural panel in the lobby of the Telephone Company's later Newark building portrays much more effectively, in the stylized bolts of electricity which radiate from Alfred E. Floegel's central figure representing mankind's control of worldwide communications, the possibilities for a modern corporate style.[31] The New York Telephone Company was extremely satisfied, however, and commissioned a chain of other office buildings with the same foliate decoration. Voorhees, Gmelin, & Walker later applied the same basic architectural ornamentation to the Salvation Army headquarters building which they completed in New York in 1930.[32]

Below

Unidentified architect entrance doors, apartment building, 7 Gracie Square, New York, c. 1928 (photo Randy Juster)

Less well known, but far more impressive in a Modernist context, was Voorhees, Gmelin, & Walker's Western Union Building on West Broadway between Thomas and Worth Streets, 1928-30. Here the architects switched to the German and Dutch Expressionist idiom of the 1910s and early '20s for the shaded brickwork on the building's exterior and its spectacular lobby. The influence of the sharply angular brickwork is seen most clearly in Peter Behrens's design for the main hall of the I. G. Farben building in Höchst, 1920-24.[33]

The son of an Austrian-born importer of glass and mirrors, *Ely Jacques Kahn* established himself in the late 1920s both as a brilliant architect and as America's leading exponent of Modernist architectural design. Kahn attended Columbia University and the Ecole des Beaux-Arts, Paris, before joining a New York architectural firm, previously Buchman and Fox, in 1915. Within ten years, Kahn, now Buchman's partner, was designing commercial buildings throughout the city, over thirty of which were erected between 1925 and 1931.[34]

Kahn is important, in the context of this book, because of his distinctly personal Modernist style of decoration. One cannot mistake the interplay of geometric motifs which recur in his entrance lobbies, elevator doors, and mail boxes, each a fresh interpretation of a common angular theme. Superior examples abound: the Film Center, Squibb Building, Holland-Plaza Building, 2 Park Avenue, the Lefcourt Clothing Center, 120 Wall Street, the Bricken Building, 111 John Street, and 1410 Broadway, to mention only some of his more spectacular entrances and vestibules.[35] Kahn's consistency can be ascribed, in part, to the fact that he had only two principal clients, Abe Abelson and Louis Adler, both of them local real estate developers. Neither appears to have been concerned with anything but the soundness, and therefore the rentability, of Kahn's buildings. This allowed his vigorous personal style to evolve and mature unhindered.

The most extravagant Art Deco façade constructed in New York was that on the Stewart & Company Building on the East side of Fifth Avenue at 56th Street, in 1929.[36] The architects Warren & Wetmore conceived of a monumental entrance consisting of six doors beneath a vast rectangular frieze flanked by two matching panels. The theme — to show that the building housed a series of women's specialty shops — was familiar in Paris a few years earlier: stylized draped nudes within lavish borders of tiered fountains, baskets of flowers, flights of birds, etc. A combination of *repoussé* aluminum, polychromed faience, and verdigris bronze brought the images sharply into low relief. This provided an increased impact on catching the sun's rays, or, at night, the rays of a lower row of concealed lights. Inside, all the public areas — lobby, stairways, elevator cabs, etc. — were decorated with silvered-nickel grilles and panels designed in the modern idiom by J. Franklin Whitman, of the firm of Whitman & Goodman.

Within eight short months the Stewart & Co. façade vanished, replaced by a faceless substitute. Bonwit Teller had purchased the building and, presumably to erase such a dominant image, retained Ely Jacques Kahn to redesign it. The resulting faceless façade in limestone, centering on a grille of metal and glass, denied the viewer even of a taste of Kahn's genius. The commission is not listed in the Kahn archives at Columbia University, suggesting that Kahn himself did not consider it more than a perfunctory remodeling job.

continued on page 170

Right

John Gabriel Beckman, in collaboration with Walter Webber and Sumner A. Spaulding (architects) Avalon Theater, Catalina Island, commissioned by William Wrigley, Jr., 1928-29. View of the proscenium fire-curtain in the auditorium, the male figure symbolizing "The Flight of Fancy Westward" superimposed on a map of Catalina Island (photo Randy Juster)

Below

John Gabriel Beckman detail of the murals in the auditorium, painted jute (burlap). Avalon Theater, Catalina Island (photo Catalina Island Museum Society, Inc.)

Below

Elsa Vick Shaw one of 14 panels depicting the musical instruments of antiquity, oil on canvas, main foyer, Severance Hall (Walker & Weeks, architects), Cleveland, 1929-31. Illustrated in *Metalcraft*, March 1931, p. 122 (photo Randy Juster)

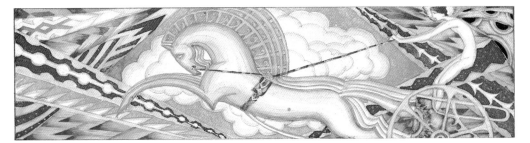

Left

Heinsbergen Decorating Company two sketches of panels for the Pantages Theater, the upper one of the central frieze above the proscenium fire-curtain, watercolor on paper, c. 1929 (photo A. T. Heinsbergen & Co.)

Left, center

Heinsbergen Decorating Company sketch of the auditorium ceiling, Pantages Theater, watercolor on paper, c. 1929 (photo A. T. Heinsbergen & Co.)

Bottom, left and right

Heinsbergen Decorating Company sketches of murals for "a little theater in San Francisco," watercolor on paper, c. 1930 (photo A. T. Heinsbergen & Co.)

Below

Heinsbergen Decorating Company sketch of a movie theater lobby and stairs, crayon on paper, 1930s (photo A. T. Heinsbergen & Co.)

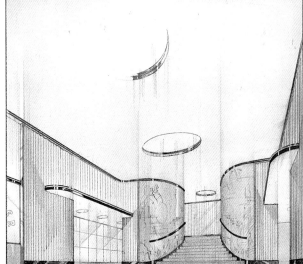

Right

Rapp & Rapp (architects) auditorium, Paramount Theater, 23 East Galena, Aurora, Illinois, 1931. The theater was renovated by Conrad Schmitt Studios, Inc. in 1978 (photo Russell B. Phillips)

Below, left

R. Harold Zook and M. Caughey (architects) asbestos fire-curtain, Pickwick Theater, 5 South Prospect, Park Ridge, Illinois. Illustrated in *The American Architect*, December 1929, p. 24 (photo Randy Juster)

Below, right

Alfred Fellheimer and Stewart Wagner (architects) Union Terminal, Central Parkway and Laurel Street, Cincinnati, 1929-33. Illustrated in *The Architectural Forum*, June 1933, p. 453 (photo Randy Juster)

Below

John Eberson (architect) lobby, Colony Theater, Shaker Boulevard, Cleveland, 1937 (photo Randy Juster)

Right

Donald Deskey living room in the apartment designed for S.L. ("Roxy") Rothafel above the Radio City Music Hall, c. 1931; with cherrywood paneling, the furnishings in lacquered and veneered wood, Bakelite, and brushed aluminum. Illustrated in *Architectural Digest*, July 1984, pp. 66-7 (courtesy *Architectural Digest*, photo William Rothschild)

John Eberson (architect) lobby, Colony Theater, Shaker Boulevard, Cleveland, 1937 (photo Randy

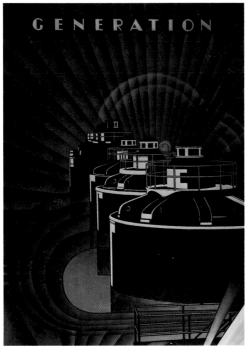

Left

Niagara Mohawk Power Corporation (Bley & Lyman, architects) four reverse-painted Vitrolite panels, artist unknown (photos Randy Juster)
Gas the design based on the Koppers type of gas manufacturing ovens
Illumination the design based on the theme "City of Tomorrow"
Generation a rendition based on the electric generators in the south end of the old Schoellkopf Hydro station at Niagara Falls
Transmission the design showing lines of force radiating from an electric substation flanked by transmission towers

Below, left

Bley & Lyman (architects) "Spirit of Light"; stainless steel figure on the front façade of the Niagara Mohawk Power Corporation Building, 28ft (8.5m) high (photo Niagara Mohawk Power Corporation)

Below

Bley & Lyman (architects) Niagara Mohawk Power Corporation, 300 Erie Blvd., West Syracuse, New York, 1930-32 (photo Niagara Mohawk Power Corporation)

Right

Frank Lloyd Wright fireplace, Hollyhock House; designed for Mrs. Alvine Barnsdall, 4808 Hollywood Boulevard, Los Angeles, 1917-20 (photo Julius Shulman)

Right, center

E. H. Faile & Co. (architects) detail of elevator cab; metal castings and aluminum strips, Goelet Building (now the Swiss Center), 608 5th Avenue, New York, 1930. Illustrated in *Metalcraft*, March 1932, p. 109 (photo Randy Juster)

Below, left

Unidentified architect street lamp, Health Department Building, corner Center and Worth Streets, New York (photo Randy Juster)

Below, right

Jean Bourdelle mural in carved linoleum; women's lounge, Union Terminal, Cincinnati. Illustrated in *The Architectural Forum*, June 1933, p. 467 (photo Randy Juster)

Left

Hoit, Price & Barnes (architects) two views of Kansas City Power and Light Company Building, 14th and Baltimore, Kansas City, 1932 (photo Bob Barrett)

Below

John Baeder "Empire Diner"; oil on canvas, 32 x 50in. (81.3 x 127cm), 1976, a romantic depiction of the Empire Diner, 10th Avenue and 22nd Street, New York, built by Fodero Diners, *c.* 1929 (collection Sydney and Frances Lewis)

Right

Anton Skislewicz (architect) Plymouth Hotel, 336 21st Street, Miami Beach, 1940 (photo Randy Juster)

Below

Alonzo H. Gentry; Voskamp & Neville; Hoit, Price & Barnes (associated architects) entrance to the Music Hall, Municipal Auditorium, 13th & Central, Kansas City, 1934 (photo Bob Barrett)

Below

Herman Sachs "Speed of Transportation"; ceiling
fresco in the porte-cochère (motor court), Bullocks
Wilshire, 3050 Wilshire Boulevard, Los Angeles, 1929
(photo Randy Juster)

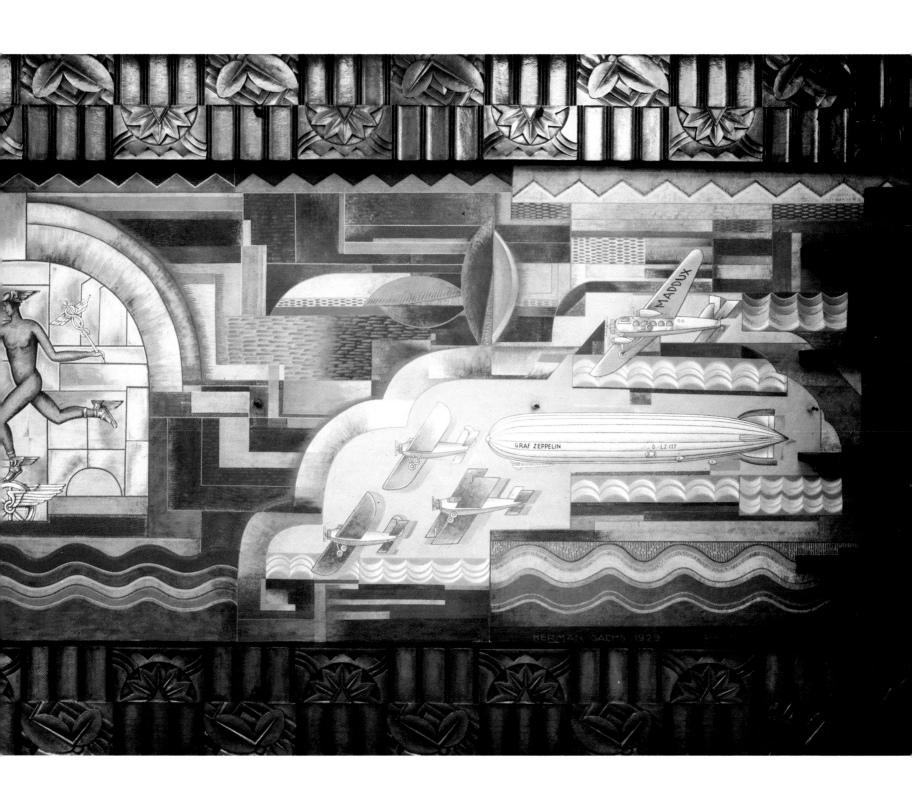

Below, left

John Wenrich perspective of the RCA Building, Rockefeller Center, 48-51st Streets, between 5th and 6th Avenues, New York, 1931-40; pencil, pastel, and gouache on paper, c. 1931 (collection Rockefeller Center, photo Scott Hyde)

Below, right

John Wenrich perspective of the RCA Building, Rockefeller Center, 48-51st Streets between 5th and 6th Avenues, New York, 1931-40 (Reinhard & Hofmeister; Corbett, Harrison, & MacMurray; Hood, Godley, & Fouilhoux, associated architects); watercolor, pencil, and gouache on board, c. 1931 (collection Rockefeller Center, photo Scott Hyde)

Opposite

Joseph Urban (architect) sketch of the façade of the Max Reinhardt Theater, between 50th and 51st Streets, New York, 1929, ink and watercolor on paper, 14¾ x 11¼in. (37.5 x 28.6cm). Illustrated in *The American Architect*, September 20, 1928, p. 362 (photo Butler Library, Columbia University)

FACADE OF THE PROPOSED MAX REINHARDT THEATRE IN NEW YORK CITY

Left

Joseph Urban (architect) sketch of the wallpaper for the Tulip Room, Central Park Casino, New York (demolished 1936); watercolor and pencil on paper. The complete interior is illustrated in *The Metal Arts*, November 1928-December 1929, p. 527; *The Architectural Record*, August 1929, p. 106; and *Architecture*, May 1934, p. 269 (photo Butler Library, Columbia University)

Left

Joseph Urban (architect) detail of wallpaper sketch for Central Park Casino (photo Butler Library, Columbia University)

Below

Joseph Urban (architect) sketch of the wallpaper for the dining room, Central Park Casino, New York; watercolor on paper. Illustrated in *Annual of American Design*, Ives Washburn, 1930/31, p. 138 (photo Butler Library, Columbia University)

Above

Joseph Urban detail of the "Joy of Life" wallpaper in the auditorium, Ziegfeld Theater, 54th Street and 6th Avenue, New York (demolished c. 1966) (photo Butler Library, Columbia University)

Above

Joseph Urban (Joseph Urban and Thomas W. Lamb, architects) view of the orchestra and balcony sections in the auditorium, Ziegfeld Theater. The wallpaper, entitled "The Joy of Life," was executed on canvas by Lillian Gaertner at the Urban Studios, Yonkers, New York. Illustrated in *The Architectural Record*, May 1927, pp. 390-92; and *The American Architect*, April 1930, p. 43

Above

Joseph Urban (Joseph Urban and Thomas W. Lamb, architects) rendering of the façade, Ziegfeld Theater, watercolor on brown paper, 1927. Illustrated in *The Architectural Record*, May 1927, p. 387; and *The Architectural Forum*, May 1927, p. 414 (photo Theater Archives, Museum of the City of New York)

Below

Joseph Urban (architect) roof garden, St. Regis Hotel, 2 East 55th Street, New York, 1927 (photo Butler Library, Columbia University)

Below

Joseph Urban (architect) façade of the Bedell department store, 17-19 West 34th Street, New York, 1926 (demolished before 1955) (photo Butler Library, Columbia University)

For a brief moment in the early 1930s, the Chrysler Building soared above all others. Today it remains the period's most exhilarating structure and romantic symbol. The building was originally designed by William van Alen for William H. Reynolds, a real estate developer, who turned over everything – the lease, architectural blueprints, *and* Van Alen – to the purchaser, Walter P. Chrysler.[37] Chrysler's goal was nothing less than the world's greatest monument . . . to himself, and, coincidentally, to capitalism. Just as Frank Woolworth had commissioned Cass Gilbert to design for him a building which would surpass both in height and architectural interest anything which preceded it, so Van Alen's brief was for a building which would not merely scrape the sky, but pierce it. Like the Woolworth Building, its ornamentation should be provocative, drawing discussion and comment to the building and, thereby, to Chrysler himself.

Stripped of its ornamentation, the building provides a characteristic example of late 1920s commercial architecture, one intended as a financial investment with 77 floors of rentable space. Its massing, studied use of fenestration as an element of design, and surface treatment are similar to many buildings under construction at the time. With its Modernist ornamentation, however, it became a classic. The excitement lies primarily in the seven floors which comprise the elongated dome, each of tiered arched form with triangular dormer windows enveloped in shimmering nickel chromed steel. Even today, surrounded by a host of taller midtown Manhattan buildings, the dome still draws the eye unerringly.

Below the top, the eagle gargoyles at the 59th floor setback and the winged radiator caps at the 31st level, enhance the novel effect, although neither amounts to more than a decorative fillip to the dome. Van Alen reserved his best feat of showmanship for last. The building's 27-ton steel spire, which pushed its height to 1,048 feet, well beyond that of H. Craig Severance's rival 927-foot skyscraper under construction at 40 Wall Street,[38] and barely beyond that of the Eiffel Tower, was assembled secretly inside the building, and hoisted through the top aperture to the astonishment of the watching world. "When the spire was finally assembled and riveted up securely . . . the signal was given, and the spire gradually emerged from the top of the dome like a butterfly from its cocoon, and in about 90 minutes was securely riveted in position, the highest piece of stationary steel in the world."[39] Van Alen had scored a double triumph, leaving his former partner, Severance, a distant second, and – in the dramatic manner of the spire's installation – providing Chrysler's building with a further mythical quality.

Not everybody was fully captivated, however. Contemporary criticism, which today seems equally valid, concentrated on the building's ornamentation, which, in one instance, was found to be superfluous, and, in another, excessive. On the exterior, the protruding eagle gargoyles at the 59th floor setback broke the symmetrical ascent of the upper floors to the spire. In the lobby, Van Alen's selection of materials, textures, and colors was found to clash badly: "An effective lighting scheme is thwarted by the highly-grained brown wall surfaces. These walls, with their strong chocolate tone, practically obscure what is probably an interesting ceiling decoration. The tone and graining of the marble are so positive that the walls of the corridors lean in threateningly toward the occupants."[40] In the attempt to provide his client with every possible novelty, Van Alen had produced

Right

Albert Kahn (architect) entrance, Kresge Administration Building, Detroit, 1930s (photo Hedrich-Blessing)

an overstrained effect. The lobby's Rouge Flambé marble walls are too forceful for such a confined space, drowning out the onyx light fixtures, Oscar Bach's metalware, and the ceiling fresco by Edward Trumbull.[41]

Notwithstanding such censure, the Chrysler Building generates an emotional response which allows the critic to forgive its excesses. Even those who found fault could not bring themselves quite to judge it as they would other buildings. As one noted, "The Chrysler Tower should not be criticized from the usual point of view of architectural design. It stands by itself, something apart and alone. It is simply the realization, the fulfillment in metal and masonry, of a one-man dream, a dream of such ambition and such magnitude as to defy the comprehension and the criticism of ordinary men or by ordinary standards."[42] In short, Van Alen had served his client well.

Van Alen is remembered as a one-building architect. He did, however, design other buildings in the modern idiom. The entrance doors for Lookout Point, Inc., in New York, for example, incorporate a successful series of contemporary motifs.[43]

Walter Chrysler hardly had time to celebrate his monument before the Empire State Building outstripped him. Its owners' ambitions were far less romantic, however. A booklet, published on May 1, 1931, couched their cold financial goals for the building in some suitably lofty prose,

Mightiest peak of New York's mighty skyline, tallest of all tall buildings . . . a marvel for the sight of men, a challenge to their awe, an inspiration and a mighty modern servant for the performance of their business requirements. . . . Up there, among the clouds, the drum-beat of New York is stilled, the nervous staccato of the city's life is left behind. In the superb heights of Empire State, the mind is free. Here the real work which is the life-blood of New York can be achieved restfully.[44]

The Empire State Building rose on the West side of Fifth Avenue between 33rd and 34th Streets, on the site previously occupied by the old Waldorf-Astoria Hotel, and, before that, John Jacob Astor's private mansion.[45] William F. Lamb, of the firm of Shreve, Lamb, & Harmon, presented sixteen plans to the consortium of owners before consensus was reached, following which a public announcement was made on August 30, 1929. Within 21 months the building was complete, its growth roughly four and a half stories per week.

The building achieves more than just height. It is an immensely skilful piece of massing, both dignified and serene, almost a natural wonder as much as a building, and one that passed quickly into popular folklore. It is not, though, as is commonly believed, a classic Art Deco building.

The building's Modernist ornamentation is restrained, even cautious, both in the lobby and, on the exterior, in the selection of cast metal spandrels and over-lapping fan-shaped motifs at each corner of the aluminum mast (intended as a dock for dirigibles to land their passengers on the upper observation platform), which crowns it. The architects' brief was entrepreneurial: a profit-making building whose size was carefully weighted against its optimum amount of rentable space. Ornamentation was not a priority, perhaps in part because it could not compete on a structure of such monumentality.

Shreve, Lamb, & Harmon were allowed far greater decorative latitude in the skyscraper which they designed at the same time at 500 Fifth Avenue.[46] Here

there is a spirited French Modernism, both in the pair of stylized Parisian female figures which surmount the entrance arch, and in the forceful geometric tracery in the vestibule (now replaced). Another Modernist commission undertaken by the architects was the R. J. Reynolds Tobacco Company Building in Winston-Salem, North Carolina (recently renovated).[47]

Like the Empire State Building, the new Waldorf-Astoria Hotel (Schultze & Weaver, architects) on Park Avenue drew on a rather conservative, even cautious, range of contemporary French motifs for its ornamentation. The entrance frieze, designed by the French artist Louis Rigal, underwent several refinements before the final, more simple, version was chosen. The restrained Modernist theme was continued in the public areas inside the hotel: the entrance vestibule, ballroom, etc.[48]

Also planned in 1927, the Chanin Building (Sloane & Robertson, architects) represented an even more self-congratulatory edifice to individual success. Irwin S. Chanin, one of two sons of an immigrant from Poltava, Russia, had, like Chrysler in automobiles, built a substantial private fortune from scratch as an architect and real estate developer. Situated diagonally across Lexington Avenue from the Chrysler Building on 42nd Street, the building "topped out" at 54 floors in just 205 days between January 3rd and August 8th, 1928. The exterior façade of the lower four floors and the interior, decorated by the Chanin design department headed by Jacques L. Delamarre in collaboration with the sculptor, René Chambellan, was based on the theme of the "City of Opportunity."

The importance given to the narrative aspect of the building becomes very evident here — thus the rich work of reliefs with allegories of the opportunities the city offers to whoever wants to improve and become a better man; in fact, they are in some way autobiographical. As with many self-made successful immigrants, they project their own experience as a general law onto the world. The city of opportunities is the leitmotif of the Chanin Building.[49]

There is no more impressive example of Modernist ornamentation than the bas-relief panels and radiator grilles by Chambellan in the building's lobby.[50] Portrayed are "the mental and physical processes by which an individual in New York City may rise from a humble beginning to wealth and influence by the power of his own mind and hands." Allegorical figures of Enlightenment, Vision, Courage, and Achievement showed the evolution of a mind bent on self-accomplishment; those of Endurance, Activity, Effort, and Success the parallel growth of the physical aspects of success.

The Modernist theme continued throughout the building, in the store fronts on the ground floor,[51] the entrance in the lobby to the Lexington Avenue subway, the Baltimore & Ohio Motor Coach Terminal on 42nd Street, the building's theater on the 50th floor, the general administrative offices, and Mr. Chanin's executive suite. The ornamentation throughout was French-inspired, except for the gates to the executive suite, for which the shameless capitalist theme was essentially Horatio Alger.

Two other buildings by the Chanin Corporation deserve mention for a more streamlined moderne look; the Majestic and Century apartment complexes on

Below

A. Stewart Walker & Gillette (architects) entrance, the Fuller Building, 57th Street and Madison Avenue, New York, 1929. Black Swedish granite and white Rockwood stone, the figures by Elie Nadelman. Illustrated in The Architectural Forum, August 1931, p. 186 (photo Randy Juster)

Central Park West, New York, built between 1930 and 1931. Here the strident Art Deco message is absent; in its place a vertical emphasis is created in the front by a stepped and ribbed façade, and in the rear by a contrasting curvilinear crown that carries the eye down the building's narrow length.[52]

Following his Chicago Tribune triumph with John M. Howells, Raymond Hood turned his attention to a host of New York commissions, four of which bore distinct Modernist ornamentation.[53] The first, the American Radiator Building at 40 W. 40th Street, opposite Bryant Park, incorporated a bold black and gold brick color scheme which emphasized the strong silhouette of the building's tower and craggy crown. Despite its lingering Gothicism, the building was hailed as a commercial breakthrough, in part because of the battery of floodlights which caused the crown to light up at night. This, as the critics noted, was an ingenious advertising ploy for a company which sold furnaces and heaters. "Aesthetically, at night, when it is artificially lighted, when the black bulk disappears and the gilded upper portion seems miraculously suspended one and two hundred feet in the air, the design has a dreamlike beauty. And if we think it a trifle crude, remember that it was designed to house a radiator company and not to commemorate a war hero nor glorify a saint."[54]

The Daily News Building on E. 42nd Street shows a more mature Hood, one well in touch with fashionable contemporary architecture.[55] The commission called simply for a factory to house the Daily News's printing plant, but Hood saw the need to dress it in the modern idiom. As he noted, "If we are going to be mentioned in the same breath with the Chrysler Building and the New York Central Building, we've just got to do something nifty."[56]

The result was a simple, yet elegant, terraced skyscraper in which height was strongly emphasized by recessed vertical bands of windows and spandrels. The façade and lobby were ultramodern, the latter paneled dramatically in black glass with a recessed central globe, a striking touch inspired by Hood's first visit to Napoleon's Tomb in Paris.[57]

For the McGraw-Hill Building, another factory-type structure to house the publishing company's offices, Hood, now in partnership with André Fouilhoux, switched gears again to create a horizontal emphasis achieved through the use of lateral windows, a technique which Walter Gropius had used in his Pagus factory twenty years earlier.[58] The McGraw-Hill Building brought Hood full circle from the historicism of the Chicago Tribune Tower and the American Radiator Building, through the modernism of the Daily News Building, to a modified version of the International Style. No other contemporary architect showed such versatility, or bravery. Only his use of color (green terracotta shading to the paler azure blue of the sky at the top), and the publisher's name in bold capital lettering along the crown (reminding some of a monumental tombstone) set the slab-shaped building fully apart from the Internationalists.

Hood's fourth significant Modernist architectural project was Rockefeller Center, which he and Fouilhoux shared with two other architectural firms: Morris, Reinhard, & Hofmeister; and Corbett, Harrison, & MacMurray. Conceived in 1927 as the new home for the Metropolitan Opera Company, the project drew the participation of John D. Rockefeller, Jr., who helped to negotiate the lease of

Below

Raymond M. Hood and John Mead Howells (architects) façade of the Daily News Building, 220 East 42nd Street at 2nd Avenue, New York, 1929-30. Illustrated in *Metal Arts*, January-September, 1930, p. 320; and *The Architectural Forum*, November 1930, pl. 130 (photo Randy Juster)

the land from its owners, Columbia University, and to develop the space around the proposed opera house for commercial use to subsidize the opera's operation. But the Depression, in addition to upheavals within the Opera Company's management, led to the latter's withdrawal from the project. Rockefeller was left with the 3-block-long parcel of land (from 5th to 6th Avenues between 48th and 51st Streets), which he decided to develop as the nation's first large-scale, privately financed, mixed-use urban renewal project.[59]

Hood's main contribution was the final draft of the 70-story RCA Building, in which he pared down the simple slab proposed by Reinhard and Hofmeister into a series of graceful knife-edged setbacks. These were purely decorative – the slab did not require setbacks to meet zoning ordinances – but Hood felt that grace, rather than function, was needed for the project's focal point.

Rockefeller Center provides the Art Deco enthusiast with an infinitely rich array of 1930s Modernist ornamentation. The façades of the twin French and British buildings facing Fifth Avenue are respectively enhanced with bronze sculptural friezes by Alfred Janniot and Paul Jennewein.[60] Between these, both in the promenade leading to the plaza and in the plaza itself, there is bronze statuary by René Chambellan and Paul Manship, including the latter's "Prometheus." The RCA Building itself offers further treasures, most particularly, Lee Lawrie's polychromed triptych above the main entrance,[61] and Leo Friedlander's twin groups symbolizing Television, which surmount the pylons flanking the building's south entrance.[62] A tour around the complex reveals other sculptural delights: for example, Hildreth Meiere's three plaques symbolizing the spirit of Song, Drama, and Dance, civilization's three moving forces.[63]

Rockefeller Center's interior decoration is dominated by Radio City Music Hall, coordinated by Donald Deskey. As on the exterior, one is provided with works by the period's foremost avant-garde artists: Witold Gordon, Louis Bouché, William Zorach, Ruth Reeves, Stuart Davis, Yasuo Kuniyoshi, Edward Buk Ulreich, Henry Varnum Poor, Henry Billings, Ezra Winter, and, most importantly, Donald Deskey himself.

Just south of Rockefeller Center, at 608 Fifth Avenue, is the little-known Goelet Building (now the Swiss Center Building). The original unabashedly French Art Deco entrance lintel has now gone,[64] but the lobby and elevator cabs have survived, providing New York with its most exuberant Modernist decoration.[65]

Upstate New York boasts one major Art Deco monument, the Niagara Mohawk Building in Syracuse (Bley & Lyman, architects). Its exterior incorporates the entire Modernist vernacular: a symmetrical ziggurat form terminating in a stepped tower, a façade sheathed in sharply contrasting materials (brick ornamented with stainless steel and black glass), a strong sense of verticality throughout, all rounded off with an arresting sculptural figure which surmounts the entrance. A source of great civic pride on its inauguration in 1932, the building continues to provide a remarkable statement of the Modernist style. The interior decoration is limited largely to the lobby, which houses some streamlined chromium-plated and frosted glass light fixtures, etched elevator doors, and a powerful set of machine-age Vitrolite panels by an unrecorded designer.

In the same period, Bley & Lyman completed the Niagara Power Company

Above

Lee Lawrie, in collaboration with Leon V. Solon (colorist) main entrance, RCA Building, Rockefeller Center, the three limestone figures representing "Wisdom" flanked by "Light" and "Sound" (photo Wurts Bros. archives, Museum of the City of New York)

building in the town of Niagara. The building's entrance traced the setback outline of the Syracuse building, its aluminum doors and pierced lintel grille embellished with an intricate geometric linear design which showed the architects' easy familiarity with contemporary design.

Across the continent, Los Angeles's grandest Art Deco building, both by day and under floodlights at night, was the Richfield Oil Building (known now as the Atlantic Richfield Building) at 6th and Flower Streets.[66] Begun in 1928 by Morgan, Walls, & Clements, the 13-story structure was surmounted by a double setback tower, itself topped by a 130 ft. Beacon Tower. The building's novel aesthetic impact lay in the architects' decision to sheath it in glazed black terracotta intersected by vertical terracotta gold ribbing. A band of gold winged figures along the parapet, symbolizing motive power, by the sculptor Haig Patigian, and a matching stepped frieze above the entrance rounded off the highly contrasting and opulent effect. The lobby provided a further splurge of color: a bank of decorated bronze elevators alternated with Belgian black marble walls trimmed in Cardiff green beneath an additional colorful composition on the ceiling.

In the late 1960s, the Atlantic Richfield Company made the fateful decision, in its need to expand, to replace the original structure with a pair of 52-story towers (one for themselves, the other for the Bank of America). Demolition began in 1968. Some of the original decoration, such as the elevator doors, is now installed at the foot of the new buildings.

Most of Los Angeles's other Art Deco masterpieces have survived, though some only barely. Two broad categories – the "zigzag moderne" of the 1920s and the streamline moderne of the 1930s – are today used to describe the range of stylistic variations which evolved.[67] The former describes the modern, largely vertical, building with setbacks, which had originated on the East Coast; the latter a horizontal structure with rounded corners and curved projecting wings and parapets, to which glass bricks and portholes were often added to provide an increased sense of movement and aerodynamics.

Notable zigzag moderne structures include the Los Angeles City Hall, the Central Library, the Selig Retail Store, the Eastern-Columbia Building,[68] the Pantages and Wiltern Theaters (discussed below), the Guaranty and Loan Association Buildings, the Oviatt Building, and the Bullocks Wilshire department store. The last two merit special mention as they both took their inspiration *directly* from Paris, unlike most others, for which Modernism came by dilution through the East Coast.

James Oviatt, the President of the Alexander & Oviatt clothing store, spent six months of each year in Europe, purchasing new fashion lines. While there in 1925, he visited the Exposition Internationale. Greatly impressed by what he saw, he summoned his store designer, Joseph Feil of Feil & Paradise, to Paris, where together they spent two months planning the decorative elements of the building which was erected three years later at 617 South Olive. They retained René Lalique and the decorating firm of Saddier et fils to assist in the decoration. Lalique responded to his only recorded California commission with designs for the entrance lobby – grill work, elevator doors, mailbox, and an illuminated glass ceiling similar to his ceiling for the Sèvres Pavilion at the Paris

Below

Ely Jacques Kahn (architect) entrance, 29th Street and 5th Avenue, New York (photo Sigurd Fischer archives, Museum of the City of New York)

continued on page 194

Above

Ely Jacques Kahn (Buchman & Kahn, architects) lobby, Bricken Building, 1441 Broadway at 40th Street, New York. Illustrated in *Architecture*, October 1934, p. 230 (photo Sigurd Fischer archives, Museum of the City of New York)

Below

Ely Jacques Kahn (architect) elevator doors, 120 Wall Street, New York, 1930 (photo Sigurd Fischer archives, Museum of the City of New York)

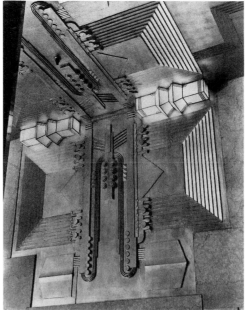

Above

Ely Jacques Kahn (architect) detail of the lobby ceiling, including light fixtures, Holland-Plaza Building, Canal, Varick, and Watts Streets, New York, 1930. Illustrated in *Architecture*, September 1930, pp. 136-37; January 1931, p. 11; and October 1934, p. 230 (photo Sigurd Fischer archives, Museum of the City of New York)

Below

Ely Jacques Kahn (architect) elevator doors, 111 John Street, New York, 1930. Illustrated in *Architecture*, May 1930, p. 319 (photo Sigurd Fischer archives, Museum of the City of New York)

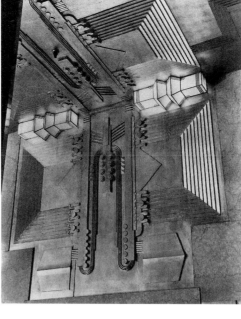

Above

Ely Jacques Kahn (architect) entrance foyer, Film Center, 44th Street and 9th Avenue, New York, 1929 (photo Sigurd Fischer archives, Museum of the City of New York)

Below

Ely Jacques Kahn (architect) elevator doors and mail box, in bronze executed by the General Bronze Corporation, entrance foyer, Film Center. Illustrated in *The Metal Arts*, November 1928-December 1929, pl. XXV; and *The Architectural Record*, October 1929, p. 315 (photo Sigurd Fischer archives, Museum of the City of New York)

Right

Ely Jacques Kahn (architect) sketch of glass mosaic mural; foyer, Film Center, 44th Street and 9th Avenue, New York, 1929 (photo Avery Library, Columbia University)

Far right

Ely Jacques Kahn (architect) entrance perspective, 1410 Broadway, New York; pencil and traces of green crayon on paper, 1931 (photo Avery Library, Columbia University)

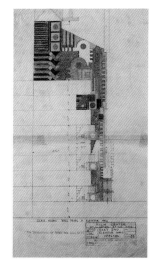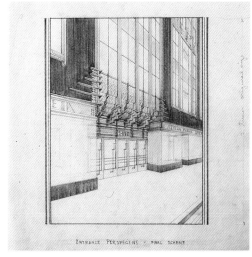

Right

Ely Jacques Kahn (Buchman & Kahn, architects) entrance in gilt-bronze, 2 Park Avenue, New York. Illustrated in *Creative Art*, Vol. 5, 1929, p. 887; and *Architecture*, October 1934, p. 231 (photo Randy Juster)

Below

Ely Jacques Kahn (architect) mail box; foyer, Film Center, 44th Street and 9th Avenue, New York. Illustrated in *Architecture*, June 1931, p. 376 (photo Randy Juster)

Left

Buchman & Kahn (architects) detail of the terracotta frieze and spandrels, 42 West 39th Street, New York, 1928 (photo Peter Mauss/ESTO 1983)

Left

Buchman & Kahn (architects) bronze mail box, 2 Park Avenue, New York 1929. Illustrated in *Creative Art,* Vol. 5, 1929, p.888; *The Architectural Record,* June 1930, pp. 505-9; and *Architecture,* June 1931, p. 384 (photo Sigurd Fischer archives, Museum of the City of New York)

Below

Arthur E. Harvey (architect) detail of glazed gold and black terracotta tiling; the Selig Retail Store Building (now a Crocker-Citizens National Bank branch office), 269-273 S. Western Avenue at W. 3rd Street, Los Angeles, 1931 (photo Randy Juster)

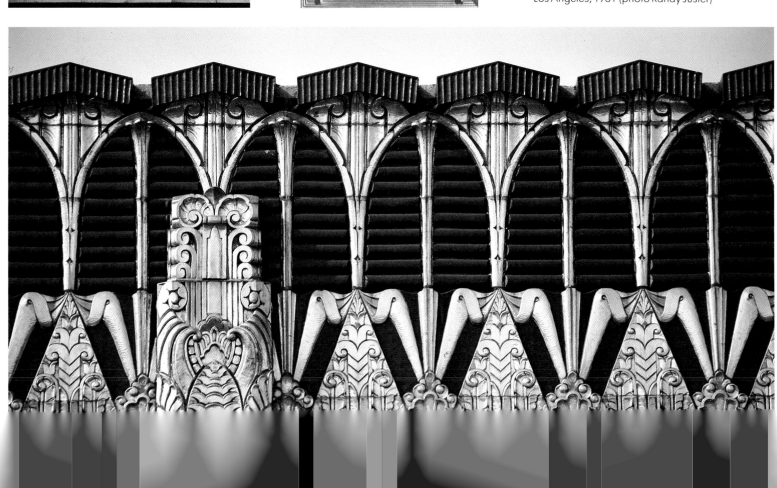

Right

Claud Beelman (architect) Eastern-Columbia Building, 849 S. Broadway, Los Angeles; glazed aquamarine and gold terracotta tiling with recessed copper spandrels, 1930. Commissioned as a retail center by Adolf Sieroty, a member of the family who owned the Eastern Clock Company (photo Randall Michelson)

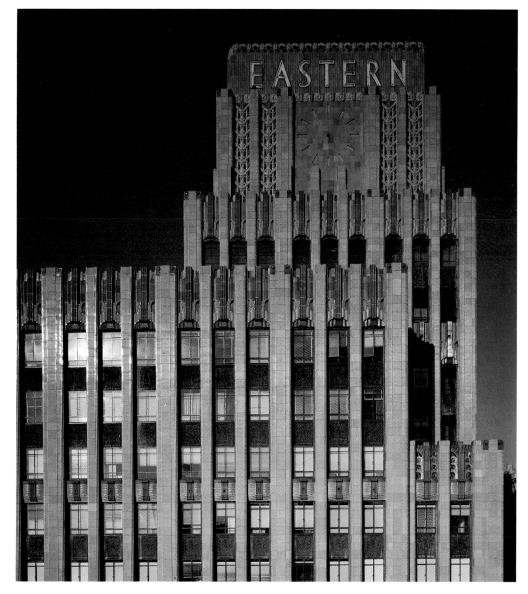

Below, left

William E. Myer (architect) detail of the façade; reinforced concrete, Lane-Wells Company Building (now Winnie & Sutch Company Building), 5610 S. Soto, Huntington Park, Los Angeles, 1938-39 (photo Randy Juster)

Below, right

Boak & Paris (architects) medallion depicting "Comedy" and "Tragedy"; polychromed terracotta, façade of the Midtown Theater, 99th Street and Broadway, New York, 1933 (photo Peter Mauss/ ESTO 1983)

Far left

Bebb & Gould (architects) entrance doors, The Seattle Art Museum, Volunteer Park, Seattle, 1933. Illustrated in *The American Architect*, January 1934, p. 29 (photo Randy Juster)

Left

Henry Hohauser (architect) detail of the terracotta façade, Hotel Taft, 1040 Washington Avenue, Miami Beach, c. 1940 (photo Randy Juster)

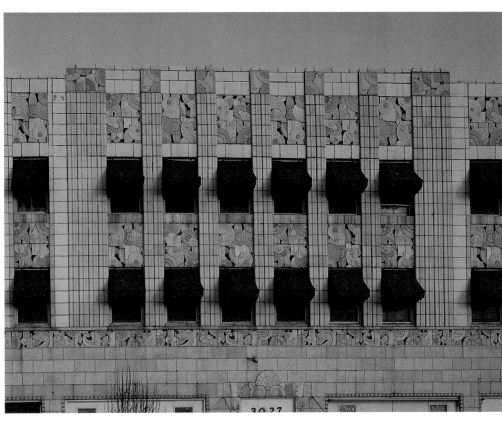

Below

Royer, Danelli & Smith (architects) Bloom High School, 10th Street and Dixie Highway, Chicago Heights, Illinois, 1931 (photo Randy Juster)

Opposite, center left

Unidentified architect apartment building, 3027 Troost Avenue, Kansas City, *c.* 1930, glazed terracotta tiling with navy-blue awnings (photo Bob Barrett)

Opposite, center right

Henry McGill (architect) entrance, Shrine of the Little Flower, Royal Oak, Michigan, 1933 (photo Randy Juster)

Opposite, bottom left

Unidentified architect façade in terracotta, Ritz 55th Garage, corner 55th and Lake Park, Chicago, 1929 (photo Randy Juster)

Opposite, bottom right

Abbott, Merkt & Co. (architects) glass brick façade, Hecht Company warehouse, 1401 New York Avenue, N.E., Washington, D.C. (photo Randy Juster)

Below

Magney & Tussler (architects) detail of elevator door; wrought iron with cast-iron applications, manufactured by the General Bronze Corporation; Foshay Tower Building, 821 Marquette Avenue, Minneapolis, 1929 (photo Randy Juster)

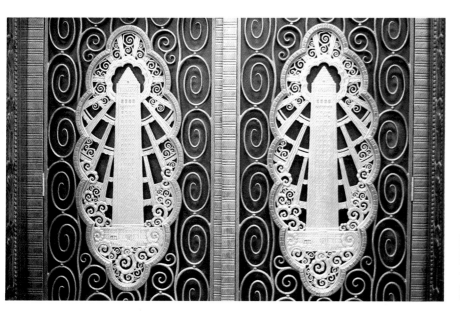

Left

Arthur P. Cramer (architect) 7-Up Bottling Company
Building, 1321 N.E. Couch, Portland, Oregon, 1940
(photo Randy Juster)

Right

Architect unidentified architectural panel, glazed beige and blue terracotta, factory building, Newark, c. 1930 (photo Randy Juster)

Opposite, far left

Louis E. Jallade (architect) entrance frieze; Navy YMCA Building, 15th Street, Philadelphia. Illustrated in *Boston Architectural Club Yearbook*, 1930, p. 98 (photo Randy Juster)

Opposite, center

James A. Wetmore (architect) detail; Main Post Office Building, Pershing Road, Kansas City, 1933-35 (photo Bob Barrett)

Opposite, right

Oskar J. W. Hansen "Spirit of Man"; bronze figure, 30ft (9.1m) high, Hoover Dam, Boulder City, 1931-35 (Arthur Powell Davis & Savage, engineers; Gordon B. Kaufmann, architectural consultant) (photo Randy Juster)

Opposite, bottom

McKecknie & Trask (architects) façade of retail store, 3935-41 Main Street at Westport Road, Kansas City, glazed terracotta tiling, c. 1929 (photo Bob Barrett)

Right

Francis Barry Byrne (architect) entrance, terracotta (possibly designed by Alfonso Iannelli), St. Thomas Apostle, 5472 S. Kimbark, Chicago, 1923/25 (photo Randy Juster)

Below, left

Walter W. Ahlschlager (architect) probably in collaboration with George Unger (interior designer) view of the lounge ceiling, Starrett Netherland Plaza Hotel, Carew Tower, 35 West 5th Street, Cincinnati, 1931. A sketch of the 13ft (4m) high brass chandelier is illustrated in *Metalcraft*, February 1931, p. 81 (photo Randy Juster)

Right, above

Walter W. Ahlschlager (architect) in collaboration with George Unger (interior designer) grille; cast nickel backed with mirror, Starrett Netherland Plaza Hotel. Illustrated in *Metalcraft*, February 1931, p. 92; and *Architecture*, February 1933, p. 114 (photo Randy Juster)

Right, below

Joseph J. Furman (architect) fireplace, 20th-Century-Fox Building, West 56th Street, New York, 1930 (now the John Jay College of Criminal Justice) (photo Randy Juster)

Right

Jock D. Peters, in collaboration with Feil & Paradise (architects) elevator doors, foyer; brass, copper, and gunmetal, Bullocks Wilshire, 3050 Wilshire Boulevard, Los Angeles, 1929 (photo Randy Juster)

Below

Robert S. Degolyer and Charles L. Morgan (architects) entrance, Powhatan apartment building, 4950 South Chicago Beach Drive at East 50th Street, Chicago, 1929 (photo Randy Juster)

Left

Clinton & Russell, Holton & George (associated architects) entrance, 60 Wall Tower, Pearl Street between Cedar and Pine Streets, New York, 1932 (photo Randy Juster)

Below, left

Clinton & Russell, Holton & George (associated architects) elevator doors, 60 Wall Tower, Pearl Street between Cedar and Pine, New York, 1932 (photo Randy Juster)

Below, center

Alfred C. Finn (architect) closet door; Gulf Building, 715 Main Street, Houston, c. 1930. A matching entrance door is illustrated in *Boston Architectural Club Yearbook*, 1930, p. 100 (photo Randy Juster)

Below, right

Rapp & Rapp (architects) elevator doors, Bismarck Hotel, North LaSalle and West Randolph, Chicago, 1926 (photo Randy Juster)

Opposite

K. M. Vitzthum & Burns (architects) lobby with bronze fixtures by the General Bronze Corporation, American National Bank Building, 1 LaSalle Street, Chicago, c. 1930. Illustrated in *Metalcraft*, July 1930, p. 14 (photo Russell B. Phillips)

Right

Wirt Rowland, in collaboration with Smith, Hinchman & Grylls, Associates Inc. (architects) elevator doors in Monel metal inset with Tiffany Favrile glass, manufactured by the Dahlstrom Metallic Door Company, the frame in Numidian red marble, Union Trust Company Building, corner Congress and Griswold Streets, Detroit, 1929 (now the Guardian Building). Illustrated in *Metal Arts*, November 1928-December 1929, p. 234; *Metalcraft*, May 1928, p. 231; and *Architecture*, May 1931, p. 274 (photo Randy Juster)

Left

Wirt Rowland, in collaboration with Smith, Hinchman & Grylls, Associates, Inc. (architects) main lobby, Union Trust Company; black Belgian and red Numidian marbles and Mankato stone. The vaulted ceiling in Rookwood ceramic tiles designed by Thomas DiLorenzo as a beehive (to symbolize Thrift and Industry) (photo Randy Juster)

Below

Wirt Rowland, in collaboration with Smith, Hinchman & Grylls, Associates, Inc. (architects) decorative frieze in glazed Pewabic ceramic tiles by Mary Chase Stratton, Union Trust Company Building, Detroit (photo Randy Juster)

Bottom

Wirt Rowland (architect) detail of the entrance, Penobscot Building, 1356 Griswold Fort, Detroit (also known as the City National Bank Building) (photo Randy Juster)

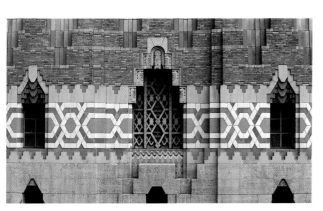

Below, left

Rubush & Hunter (architects) entrance, Circle Tower Building, 5 East Market, Indianapolis; carved limestone with bronze doors, 1929-30. Illustrated in *Metalcraft*, July 1930, p. 28 (photo Randy Juster)

Below, right

Rubush & Hunter (architects) bronze mail box and chute, Circle Tower Building. Illustrated in *Metalcraft*, July 1930, p. 29 (photo Randy Juster)

Opposite, above left

Ralph Walker (architect) mail box, Western Union Building, West Broadway between Thomas and Worth Streets, New York, 1928-30. Illustrated in *Architecture*, June 1931, p. 371 (photo Randy Juster)

Opposite, above center

Hewitt & Brown (architects) mail box, silvered bronze, Northwestern Bell Telephone Company Building (photo Randy Juster)

Opposite, below left

Hewitt & Brown (architects) elevator doors in silvered bronze, Northwestern Bell Telephone Company Building, 200 South 5th Street, Minneapolis, 1931. Illustrated in *The Kaleidoscope*, January 1933, p. 10 (photo Randy Juster)

Opposite, right

Edgar Brandt entrance doors; wrought iron with gilt-bronze applications, Cheney Brothers, Madison Avenue at 34th Street, New York (Howard Greenley, architect), c. 1925. Illustrated in *The Art News*, October 24, 1925, p. 10; *The Decorative Furnisher*, November 1925, p. 91; *The American Architect*, November 20, 1925, p. 318; and *Arts and Decoration*, December 1925, p. 74 (photo Randy Juster)

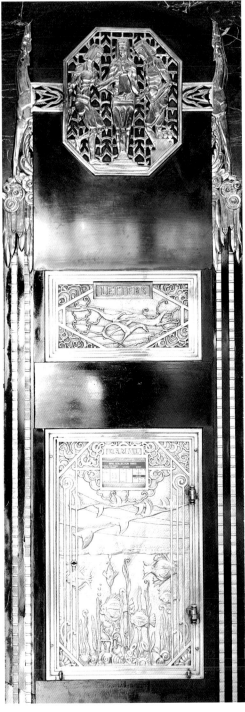

Juster)

Opposite, left

William van Alen (architect) view from the 67th floor
to the spire of the Chrysler Building, 1046ft. above
Lexington Avenue at 42nd Street, New York, showing
the construction of the stainless steel dome, 1930
(photo collection of David and Amy Stravitz)

Opposite, right

William van Alen (architect) maintenance men on the
steel eagle gargoyle at the 59th floor level of the
Chrysler Building, c. 1934 (photo collection David
and Amy Stravitz)

Below

Mark D. Kalischer (architect) terrazzo floor; lobby,
Adelphi Theater, 7074 N. Clark, Chicago, c. 1930
(photo Randy Juster)

Below

Holabird & Root (architects) silvered-metal elevator doors, Daily News Building, 400 West Madison, Chicago, 1929. Illustrated in *The Architectural Record*, January 1930, p. 13 (photo Randy Juster)

Below

Weary & Alford (architects) aluminum entrance, 1st National Bank, 120 North Robinson, Oklahoma City, 1932. Illustrated in *Metalcraft*, February 1932, p. 64 (photo Hedrich-Blessing)

Below

Weary & Alford (architects) stairway with cast aluminum light fixture, City Hall, Kalamazoo, c. 1930. Illustrated in *The Architectural Forum*, February 1932, p. 136 (photo Hedrich-Blessing)

Exposition.[69] Saddier et fils furnished the store's interior and Mr. Oviatt's penthouse on the top of the 13-story building. Unsurprisingly, a distinct French flavor prevails, not least in the penthouse bar, which includes a duplicate set of the bar-room stools which Saddier had introduced at the 1927 Salon of the Société des Artistes-Décorateurs in Paris.

In the 1960s the Oviatt Building followed the rest of downtown Los Angeles into decline. It closed in 1969, the Oviatt Corporation relinquishing its leasehold to the Archdiocese of Los Angeles six years later. In 1977 it was purchased by Ratkovich, Bowers, Inc., who have renovated what had survived, including the lobby. The original haberdashery on the ground floor has been remodeled into a restaurant.

The co-founder of the Bullocks Wilshire department store, P. G. Winnett, also visited the Paris Exposition in 1925, returning to Los Angeles with a determination to model his intended new store in the Modernist idiom.[70] Contemporary artists were commissioned to decorate it: "They flocked to the cause . . . great names and unknowns . . . artists the world over, all anxious to be a part of this exciting new venture. Mr. Winnett himself once said his biggest problem was to get the artists to stop working, for they were constantly finding new ways to do the work they had already completed and begged for permission to begin the projects anew."[71] The building has survived in its original condition, providing today's historian, in its symmetrical setback architecture and treasure trove of interior decoration, with a rare encyclopaedic record of 1920s avant-garde art.

Examples of the 1930s streamline moderne in Los Angeles include the Pan-Pacific Auditorium, the Coca-Cola Bottling Company plant, the California Petroleum Service Station (on Wilshire Boulevard), and a host of now forgotten roadside diners. The Union Railroad Terminal provides an unusual blend of streamlined modernism with Spanish Colonialism.

Two examples of Frank Lloyd Wright's 1920s architecture in Los Angeles are included here despite the fact that his style is beyond the scope of this book. One, the fireplace overmantel in the Barnsdale house, contains a powerful abstract geometric design in which a vertical band of stylized hollyhock motifs repeats itself in bands on the house's exterior. The other, the interior of the Ennis house, shows Wright's conversance with pre-cast concrete block construction and the effective manner in which he applied it.[72] His facility with contemporary architecture and building materials touched continually on all aspects of the Modernist movement.[73]

In San Francisco, the movement found a most gifted disciple in *Timothy L. Pflueger*, of the architectural firm of J. R. Miller & T. L. Pflueger. Pflueger designed several important commissions in the new idiom, in particular the Medical and Dental Building at 450 Sutter Street.[74] The architect's choice of a stylized Mayan theme to decorate a medical center seems highly inappropriate today, yet contemporary critics did not question this. What was found newsworthy was the use of broad bands of incised hieroglyphics to span the building between its rows of windows, providing the effect, from a distance, of a giant woven tapestry. The entrance and lobby repeated the theme in tones of golden brown.[75]

The Luncheon Club in the San Francisco Stock Exchange was a further commis-

Below

Timothy L. Pflueger (Miller & Pflueger, architects) lobby, gilt-bronze and cast iron, Medical and Dental Building, 450 Sutter Street, San Francisco, 1930. Illustrated in *Metalcraft*, August 1930, pp. 80-81 (photo Gabriel Moulin)

Above

Timothy L. Pflueger (architect) women's lounge, lower level, Oakland Paramount Theater, 2025 Broadway, Oakland, 1931. The mural was designed by Charles Stafford Duncan (photo Library of Congress, Washington, D.C.)

Below

Timothy L. Pflueger (architect) auditorium, Oakland Paramount Theater. The sculpted plaster decoration above the orchestra pit (top left), designed and executed by Robert Howard and Ralph Stackpole, depicts Poseidon rising from the sea (photo Library of Congress, Washington, D.C.)

sion which Pflueger designed as a modern interior.[76] This time the effect was strongly Parisian; the room's furniture and pilasters incorporated broad reeded supports and capitals terminating in scrolls in a manner suggesting certain pieces by Süe et Mare some years earlier.

Pflueger's most celebrated architectural achievement was the theater which he designed for Paramount-Publix, a giant studio-theater chain, across the Bay in Oakland. Ground-breaking began in December, 1930. The Oakland Paramount matched, in its massive scale and splendor, any movie palace built: "more than a mile of neon tubing in the marquee and sign, and the two together, suspended above the sidewalk, weighed twenty tons . . ."[77] The theater's management claimed innumerable additional records for the Paramount's interior, but in reality it was no larger or spectacular than the other movie palace giants. Pflueger's creation had, however, met precisely the owners' brief to provide an antidote for its underprivileged patrons, a momentary Shangri-La away from life's realities. The Oakland *Post Enquirer* hailed it as a "knockout for pessimism, for gloomy doubt."[78]

In the Midwest, following the Tribune Tower competition, Chicago played host to several Art Deco buildings at the end of the decade. The city's leading practitioners of the style were John A. Holabird and John Wellborn Root, Jr.,[79] the respective sons of William Holabird and John Wellborn Root, two of the leading architects of the Chicago School. The pair teamed up after Holabird's partner, Martin Roche, died in 1927. Breaking with Chicago's Beaux-Arts and Gothic classicism, Holabird & Root dressed several buildings between 1928 and 1930 in Modernist ornamentation: for example, the Palmolive Building,[80] 333 North Michigan, the Chicago Daily News Building, the Chicago Board of Trade Building, and the Michigan Square Building.

Of these, the Chicago Daily News Building warrants mention, not only because it has survived intact, but because it is enhanced with an unusually broad and spirited blend of Modernist art: in particular, the ceiling mural in the main concourse, entitled "The Printing of the News," by John W. Norton, exterior fountain statuary and reliefs by Alvin W. Meyer, and striking Modernist elevator doors.[81]

In the same year, the Michigan Square Building provided the architects with a forceful expression of Modernist design, especially in the building's central Diana Court, and its row of street-front shops. Unfortunately, the building was demolished in two stages, the final part to make way for a rather bland Marriott Hotel.[82]

Directly across the Chicago River from the Daily News Building is the 44-story Chicago Civic Opera Building, completed by the firm of Graham, Anderson, Probst, & White in 1929. The exterior is decorated at the setbacks with rows of circular windows and balustrades. Elsewhere, the façade is decorated with charming pairs of stylized theatrical masks depicting "Comedy" and "Tragedy."[83]

The new Union Trust Building in Detroit stands unquestionably as America's premier Art Deco bank building, the theme and scale of its Modernist decoration justifying the soubriquet which it acquired when it opened in 1929, the "Cathedral

Left

Abel Faidy Airplane Room, Hotel Sherman, N.W. corner of Clark and Randolph, Chicago, 1932 (demolished 1980) (photo Hedrich-Blessing)

Opposite, top left

Robert V. Derrah (architect) the Coca-Cola Bottling Company Plant, 1334 S. Central Avenue, Los Angeles, 1936. The steamship design was chosen in acknowledgment of the Board Chairman's strong interest in ships. The building replaced five older warehouses on the same site (photo Herbert Bruce Cross)

Opposite, top right

Robert V. Derrah (architect) the Coca-Cola Bottling Company Plant; detail of the building's façade, showing port-hole windows and doors designed as ship hatches (photo Library of Congress, Washington, D.C.)

Below

C. A. Eckstorm (architect) the Samovar Café, the Blum Building, 624 S. Michigan Avenue, Chicago, built in 1908, renovated in the late 1920s (photo Hedrich-Blessing)

Opposite, center left

Donald McCormick (architect) "Diamond" gas station for the Mid-Continental Petroleum Company, Sapulpa, Oklahoma, c. 1928-29. Black and ivory Vitrolite and aluminum. Illustrated in *The American Architect*, July 1931, p. 97 (photo Donald McCormick)

Opposite, center right

Walter Wurdemann and Welton Becket (architects) Pan-Pacific auditorium, 7600 Beverly Boulevard, Los Angeles, 1935-38 (photo Becket Associates)

Below, left

Hanns Teichert murals in the main floor bar, Boulevard Bridge Restaurant, Chicago, 1933. The bar in walnut and lace wood with stainless steel trim. Illustrated in *The Architectural Forum*, March 1934, p. 189 (photo Hedrich-Blessing)

Below, right

Unidentified architect Fountain Drive-In, corner of Ward Parkway and Main Street, Kansas City, Missouri, c. 1940 (photo Hedrich-Blessing)

Below

Gilbert Stanley Underwood (architect) Omaha Train
Station, 801 South 10th Street, Omaha, the exterior in
glazed terracotta, 1929-31 (photo Randy Juster)

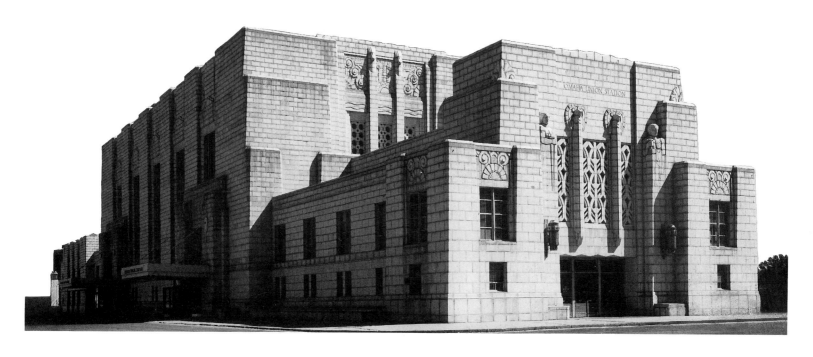

of Finance." The Union Trust Company had originally commissioned Smith, Hinchman, & Grylls, Associates, to build their new offices, but the $12 million project was turned over to Wirt Rowland, who had dressed his most recent architectural commission, the City National Bank Building (the Penobscot), in Detroit, with Modernist ornamentation. The Union Trust Company, a new banking group anxious to project a concerned and public-spirited image, gave Rowland broad latitude to develop a decorative theme which would impart this message. Rowland began at the front door, decorating its upper half-dome with a central figure symbolizing progress, flanked by three medallions representing agriculture, transportation, and industry. On each side of the entrance were sculpted stone figures, one holding a sword to represent the banking institution's power, and the other a key to signify its security (the latter an ill omen, as quickly became evident). The arch above the side entrance on Congress Street continued the theme with a tiled beehive (to symbolize thrift and industry), an eagle (representing money), and a caduceus (representing authority and commerce).

To draw the passerby's attention, Rowland also dressed the building's exterior with bright horizontal bands of green, tan, and red-brown ceramic tiles, assembled as interlocking hexagons, which contrasted sharply with the building's sheath of orange-tan bricks. Color combinations within the bands likewise varied as the eye followed them up to the latticed gold and black tower which topped the entire structure.

The emphasis on color continued within the building, the main lobby's vast vaulted ceiling repeating the beehive theme in bright Rookwood ceramic tiles. Imported Travertine marble columns, Mankato stone, Belgian black marble, and red Numidian marble walls compounded a kaleidoscopic effect further set off by the glistening Monel metal elevator doors, check desks, and trim. A vast Monel ornamental grille centering a star-formed clock likened the vaulted room to a cathedral.[84]

Within six months of the building's completion, the Union Trust Company failed in the wake of the stock market crash. The Company reorganized in March, 1930, under the name of the Union Guardian Trust Company. In 1949 bankruptcy again occurred, and the building was sold at public auction to the Guardian Building Company of the Michigan Corporation. Despite further later financial vicissitudes and transfers of ownership — most of which entailed remodeling of the building's upper floors — the exterior and lower floors have remained relatively unchanged. To many, the building's rich imagery exceeds even that of the Chrysler Building.

Kansas City has, until very recently, been America's unheralded Art Deco mecca. Unlike St. Louis, which is fundamentally a nineteenth-century city, Kansas City underwent a building boom in the 1920/30s. The result has provided a bonanza for Art Deco devotees: a wide range of well-preserved architectural elements on parking garages, apartment houses, and commercial and municipal buildings. The prize is the Kansas City Power and Light Co. Building, which has retained its spectacular illuminated tower and almost all the metalware in its lobby.

Kansas City's real Art Deco charm, however, lies in the scores of glazed

Below

Loewenberg & Loewenberg (architects) entrance, Studebaker Building, 25th and Federal, Chicago, 1930s (photo Hedrich-Blessing)

terracotta friezes which adorn its commercial buildings. It is extraordinary, considering the attrition rate of similar factories and shops across the country, how many have survived.

Two further Midwestern Art Deco masterpieces, erected at the same time in Cincinnati, have had a far less certain road to survival. The Union Terminal, designed by Fellheimer & Wagner, is today a makeshift shopping arcade, the vast sweep of its rotunda playing host to similar projects since the station closed in 1972. Built to consolidate Cincinnati's railroad system under one roof (the city had been serviced by five separate stations until that time), the Terminal's exterior has an ascetic grandeur that touches on the International Style. A host of decorative elements awaits the traveler on the inside, however – a tea room paneled in ceramic tiles from the local Rookwood Pottery, a mosaic mural by Winold Reiss, terrazzo floors, and a women's lounge adorned with tooled leather walls by Jean Bourdelle. Machine Age chromed furnishings and accessories rounded off the sparkling moderne look.[85]

The other Cincinnati Art Deco landmark achieves an entirely different effect. Part of the Carew Tower, designed by Walter Ahlschlager of Chicago, and Delano & Aldrich, associate architects from New York, as one of America's first multi-purpose commercial buildings, the Starrett Netherland Plaza Hotel shared its block-long quarters with two large department stores, a garage, a restaurant, and business offices. The hotel's interior, recently restored, reflects a jumble of styles.[86] Art Deco predominates among an eclectic mix of Beaux-Arts, rococo, and Egyptian Revival themes. The Art Deco decoration was plucked unashamedly from 1925 Paris; designs by Edgar Brandt, in particular, are repeated in balustrades, chandeliers, and the molded borders on the rococo-style ceiling murals.[87] The Continental Room, the Hall of Mirrors, and the Palm Court, the last-mentioned with sea-horse *torchères* and a fountain in Rookwood Pottery, are replete with replicas of high style French art moderne. The lavish ambience, so unexpected in Midwestern America, continues to astonish today's hotel guests.

Another surviving Midwest gem is the Circle Tower in Indianapolis, its stepped pyramid shape conforming to the city's 1922 zoning law. The limestone entrance frieze is sumptuously ornamented with a profusion of carved botanical motifs, including bellflowers, vines, and sunflowers, encompassing a pierced bronze overdoor cast with a stylized Egyptian scene of pharaohs, courtiers and beasts. The elaboration continues inside the lobby. Cast bronze elevator doors, plaques, screens, and reliefs, all Art Deco, contrast with alternating gold-veined black marble and plain black marble walls and a floor adorned with gray-green, cream, and black terrazzo chevrons.

One further delight lurks beyond the lobby. An upstairs barber's shop has retained its original Modernist mural decoration of barber's tools, aircraft, and linear patterns in silver on a black ground. The entire effect is so authentic and timeless that a recent visitor left with the certainty that the barber and the floor clippings were likewise original![88]

Like Kansas City to its north, Tulsa boasted numerous Art Deco-inspired buildings. The 7-story Halliburton-Abbott department store building (Frank C. Walter, 1929) incorporated along its cornice a brightly colored band of scrolled foliate

Below

George Keister (architect), in collaboration with Joseph J. Babolnay (designer) mezzanine lounge, Earl Carroll Theater, 50th Street and 7th Avenue, New York, 1930-31 (demolished). Illustrated in *Metalcraft*, October 1931, pp. 132-33; and *The Architectural Forum*, November 1931, p. 569

panels in terracotta by the Northwestern Terra Cotta Company.[89] The plaster moldings on the building's interior repeated the stylized Parisian theme. Known also as the Skaggs Building, the Halliburton-Abbott was recently torn down and replaced by a 47-story tower. The Gillette-Tyrrell (Edward W. Saunders, architect) was another Tulsa building at the time to be clothed in modern French ornament, likewise in terracotta and plaster.[90] Elsewhere in the city, an interchangeable range of decorative motifs brought color and interest to a host of otherwise nondescript store fronts and factories.

Nowhere in the United States did Art Deco architecture manifest itself with more uniformity than in Miami Beach. Incorporated in 1915 on an island bounded on the west by the intercoastal waterway and on the east by the Atlantic Ocean, Miami Beach emerged as an island paradise for those working-class people who could not meet the prices and exclusivity of its northern neighbor, Palm Beach. Following ruinous hurricanes and flooding in the late 1920s, a new style of architecture appeared, one that joined the Modernist vision with the fanciful colors and idiosyncrasies of the subtropics. Confined roughly to a square mile in south Miami Beach between 5th and 23rd Streets, a small city of holiday hotels and winter homes arose to lure a Depression-racked nation. A distinctly regional architecture evolved.[91] Not only were the buildings generally of the same height (none exceed twelve or thirteen stories), but basic elements recurred in various combinations from street to street. Most buildings show a crisply streamlined, horizontal line intersected in the center by a series of strong vertical lines culminating in a Buck Rogers-type finned tower or cupola.[92] Diversity was provided by a marvelous range of subtropical pastels: white stucco alternating with pink, green, peach, and lavender façades or trim. In recognition of their setting, windows were etched with flamingoes, herons, seashells, palms, and, most significant of all, sunbursts. Neon lighting and flagstaffs completed the effect.

The area flourished as a resort until the late 1940s, playing host to the same set of northern holidaymakers. But by the end of the decade both the buildings and their clientele were aging. Bigger hotels a few miles to the north lured the new vacationers. Soon guests became residents and hotels became rooming houses. Neighborhood decline set in. Almost the entire district has survived, however, thanks to an energetic local Preservation League which has overseen the remodeling of such fine examples of period architecture as the Greystone, Versailles, Plymouth, Delano, Adams, Governor, Collins Park, and Abbey, all hotels.[93]

The local movie theater provided most of the American population with their only first-hand exposure to the modern style. It was not by accident that cinemas in the 1920s were termed "movie palaces." Aware that most of the working class eked out a drab livelihood far beneath the American dream, owners erected glittering theaters across the nation as a palliative to life's daily grind. Here one could retreat for an hour into a fantasy world with one's matinee idol on the silver screen, propelled along the way by the most lavish and exotic surroundings conceivable. Extravagance became the keynote to 1920s theater design. To this end the entire building — its façade, marquee, entrance vestibule, lobby and auditorium — was transformed into a palatial fairyland. A contemporary writer noted the marketing strategy behind the glitter.

Opposite, top left

Jack Liebenberg (Liebenberg & Kaplan, architects) rendering of the new entrance on Superior Street, Norshor Theater, Duluth, 1940-41 (photo Northwest Architectural Archives, University of Minnesota)

Opposite, top right

Jack Liebenberg (Liebenberg & Kaplan, architects) rendering of the Uptown Theater, Minneapolis (built in 1916, re-modeled 1937-39); graphite, red chalk, and colored crayons on tracing paper, 22¼ x 31½in. (56.5 x 80cm), signed l/r RI 38 (photo Northwest Architectural Archives, University of Minnesota)

Opposite, center right

Jack Liebenberg (Liebenberg & Kaplan, architects) "Looking Towards Proscenium Showing Lighting Treatment," rendering of the auditorium for the Astor Theater; black crayon on tracing paper, 12⅛ x 20¾in. (30.8 x 52.7cm), initialed and dated l/r JJL '31 (photo Northwest Architectural Archives, University of Minnesota)

Opposite, bottom left

Jack Liebenberg (Liebenberg & Kaplan, architects) rendering of the Uptown Theater, Minneapolis, 1937-39; graphite, black crayon and colored pencils over black line print on paper 32 x 25¾in. (81.1 x 65.4cm), dated l/r 6-1-39 (photo Northwest Architectural Archives, University of Minnesota)

Opposite, bottom center

Jack Liebenberg (Liebenberg & Kaplan, architects) rendering of the Hollywood Theater, La Crosse, Wisconsin, 1936-37 (photo Northwest Architectural Archives, University of Minnesota)

Opposite, bottom right

Jack Liebenberg (Liebenberg & Kaplan, architects) rendering of the Egyptian Theater, Sioux Falls, 1938; graphite over black line print on paper, 28⅜ x 20in. (73 x 50.8cm) (photo Northwest Architectural Archives, University of Minnesota)

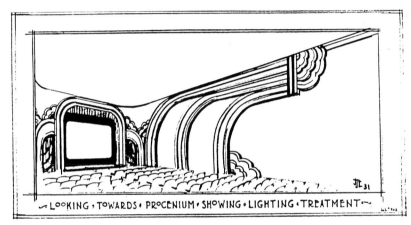

~LOOKING · TOWARDS · PROCENIUM · SHOWING · LIGHTING · TREATMENT~

Theater owners, almost universally, are of the opinion that the average theater-goer comes to the theater to get the thrill of rubbing shoulders with the elite and basking in luxuries that their homes cannot afford. They claim that the audiences increase in proportion to the amount of ornamentation. They insist that a theater designed in the character of one of the old styles and periods will immediately attract a regular following, while the house that lacks rich, elaborate and gorgeous ornamentation will be half empty at every performance.[94]

Designers switched from one national style to another with equal facility. Several theaters are noteworthy for their sheer size and attention to sumptuous detail: Grauman's Chinese Theater, Hollywood (Chinese); the Fisher Theater, Detroit, and the Mayan Theater, Los Angeles (Aztec and Mayan); the Maute Theater, Irwin, Pa., and the KiMo Theater, Albuquerque, New Mexico (American Indian); the Corona Theater, Corona, California (Spanish Colonial); the Tampa Theater, Tampa, Florida, and the Belasco Theater, Hollywood, L.A. (Italian Renaissance and Baroque); the Metropolitan Theater, Houston, Texas (Egyptian); and the Guild Theater, New York, and the Harris Theater, Chicago (Elizabethan). At one point, theaters designed as Greek and Mayan temples faced each other on a Los Angeles boulevard, a short block from another embellished as a Chinese pagoda. The actual theme of the decor did not matter, though, only the degree to which it was romantically applied. Theaters were designed as the Alhambra, Granada, Tivoli, and Coliseum. Others, such as the Avalon, Palace, Paradise, and Ritz, offered an equally grand, but less specific, flight into fantasy.

To the theater manager, the arrival of the Modernist idiom, based on the prevailing French Art Deco "high style," simply meant that there was another choice in his decorative vernacular. That it was modern mattered considerably less than that it was lavish. Architects and impresarios such as Marcus B. Priteca and S. L. ("Roxy") Rothafel oversaw the decoration of theaters in which every available inch was crammed with Modernist Parisian motifs – chevrons, tiered fountains, bouquets of summer flowers, sunbursts, etc. Foremost among these were the Pantages and Wiltern, both in Los Angeles, and the Paramount in Oakland, all recently restored to their former splendor. Others equally exuberant were the Uptown Theater, Philadelphia,[95] and the Fox Detroit Theater, Detroit. Less gaudy examples included the State Theater, Philadelphia; the Pickwick Theater, Park Ridge, Illinois;[96] the Paramount in Aurora, Illinois; the Fox in Brooklyn; the Avalon, Catalina Island, California; and the St. George Playhouse, Brooklyn.[97]

It was the advent of the sound motion picture, or "talkie," that paved the way for Modernism, rather than any disenchantment by the public with period interiors. The attempt to recreate historic settings had led earlier to the "atmospheric interior," in which buildings – palaces, temples, etc. – were reproduced in plaster around the circumference of the auditorium. The entire façade of a Florentine palace, replete with balustraded balconies and niches enclosing statuary, gave the audience the impression of sitting down in the heart of Tuscany. The protruding walls of the make-believe palace created acoustical problems, however, catching or diverting the sound waves of Hollywood's most recent invention. "Atmospheric interiors" were suddenly regarded as encumbrances:

Right

John Frederick Coman (architect) façade of Delettrez store, 5th Avenue, New York, c. 1927 (demolished). Illustrated in *The American Architect,* January 20, 1928, p. 89

Below

Unidentified architect Hotel Apollo, Atlantic City, New Jersey, 1926 (demolished) (photo collection Vicki Gold Levi)

trappings of the silent motion picture era which was itself facing extinction.

Streamlined modern theater design emerged gradually in the 1930s. Some of the designers who had created the elaborate historical interiors, such as John Eberson and the Rambusch Decorating Company, switched readily to the new idiom. The movement's protagonists claimed that the screen should be the only focal point, its flanking ornamentation, if any, orchestrated largely by clever color lighting effects. Out of fashion now, with the older period interiors, were the Art Deco excesses of the Pantages Theater. Decoration became more restrained. Emphasis was placed increasingly on curvilinear forms, as exemplified by the stepped contours of the auditorium in Radio City Music Hall and, ultimately, the bold sweep of Eberson's Colony Theater in Cleveland. Other fine examples of streamlined theater design included the Earl Carroll Theater, New York,[98] the Trans-Lux in Washington, D.C.; the Cape Cinema, Dennis, Mass.,[99] and the Chanin Building auditorium (all now demolished). Black glass, mirror, and chromium-plated sheet metal paneling provided the new mood.

Most movie theater chains, especially the giant Loew's, restyled their facilities as the opportunity to modernize arose. Changes were, for the most part, superficial, limited to the building's exterior façade. Frequently, a brand-new neon marquee was considered adequate.

No mention of American theaters in the 1920/30s can omit a reference to *Joseph Urban.* Whereas his influence was profound in both architecture and the arts, it is for his theater designs that he was principally recognized.

Urban was born on May 26, 1872, in Vienna, where he studied at the Imperial & Royal Academy of Fine Arts and the Polytechnicum. His first architectural commission is listed as a restoration of two churches in 1893. By 1900 his versatility had established itself in a range of canvases, book illustrations, architectural commissions, and interiors. His manifold talents brooked no boundaries between disciplines, a fact to which countless European awards attested. In 1901 Urban made his maiden visit to the United States in preparation for his design of the Austrian Pavilion at the St. Louis Exposition three years later (for which he received a gold medal). On returning to Vienna, he continued to participate actively in the Hagenbund exhibitions, but turned his attention increasingly to operatic stage design. In 1911 he accepted the Art Directorship of the Boston Opera House, and settled permanently in the United States.

Urban's style, both architectural and theatrical, defies easy categorization. It remained, above all, Viennese Secession in its inspiration and whimsicality. One sees, in the "Joy of Life" wallpaper for the Ziegfeld Theater, the same selection of fanciful figures and kaleidoscopic color that had vitalized the Austrian capital a quarter century earlier.[100] Urban designed the Ziegfeld to house the lighter forms of entertainment: operettas, musical comedies, and vaudeville. "The painting of the auditorium has no tale to tell, no continuous action as its basis. Under a roof of flowers and foliage, among castles and hamlets, on meadows and in woods, hunting, laughing, running, leaping, music-making, singing, kissing, loving – human beings in mad, happy medley – no deep meaning, no serious thoughts or feelings, only joy, happiness – a veritable trance of color."[101] Color predominated, as it did in Urban's design for the Max Reinhardt Theater and the Central

John Sloan and Markoe T. Robertson (architects) entrance, Baltimore and Ohio Terminal, Chanin Building, 42nd Street and Lexington Avenue, New York, 1927-29. Illustrated in *A Romance with the City: Irwin S. Chanin*, Cooper Union Press, 1982, p. 51 (photo Gottscho-Schleisner archives, Museum of the City of New York)

Left

John Sloan and Markoe T. Robertson (architects) cast aluminum mail box, lobby, 29 Broadway, New York, 1931. Illustrated in *Architecture*, June 1931, p. 381; *The Architectural Forum*, November 1931, p. 578; and *The American Architect*, December 1932, p. 30 (photo Randy Juster)

Below

René Lalique panel in etched glass for the Wanamaker's men's store, Broad Street and Penn Square, Philadelphia, 107in. (271.8cm) high, signed and dated R. LALIQUE 1932 (collection The Corning Museum of Glass, gift of Benjamin D. Bernstein)

Below

René Lalique elevator doors in molded glass and *maillechort*, lobby of the James Oviatt Building, 1928. Illustrated in *Architecture*, June 1930, p. 313 (photo Randy Juster)

Below

René Lalique mail box in *maillechort* (an alloy of copper, zinc, and nickel); James Oviatt Building (Albert Raymond Walker and Perry Augustus Eisen, architects), 617 S. Olive Street, Los Angeles, 1928. Designed as the Alexander & Oviatt clothing store, the building was renovated by Walter Ratkovich, Bowers, Inc., 1981 (photo Randy Juster)

Right

Voorhees, Gmelin, & Walker (architects) bronze mail box, New Jersey Bell Headquarters Building, 540 Broad Street, Newark, 1929. Illustrated in *Metalcraft*, May 1929, p. 224; *Boston Architectural Club Yearbook*, 1929, p. 91; *Architecture*, June 1931, p. 384, and October 1934, p. 236 (photo Randy Juster)

Far right

Warren & Wetmore (architects) entrance, Stewart and Company Building, 5th Avenue and 56th Street, New York, 1929. The frieze, sculpted by Trygve Hammer and cast in aluminum and bronze by the General Bronze Corporation, depicts the fountains of youth and beauty. Illustrated in *Metalcraft*, November 1929, p. 203; *The American Architect*, December 1929, pp. 48-51; and *The Metal Arts*, November 1928-December 1929, pp. 498-502

Below

René Paul Chambellan, in collaboration with Jacques Delamarre "Endurance"; bronze plaque and grille executed by the Reliance Fireproof Door Company, lobby, Chanin Building, 42nd Street and Lexington Avenue, New York, 1927-29, one of the series entitled "New York – City of Opportunity" installed in the lobby. Illustrated in *The Metal Arts*, November 1928-December 1929, pl. XI (photo Irwin S. Chanin)

Below

René Paul Chambellan, in collaboration with Jacques Delamarre "Enlightenment"; bronze plaque and grille executed by the Reliance Fireproof Door Company, lobby, Chanin Building, New York, 1927-29, one of the series entitled "New York – City of Opportunity" installed in the lobby. Illustrated in *The Metal Arts*, November 1928-December 1929, pl. XI (photo Irwin S. Chanin)

Below

René Paul Chambellan (attributed to) bronze entrance doors executed by the Reliance Fireproof Door Company, Executive Suite, 52nd floor, Chanin Building, 1927-29. The doors depict the power of industry supported by capital (represented by the lower piles of coins). Illustrated in *A Romance with the City: Irwin S. Chanin*, Cooper Union Press, 1982, cover illustration and p. 71 (photo Randy Juster)

Park Casino.[102] Department store interiors, such as the Bedell in New York, and Kaufmann's in Pittsburgh, showed an additional preoccupation with striking lighting effects. In summary, Urban's work cannot be categorized as "Art Deco" *per se*, by the criteria applied today. Its energy and innovative flare, however, greatly influenced the Modernist movement in the United States.

Art Deco nightclubs and cocktail lounges have suffered an even faster rate of attrition than theaters. The Bal Tabarin and the Circus Room lounge (in the Fairmount Hotel), both built in San Francisco in the early 1930s, combined a jazzy mix of colored lights and geometric patterns in mirrored glass, a classic Art Deco look revived by Régine's and other nightclubs in the 1970s. Winold Reiss provided a variation in the ballrom which he designed for the St. George Hotel, Brooklyn, in 1931; a "color organ," in which the lighting system was linked to the organist's keyboard, flooded the room's white walls with hues synchronized to the music.

Art Deco ornamentation began to wane in the mid-1930s, its eclipse linked, in part, to the decline of the skyscraper. The RCA Building in Rockefeller Center was the last great commercial structure to be built. The critic Henry McBride's 1931 prediction regarding the skyscraper's future proved uncannily correct: "Preaching at skyscrapers won't do away with them. I think they come about through economics and when the time comes to destroy them economics will be the weapon employed. When it pays to spend $56 million in building an Empire State Building, skyscrapers will continue to be built. When millions are lost in their construction, they will no longer be constructed."[103]

The fall-off in the number of such giant "cathedrals of commerce" was matched by a similar reduction in the number of large federal and municipal buildings undertaken at the advent of World War II.[104] The ornamentation decorating these structures was also seen as inappropriate, a romantic throwback to 1920s optimism, out of keeping with the new decade's austerity.

Left

Beaux-Arts Ball, Hotel Astor, New York, 23 January 1931 architects dressed in costumes representing the buildings they had designed; *from the left*: A. Stewart Walker as the Fuller Building; Leonard Schultze as the New Waldorf-Astoria; Ely Jacques Kahn as the Squibb Building; William van Alen as the Chrysler Building; Ralph T. Walker as the Wall Street Building; and Joseph H. Freedlander as the Museum of the City of New York

The evolution of an American "Art Deco" style in sculpture was more complex than the style's evolution in most of the disciplines discussed in this book.[1] On the one hand, it was only one of several interrelated vanguard movements which occurred simultaneously in the fine arts in the United States between 1910 and 1930, and, on the other, its growth and establishment depended largely on the efforts of immigrant sculptors. As the cream of America's young sculptors crossed the Atlantic to complete their training in Europe, a group of gifted Europeans set sail in the other direction. From France came Gaston Lachaise and Robert Laurent; from Russia, William Zorach, Boris Lovet-Lorski, and Alexander Archipenko; from Poland, Elie Nadelman; from Germany, Wilhelm Hunt Diederich and the 17-year-old Carl Paul Jennewein; from Sweden, Carl Milles; and from Yugoslavia, Ivan Mestrovic. All these artists were instilled with the hope that twentieth-century avant-garde art would be afforded in the USA the same degree of tolerance that it had been given in Europe (particularly France). The East Europeans among them hoped that their adopted country would also offer them political freedoms.

In fact, America's conservative academic community and public were even less prepared for any form of Modernist sculpture than they were for the parent movement in painting. Sculpture virtually missed the impact of the celebrated 1913 Armory Show which was so decisive for American contemporary painting. The belief that form could exist independently of content, that it could express purely aesthetic or personal ideals without regard to representation, progressed far more rapdily on canvas than it did in bronze or stone. Traditional American sculpture was simply not ready for the waves of abstract European Modernist art with which it was confronted between 1910 and 1920: Cubism, Constructivism, Futurism, the machine aesthetic, and French "Art Deco." The esteemed National Sculptural Society, which had been founded in the wake of the public's enthusiastic response to the monumental outdoor statuary at the 1893 Columbian Exposition in Chicago, continued to represent the most conservative factions of American sculpture. The human figure, drawn from classical art, remained the medium's primary means of expression, and sculpture's materials also remained traditional.

Progress toward the new and the radical came slowly, in part because the

Below

Louis Paul Jonas "Giant Sable Antelope"; bronze, inscribed and dated © LPJ Sc 1928 and impressed ROMAN BRONZE WORKS N.Y., 15in. (38.1cm) high (collection Brookgreen Gardens)

Above, left

Elie Nadelman "Resting Stag"; bronze, 16½in. (41.9cm) high, c. 1917. An identical model is illustrated in *Elie Nadelman*, Lincoln Kirstein, Eakins Press, 1973, #56 (collection Brookgreen Gardens)

Above, right

Elie Nadelman "Tango"; painted and gessoed rosewood, 33½in. (85.1cm) high, c. 1918. Illustrated in *Elie Nadelman*, Lincoln Kirstein, Eakins Press, 1973, #115 (photo Sotheby's, New York)

National Sculptural Society continued to control the allocation of important public commissions, scholarships, prizes, and appointments. This fact in itself proved an important deterrent to those local sculptors who were tempted to explore Modernist expression. Official patronage was, after all, the bedrock of their careers, official recognition their livelihood. So Modernism's advance in the USA was piecemeal, its achievements those of the individual artist rather than the school. Experiments in form, technique, and expression were carried out independently. As long as public commissions were not forthcoming, a private clientele had to be nurtured. Garden sculpture, especially, became an important middle ground between the Modernist and his customer because abstraction or distortion of the animal form was more palatable to most than distortion of the human figure.

No analysis of Modernist American sculpture can begin without brief reference and tribute to *Elie Nadelman*, whose monolithic talent dominated the medium in the USA from his arrival at the end of World War I.[2] Nadelman's individual, avant-garde style defies easy categorization, but its beauty inspired a host of young sculptors to forgo their traditional training. Although the main body of his work falls beyond the scope of this book, certain pieces evoke the sleek French Modernism of the later Art Deco movement.

Three factors came together in the 1920s to facilitate the introduction of a distinct twentieth-century style of American sculpture: the influx of European avant-garde artists, as noted; the return home of the latest wave of young European-trained American sculptors eager to provide their own, somewhat diluted and cautious, interpretation of vanguard European art; and the emergence of the new setback skyscraper form of architecture.

Among the immigrant sculptors, only Lovet-Lorski and Hunt Diederich (the latter primarily a metalworker, see Chapter 5) worked consistently in the Art Deco idiom. Most of the others, such as Lachaise and Storrs, produced the infrequent masterpiece in the 1920s French style among a larger body of more abstract

Opposite

Paul Manship "Diana"; bronze group, inscribed and dated PAUL MANSHIP 1921 © No. 3, 37½in. (95.3cm) high. The model illustrated in *Arts and Decoration*, March 1922, p. 33; *Paul Manship*, retrospective exhibition catalogue, Smithsonian Institution, 1958, cover illustration; and *Paul Manship*, Edwin Murtha, 1957, p. 161 (photo Christie's, New York)

Below

Paul Manship "The Four Elements"; parcel-gilt bronze plaques executed by the William H. Jackson Company, inspired by themes in the Ancient Tower of the Winds, Athens, for the A.T.& T Headquarters Building, 195 Broadway, New York (Welles Bosworth, architect), c. 1930. Illustrated in *The Metal Arts*, January-September, 1930, pl.xxxv; and *Fortune*, February 1931, p. 31 (photos Christine Roussel)

Below, left

"Air"; 37½ x 64in. (95.3 x 162.6cm)

Below, right

"Water"; 37½ x 65½in. (95.3 x 166.4cm)

Bottom, left

"Earth"; 37½ x 64in. (95.3 x 162.6cm)

Bottom, right

"Fire"; 37⅜ x 65½in. (94.9 x 166.4cm)

Below

Paul Manship reduced models of two of the four groups representing "The Moods of Time" commissioned by the Board of Design of the Fair Corporation of the New York 1939 World's Fair which Manship designed as fountains to surround his sundial, "Time, the Fates, and the Thread of Life," in Constitution Mall at the fairgrounds

Left: "Day"; bronze group, signed and dated *Paul Manship 1938,* 14½in. (36.8cm) high
Right: "Evening"; bronze group, signed and dated *Paul Manship 1938,* 13¾in. (34.9cm) high (collection The National Museum of American Art, Smithsonian Institution, gift of the artist)

Right

Paul Manship "Flight of Europa"; gilt-bronze, signed and dated *P. Manship 1925,* 20½in. (52.1cm) high. The model illustrated in *Paul Manship,* Paul Vitry, 1927, pls. 25 and 26; *New York Sculpture by Paul Manship,* Averell House, 1933, p. 11; and *Paul Manship,* Edwin Murtha, 1957, pl. 30 (photo Sotheby's, New York)

Left, above

Paul Manship group of six birds; gilt-bronze on lapis lazuli bases, all inscribed and dated PM© 1932. *Left to right: Crowned Crane*, 13⅝in. (34.6cm) high; *Concave-casqued Hornbill*, 9½in. (24.1cm) high; *Black-Neck Stork*, 16in. (40.6cm) high; *Goliath Heron*, 12⅝in. (32.1cm) high; *Flamingo (#1)*, 16¼in. (41.3cm) high; and *Pelican*, 9⅝in. (24.4cm) high (collection The National Museum of American Art, Smithsonian Institution, gift of the artist)

Left

Paul Manship "Acteon"; bronze group, companion piece to "Diana," inscribed and dated PAUL MANSHIP SCULT 1925, 48in. (121.9cm) high. Illustrated in *Arts and Decoration*, March 1925, p. 33 (collection The National Museum of American Art, Smithsonian Institution, gift of the artist, photo Edward Owen)

Below, left and right

Paul Manship "Indian Hunter" and "Pronghorn Antelope"; pair of bronze figures, 14½in. (36.8cm) height of Indian, 13⁹⁄₁₆in. (34.4cm) height of antelope, both inscribed and dated PAUL MANSHIP © 1914. Illustrated in *House and Garden*, June 1921, p. 62 (collection The National Museum of American Art, Smithsonian Institution, gift of the artist, photo Edward Owen)

Above

Carl Milles "Europa and the Bull"; bronze, inscribed C MILLES and L. RASMUSSEN KOPENHAVEN, 31 in. (78.7cm) high, c. 1926. The model is illustrated in *Carl Milles: An Interpretation of His Work*, M. R. Rogers, 1973, p. 52, pls. 33-44. Another example, in the collection of the Cranbrook Academy of Art Museum, is illustrated in *Design in America, The Cranbrook Vision 1925-1950*, exhibition catalogue, The Detroit Institute of Arts and the Metropolitan Museum of Art, 1983, p. 240 (photo Christie's, New York)

Right

Carl Milles "Times of the Day"; annular clock, white marble, signed and dated C MILLES 1918, 28 in. (71.1cm) high. The model illustrated in *Carl Milles*, S. Strombon, 1948, p. 17; and *Carl Milles*, H. Cornell, 1963, pp. 240-1 (photo Christie's, New York)

Below

Carl Milles "Dancing Maenad"; sandstone frieze, 42¾in. (108.6cm) high, c. 1914 (The Detroit Institute of Arts, Founders Society Purchase, Robert H. Tannahill Foundation Fund, Eleanor and Edsel Ford Exhibition and Acquisition Fund, and Dexter M. Ferry, Jr., Fund, 81.696)

avant-garde works. These artists embraced the human form and realism – the traditional means of artistic expression – only to varying degrees, and also found wanting the rather effete floral bouquets and garlanded maidens of Paris of the 1920s. They needed symbols that would express their vision of the new industrial age, and, ironically, they chose to search for these by looking back to Modernism's roots in France at the turn of the century, taking the early works of Picasso, Braque, etc., as their starting point.

An appreciation is only now growing of the importance of *Boris Lovet-Lorski*'s sculpture. Accorded substantial press coverage and acclaim in his lifetime, Lovet-Lorski's work later slipped into obscurity, in large part because most of it was commissioned by private clients and did not reappear on the market for several decades.

Born in 1894 in Lithuania, Lovet-Lorski studied at the Imperial Academy of Art in St. Petersburg, where he worked, briefly, as an architect before moving in 1920 to the USA. He settled in New York, taking American citizenship five years later.

Lovet-Lorski's style, like his choice of materials, was eclectic: a heady mix of Modernist, Oriental, tribal, archaic (Greek and Cretan), and Teutonic influences is evident in illustrations of his sculpture in contemporary publications.[3] But it is his work in the modern style which is by far the most individualistic and impressive. An early, rather stiff Modernism gave way to a more sophisticated, yet simplified, distribution of forms and mass. The female nude became Lovet-Lorski's forte, the bold sweep of the body capturing its innate rhythm and grace. Even his torsos, though often cut off across the crown of the head, convey a feeling of motion and energy, no doubt partly due to the simplifying and streamlining of facial features and hair.[4] No other sculptor in America caught the prevailing French Art Deco mood as effectively or poignantly.

Lovet-Lorski worked in an exhaustive range of materials, including pewter, lava from Sicily and Stromboli, plaster, bronze, Swedish marble, silver, brass, Belgian black marble, linden wood, Egyptian granite, Carrara marble, slate, Mexican onyx, and jade. Marble imparted a special beauty and nobility, as noted by Mary Fenton Roberts in a 1929 article in *Arts and Decoration*: "The work of this man gives one a sense of great power and reserve strength. He does not seem to exhaust himself on any subject, but in every case you are given all the beauty and strange calm that marble so wonderfully lends itself to expressing . . . a curious combination of old Greek simplicity and Russian intensity."[5] Lovet-Lorski's selection of materials was sometimes unsuited to his subject; for example, he used Egyptian serpentine marble, which has a pronounced speckled grain, for portrait busts, giving the subject a sickly appearance.

Lovet-Lorski's New York studio was at 131 E. 69th Street and his work was exhibited by at least three galleries in the city: Wildenstein and Co., Reinhardt, and the Grand Central Art Galleries. He also participated in the annual Salon d'Automne in Paris. He shared space in an *atelier*, owned by a local artist, where he sculpted his Salon entries. In 1983, ten years after Lovet-Lorski's death, a broad selection of his major 1920s and 1930s marbles and plasters was discovered in the *atelier* – a further reason why his work has not been as broadly known as it should have been.

Above

Mary Andersen goat; plaster, 25½in. (67.8 cm) high, c. 1935 (collection The National Museum of American Art, Smithsonian Institution, gift of Louis Cheskin, 1977.42.2)

Below

Bruce Moore "Panther"; bronze, 14½in. (36.8cm) high, 1929. Illustrated in *The American Magazine of Art*, January-June 1932, p. 97 (collection The Whitney Museum of American Art)

Right

Wilhelm Hunt Diederich "The Jockey"; bronze, signed and dated *H. Diederich 1924,* 23¼in. (59.7cm) high. Illustrated in *American Bronze Sculpture,* The Newark Museum, 1984, p. 46, #54; and *Good Furniture Magazine,* January 1928, p. 34. Shown in the 1928 "Venturus" exhibition at Wanamaker's, New York (collection The Newark Museum, gift of Mr. and Mrs. Felix Fuld, 1927)

Wilhelm Hunt Diederich brought to sculpture the same fascination with flatness and the silhouette that he brought to his metal screens, chandeliers, and weathervanes. The bronze pieces which he created in the round, such as *Playing Dogs*[6] and *The Jockey,* show, in their squared limbs, a distinctly individual angularity which appears to have been limited to an occasional sculptural commission.

Carl Paul Jennewein was born in Stuttgart, Germany, on December 2, 1890.[7] He came to the USA in 1907, and studied at the Art Students League in New York from 1908 to 1911, before returning to Europe and the Middle East for two years. In 1916 he received the Prix de Rome and returned to Europe for four years of advanced study. During this period he produced *Cupid and Gazelles* (1919), the forerunner and companion piece to *Cupid and Crane* five years later.[8] A highly important sculptural commission was forthcoming on his return to the USA, for the pediment of the west wing of the Philadelphia Museum of Art, which he executed in the Hellenistic style in polychromed terracotta. On a return trip to Rome to formulate his design for the pediment, Jennewein created an enduring Art Deco classic, *The Greek Dance,* which was cast in an edition of 25 in bronze, and a smaller number in silver. Other free-standing works created at the same time, such as studies of his children and animals, show an intimacy and sensitivity often lacking in his formal body of work.

In the 1920s and 1930s Jennewein worked on several important architectural commissions in Washington, D.C., occasioned by the Government's construction of a series of federal office buildings. Jennewein was asked to provide sculptural ornamentation for several of these, most notably the Department of Justice building on Pennsylvania Avenue, for which he designed four allegorical marble statues depicting the Four Elements, various reliefs, pediments, and decorative elements.[9] At the same time he was retained by the prominent New York

Below

Carl Paul Jennewein "Greek Dance"; gilt-bronze, inscribed C.P. JENNEWEIN and impressed P.P.B.U. Co. MUNCHEN MADE IN GERMANY, 18in. (45.7cm) high, c. 1926. Illustrated in *C.P. Jennewein, Sculptor*, Tampa Museum, 1980, p. 86 (photo Christie's, New York)

Opposite, above

Boris Lovet-Lorski bust of a young girl; white marble, inscribed BORIS LOVET-LORSKI, 25⅞in. (65.7cm) high, c. 1927 (collection William Hill)

Opposite, center

Boris Lovet-Lorski bust; black Belgian marble, inscribed BORIS LOVET-LORSKI, 20in. (50.8cm) high (collection William Hill)

Opposite, below

Boris Lovet-Lorski three-quarter-length figure; black Belgian marble, inscribed BORIS LOVET-LORSKI, 25in. (63.5cm) high (collection William Hill)

Opposite, far right

Boris Lovet-Lorski model for a fountain; plaster, signed and dated BORIS LOVET-LORSKI 1929, 43¼in. (109.8cm) high (collection William Hill)

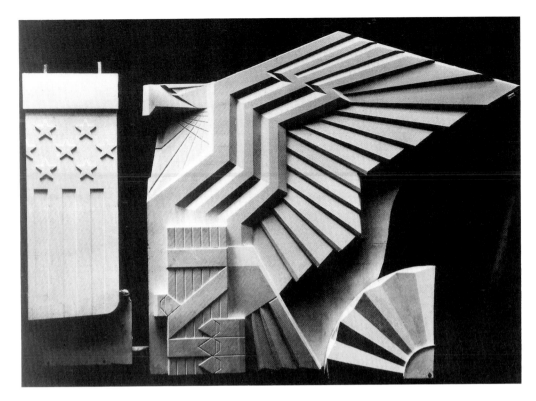 

architectural firm of McKim, Mead, & White to create statuary for the Arlington Memorial Bridge. The four large eagles positioned on the pylons at the bridge's west end, and the circular eagle reliefs on its nine spans were Neoclassical, in keeping with the bridge's traditional design.

In the 1930s Jennewein sculpted several powerful Modernist works far removed in feeling from the bulk of the classically inspired commissions which were his livelihood. Principal among these was his entrance to the British Empire Building in Rockefeller Center (1933);[10] a charming Modernist frieze for the entrance to an apartment building at 19 E. 72nd Street, New York (1937);[11] and four stone pylons representing the Four Elements for the 1939 New York World's Fair.

A review of Jennewein's work reveals a dichotomy: whereas his small-scale models show a considerable Modernist influence, the larger architectural pieces remained traditional. This is no doubt largely explained by the fact that traditionalism was often a prerequisite for obtaining a commission. Only one of Jennewein's designs defies categorization: his eagle relief for the Federal Office Building in New York in which geometric stylization is taken to a point not far short of abstraction.

Known primarily for his series of oversized, buxom models of his wife, Isabel Nagel, *Gaston Lachaise* used a more commercially popular style for a range of lesser-known portrait busts and animal group commissions throughout his career.[12] Foremost among these were the figure of a seal and *Dolphin Fountain* which he created for Gertrude Vanderbilt Whitney in 1924. The *Dolphin Fountain* — one of several pieces, including a radiator cap, designed by Lachaise on the same subject — is an example of the sculptor at his most sensitive and alluring; the animals' characteristic playfulness and grace are caught precisely in the flow of their undulating bodies. Other commercial commissions, such as the frieze in the lobby of the A. T. & T. Building, New York, the bas-reliefs on the RCA building,[13]

and the large plaster relief for the Chicago Century of Progress Exposition, also showed, though less successfully, Lachaise's ability to harness his highly distinctive personal style to the conservative needs of his American clients, when necessary. (It is interesting to note here that Aristide Maillol, whose sculptural style was closely related to Lachaise's in its infatuation with the human body, received a much more enthusiastic response in France than Lachaise did in the USA at the same time.)

Carl Milles's style showed considerable variations throughout an early career in Europe and subsequent move to America, where he settled in 1931 at the age of 57. His remaining working years were spent as Director of the sculpture department at the Cranbrook Institute.[14] The critic Helen Appleton Read remarked on the multiple influences evident in his work in a review of his first American exhibition, which was held at the 56th Street Galleries, New York, in 1929, "The mysticism, humour, and fine fantasy of Scandinavian folklore, the Norseman's nostalgia for the South, and Stockholm's cultural eclecticism are aesthettic elements that compose the work of Carl Milles."[15] Steeped in classicism, the artist brought to his mythological figures a light Modernist interpretation which set his work apart from other traditionalists.

Immigrant Modernist sculptors imported a strong belief in the technique of direct carving, in preference to bronze casting, as the principal means of sculptural expression. This was partly a reaction against academic tradition in Europe, which had always favored bronze over other materials. America, too, had a long-standing affiliation and affection for bronze, particularly in small-scale editions of public statuary (such as Civil War heroes). This limited the direct carvers' success in the 1920s to a small audience, often courted through one-man exhibitions. However, sculptors such as Robert Laurent, William and Marguerite Zorach, José de Creeft, Heinz Warneke, John Flannagan, and Chaim Gross promoted the use of primary materials such as stone, wood, and alabaster.[16] This not only involved the sculptor in the entire creative process, allowing him to "lay his hands on the work," as it were, but also provided him with a spontaneous approach to composition. Laurent explained his preference for direct carving:

I have always preferred cutting directly in materials such as stone, wood, and on irregular shapes in any material, I find [this] always most inspiring – I often start without any preconceived idea, *cherchant dans la matière* – so to speak. I do not especially enjoy modelling in clay, I prefer a material more resistant . . . Generally, I start cutting without a preconceived idea – it keeps me more alert and open to surprises that always develop.[17]

Like Laurent, *William Zorach* chose to express himself in primary materials, especially wood, to "keep a consistent vision of his completed work, a continual sense of the vital, living thing he is trying to release."[18] His style revealed a corresponding ruggedness and tactile quality appropriate to the range of informal animal and children studies which constituted the bulk of his work.[19] A sense of primitive and folk art frequently reveals itself.[20] One of his larger works, a kneeling nude depicting "The Spirit of the Dance," commissioned for the interior of Radio City Music Hall, brought Zorach notoriety when it was removed from public view by the theater's impresario, "Roxy" Rothafel, because of its "lasciviousness."

Top row

William Zorach *Left*: pigeon; cast and patinated plaster, unsigned, 6in. (15.2cm) high. *Center*: Mother and Child (Dike and Mirene); cast and patinated plaster, incised *Zorach*, 14⅞in. (37.8cm) high. *Right*: seated girl, cast and patinated plaster, inscribed *Zorach*, 7⅝in. (19.4cm) high (collection The National Museum of American Art, Smithsonian Institution, gift of Tessim Zorach and Dahlov Ipcar)

Bottom, left

Heinz Warneke "Wild Boars"; granite, inscribed HEINZ WARNEKE, 18in. (45.7cm) high, 1943 (collection The National Museum of American Art, Smithsonian Institution, subject to Interim Trust)

Bottom, right

Bruce Moore "Black Panther"; bronze, 13½in. (34.3cm) high, 1929 (collection The National Museum of American Art, Smithsonian Institution, promised gift of Mrs. Bruce Moore)

Right

Gaston Lachaise "Dolphin Fountain"; bronze, 17in. (43.2cm) high, 1924. Illustrated in *The American Magazine of Art*, January-June 1932, p. 97; and *Gaston Lachaise*, Whitney Museum of American Art, 50th anniversary exhibition catalogue, 1980, p. 16 (collection The Whitney Museum of American Art, gift of Gertrude Vanderbilt Whitney)

Bottom, left

Ivan Mestrovic "American Indian"; one of two equestrian groups installed at each side of the esplanade at the entrance to Grant Park, Chicago. Bronze cast in Zagreb, commissioned by the Chicago Art Institute, October 1928, 17ft (5.2m) high. Illustrated in *Arts and Decoration*, November 1928, p. 67; *The American Magazine of Art*, Vol. 19, 1928, p. 632; and *The Studio*, January-June 1935, p. 52 (photo Randy Juster)

Bottom, center

Frank Lloyd Wright "Nakoma" and "Nakomis"; pair of figures designed as a memorial to the Winnebago Indians (Nakoma, the warrior, teaches his son to offer his bow to the Sun God; Nakomis, the mother, symbolizes fertility), cast in 1924 in terracotta with a platinum glaze, re-cast in bronze in 1974. Nakoma, 15¾in. (40cm) high; Nakomis, 12¼in. (31.1cm) high (collection the Frank Lloyd Wright Foundation, Scottsdale, photo Carla Breeze)

Bottom, right

Cesare Stea commission for the Works of Art Project; cast aluminum impressed *N.Y.C. Art Project W.P.A. #318*, 31in. (78.7cm) high, exhibited in the outdoor sculpture exhibition, Central Park, New York, 1938. Illustrated in *Brave New Worlds: America's Futurist Vision*, exhibition catalogue, the Mitchell Wolfson, Jr., Collection of Decorative and Propaganda Arts, 1984, p. 22, #195 (collection Mitchell Wolfson, Jr., Miami-Dade Community College)

Center

Gaston Lachaise "Peacocks"; parcel gilt bronze, inscribed and dated *Lachaise 1922* and impressed ROMAN BRONZE WORKS N.Y., 23½in. (58.7cm) high. The model illustrated in *Vanguard American Sculpture 1913-1939*, exhibition catalogue, Rutgers University Art Gallery, 1979, p. 98, #156; and *Carved and Modelled American Sculpture 1810-1940*, Hirschl & Adler, exhibition catalogue, 20 April-4 June, 1982, p. 86, #53 (collection Diane Wolf)

The second primary influence on American Modernist sculpture was the young American artist himself. By tradition he had to complete his training in Europe, usually either in Rome or Paris. Both centers were acceptable, despite the fact that the education they offered was fundamentally different.

In the nineteenth century, Italy had been on the crest of a classical revival, drawing America's advanced sculptural talents to study under its masters. Horatio Greenough and Hiram Powers, for example, used the opportunity as a springboard to careers back home, absorbing the sculptural techniques and iconography of antiquity (Archaistic, and Hellenistic and Roman Classicism) and the Italian Renaissance and evolving from this fund of historical sources their own individual styles.

By the early 1900s Rome's ascendancy was threatened, though the cream of America's young sculptors, almost by force of habit, continued to apply for the Prix de Rome, the annual scholarship of the American Academy in Rome. Even Paul Manship, whose style and fame evolved more than any other American Modernist sculptor directly from his Italian experience, later admitted that he had had "no particular desire to go to Rome, having always looked upon Paris as the art mecca."[21] For a sculptor of his generation, setting out on his career before or just after World War I, Rome was viewed as an artistic backwater. One artist even remarked, in reference to the hallowed American Academy, "I pity any artist doomed to Rome for 3 years. Art is certainly dead there and you might as well bury him as let him go to Rome."[22]

In Paris, the art world was immeasurably more up-to-date. As the critic Charles Caffin noted in 1913, "It is the world's clearing-house of artistic currency."[23] The city's appeal derived from a vibrant academic tradition spanning everything from the Ecole des Beaux-Arts to the annual Salons. Most importantly, the system had developed a built-in tolerance for radical thought and expression. In the same manner that the adherents of Art Nouveau had rejected the ornately textured academic statuary of Carpeaux, Carrier-Belleuse, and Gérôme, avant-garde sculptors of the 1920s threw out the Belle Epoque nymph and floral hybrids of Bouval and Korschann. Even if one's entry to the Salons were refused by its ultraconservative jury, as happened to the prominent turn-of-the-century sculptor Rupert Carabin, the system provided other means through which an avant-garde artist could show his work. Modernists grouped and regrouped continually in independent gallery exhibitions to foster their cause, until, with the next wave of vanguard art, they were themselves absorbed into the same conservative establishment by which they had originally been spurned. This French tolerance of progress instilled in the visiting American Modernist sculptor a confidence on which he could draw when he returned to America. Not only did vanguard French sculptors of the 1920s, such as Gustave Miklos, Jean Chauvin, and Joseph Csaky, earn a livelihood from their work, but they were provided by contemporary critics with the kind of enthusiastic editorial coverage that was not to be given their American counterparts until after World War II.

Another commercial incentive for the visiting American in Paris, one lacking in Rome and New York, was the host of foundries which frequented the Salons to purchase models for reproduction in limited bronze editions.

Above

Harriet W. Fishmuth "Speed"; radiator cap executed by the Gorham Company, electro-plated bronze, 6in. (15.2cm) high, c. 1925

Below

Ernest Wise Keyser "Lady of the Lotus"; designed as a fountain for the Newark Museum Court, bronze, cast by Gargani & Sons, signed and dated 1926, 64in. (162.6cm) high. Illustrated in *The American Magazine of Art*, Vol. 17, 1926, p. 591; and *Brookgreen Gardens, Sculpture by Ernest Wise Keyser*, monograph series, 1937, unpaginated (collection The Newark Museum, gift of Louis Bamberger, 1926)

Of the returning Americans, none was better prepared than *Paul Manship*. Born in St. Paul, Minnesota, on Christmas Day, 1885, Manship studied painting and modeling at the St. Paul Institute before moving in 1905 to New York.[24] Enrolled at the Art Students League, he gained practical experience by working as an assistant to Solon Borglum, the noted Western sculptor. Further tuition at the Pennsylvania Academy of Fine Arts under Charles Grafly was followed by apprenticeship in the studio of the Viennese-American Isidore Konti, who encouraged Manship to apply for a scholarship to the American Academy in Rome. He was awarded the Prix de Rome in 1909.

Manship spent the years 1909-13 based in Italy, traveling extensively in Greece and the Middle East to study the iconography and techniques of archaic and Greco-Roman sculpture. The style which he evolved was a highly personal interpretation of antiquity, one which academicians saw as both fresh and at the same time a proper continuation of the American tradition. It did raise certain doubts, however, among contemporary critics concerning its origins and therefore its legitimacy. "Whether Paul Manship's sculpture is classical or modern has proved perplexing," noted one critic, "but the fact is, it is both. It shows great simplification and directness in treatment, but it has the dignity and the quality of universality which is associated with the great art of the past."[25] A predilection for elaborate bas-relief detailing on the bases of his sculpture, and the use of imitation verdigris or brushed gold patinas bound Manship further to classical and Renaissance sculptural traditions.

Manship met with immediate success on his return from Rome, a period when he was adding Indian and European medieval influences to his archaism. By 1925, a brilliant and prodigious body of work had propelled him to pre-eminence within the American sculpture establishment. In the 1920s he achieved the highpoint of a highly individual style, which appears in retrospect to be exemplary Art Deco. Commissions in the 1930s, such as his "Moods of Time," executed in 1937/8 for the New York World's Fair, and his Celestial Sphere for the Woodrow Wilson Memorial in Geneva (1939) show an equally vigorous, but now more streamlined, Modernism.[26]

Manship digressed from his usual archaistic style in 1934 in a series of charming animal and bird studies. These were initiated by the commission from Mrs. Grace Rainey Rogers to design a pair of gates for the main entrance to the New York Zoological Park in the Bronx in memory of her brother, Paul J. Rainey, an explorer and big-game hunter.[27] For this large project – approximately 36 ft. high by 42 ft. wide (10.9m x 12.8m) – Manship designed a double gateway in bronze. The flanking columns and surmounting lunettes were conceived as stylized trees and foliage populated by birds and animals. A lion, the king of beasts, crowned the central tree, as guardian of the entranceway. Beneath him was a menagerie of birds and animals perched among the leaves. These, subsequently issued by Manship in individual editions, were modeled in an uncharacteristically expressive manner. The birds, in particular, reveal their personalities through a range of lightly humorous expressions, recalling contemporary works by the French *animalier* masters, Edouard Sandoz and François Pompon.

Manship did not often pursue this mood of relaxed expressionism. Although his

Below

Avard T. Fairbanks "Rain"; bronze, inscribed and dated *Avard Fairbanks 1933* and impressed ROMAN BRONZE WORKS N.Y. monograph series, 42in. (106.7cm) high. Illustrated in *Brookgreen Gardens, Sculpture by Avard Fairbanks*, 1937, cover illustration (collection Brookgreen Gardens)

William Church Osborn Memorial Gateway in Central Park, New York City, completed in 1952, uses a similar theme of animals among foliage, it lacks the levity and spontaneity of the Bronx Zoo model.

Manship's celebrity did not preclude — in fact, it probably provoked — occasional censure, some of it malicious. e.e. cummings, for example, wrote in 1920,

One wonders whether his winning the Prix de Rome accounts for the fact that in the last analysis Manship is neither a sincere alternative to thinking, nor an appeal to the pure intelligence, but a very ingenious titillation of that well-known element, the highly sophisticated unintelligence. . . . His work is, of course, superior to the masterpieces of such people as French, Barnard, Bartlett, the Borglums, and Bela Pratt — in so far as something which is thoroughly dead is superior to something which has never been alive.[28]

In the 1950s, especially, when America's changing taste in sculpture generated a critical reevaluation of its antecedents, Manship's classicism was seen as being at the root of the earlier academic misdirection. Today, taste has again turned, and his work is being reassessed with considerable enthusiasm.

Born in Missoula, Montana, on June 8, 1896, *Allan Clark* studied with Albin Polasek at the Art Institute of Chicago, and later with Robert Aitken at the Art Students League in New York.[29] In 1924 he left for Japan to experiment with the technique of polychromed sculpture. Three years of travel and study in the Far East, including trips to Korea, China, and later to the Turkestan border with a Fogg Museum archaeological expedition, gave Clark's sculpture a pronounced exoticism.

Bedaja and *Study for a Garden Pool* show Clark's graceful marriage of Oriental and Modernist influences. His treatment of clothing, in which the garment's folds were simplified into sweeping lines, was particularly successful. A pair of

Opposite

John Gregory Top row, left: "Philomela"; bronze, signed and dated JOHN GREGORY 1922 © PHILOMELA ROMAN BRONZE WORKS NY No 14, 12¼in. (31.1cm) high. Illustrated in *Architectural Record*, April 1924, pp. 401-4

John Gregory Top row, right: figure of a nymph; bronze, signed and dated JOHN GREGORY 1927 © ROMAN BRONZE WORKS NY No 4, 11in. (27.9cm) high. Illustrated in *Brookgreen Gardens Sculpture*, B.G. Proske, 1968, p. 303

Paul Manship Bottom row, left: "Lyric Muse"; bronze, signed and dated PAUL MANSHIP © ROMAN BRONZE WORKS NY, 11⅞in. (30.2cm) high. Illustrated in *Paul Manship*, Edwin Murtha, 1957, pl. 4, #19

Carl Paul Jennewein Bottom row, right: "Mimi and the Squirrel"; bronze group inscribed C.P. JENNEWEIN SC. © and impressed P.B. CO MUNCHEN MADE IN GERMANY, 9⅝in. (24.4cm) high, c. 1925. Mimi was the sculptor's daughter (photo Christie's, New York)

Right

John Gregory "Orpheus"; bronze group, inscribed and dated ORPHEUS JOHN GREGORY 1941, 67in. (170.2cm) high. A similar group is illustrated in *The Metal Arts*, November 1928-December 1929, p. 315 (collection Brookgreen Gardens)

Caucasian figures, *Forever Young* and *Forever Painting*, issued in editions of 15 by the Gorham Company, show the same engaging youthfulness and energy.[30] Unfortunately, most of Clark's works were unique castings commissioned by private clients; the whereabouts of many of them have remained unrecorded.

Sidney Biehler Waugh was born in Amherst, Massachusetts, in 1904. After attending Amherst College and the School of Architecture at MIT, he went in 1925 to Europe, where he studied in Paris under Emile Bourdelle and later, as an assistant, with Henri Bouchard. In 1929, Waugh was awarded the Prix de Rome, which allowed him three further years of study abroad. Returning to the USA in 1932, he concentrated on architectural sculpture, including the decoration of federal buildings in Washington, D.C. The following year he was retained by the Steuben division of the Corning Glass Works to design a range of glassware (see Chapter 7). By 1935 Waugh's early classicism had yielded completely to a robust contemporary style in which the human body was given exaggerated musculatory emphasis. Secondary detailing, such as trailing drapery and background foliage, was reduced to its basic geometric elements.[31] The technique proved particularly effective in Waugh's architectural reliefs, to which he applied deep carving to accentuate the bold bodily features of his subjects. The group of friezes on the Buhl Planetarium & Institute of Popular Science in Pittsburgh shows the artist at his most expressive and modern. His monumental group, *Manhattan*, at the 1939 New York World's Fair, was an example of the same distinctive stylization applied in the round.

Edmond Amateis, another Prix de Rome winner, embraced a distinctly Parisian, rather than Italian, style. Born in Rome to American parents on February 7, 1897, Amateis began his studies at the Beaux-Arts Institute of Design, New York, in 1916.[32] He was mobilized almost immediately and returned to fight in France. After the war he spent four months at the Académie Julian. Back in New York to complete his education at the Beaux-Arts Institute, Amateis worked part-time in the studios of sculptors Henry Shrady and John Gregory. Upon receiving the Prix de Rome in 1921, he spent the next three years at the American Academy in Rome. Several important commissions awaited his return to New York, including architectural ornamentation for the Buffalo Historical Society and the Rochester Times-Union buildings. Like Jennewein, Amateis made use of a range of historical and modern styles. Notable among the latter were his designs for the Baltimore War Memorial, his *Pastoral* marble group in Brookgreen Gardens,[33] and the large pewter urn, decorated with a band of camels, which he designed for Ely Jacques Kahn's garden exhibit at the 1929 "The Architect and the Industrial Arts" show at the Metropolitan Museum of Art, New York.[34]

John Storrs's sculpture defies easy categorization. No single theme predominated in his work. The artist moved freely between figurative and abstract art, drawing both on classical iconography and on a blend of themes from avant-garde twentieth-century abstract art: Cubism, French Modernism, and the machine aesthetic. His ability to explore every form of artistic expression placed Storrs in a category of his own within the context of twentieth-century American sculpture.

Born on June 28, 1885, in Chicago, Storrs was the son of an architect and real

Above

Allan Clark "Study for a Garden Pool"; bronze, inscribed ALLEN (*sic*) CLARK © No. 3, and impressed ROMAN BRONZE WORKS N.Y., 18½in. (47cm) high, 1925. Illustrated in *Brookgreen Gardens, Sculpture by Allan Clark*, monograph series, 1937, cover illustration (collection Brookgreen Gardens)

Below

Edmond Amateis "Pastoral"; Tennessee marble, inscribed EDMOND AMATEIS, 54½in. (138.4cm) high, 1924. Illustrated in *Brookgreen Gardens, Sculpture by Edmond Amateis*, monograph series, 1937, cover illustration (collection Brookgreen Gardens)

Right

Sidney Biehler Waugh "Lion"; black granite, 26½in. (67.3cm) high, 1933. Illustrated in *Sidney Waugh*, American Sculptors Series 6, W. W. Norton, 1948, p. 20 (collection Brookgreen Gardens)

Right

Sidney Biehler Waugh "Primitive Science"; gilt-bronze on a red granite ground, Buhl Planetarium and Institute of Popular Science (now the Buhl Science Center), Allegheny Square, Pittsburgh (Ingham & Boyd, architects), 1939. Illustrated in *Sidney Waugh*, American Sculptors Series 6, W. W. Norton, 1948, p. 42; and *Discovering Pittsburgh's Sculpture*, University of Pittsburgh Press, 1983, p. 40. 144 x 62in. (365.8 x 157.5cm) (photo Vernon Gay)

Far right

Sidney Biehler Waugh "The Heavens"; limestone carved by Joseph Geratti, the Buhl Planetarium and Institute of Popular Science (now the Buhl Science Center), Allegheny Square, Pittsburgh (Ingham & Boyd, architects), 1940. Illustrated in *Sidney Waugh*, American Sculptors Series 6, W. W. Norton, 1948, p. 10, and *Discovering Pittsburgh's Sculpture*, University of Pittsburgh Press, 1983, p. 41. 115 x 115in. (292.1 x 292.1cm) (photo Vernon Gay)

Bottom right

Sidney Biehler Waugh "Day"; limestone carved by Joseph Geratti, the Buhl Planetarium and Institute of Popular Science (now the Buhl Science Center), Allegheny Square, Pittsburgh (Ingham & Boyd, architects), 1940. Illustrated in *Sidney Waugh*, American Sculptors Series 6, W. W. Norton, 1948, p. 23; and *Discovering Pittsburgh's Sculpture*, University of Pittsburgh Press, 1983, p. 43. 36 x 38in. (91.4 x 96.5cm) (photo Vernon Gay)

estate developer.[35] His art training began in earnest in 1905 with a trip to Europe, which led to countless transatlantic crossings during his career as he divided his time between the USA and France. He ended up spending most of his time as an expatriate in Orléans, his wife's birthplace.

Storrs studied in Paris and Hamburg in 1906-07. The following year he returned to Chicago to learn anatomy and modeling from the sculptor Charles J. Mulligan, and to attend the Art Institute of Chicago and the Chicago Academy of Fine Arts. In 1910, he studied under Bela Pratt at the Boston Museum School of Fine Arts, and a year later under Charles Grafly at the Pennsylvania Academy of Fine Arts in Philadelphia. In 1912 he was back in Paris, continuing his formal education at La Grande Chaumière, the Académie Julian, the Ecole des Beaux-Arts, and the Académie Colarossi. In 1914, this extraordinarily long and diverse spell of education culminated in an invitation from Auguste Rodin to join his *atelier*. Storrs later traveled to San Francisco to install the master's exhibition at the Panama-Pacific International Exhibition of 1915. Now a mature and independent sculptor in his own right, Storrs launched his career in Paris, and his inaugural American one-man show was staged at the Folson Gallery, New York, in 1920.[36]

Storrs's career in the 1920s and 1930s, during which time he added paintings and rug designs to his sculpture, was studded with gallery exhibitions on both sides of the Atlantic. By 1920 he had already developed a distinctive non-representational style in which he explored the simplification of form into planes and volumes. One approach entailed his use of faceted surfaces to achieve a range of cubist shadow and light effects in the manner of Picasso, Gris, and Laurens; another was his reduction of mass into its basic geometric components.

Below, left

John Storrs "New York"; bronze, 21in. (53.3cm) high, c. 1925 (collection The Indianapolis Museum of Art, Director's Discretionary Fund)

Below, center

John Storrs "Forms in Space"; aluminum, brass, copper, and wood on a black marble base, 28¾in. (73cm) high, c. 1924 (collection The Whitney Museum of Art, photo Robert Schoelkopf Gallery)

Below

John Storrs "The Spirit of Walt Whitman"; study for a monument to the poet, bronze, impressed *Cire Perdue* with the Valsuani foundry mark, 13¼in. (33.7cm) high, c. 1920 (collection The Art Institute of Chicago, Friends of American Art, 1921.91)

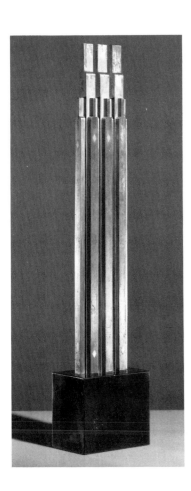

Storrs had grown up with a strong interest in architecture and its interdependence with sculpture. His thoughts on architectonic sculpture, noted in the press as early as 1917 and frequently after that, mirrored Louis Sullivan's comments on the emerging tall building, "every inch a proud and soaring thing, rising in sheer exultation . . . ." In the 1920s Storrs created a series of sheer architectural pieces inspired by skyscrapers, among them *Forms in Space* and *Study in Forms* (c. 1924) and *Forms in Space No. 1* (1927). The elegant setback structures, enhanced with color accents, inspired a reviewer in *The Christian Science Monitor* to remark on their crispness: "I would like to see the new towers of Manhattan rise up in such a burnished beauty as Mr. Storrs indicates, with a new and rigid economy of material and architectural detail that would let them express all the shining efficiency of our metallic age."[37] Allied to his interest in architecture was the artist's growing fascination with industrial art. Machine parts formed the subject of several later pieces – for example, *Opposing Forms* and *Composition around Two Voids*, both executed in 1932.

In an Art Deco context, Storrs's figure of Ceres to surmount the Chicago Board of Trade Building in 1928 captures, more than any of his other pieces, the Modernist spirit.[38] For this important commission, the artist transformed the features of the mythological Goddess of the Harvest into a graceful 30-ft. (9.1m) vertical mass pared down to those elements visible in silhouette from the street. Art Deco stylization in other works by Storrs is often interposed with more abstract forms, simultaneously disguising its presence and stressing the artist's ability to assimilate different influences.

Architecture was the third factor to influence modern sculptural expression in the United States. The advent of the new American tall building, and the architect's rejection of historical ornamentation provided the avant-garde sculptor with a new vehicle for his art. In place of fussy traditional decoration, architects demanded fresh images and forms to accent their towering new structures. The function and even the relevance of modern architectural sculpture was carefully analyzed. It should have, said one critic, "sufficient intrinsic importance to justify its existence, yet it must not obtrude so as unduly to draw attention to itself. Its primary duty is to be an organic part of the building it decorates . . . . For wall decoration, it is obvious that designs of a geometric character in low relief, or even incised in the stone, are better suited to the flat surfaces of modern buildings than the high reliefs of the classical and baroque styles."[39] Understatement became the key to sculpture's interrelationship with architecture; the function of sculpture was to soften the harsh transitions between a building's separate parts. Several sculptors responded to this task with rich imagination.[40]

Despite his French-sounding name and sculptural style, *René Paul Chambellan* was born in West Hoboken, New Jersey, in 1893.[41] Following a formal education at New York University from 1912 to 1914, and at the Académie Julian in Paris, Chambellan was mobilized in World War I, serving as a sergeant in the 11th US Engineers Corps. After the Armistice he established himself in the late 1920s as a leading architectural sculptor. His vigorous Modernist style attracted numerous important commissions, both public and private. The former included, in the New

Below

John Storrs "Ceres"; cast chromium-plated steel, inscribed *Storrs Cast by American Art Bronze Foundry Chicago,* 26in. (66cm) high, 1928. The figure was a model of the figure to surmount the Chicago Board of Trade Building (Holabird & Root, architects). It was illustrated in *Creative Art,* Vol. 6, 1930, supp. p. 117 (collection The Art Institute of Chicago, gift of John N. Stern)

Left

René Paul Chambellan, in collaboration with Oronzio Maldarelli wall panel in the Center Theater, Rockefeller Center, New York; steel aluminum and wood veneer executed by Oscar B. Bach, c. 1934. Illustrated in *Architecture*, October 1934, p. 204; and *The American Architect*, December 1932, p. 47

Right

René Paul Chambellan "Achievement"; one of the panels in the lobby of the Chanin Building, c. 1928, illustrated in *The American Architect*, April 1930, p. 49

Left

John David Brcin "Romanza"; frieze displayed at the exhibition of Contemporary American Sculpture, the California Palace of the Legion of Honor, San Francisco, April-September, 1929. Illustrated in *The American Architect*, April 20, 1929, p. 554

Left

John David Brcin "Sign Language," in collaboration with John and Alan McDonald (architects); pink Georgia marble, for the Joslyn Memorial, Omaha, c. 1932. Illustrated in *Architecture*, February 1933, p. 100

York area, ornamentation for the Criminal Courts building and jail, the New York State Office building, King's County Hospital, Queen's County Hospital, the North Corona Gate at the 1939 World's Fair, and the East Side Airlines Terminal. Private commissions included the façades of Raymond Hood's American Radiator and Daily News Buildings, the Stewart and Co. Building, the New York Life Insurance Building, the Crowell-Collier Building, and, most importantly in an Art Deco context, the panels in the foyer of the Chanin Building and the Fountain Court and ceiling of the RKO Center Theater in Rockefeller Center.[42]

Chambellan's angular style, implemented in a flat, two-dimensional manner for architectural purposes,[43] displayed an even more forceful Modernism than that of most of his contemporaries in France, except perhaps Joseph Csaky and the Martel brothers, Jan and Joël. Unfortunately, much of his work remains unidentified because its authorship is concealed under the name of the building's retaining architect.

Lee Lawrie had established himself as a major exponent of Modernist architectural sculpture by the late 1920s, in large part through his association with the architect Bertram G. Goodhue. Goodhue, a strict traditionalist by training, retained Lawrie to design a Gothic-style reredos for the St. Thomas Church, New York, which Goodhue began to build in 1914. This led before long to the first major commission in which the architect tried his hand at designing a structure in the modern idiom: the Nebraska State Capitol Building (1922-32) in Lincoln, Nebraska.[44] Lawrie was Goodhue's automatic choice for the Capitol's ornamentation, despite the sculptor's penchant for Neoclassicism and his relative unfamiliarity with the new style. Lawrie's designs, ranging from flat and bas-relief wood frescoes to free-standing stone statuary, provide an extraordinary mix of materials and influences.[45] A contemporary critic noted the artist's versatility,

There is something astonishing in the adaptability of an imagination which can compass, as it were in a breath, the Biblical, the Classical, the Romantic, and the Modernist . . . . To

Below, left

Lee Lawrie doors; carved polychromed wood, Senate Chamber, Nebraska State Capitol, 15th and K Streets, Lincoln, c. 1934. Illustrated in *American Architect*, October 1934, p. 75

Below, right

Lee Lawrie frieze; carved granite, on the steps to the North entrance, Nebraska State Capitol, 15th and K Streets, Lincoln, c. 1934. The inscription on the buffalo is taken from tribal hymns of the Sioux Indians. Illustrated in *American Architect*, October 1934, p. 47

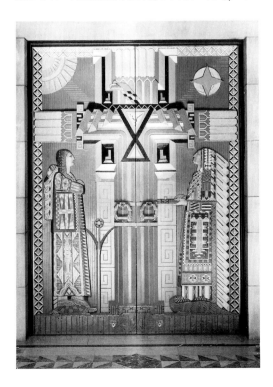

take but the Modernism of the "Childhood" and "Youth" for Nebraska — the mere radiance of these images is superb. The conventionalized sun's rays form in each the key to the symbol, but this key, or signature, is developed into a multitude of linear subtleties and into a shimmering patina of color, caught in the values, which manifolds each surface with meaning.[46]

In his work for Goodhue's Los Angeles Public Library (1922-26) Lawrie showed himself to be by now fully conversant with Modernism.[47] Certain detailing, such as the corbel of the hemisphere surmounting the children's entrance, represents the style at its most virile in the United States. The profusion of geometric ornamentation throughout the building — stylized plant, animal, and human forms — has an invigorating freshness and exuberance.[48] Lawrie incorporated similar

Left

Leo Friedlander "Reception," one of two sculptural groups depicting Television (the other called "Production") on top of the pylons flanking the south entrance of the RCA Building, Rockefeller Center, New York, carved stone, c. 1933. Illustrated in *The Architectural Forum*, February 1933, p. 131; and December 1936, p. 538 (photo Wurtz Bros. Archives, The Museum of the City of New York)

Below, left

Wheeler Williams "Venus Bringing the Arts to Manhattan"; cast aluminum, façade of ex-Sotheby's building, Madison Avenue at 75th Street, New York, 1940s (photo Sotheby's, New York)

Below

Wheeler Williams "Euterpe"; cast stone, signed and dated *Wheeler Williams* MCMXXVI, 51in. (129.5cm) high. Exhibited in the Railroad Building at the New York World's Fair, 1939. Illustrated in *Wheeler Williams*, American Sculptors Series, 1947, p. 15 (photo Sotheby's, New York)

Modernist decoration in subsequent commissions; for example, the National Academy of Sciences, Washington, D.C. (Bertram G. Goodhue), the Church of the Heavenly Rest, New York (Mayers, Murray & Phillip), the Education Building of the Soldiers and Sailors' Memorial Bridge, Harrisburg, Pa. (Ellerbe & Co., Holabird & Root, associate architects).

Leo Friedlander was another artist who specialized in architectural sculpture. An excellent, but mixed, academic education – the Ecole des Beaux-Arts, Paris; the Beaux-Arts, Brussels; and the American Academy in Rome (1913-17)[49] – left him with the conviction that he should ally himself as a sculptor closely with architecture, the "mother art."[50] A broad body of formal academic commissions, mostly on a heroic scale, for traditional architects such as McKim, Mead & White,[51] Cass Gilbert, and Paul P. Cret,[52] established Friedlander's reputation for strong, monumental works, many of which incorporated male figures of exaggerated musculature. These were supplemented in the late 1920s by a selection of Modernist works: most notably, the pylons flanking the north and south entrances to Radio City Music Hall in Rockefeller Center,[53] and Modernist panels for the New York Telephone Company Building in Buffalo (Voorhees, Gmelin, & Walker, architects).[54] For the Jefferson County Court House in Birmingham, Alabama (Holabird & Root), Friedlander designed a frieze of twenty limestone panels with angular allegorical figures of Mercury, Vigilance, Power, etc.[55] For these, he addressed a favorite issue, that of modeling his figures to correct the distortion caused by their being viewed at a considerable height above eye level.

Contemporary architectural reviews show Modernist examples by other sculptors: for example, Alfonso Iannelli, Paul Fjelde, Maxfield Keck, and Alvin Meyer.[56] Many more await discovery and identification on buildings erected in the 1920s and 1930s across the country.

Right

Emory P. Seidel centerpiece, bronze, inscribed © *E.P.Seidel* and impressed ROMAN BRONZE WORKS N.Y. 8.11., 9⅞in. (25.1cm) high, c. 1920 (photo Christie's, New York)

PAINTING AND GRAPHICS

One has to search hard to find an Art Deco influence in American paintings of the 1920s and 1930s. Among the various strains of modern art which took root in the United States at that time, the flamboyant stylizations that gained favor in Paris around 1925 were far less in evidence than those of the French abstract art movements which had matured before World War I. Such impact as Art Deco had in America was linked to the modern art movement in general, and must therefore be analyzed as part of it.

The photographer Alfred Stieglitz had perhaps the greatest influence on the progress of modern American art in the early years of this century. In 1905, he opened his Photo-Secession Gallery, later known as "291," where he exhibited both his own photographs and those of others.[1] Two years later, he widened the scope of his exhibitions to include avant-garde paintings and sculpture. Many artists who were later recognized as the forerunners of European modern art made their American debuts at "291" – for example, Rodin, Matisse, Cézanne, Le Douanier Rousseau, and Brancusi. At the time that Stieglitz began his role as a conveyor of modern art, several American artists returned home from Paris imbued with the same radicalism. Among the first was Max Weber, who had been greatly influenced by the early work of Braque and Picasso in Paris. Later American vanguard painters who exhibited at Gallery "291" included John Marin, Marsden Hartley, Arthur Dove, Alfred Maurer, and Georgia O'Keeffe. The gallery closed in 1917, having provided the American public with 79 exhibitions of modern photography, painting, and sculpture in its twelve years of existence.

Another milestone in modern art in the USA was the celebrated International Exhibition of Modern Art, held at the 69th Regiment Armory, New York, between February 15 and March 15, 1913.[2] The Armory Show, as it became known, transformed American art. The artistic revolution, which until then had been confined to "291" and small art groups, now became a front-page phenomenon. No longer could the "madmen," "fakers," and "degenerates" of contemporary art be silenced or ignored: the show's impact, both in the press and by public consensus, attracted vast attention, which, though often hostile, was better than no attention at all. As one critic observed, "Official art acted like an outraged virgin, furious, shocked, and bewildered that such things went on. The public, abetted by the newspapers, came to scoff, had their laugh, but left in bewilderment. Ignorance and misunderstanding were rife, but it was a grand circus nonetheless."[3]

After the Armory Show, American art underwent systematic change. The National Academy of Design, painting's official academic body, became increasingly isolated as modern art asserted itself and grew stronger. The Show, which had included an estimated 1,600 works, was actually two exhibitions in one: a selection of vanguard European art and a cross-section of more restrained contemporary American art weighted heavily in favor of the younger, more radical group of painters based in the East. Noticeably absent from the European representation was much of the German Expressionist movement and Italian Futurism. Duchamp's *Nude Descending a Staircase* received the brunt of the press's disdain and was singled out as proof of the incomprehensibility and

Right

Raymond Loewy advertisement for Saks Fifth Avenue, illustrated in *Vogue*, March 15, 1927

decadence of Modernism. Other artists, such as Van Gogh, Gauguin, and especially Matisse, were treated to a similar barrage of derision.

Modernism survived its initiation, however, and was carried forward from the Armory Show by its young American disciples. Following World War I, they gained ground steadily. Official respect and sanction were granted by the two exhibitions staged at the Pennsylvania Academy of Arts in 1920 and 1921. Also in 1921, the Metropolitan Museum of Art held its respected Modernist show.[4] Suddenly, within a relatively few years, the old-line academic painters were superseded.

In American painting in the 1920s numerous cross-influences and temporary alliances are evident as vanguard artists experimented with the different Modernist strains imported from Europe, in particular, Cubism, Fauvism, the pattern-making of Matisse, and the Post-Impressionism of Cézanne. Cubism, for example, was given different interpretations by artists such as Stuart Davis and Arthur G. Dove. To some, it represented a way to break mass down into its simplest components; to others it was a means of achieving greater abstraction. Abstraction itself was pursued by artists such as Man Ray (until he moved to Paris in the early 1920s), Joseph Stella, and Konrad Cramer. Charles Sheeler and Charles Demuth headed a movement towards photorealism as a means of depicting the coldness and mechanical precision of the new industrial civilization. Curiously, however, the machine was largely avoided as a theme by American artists, who saw the human element in industrial society, rather than the machine itself, as a source of inspiration. The mechanical theme which had inspired the Italian Futurists virtually passed America by.

There is very little of the stylized 1920s French Art Deco idiom in the above experimentation. As in sculpture, the young American artist looked back for inspiration primarily to the inception of modern art at the turn of the century, rather than to his contemporaries in Paris. The highly distinctive Art Deco graphics of Jean Dupas, Tamara de Lempicka, Paul Colin, and Eugene Robert Pougheon were not emulated in the USA beyond the field of commercial and poster art, in which a handful of immigrants employed them successfully. One can detect a certain Art Deco influence – if not in style, then in the use of images such as the skyscraper – in paintings by Georgia O'Keeffe, Rockwell Kent, and others, but Art Deco did not become a significant force in American painting on canvas.[5] It was more readily applied in the case of murals and ceilings. Artists such as Arthur S. Covey and Kimon Nicoläides adopted an Art Deco style in several architectural commissions around 1929/30.[6] Of particular importance, in this type of painted decoration, was Rockefeller Center.

Described at the time as "the last monument to the spirit of 1929," Rockefeller Center generated the most ambitious privately endorsed art project of the inter-war years, and its completion preceded, by only a few months, the introduction of FDR's New Deal programs. Donald Deskey and Eugene Schoen, who coordinated the decoration of the two theaters in the complex – Radio City Music Hall and the RKO Center Theater – drew on a rich array of vanguard artists and muralists. Of those originally invited to participate, Georgia O'Keeffe declined, and Diego Rivera saw his mural "Man at the Crossroads Looking with Hope and

Right

Vladimir Bobritsky advertisement for Saks Fifth
Avenue, illustrated in *Vogue,* March 1928, p. 164

High Vision to the Choosing of a New and Better Future" destroyed at Nelson
Rockefeller's instruction when it was two-thirds complete because he refused to
remove Lenin's figure from his composition.[7]

For the RKO Center Theater, Schoen invited Boardman Robinson to provide the
mural in the lobby, and Edward Steichen the photo-mural of aviation in the men's
basement lounge.[8] For the much larger, and more ambitious, Radio City Music
Hall project, Deskey retained a host of established American artists to decorate
the labyrinth of lobbies, smoking rooms, foyers, and lounges dispersed over five
floors. Included, most notably, were Ezra Winters ("The Fountain of Youth"), Louis
Bouché ("The Phantasmagoria of the Theater"), Witold Gordon ("A History of
Cosmetics", and a group of maps), Buk Ulreich ("Wild West"), Yasuo Kuniyoshi
(a floral mural), Stuart Davis ("Men without Women"), Henry Billings (a mural of
wild animals), and Donald Deskey himself ("Nicotine," a block-printed aluminum wallpaper).[9]

Left

Constance Hacker illustration for *Cinematic Design*, Leonard Hacker, published by the American Photographic Publishing Co., Boston, 1931, 8×5in. (20.3×12.7cm) (collection Mitchell Wolfson, Jr., Miami-Dade Community College)

A strong Modernist spirit pervades the wide range of styles represented. Only Davis's "Men without Women" (which was removed and transferred to the Museum of Modern Art in 1975) shows considerable abstraction. The rest have a light theatrical charm well-suited to their location.

The issue of whether such a munificent gift of art by the Rockefeller family to the City of New York could sustain itself financially was raised at the time. "Can the city maintain so colossal a development?" one critic asked. "Beautiful as it may be – and the artistic quality evidenced in the theaters represents a tremendous advance – it is not, primarily, the result of a need, but of a fortune seeking to find monumental expression."[10] These words proved prophetic when the Music Hall posted the first of its annual deficits in 1969, leading to serious consideration, in 1977, as to whether it should be closed and demolished.[11]

The French Art Deco graphic style manifested itself most strongly in the United States in the fields of advertising and poster art. America could not match the diversity of talents that had aligned themselves to the related decorative arts movement in Paris – for example, Robert Bonfils, George Barbier, A. M. Cassandre, and Georges Lepape – but a handful of commercial artists, whose style can be defined as Art Deco, came to the fore. Of these, Joseph Binder demands pride of place for a distinctive angular style which echoed that of the top French designers of advertising material.[12] Born in Vienna, where he studied at the Kunstgewerbeschule, Binder came to the USA in 1933 and lectured on contemporary advertising design at the Art Institute of Chicago; the Layton School of Art, Milwaukee; the Minneapolis School of Art; and the Chouinard School of Art, Los Angeles. Binder produced a range of covers for magazines such as *Fortune* and *Modern Packaging,* and posters for travel companies, capping his work in the 1930s with the commission to design the official poster for the 1939 New York World's Fair.

Ilonka Karasz was another designer to apply the Art Deco idiom to graphics. Born in Budapest in 1896, Karasz attended the Royal School of Arts and Crafts in her native city before emigrating to the USA in 1913.[13] One of the first Modernists in her adoped land, Karasz settled in Greenwich Village, New York, where she turned her talents to almost every aspect of the fine and applied arts: silverware, ceramics, furniture, fabrics, rugs, and graphics. Among the last-mentioned were covers and illustrations for *The New Yorker* and *Vanity Fair* which show an engaging, angular style. Karasz worked on numerous projects with her younger sister, Mariska, a needlework designer, artist, and author.[14]

Another Hungarian, *Emil J. Bisttram,* was born in 1895 and came to the USA with his parents at the age of twelve.[15] He settled on New York's East Side, taking a series of jobs to supplement his tuition fees at the National Academy of Design, the Parsons School of Art, Cooper Union, and the Art Students League. By 1920 he had established his own advertising agency, while also serving as art director of other local agencies. His career in painting was launched during this period with a series of New England seascapes. By the mid-1920s his realism had yielded to an energetic Art Deco style in which hard-edged geometry – which Bisttram termed dynamic symmetry – predominated. A delightful Parisian air of levity pervades his paintings of this period. Later works revealed a more abstract, Kandinsky-inspired, influence. Bisttram settled in the late 1930s in Taos, New Mexico, where he opened his own painting school in 1941. Later he moved to Los Angeles.

The entries for the annual Advertising Art competition, published annually by the Art Directors Club of New York, show a smattering of stylized Art Deco designs by Vladimir Bobritsky for Saks-Fifth Avenue, and by S. Garnett Goesle for the International Mercantile Company.[16] Similar advertisements by other commercial artists appeared in *Vogue* and *House and Garden* from 1925 to 1935.

The industrial designer *John Vassos* applied his multiple talents to both book illustrations and bindings.[17] The latter in particular showed a forceful interpretation of machine-age forms and geometry, in keeping with contemporary book design in Paris by Pierre Legrain, Rose Adler, Henri Creuzevault, and Paul Bonet. In the same years, 1928-31, the American book market was inundated with volumes on the country's new architecture. Renderings of soaring, setback

Left

John Vassos   untitled illustration #11, for *Ultimo*, gouache on board, 20×15 in. (50.8×38.1 cm)

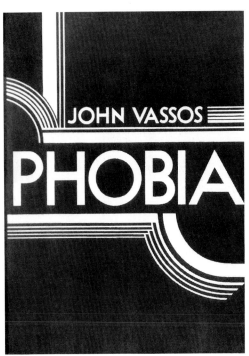

Far left

John Vassos   bookbinding for *Contempo*, Ruth Vassos, published by E. P. Dutton, New York, 1929; quarto, blue cloth on board. Illustrated in *Brave New Worlds: America's Futurist Vision*, exhibition catalogue, Mitchell Wolfson New World Center Campus, 1984, #53 (collection Mitchell Wolfson, Jr., Miami-Dade Community College)

Left

John Vassos   bookbinding for *Phobia*, John Vassos, published by Covici-Friede, New York, 1931; quarto, silver on black cloth on board. Illustrated in *Brave New Worlds: America's Futurist Vision*, exhibition catalogue, Mitchell Wolfson New World Center Campus, 1984, #54 (collection Mitchell Wolfson, Jr., Miami-Dade Community College)

Right

Alvin Lustig "The Dying Phoenix"; illustration in *The Ghost of the Underblows*, Alvin Lustig, published by the Ward Ritchie Press, Los Angeles, 1940, 9⅛ x 6¼in. (23.2 x 15.9cm). Illustrated in *Brave New Worlds: America's Futurist Vision*, exhibition catalogue, Mitchell Wolfson New World Center Campus, 1984, #43, cover illustration (collection Mitchell Wolfson, Jr., Miami-Dade Community College)

Below, left

John Vassos bookbinding for *Ultimo*, Ruth Vassos, published by E. P. Dutton, New York, 1930, 10½ x 8in. (26.7 x 20.3cm). Illustrated in *Brave New Worlds: America's Futurist Vision*, exhibition catalogue, Mitchell Wolfson New World Center Campus, 1984, #55 (collection Mitchell Wolfson, Jr., Miami-Dade Community College)

Below, center

William P. Welsh slip cover for *Chicago*, published by the Miehle Press and Printing Company, Chicago, 1928, 12 x 9⅛in. (30.5 x 23.2cm) (collection Mitchell Wolfson, Jr., Miami-Dade Community College)

Below, right

Joseph Binder cover illustration of *Fortune*, December 1937, 14 x 11¼in. (35.6 x 38.6cm)

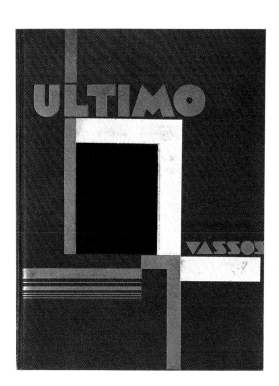

structures were undertaken by illustrators such as Louis Lozowick, W. K. Oltar-Jevsky, and, master of the romantic impression, Hugh Ferriss. The same theme was adopted by Howard Cook, Samuel L. Margolies, and William C. McNulty, in editions of lithographs and wood engravings.

If the 1920s was the decade of Modernism, the 1930s was that of social art. The stock market crash had a profound effect on American painters, many of whom felt a responsibility to depict in their art the hardships brought about by unrestrained capitalism. Artists such as Thomas H. Benton and William Gropper turned to realism to portray urban squalor in a style similar to that of the Ash Can School at the turn of the century.

The Crash generated a vacuum in private art sponsorship, which was at best limited to the purchase of European paintings by a few wealthy American art patrons and connoisseurs. However, the vacuum was more than filled by the seven federal programs launched between 1933 and 1943. Of these, the Works Progress Administration (WPA), initiated by the Roosevelt Administration in May 1935, was by far the most effective from the artist's standpoint.[18]

The WPA was set up to provide jobs for the "employable unemployed." It marked a distinct departure from its predecessors, the Public Works Administration (PWA),[19] and the Civil Works Administration (CWA), which had been established primarily to create jobs, *whether needed or not*. By 1935, analysis of the two existing programs showed that, within the community of the unemployed, work relief was more popular than direct relief, and that work relief, to be really effective, should be structured to provide the various occupational groups with jobs suited to their training and experience. The earlier charity relief of the PWA and CWA projects yielded to a vast and complicated government system in which commissions were awarded by competition. The division of the WPA relating to the arts was called the Federal Arts Project and was divided into separate divisions for music, theater, and painting.

The government's experimentation caused a minor cultural revolution in America. As a critic noted,

They brought the American audience and the American artist face to face for the first time in their respective lives. And the result was an astonishment needled with excitement such as neither the American artist nor the American audience had ever felt before. Down to the beginning of these experiments neither the American audience nor the American artist had ever guessed that the American audience existed. The American audience as the American artist saw it was a small group of American millionaires who bought pictures not because they liked pictures but because the possession of certain pictures was the surest and most cheaply acquired sign of culture. Since all pictures, to qualify, must necessarily have been sold first for a high price at Christie's in London this audience did not do much for American painters.[20]

Within a few months, however, the Federal Painters' Project had established 28 art galleries and centers in Southern towns where art had never previously been exhibited. In the first year, more than a million people were estimated to have been exposed to art for the first time, through classes, exhibitions, and lectures.

By 1936, Holger Cahill, the Director of the Federal Painters' Project, had created a program which, as far as was practicable, drew on the talents of *all* artists – i.e., good *and* not so good, for the government could not select only starving geniuses. This, in effect, committed the federal government to the formation of the broad base necessary for a genuine national art movement. As Cahill explained,

The organization of the Project has proceeded on the principle that it is not the solitary genius but a sound general movement which maintains art as a vital functioning part of any cultural scheme. Art is not a matter of rare occasional masterpieces. The emphasis upon masterpieces is a nineteenth-century phenomenon. It is primarily a collector's idea and had little relation to an art movement . . . in a genuine art movement a great reservoir of art is created in many forms both major and minor.[21]

The New Deal projects achieved two goals in parallel: on the one hand, over 5,000 jobs were provided for artists, and, on the other, the public was exposed to, and educated in, art. A legacy of over 225,000 works was created by the WPA program for placement in federal schools, hospitals, post offices, and office buildings. The only formal guidelines were that the subject matter be "American," and preferably of local historical significance.

A variety of styles were represented in the WPA projects, ranging from the strictly representational to the surreal and abstract. Predictably, a fair number portrayed either an Art Deco or "streamlined" imagery. Recent interest in the WPA program has initiated research into the artists involved, many of whom have remained unknown, along with their works, which have frequently been destroyed or painted over.[22] In the case of a number of artists, however, notably Jackson Pollock, Mark Rothko, and David Smith, the experience proved to be the means by which they eventually achieved recognition and even celebrity.

Right

Leo Rackow cover design, A.C.F. (American Car and Foundry Co.) sales booklet, c. 1938, 10x14 in. (25.4x35.6cm). Shown is a rendering of Raymond Loewy's "Ultraliner" train

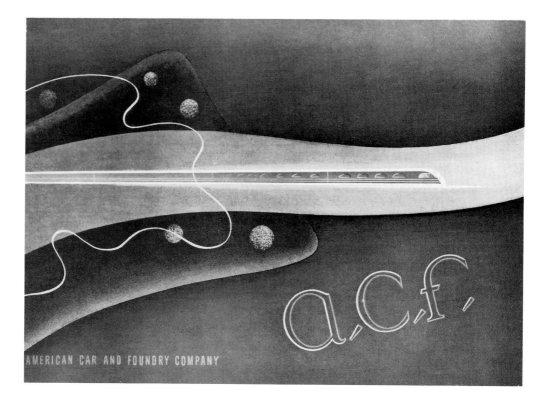

Opposite

Emil Bisttram "Pearls, and things and Palm Beach (The Breakers)"; watercolor, 16¾ x 11⅝in. (42.5 x 29.5cm), 1925 (collection Herb S. Adler)

Right

William E. Hentschel silkscreen; signed in pencil l/l, 14½ x 11in. (36.9 x 27.9cm) (collection Denis Gallion and Daniel Morris)

Right, below

Henry Lyman Säyen "The Thundershower"; tempera on wood, 36 x 46in. (91.4 x 116.8cm), 1917-18 (The National Museum of American Art, Smithsonian Institution, gift of H. Lyman Säyen to his Nation)

Below

Ilonka Karasz magazine cover for *The New Yorker*, January 8, 1927; watercolor, 14¼ x 10in. (36.2 x 25.4cm) (collection 50-Fifty Gallery)

≣JEWELRY≣

American jewelry design in the 1920s was largely derivative. No clear national style emerged, only a pastiche of earlier European ones: classical, medieval, Renaissance, and Victorian. The Egyptian revival jewelry generated by Carter's 1922 discovery of Tutankhamun's tomb was typical of America's alliance with the past. Jewelers were inspired from outside and neglected indigenous historical sources — most obviously, the American Indian, Pre-Columbian, and Eskimo heritages. It was predictable, therefore, that a certain amount of French Modernist jewelry would be reproduced. Innate American conservatism, however, prevented jewelers from embracing the mode with real enthusiasm. What resulted was a dilution. The fact that Tiffany & Co., the country's premier silversmith and jeweler, could afford virtually to ignore the modern style shows that domestic demand for Parisian trends — contemporary ones, at least — was not pronounced. Louis Comfort Tiffany remained Director of the Design Department at Tiffany's after his father's death in 1902. His aversion to the 1925 style is evident in its nearly total absence from the jewelry which the company produced between the two World Wars. Certainly the firm's salesmen would have urged a belated adoption of French Modernism after Tiffany's own death in 1933 if that were felt necessary, yet examination of the firm's sketch books from the period indicates that very few Art Deco designs were put into production.[1] The taste in jewelry among America's wealthiest families — the bedrock of Tiffany's business and esteem — remained rooted in the past, especially that of the nineteenth-century French and Russian aristocracies.

Apart from Tiffany & Co., America's foremost jewelers of the 1920s and '30s were Black, Starr & Frost, and Udall & Ballou (New York); J. E. Caldwell & Co., and Bailey, Banks, & Biddle (Philadelphia); and C. D. Peacock, and Spaulding-Gorham, Inc. (Chicago). All of these offered a restrained selection of French-inspired Modernist jewelry among more traditional wares.[2] None, however, approached the lavish "high style" examples of Cartier, Mauboussin, and Van Cleef & Arpels in France. Some firms even had their more complex Modernist designs — those which incorporated a range of hardstones, rock crystal, and enameled gold — manufactured in Paris for the American market.

It was left to other firms to produce the bulk of the Modernist jewelry which reached the American market between 1925 and 1939. Many of these have

Below

Gorham cigarette box; rose-cut diamonds and enameled gold, signed, c. 1925

remained totally unknown, their creations bearing the name tags of the retail stores through which they were marketed. Included were a host of commercially successful jewelers; in particular, Oscar Heyman & Brothers, Jacob Mehrlust, the Bonner Manufacturing Company, Walter P. McTeigue, Inc., and Hirsch & Leff (New York); J. Milhening, Inc., Juergens & Andersen, and W. R. Anderson & Co. (Chicago); and Dorst & Co. and Letwin & Sons (Cincinnati).[3]

It may seem strange that a jeweler would accept such anonymity, but the industry has by tradition comprised small family businesses that lack the means of distributing their merchandise. Their role has become, in effect, that of the jeweler's jeweler; to provide prestigious retailers, such as Marcus & Co., Saks Fifth Avenue, and Gattle, with their creations. This silent partnership, fundamental to the industry, satisfied both sides: the retailer enjoyed a reputation for fine wares while the manufacturer could concentrate on designing jewelry, with price a function of design rather than the reverse.[4]

The "high style" design excesses of the French art moderne movement, avoided in large part by the jewelers and retailers discussed above, found their way on to a range of inexpensive jewelry and accessories produced by several short-lived American firms. The Elgin American Manufacturing Company, of Illinois, for example, offered "Chic de Paris" silvered vanities decorated with a series of stylized geometric designs in applied enamels. Similar frivolous Modernist boudoir sets and costume bags à la Poiret, priced from $2 to $10, were offered by Victor A. Picard & Co., New York, and Whiting & Davis, Plainsville,

Below

Hirsch & Leff designs for jewelry, illustrated in *The Jeweler's Circular*, February 27, 1930, p. 95

Below, right

Walter P. McTeigue, Inc. jewelry designs, illustrated in *The Jeweler's Circular*, February 21, 1929, p. 155

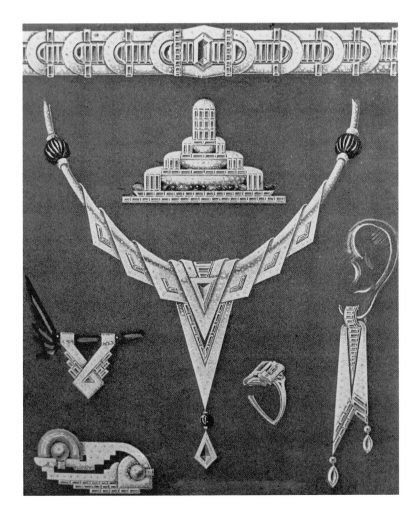

Left

Paul Flato brooch; baguette and pavé-set diamonds and oval rubies, mounted in platinum, signed, c. 1933

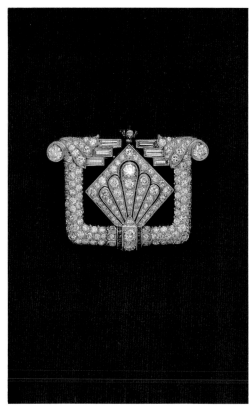

Far left

J.E. Caldwell & Co. brooch; onyx, calibré-cut rubies, and pavé-set diamonds, mounted in platinum, signed (photo Christie's, New York)

Left

J.E. Caldwell & Co. lapel watch; baguette diamonds and calibré-cut emeralds, mounted in platinum, signed, c. 1925 (photo Sotheby's, New York)

Right

Gattle brooch; hexagonal-cut and calibré-cut emeralds, baguette diamonds, and black enamel, mounted in platinum, signed, c. 1930

Right

Black, Starr & Frost bracelet, calibré-cut sapphires and pavé-set diamonds, mounted in platinum, signed, c. 1925 (photo Christie's, New York)

Far right

Charlton bracelet; rubies and diamonds, signed, c. 1930

Below

Yard pendant watch; circular-cut diamonds, onyx, and cabochon sapphires, signed, c. 1930

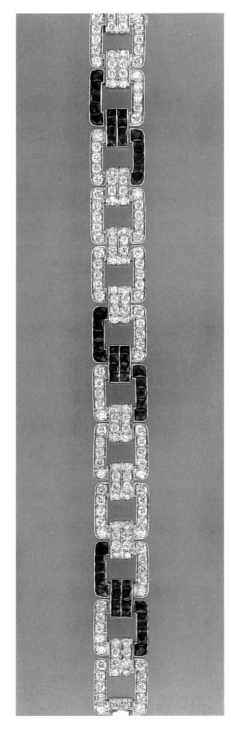

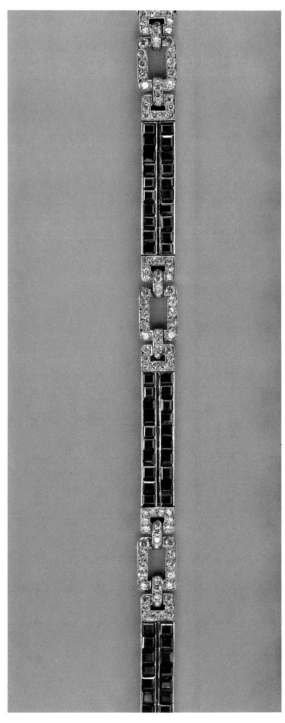

JUERGENS & ANDERSEN CO.

Left

Juergens & Andersen Co. jewelry designs, illustrated in *The Jeweler's Circular*, February 2, 1927, p. 165

Below

Bonner Manufacturing Co. designs for brooches and necklaces, illustrated in *The Jeweler's Circular*, February 2, 1927, p. 149

BONNER MFG. CO.

Massachusetts. Invariably unsigned, these often surface today at antique fairs as "French," an attribution which, despite their place of manufacture, is artistically correct.[5]

The American jeweler could keep pace with his European counterpart through a handful of periodicals which reviewed changes in jewelry fashion and technology. In America, *The Jeweler's Circular* and *Gem Creations*; in Europe, *Art et bijoux*, *La Perle*, and *Dessins – Joaillerie – Paris* (Paris); and *Deutsche Goldschmiede-Zeitung* (Leipzig). American fashion magazines, especially *Vogue*, provided further clues to the changing modes which could precipitate a corresponding change in jewelry design.

The Parisian influence on the American jewelers who designed a range of Modernist jewelry between 1925 and 1927 was immense, if not total. Color was rampant, design secondary. This effect, called color massing, was achieved by placing large numbers of small gemstones in pavé settings within color neutral borders, such as brilliants or platinum. Black or white accents were provided by onyx or diamonds. Single splashes of red or blue (rubies or sapphires) caught the mid-1920s mood of exuberance and boundless optimism. This was not a moment for half-measures, or half-tints. Later, when the impact of a single bold color was considered too forceful, the effect was toned down by shading between complementary colors.

Despite overwhelming evidence to the contrary, the American jeweler claimed by early 1927 that he was completely independent of his European counterpart. The editor of *The Jeweler's Circular* summarized the magazine's survey of the leading jewelers in the USA:

There can be little doubt from the opinions expressed by those who know, that the American designer, as the final arbiter, has come into his own, and that Paris no longer dominates American jewelry design as it may have done in the past.[6]

In retrospect, this expression of self-confidence seems to have been premature, if not pure fantasy. The designs illustrated in contemporary American jewelry reviews show all too clearly that a national style did not exist. More plausible was the American jeweler's claim that his technical expertise exceeded that in Europe. Since the nucleus of the American jewelry industry consisted of immigrant families – mostly East Europeans – it is not surprising that the local quality of artisanship was high. American jewelers also had the advantage of superior materials – the platinum in the USA, in particular, was harder and more durable than that used in Europe, so that jewelry mounts had a more beautiful contour and a longer life.

The jewelry industry depended largely on the related field of fashion. The four seasons provided a regular cycle of new designs in gemstones within the calendar year. Summer formal evening wear, for example, required delicately colored gems with understated mounts: opals, pink and red coral, peridots, green beryls, tourmalines, topazes, and pearls. Autumn and winter brought more somber hues: beige, silver, white, and black, the new mood translated into corn-colored sapphires, amber, jasper, diamonds and onyx.[7]

Fashions were also geared to further change from year to year. The boyish tailored mode which swept Paris in 1925 manifested itself in a corresponding

Left

Greenleaf & Crosby mantel clock; crystal and enameled metal, the movement by Vacheron & Constantin, c. 1929 (photo Christie's, New York)

Above

Marcus & Co. brooch; opal and enameled gold, signed, c. 1922

Right

Marcus & Co. brooch; circular-cut rubies, old mine-cut diamonds, natural baroque pearls, sapphires, tourmalines, enameled gold and platinum, signed

Below, left

Oscar Heyman & Bros. designs for jewelry in diamonds, enamels, and colored gems, illustrated in *The Jewellers' Circular*, February 3, 1926, p. 171

Below, center

Oscar Heyman & Bros. sketch of a necklace; diamonds and sapphires, c. 1928 (photo Oscar Heyman & Bros.)

Below, right

Oscar Heyman & Bros. sketch of a necklace; diamonds, emeralds and onyx, c. 1930 (photo Oscar Heyman & Bros.)

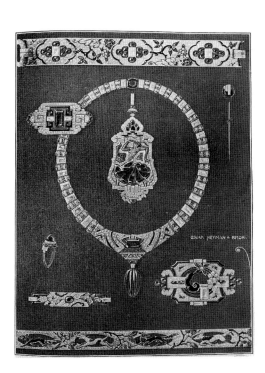

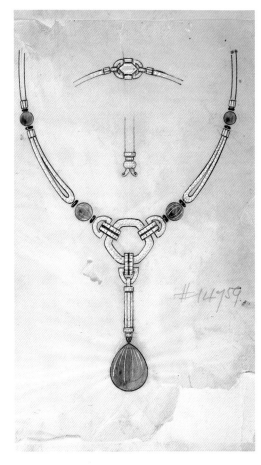

range of jewelry styles in the USA. Short, bobbed hair and the false chignon, the latter introduced to hide the evidence of growing hair, laid bare a large expanse of neck. The jeweler responded with a selection of elaborate earrings and neck-laces.

Another French influence, specifically Cartier, was seen in a range of charming animal, fruit, and flower brooches, introduced between 1926 and 1928. Realism was achieved by the use of emeralds and peridots for grass and green leaves; rubies and pink-tinted tourmalines for roses; and beryls, sapphires, aquamarines and lapis for sky and birds. Definition was sharpened by intricate carving within a border of baguette- or marquise-cut diamonds.

The brooch became a particularly popular piece of jewelry in 1928, with the shift by Paris couturiers to a new, streamlined, feminine silhouette. The American Modernist jeweler was provided with the opportunity to introduce a range of brooches as dress fasteners. Richard F. Bach, of the Metropolitan Museum of Art, explained the carry-over marketing effect:

Modern woman does not think of a gown as a dress, but as something which expresses her own figure and character. A gown is an accessory to the figure, not only a covering for it. Economical as her garb may be, she will wear ornaments.[8]

In addition to its traditional function as a corsage ornament, the brooch was worn in the late 1920s on the shoulder and as a scarf pin, hat trimmer, and glove or slipper buckle.

The 1928 return to grace and femininity also saw the demise of bobbed hair. Hair length trebled and coiffure ornaments returned, generating a new selection of gem-encrusted hairpieces, such as headbands and tiaras.

The brief return to favor of the muff a few years later brought an increased demand for rings (if muffs were "in," gloves, which concealed the fingers, were "out"), and a corresponding decline in bracelets.

An infrequent attempt was made to link modern jewelry design to the corresponding movement in contemporary furniture, textiles, and architecture.[9] But the latter's common denominators — fluted detailing, streamlined contours, and subdued colors — were virtually absent from jewelry design until the early 1930s. Most noticeably missing, in America, was any adoption of the skyscraper's setback form, a strange omission for those who claimed autonomy from Europe.

In 1930 the American jewelry industry announced that simplicity and strength were its new characteristics. Gone, in keeping with the economic climate, were lavishness and opulence; in their place leaner, cleaner lines. Whereas fancy-cut gemstones had predominated, now broad unornamented surfaces emphasized the material's intrinsic worth. As Ima Thompson wrote in 1929, "In the designing of the new jewels, this *vide* is gained by the use of the matt finishes on the ground of platinum or gold. . . . It is a matter of the absence of finickiness in modern jewelry designing."[10]

Everything was simplified; the truly distinguished woman was identified by *simple* elegance.[11] Jewelers did not, of course, suddenly drop production of their traditional gem-set jewelry, but a range of designs was added in which combinations of red and yellow gold, silver, or platinum provided a sleekly contoured alternative to more expensive, and ostentatious, jeweled wares. "Dynamic symmetry" became the new cry, its components utility, beauty, grace, and workmanship.

In acknowledgment of the Depression and its own precariousness in such times, the jewelry industry introduced a range of combination pieces to meet reduced budgets: chokers which could be separated into a pair of bracelets and a brooch, or brooches that divided into two clips. Solitaire rings were designed with detachable bezels that permitted the central stone to be interchanged with others of a different color. Ownership of a few prized pieces was promoted in preference to a host of trinkets.

In 1933 the road to prosperity seemed for a moment visible. Jewelers took heart in the likely acceleration of sales, and one of them wrote,

If prosperity does not reveal itself this spring, many postponed weddings will be determined upon and June may be the royal month of marriage, which is good grist to the mill of the retail jeweler and, in turn, the manufacturer.[12]

By the mid-1930s American Modernist jewelry had become as nondescript as its European counterpart. The trend was to larger pieces in gold enhanced with bold color accents, a prelude to the 1940s style now commonly referred to as "chunky" jewelery.

Right

Dreicer & Co. lapel watch; cabochon and calibré-cut emeralds, round and baguette diamonds, mounted in platinum, signed, *c.* 1930

Left

Tiffany & Co. desk clock; jade, rose-cut diamonds, onyx, citrines, and enameled gold, signed, 4¾in. (12.1cm) high (photo Christie's, Geneva)

Opposite

Tiffany & Co. desk clock; silver, jade, rock crystal, black onyx, and enamel, signed, 5in. (12.7cm) high (photo Christie's, Geneva)

Below, left

Tiffany & Co. sketch of a ring; coral, onyx, and diamonds, mounted in platinum, c. 1930 (photo Tiffany & Co.)

Below, center

Tiffany & Co. sketch of a brooch; diamonds and rubies, mounted in platinum, c. 1929 (photo Tiffany & Co.)

Below

Tiffany & Co. brooch; rose-cut and old European-cut diamonds, emeralds and a sapphire, mounted in platinum, signed, 1936 (photo Sotheby's, New York)

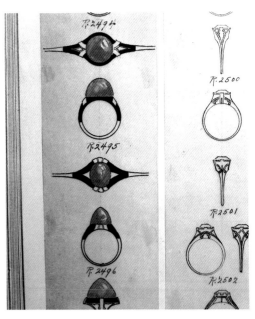

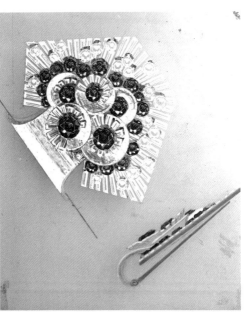

≡WORLD FAIRS≡

T he major world fairs held in the United States in the 1930s continued in the tradition of their international predecessors with one important distinction: they were also meant to provide an antidote to the country's pervasive economic gloom. For the masses, in need of distraction from the realities of daily life in the Depression, the fairs' futurist imagery and ideology offered a welcome flight into fantasy, one that matched the Hollywood comedies and dance extravaganzas of the time.

Today it is hard to appreciate the excitement, even euphoria, surrounding a world fair in the 1930s. The promotion of business and national prosperity – the principal goal of these events – tends now to be handled by individual firms themselves in a world of expanded international marketing techniques. Governments, too, are less keen on hosting world exhibitions now unlikely to be profitable. For the public, there is a sense of déja vu to today's fairs, for futurist themes such as "The World of Tomorrow" are commonplace on television and cinema screens. Even the amusement parks that were usually an element in the fairs seem dated. For people of the 1930s, however, the world fair provided a glimpse of the way ahead, presented in a utopian and nationalistic package.

It is primarily the architecture and accompanying sculpture and murals of the inter-War fairs which warrant our attention. The souvenirs manufactured for the exhibition visitor to purchase were a predictable selection of ephemera: programs, postcards, commemorative stamps and medallions, pennants, and souvenir spoons.[1] The architecture, however, was often avant-garde and provocative; its short life-span encouraged the use of novel forms, materials, and building techniques. The sculpture commissioned by the fairs' supervisory committees, much of it executed in plaster or terracotta to underline its impermanence, was also original. The same freedoms awaited the muralist who adorned the exhibition pavilions and whose creations, even more certainly than those of the sculptor (which might be disassembled and salvaged), awaited demolition on the fair's closure.

Four expositions created a significant impact on design, all in the 1930s:[2] the Century of Progress Exposition (1933/1934), the Dallas Centenary Exposition (1936), the New York World's Fair (1939/1940), and the Golden Gate International Exposition (1939).

Below

E.H. Bennett, H. Burnham, and J.A. Holabird (architects) Travel and Transportation Building, A Century of Progress Exposition, Chicago, 1933, the roof formed of metal plates suspended by steel support cables from 12 steel towers anchored by concrete slabs. Illustrated in *The American Architect*, May 1932, p. 28; and *The Architectural Forum*, October 1931, p. 449 (photo Hedrich-Blessing)

The idea for the Century of Progress Expostion – in effect, a 100th birthday celebration for the City of Chicago – was conceived at the height of the financial boom of the 1920s. Despite the fact that several of the fair's more ambitious projects – for example, a revolving aerial restaurant and an underwater aquamarine restaurant by Norman Bel Geddes,[3] and a network of moving sidewalks and escalators – had to be abandoned or scaled down to match shrinking budgets, the exhibition opened as scheduled on May 27, 1933, and ran a full year beyond its intended five-months duration.[4]

The mass appeal of the exhibition surprised everyone. It drew 38 million visitors to the 424-acre parcel of reclaimed land on the edge of Lake Michigan.[5] It also turned a handsome profit – something unprecedented in world fair history – and it did so at the depths of the Depression. Such success was surprising in view of the fair's obvious weaknesses, cited constantly by contemporary critics frustrated by its haphazard assembly. As one noted,

The Exposition witnessed the breakdown of the old scheme of exhibit arrangement. At previous fairs exhibits had been organized with a certain amount of consistency; the products of related industries had usually been collectively housed in individual buildings, lending coherence and logic to mass displays. At Chicago, the individual exhibitor took precedence over orderly arrangement. The grounds were dotted by the buildings of individual exhibitors, placed without regard to the product displayed. There were no specific areas set aside for separate phases of modern life and commerce. In spite of the fact that a good number of private buildings were excellently designed and contained admirable exhibits, the general effect for the average visitor was one of confusion and incoherence. The relationships of the various developments in modern science were not made clear. In schematic arrangement, the Exposition represented a sort of jigsaw, which the visitor, if he possessed the strength and the imagination, might piece together for himself.[6]

It remained for architects to create individual works of interest amid the disarray. Several masterful structures were conceived – in particular, the Travel and Transportation Building and the Administration Building (Edward H. Bennett, Hubert Burnham, and John A. Holabird, architects),[7] the Hall of Science (Paul P. Cret, architect),[8] and the Electrical Building (Raymond M. Hood, architect). The ephemeral nature of the fair encouraged experimentation and theatricality, both promoted further by Joseph Urban, who had been appointed the fair's Director of Color-Coordination. Urban used a selection of 23 hues to unify the entire site. Most buildings were composed of 3 to 4 colors. Harmony between neighboring structures was achieved by dressing the flagpoles, railings, and kiosks in intermediate spaces in complementary colors. At night, Urban's color scheme was turned into a kaleidoscopic fairyland by an intricate system of architectural illumination, which included the first use of neon tubing.

The fair's architecture was experimental, combining the vigorous, sharply angular Modernism of the 1925 Exposition Internationale in Paris, with materials – steel, asbestos wallboard, and Bakelite – better suited to the new decade's austerity. No attempt was made to imitate the masonry architecture of past shows. As a critic observed,

Whether such experiments are themselves of lasting value or not, whether they affect the

Below

E.H. Bennett, H. Burnham, and J.A. Holabird (architects) Administration Building, A Century of Progress Exposition, Chicago, 1933; midnight blue, white, pale blue, and light gray with red trim. Illustrated in *The Architectural Forum*, August 1931, pp. 133, 135 (photo Hedrich-Blessing)

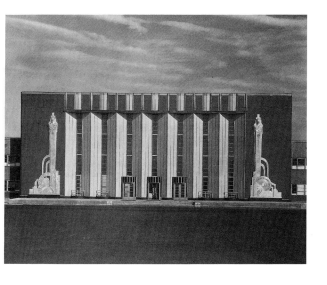

Far left

Alfonso Iannelli "Lecture News Advertising"; painted plaster *maquette* of the frieze on the north-west entrance to the Social Science Building (Raymond M. Hood, architect), A Century of Progress Exposition, Chicago, 1933, 25½ x 17½in. (64.8 x 44.5cm) (collection Mitchell Wolfson, Jr., Miami-Dade Community College)

Left

Alfonso Iannelli "S.O.S."; painted plaster *maquette* of the frieze on the north-west entrance to the Social Science Building (Raymond M. Hood, architect), A Century of Progress Exposition, Chicago, 1933, 25 x 15½in. (63.5 x 39.4cm) (collection Mitchell Wolfson, Jr., Miami-Dade Community College)

Below

Artist unidentified Micarta panel; A Century of Progress Exposition, Chicago, 1933, probably from the General Electric-Westinghouse Building (collection Mitchell Wolfson, Jr., Miami-Dade Community College)

Right

Charles Murphy ceramic commemorative plate for the 1939 New York World's Fair; designed for the Homer Laughlin Company, signed within a gold circle *Decoration by Charles Murphy 150th ANNIVERSARY OF GEORGE WASHINGTON AS FIRST PRESIDENT OF THE UNITED STATES*, with underglaze signature HOMER LAUGHLIN MADE IN U.S.A. M38 N6, 10¼in. (26cm) diameter

Right, below

Charles Murphy (attributed to) ceramic commemorative plate for the Golden Gate International Exposition, San Francisco, 1939/40; designed for the Homer Laughlin Company, signed GOLDEN GATE INTERNATIONAL EXPOSITION AN OFFICIAL SOUVENIR COPYRIGHTED LICENSE 63C, with underglaze signature HOMER LAUGHLIN MADE IN U.S.A., 10¼in. (26cm) diameter

future of architectural design or are later looked upon as whims of the moment, an exposition affords the best opportunity to try them out. We must not ask our architects to adhere to conservative ideals at such a show. We must welcome their attempts at originality, even when they verge on the bizarre, for they will tell us either what to do in the future or what not to do. On the other hand, knowing that the architect is using forms and materials that are new to him, we should not look upon this, or any other exposition, as a revealed gospel. It isn't such a thing.[9]

The most interesting building, in this respect, was the Travel and Transportation Building, which was suspended by the first "Skyhooks," to free the exhibition galleries on the inside from columns and other structural encumbrances.[10]

The fair's architectural ornamentation was coordinated by the sculptor Lee Lawrie. Emphasis was given to bas-reliefs by Lawrie and other noted sculptors, such as Leo Friedlander and Alfonso Iannelli, which depicted the fair's theme of Science in Industry.[11] Allegorical figures, representing Electricity, Power, and the Four Elements, graced the façades facing Lake Michigan, their stylized Art Deco forms matching the 1920s conception of the building themselves. Elsewhere in the fair, the evolving streamlined aesthetic made its first public appearance in the shape of the Burlington Zephyr, a 100 m.p.h. diesel-powered train manufactured by the E. G. Budd Company, and Buckminster Fuller's teardrop-form, 3-wheeled "Dymaxion" car, which was included in the Pageant of Transportation, an exhibit tracing 100 years of transportation history.

The 1936 Dallas Centenary Exposition marked the anniversary of the battle of San Jacinto in which Texas independence had been wrested from Mexico 100 years earlier.[12] A wedge-shaped 277-acre piece of land was chosen for the site, which included Dallas's existing fairgrounds in which the Cotton Bowl had been erected in 1930.[13]

Though inspired by the financial success of the Century of Progress Exposition, the Dallas show was more regional in scope. There were no international pavilions, and few other states participated, beyond related business representation. Notwithstanding, the exposition's inauguration by President Franklin D. Roosevelt drew a crowd of 117,625, exceeding that on Chicago's opening day.[14] The $25 million project, coordinated by Dallas architect George Dahl, included roughly fifty temporary and permanent structures, many of which have remained to provide today's world fair enthusiast with America's best surviving exposition site from the period. The architecture, which was described at the time as "Classic-Modern," mixed tall, stepped structures with liberal splashes of color and clever nocturnal illumination. The automobile giants — in particular, Ford, General Motors, and Chrysler — responded to the Southwest's expanding market with imposing pavilions and displays. Several other buildings were decorated with Modernist murals, carved reliefs, and free-standing statuary. Many of these have survived, notably the Transportation Building (now the Centennial Building) and the Hall of Administration (now the Fair Park Maintenance Building). The fair's most arresting Art Deco ornamentation was created by Pierre Bourdelle, who enhanced the pair of cement pylons and fountain at the west end of the Esplanade of State with frescoes of mythological horses and sirens. Bourdelle also designed the mural on the Transportation Building, in which he depicted the

Above

Ulrich H. Ellerhusen "Light" mural symbolizing Stellar Energy; circular court, the Electrical Building (Raymond M. Hood, architect), A Century of Progress Exposition, Chicago, 1933 (photo Hedrich-Blessing)

Below

Lee Lawrie twin pylons of the Water Gate, the Electrical Building (Raymond M. Hood, architect), A Century of Progress Exposition, Chicago, 1933, bas-relief panels, 40 ft. (12.2m) high, one representing Atomic Energy, the other Stellar Energy (photo Hedrich-Blessing)

different modes of transportation in a lively Modernist style. The Hall of State Building (now the State of Texas Building) emerged as the exposition's architectural centerpiece, its entrance dominated by a heroic bronze figure by Allie V. Tennant of a Tejas Indian raised on a 20-foot-high dais, the warrior's powerful frame standing out against a wall of deep blue and orange ceramic tiles.

The 1939 New York World's Fair provided a welcome escape at the end of a grim decade. The consumer was offered a vast mixture of future products and services, including technological marvels, robots, synthetic speech synthesizers, and an array of labor-saving household appliances. Situated on roughly 1,200 acres at Flushing Park Meadow, in view of Manhattan across the East River, the fair opened on April 30, 1939, officially to celebrate the 150th anniversary of George Washington's inauguration as the first President of the United States.[15]

The fair's theme was to "build the World of Tomorrow", an ill-chosen motto on the eve of World War II. Whereas the great international expositions of the past had *reviewed* man's accomplishments, this one coordinated man's accumulated knowledge to propel him to a higher general standard of living *in the future*. In this, the machine played a pivotal role, its impact on twentieth-century society having created new modes of behavior and cultural standards.

The fair's theme was symbolized by its Theme Center — two structures designed by Wallace K. Harrison and André Fouilhoux — the Trylon and Perisphere.[16] The latter, a 200-foot-wide sphere, housed Henry Dreyfuss's *Democracity*, a diorama of the City of Tomorrow which was viewed by visitors from an upper circular rotunda. The Trylon and Perisphere formed the center of the main exhibition area, in which the pavilions were grouped along three diagonal avenues coordinated by color to aid the visitor in his passage through the fair.

An important aspect of the New York World's Fair was the official sanction accorded to industrial designers — a newly formed profession — because they were "supposed to understand public taste and be able to speak in the popular tongue, and because as a profession they are bound to disregard the traditional forms and solutions and to think in terms of today and tomorrow."[17] Walter Dorwin Teague, Norman Bel Geddes, Henry Dreyfuss, Raymond Loewy, Russel Wright, Donald Deskey, and Egmont Arens prepared major exhibits.

The pavilions incorporated a wide range of avant-garde architectural forms, in keeping with the Fair Design Committee's wish that uniformity be avoided except in overall scale and color coordination, for which guidelines were issued. Due to the fair's impermanence, experimentation was strongly encouraged, especially in the use of new building materials. Certain buildings, such as the United States Steel Exhibit by Teague, were deliberately left unfinished so that the public could see the underlying structural steel skeleton.[18]

The fair's sculpture, often on a heroic scale, included over sixty pieces by thirty-five of the foremost American artists; in particular, Paul Manship ("The Moods of Time," "Time and the Fates of Man," and "The Celestial Sphere"); Edmond Amateis ("Benevolence, Humility, and Efficiency"); René Chambellan ("The Spirit of the Wheel"); Leo Friedlander ("Four Freedoms"); John Gregory ("The Four Victories of Peace"); Waylande Gregory ("The Fountain of the Atom"); Carl Paul Jennewein ("The Four Elements"); Carl Milles ("The

Below

Leo Friedlander "The Pylons"; gypsum, representing the four base elements, north entrance, Hall of Social Science Building (Raymond M. Hood, architect), A Century of Progress Exposition, Chicago, 1933 (photo Hedrich-Blessing)

Opposite

Allie V. Tennant "Tejas Warrior"; gilt bronze, Hall of State Building, 11 ft (3.3m) high, Texas Centennial Exposition, Dallas, 1936/37 (photo The Dallas Historical Society)

Right

Wallace K. Harrison and André Fouilhoux (architects) the Trylon and Perisphere, the 1939 New York World's Fair (Gottscho archives, Library of Congress, Washington D.C.)

Below

Raoul Josset "Spirit of the Centennial" figure and fountain, executed by José Martin, Texas Centennial Exposition, Dallas, 1936/37. The rear mural, designed by Carlo Ciampaglia, depicts the Lone Star of Texas, a longhorn steer, a map of Texas with Dallas highlighted by a ray of light, a yucca plant, and two diagonal bands of Texas animals (photo The Dallas Historical Society)

Astronomer"); Sidney Biehler Waugh ("Manhattan"); and William Zorach ("Builders of the Future"). Contemporary illustrations show vigorously sculpted Modernist groups adorning the fair's buildings, thoroughfares, and plazas.[19] Unfortunately, almost all of these were executed in plaster and later destroyed.

To complement the sculpture, the fair's Board of Design commissioned 105 murals from 33 artists, including several who had participated in Radio City Music Hall seven years earlier: Witold Gordon (a mural on the Food Building); Ezra Winter (the entrance to the Court of States); Hildreth Meiere (the Medicine and Public Health and Science and Education Buildings); and Henry Billings (the Chrysler Motors Building).[20] Also included was Winold Reiss (the "Music and Dance" mural in metal and glass on the Music Hall).

Across the continent, San Francisco responded with an extravaganza of its own, the Golden Gate International Exposition, which ran from February 12 to December 2, 1939. Twenty-eight foreign countries and fifteen American States participated. An island of reclaimed land, called Treasure Island, was constructed in San Francisco Bay alongside Yerba Buena Island to house the exposition, all of which was disassembled and scrapped when it closed.[21]

The exposition's buildings were erected on two main axes, one north-south , the other east-west. In many of its features, the architecture, coordinated by a committee which included the Modernist Timothy Pflueger, exceeded in interest that of the New York World's Fair. A rich blend of European, Middle Eastern, Oriental, and Pre-Columbian influences abounded in the façades of the pavilions, reinforcing the fair's claim to internationalism. Many of the structures, such as the Elephant Towers at the main entrance, and the Tower of the South, had an exotic, almost ethereal quality, especially when bathed in colored light at night.[22]

Lighting played a significant role in the fair's architectural impact. Thousands of hidden bulbs projected a symphony of colors at nightfall on to both the stepped silhouettes of the pavilions and the surrounding expanses of water and lawn. Colored lighting was used everywhere to create "a magical city."[23] To ensure constant lighting in the exhibition galleries, windows were eliminated from all the buildings and artificial light introduced.

Modernist design dominated throughout the fair, especially in the stepped crowns of the architecture and the sculptural decoration with which the façades and malls were adorned. Artists from the Bay area were retained to provide the sculpture, much of which was executed in a chic, Modernist idiom. Works by Haig Patigian, Carlo Taliabue, Gordon Huff, Adeline Kent, and William Tognelli showed the movement's influence among the country's lesser-known West Coast artists. Murals by California painters such as Dorothy W. Puccinelli, Hugo Ballin, Millard Sheets, and Armin C. Hansen continued the theme on the pavilions which housed, on the interior walls, ensembles by Paul Frankl, William Haines, Rena Rosenthal, Gilbert Rohde, Kem Weber, Victoria Proetz, Robert Locher, and Marcel Breuer.[24] Great Britain's declaration of war against Germany in September, 1939, brought to a halt the prospect of the fair being extended into 1940.

Below

Portals of the Pacific, also known as the Elephant Towers (Ernest E. Weihe and John Bakewell, architects), and the Tower of the Sun (Arthur Brown, Jr., architect) Golden Gate International Exposition, San Francisco, 1939 (photo San Francisco archives, the San Francisco Public Library)

INDUSTRIAL DESIGN

I ndustrial design became an essential component of the manufacturing process in the late 1920s,[1] when the huge advances made during the war years in mass production resulted in a market saturated with competing products of equal performance, and closed the gap between consumer demand and available supply.[2]

That the market for a particular product could reach saturation point was a fact not every manufacturer learned early enough. Henry Ford, for example, found his maxim about the Model T – "They can have it in any color so long as it's black" – coming back to haunt him.[3] By the late 1920s, every car was more or less as sophisticated mechanically as its competitors, so there was no reason, except design, to prefer one over another. In 1927, Ford found himself losing ground to General Motors, whose President, Alfred P. Sloan, introduced a range of colors and chassis styles to combat the success of Ford's Tin Lizzie. The public responded enthusiastically to the choice presented them, unaware that they were encouraging what within five years would become a standard marketing ploy – planned obsolescence. Forced to suspend production of the Model T, and to spend millions on retooling for a more stylish Model A, Ford learned what one observer termed "the most expensive art lesson in history."[4]

Manufacturers throughout the consumer goods industry took careful note of Ford's mistake. Marketing executives were quick to realize that in most cases it was only an object's appearance which distinguished it from other similar products. A new merchandising plan was thus required to boost one's share in a competitive market. Product redesign was seen as the most likely solution.[5]

The men who could supply this new sort of expertise were a varied group of ex-commercial artists, stage designers, advertising men, and former craftsmen. As soon became evident, the ability to lure the consumer by creating illusions became more important than producing a better product.

This new breed of "industrial designers," as they preferred to be called, established themselves mostly as independent, freelance consultants. By the mid-1930s as much celebrity had been injected into the profession itself as into its products. Gilbert Rohde wrote in 1936,

"Industrial Design" has become a glamorous name. Certain magazine articles, calculated to "dramatize" a new profession, have drawn a picture of industrial design as being

Below

Mills Industries "Empress" juke box; die-cast metal and marbelized plastic, 1939. Illustrated in *Jukebox: The Golden Age*, Lancaster-Miller, 1981, #30 (photo Kaz Tsuruta)

Opposite, left

Stewart & McQuire peanut dispenser; impressed STEWART & McQUIRE 350 5TH AVE NYC NY with patent numbers, 19in. (48.3cm) high, late 1930s (collection Ronald and Norma Keno)

Opposite, right

Harold van Doren and John Gordon Rideout "Air King" radio designed for the Air-King Products Company; red "Plaskon," signed AIR KING PRODUCTS INC B'KLYN N.Y. USA, 12in. (30.5cm) high. A similar model is illustrated in *Decorative Art 1934*, Yearbook of The Studio, 1934, p. 137 (collection Ronald and Norma Keno)

Opposite, right

Gordon Buehrig "Cord" 810 Westchester Sedan designed for the Auburn Automobile Company, 1936 (photo Auburn-Duesenberg Museum, Auburn, Indiana)

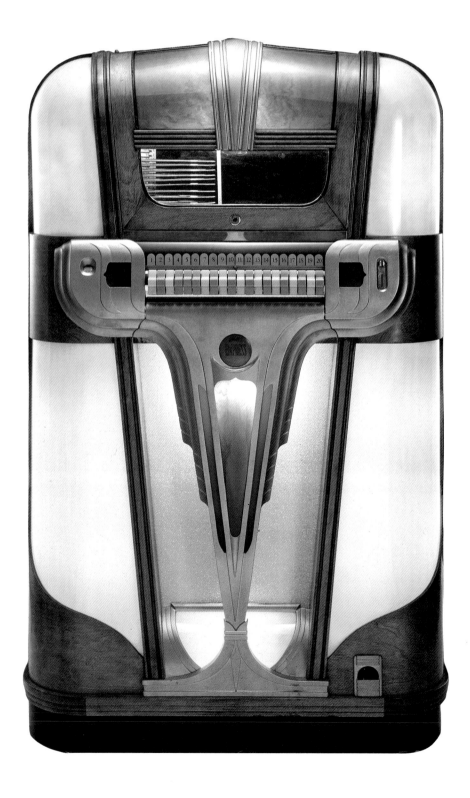

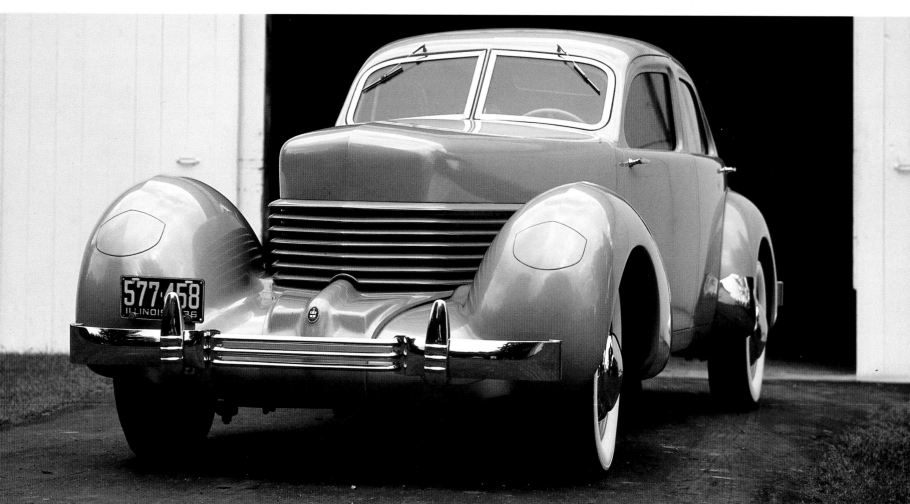

the exclusive and mysterious possession of a handful of super-men who are revolutioniz-ing everything from hairpins to locomotives at a fabulous price. The stories are exagger-ated. . . . Stripped of hocus-pocus, industrial design is a very simple matter; it is design brought up to date, design in terms of a mass production economy instead of a handcraft economy.[6]

Rohde, who at the time established a Design Laboratory in New York to teach industrial design under the Federal Arts Project of the WPA, went on to define the profession's required skills as "a modicum of art and engineering abilities . . . it is the combination which is important."[7]

This rather vague job description caused some to question whether the job itself was superficial.[8] Many felt that it was. Eugene Schoen, for example, took the view that the

attempts to inject abstract beauty into factory-made articles through the use of persons whose training is simply esthetic and who have not the fundamental prime contact with the object to be created, are likely to be frustrated and merely result in a sort of dressing-up that has little or no esthetic value. Plainly the industrial designer per se should be discouraged and design in industry by the creators of the objects themselves should be stressed and encouraged by all those who believe that modern machines can be made the complete servants of man . . .[9]

It did not help the image of industrial design that some of the new profession's leading lights – in particular, Norman Bel Geddes and Raymond Loewy – pro-jected a brand of showmanship which seemed to focus less on their designs than on themselves.

The industrial designer's attempt to modernize consumer goods as a means of boosting sales led him in the 1930s to the pursuit of a new style, one which evolved from the preceding fashionable Art Deco style of the 1920s and could be applied to industrial products.[10] Whereas the skyscraper had inspired an angu-lar, setback style that expressed the 1920s age of jazz and unbridled entre-preneurship, it was totally unsuited to the sober economic mood that followed the Wall Street crash. An authentic new image was needed to unify industry and to propel it out of economic stagnation. The image that answered this need was the streamlined form. Based on sound aerodynamic principles, the form came to symbolize industrial progress. Siegfried Giedion explained why streamlining was suitable for the 1930s: "It is only natural that an age of movement should adopt a form associated with movement as its symbol, using it in all places at all occasions."[11]

The optimum streamlined form became that of the teardrop, or parabolic curve, providing an image of fluid, energy-efficient motion. A critic explained,

Streamlining means exactly what one would think, the smoothing down of the form of an object, leveling the bumps and hollows until a shape is achieved which suggests a bullet, tear drop or one of the simpler fishes. It was developed in the design of planes and racing automobiles and boats, in order that delay due to surface friction might be reduced and speed, consequently, increased.[12]

The industrial designer set about restyling practically everything, and particularly household goods, so that existing models would quickly appear outdated. Philip Johnson explained the marketing strategy behind this in his introduction to the

Below

Chrysler Corporation "Airflow" brochure, 27×21in. (68.6×53.3cm), 1934

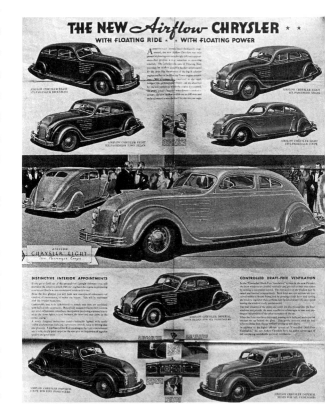

catalogue of the *Machine Art* exhibition held at the Museum of Modern Art in 1934: "In the 1920s there developed in America a desire for 'restyling' objects for advertising. Styling a commercial object gives it more 'eye-appeal' and therefore helps sales."[13]

No attempt was made to distinguish in form between functional and non-functional streamlining.[14] All objects, moving or stationary, were cased in sleek, aerodynamic bodies emblematic of the 1930s obsession with speed and efficiency.[15] The technical fact that at most speeds streamlined styling did not, in fact, save much energy and that, in stationary objects, it saved none at all was ignored completely. Nevertheless, this style came to represent the machine and the hope that it held for the future, though the manufacturer was only too aware of the risks of adopting a styling so exaggerated that the public would no longer buy his products. The costs of retooling a modern plant were enormous.

Not everybody was convinced by the doctrine of streamlining, however. The critic John McArthur commented that

streamlined paper cups, if dropped, would fall with less wind-resistance; they are no better than the old ones for the purpose for which they are actually intended, namely, drinking. The Bauhaus was closed about the time the streamline mania began, but it would have rejected the streamlined form for objects such as cocktail shakers and fountain pens where its use is nonsense. Typical Bauhaus designs, whether for chairs, lighting fixtures, or ash trays, are free of both modernistic and streamlined aberrations; sound Bauhaus training would not permit them.[16]

Another critic was equally exasperated: "Streamlining has been perverted from functional design to a mere selling trick. The small radio is one of thousands of examples that might have been selected. Occasionally this tendency is carried to sheer idiocy, as in the case of a coffin manufacturer who asked his designer for the latest in streamlined caskets."[17]

By the mid-1940s streamlining was seen as the expression of a false optimism.[18] The public was bored with a style which after fifteen years had become institutionalized. In addition, several industrial designers had been commissioned from 1941 to design war-related projects, and their absence caused the movement to lose continuity and momentum. After World War II the American people saw the obverse side of the machine — its potential for destruction. It was harder, after Hitler and Hiroshima, to sell the machine as society's savior. Streamlining suffered accordingly, and the bold sweep which had dominated the consumer market of the 1930s was relegated largely to automobile tailfins.

The leaders of the industrial design profession in its formative years came from a variety of backgrounds and responded in varying degrees to the philosophy of streamlining. To some, the Bauhaus functionalist doctrine remained inviolate; to others, the new style, although flawed, seemed to provide greater opportunities.

Walter Dorwin Teague projected the most businesslike image of all the industrial designers. A realist who insisted on collaborating with a company's production engineers rather than merely submitting sketches, Teague's thoroughness gained the confidence of industry. In the case of Kodak, for example, this preoccupation with detail won him the firm's business for upward of thirty years. By

Below

Bohn Aluminum & Brass Corporation advertisement with streamlined tractor design, 10 ⅜ × 13 in. (26.4 × 33 cm), *Fortune* magazine, 1943

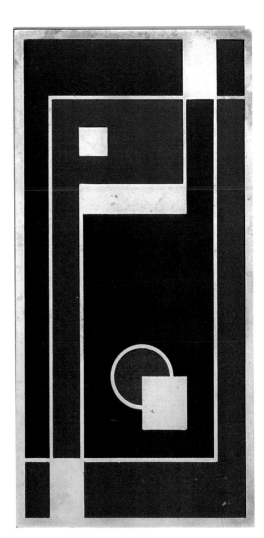

Left

Walter Dorwin Teague camera box; enameled metal and wood, 8⅞in. (22.5cm) long, c. 1936. Illustrated in *Brave New Worlds: America's Futurist Vision*, Mitchell Wolfson New World Center Campus, exhibition catalogue, 1984, p. 37, #304 (collection Mitchell Wolfson, Jr., Miami-Dade Community College)

Below

Walter Dorwin Teague "Bantam Special" camera designed for Eastman Kodak; enameled metal, signed KODAK BANTAM SPECIAL MADE IN USA, Eastman Kodak Company, Rochester, N.Y., 3in. (7.6cm) high, 1934 (collection Mitchell Wolfson, Jr., Miami-Dade Community College)

Left

Ronson Company "Touch Tip" lighter; enameled brass, impressed RONSON "TOUCH TIP" LIGHTER with patent numbers, 3½in. (8.9cm) high. Illustrated in *Brave New Worlds: America's Futurist Vision*, Mitchell Wolfson New World Center Campus, exhibition catalogue, 1984, p. 36, #299 (collection Mitchell Wolfson, Jr., Miami-Dade Community College)

1940 Teague had established himself as the United States' most respected designer, hailed as "industry's businesslike artist-collaborator, the industrial-design profession's ambassador."[19]

Born in 1883 in Decatur, Indiana, Teague grew up in Pendleton, near Indianapolis.[20] On graduating from high school in 1902, he set off for New York, where he supported himself with daytime commercial art commissions through five years of night classes at the Art Students League. A faltering career was reversed in 1908 when he joined the art department of the noted advertising agency, Calkins & Holden. In 1927, by which time he had become an independent freelance artist and an acknowledged authority on typography, Teague began to apply his advertising expertise to "the organization of a manufactured product to increase its desirability, and hence its sales".[21] Teague was motivated by the sincere belief that the use of better business methods and products would improve the quality of life for the ordinary person.[22]

In 1928 Richard Bach at the Metropolitan Museum of Art recommended Teague to Adolph Stuber, son of the president of Eastman Kodak. Teague's design for the Bantam Special camera in 1934 was only one of many successes in a career which contained several blue-chip customer accounts:[23] for example, Westinghouse, the A.B. Dick Co., Steuben Glass, the Pittsburgh Plate Glass Co., Texaco, and Steinway & Sons. He worked on a wide range of products, including X-ray equipment, gasoline stations, railroad coaches, glassware, cash registers, radio cabinets, shop-fronts, etc. At the 1939 New York World's Fair alone, the Ford Motor Co., United States Steel, Consolidated Edison, Du Pont, Eastman Kodak, and the National Cash Register Co. were among his clients.

Right

Ronson Company "Touch Tip" cocktail bar smoker's accessories: enameled and chromium-plated metal, both impressed ART METAL WORKS INC NEWARK, NJ USA, with patent numbers: *left:* 7½in. (19.1cm) high, *right:* 6⅞in. (17.5 cm) high (collection John P. Axelrod)

Apart from the Kodak Bantam Special camera, Teague is perhaps best identified by the service stations which he designed nationwide for Texaco in the mid-1930s. Many of these streamlined structures, which were painted white with green trim, have survived.

Born in Paris in 1893, *Raymond Loewy* injected a personal Gallic flair and elegance into the beleaguered American consumer market of the 1930s.[24] Loewy had three years of specialized engineering training before he was mobilized in World War I. Following the Armistice and an unsuccessful search for employment in Paris, he set sail for the United States in 1919. A chance meeting on board ship afforded him an introduction to the publisher of *Vogue* and a job as a fashion illustrator for the magazine.

Loewy's career as a commercial artist began to shift towards industrial design in late 1929, when he was hired by Sigmund Gestetner, an Englishman, to modernize the appearance of the Gestetner mimeograph machine. Loewy later claimed to have been "esthetically shocked" by the vulgarity of American products in the 1920s. Although the Gestetner commission provided Loewy with no immediate publicity, since it was not manufactured until 1933, it gave him the confidence to pursue other clients. In 1930, he opened his own office in New York. Random commissions, such as that for Shelton Looms, a textile company, came his way. By the time he designed the Hupmobile for the Hupp Motor Company in 1932, Loewy finally reached the audience he had been seeking.[25] In 1935 his revamped design of the Sears, Roebuck, box refrigerator assured his success. In its first year Loewy's updated version, a sparklingly modern unit called the Coldspot "Super Six," jumped from eleventh to fourth place in a highly competitive national market. The Coldspot's success brought Loewy to the attention of executives in other major industries, and by 1936 he had expanded his staff to twelve, and had offices in Chicago and London.[26]

Today, many of Loewy's designs of the 1930s appear blatantly commercial, their aerodynamic forms giving them a futuristic appearance. In particular, his renderings of vehicles – taxis, automobiles, and trains – published throughout the decade, showed a preoccupation with speed in preference to practical design considerations.[27] Photographs of the designer posing in front of his creations reinforced an image of flamboyance and opportunism which tended to mask his more serious accomplishments: for example, his series of locomotives for the Pennsylvania Railroad, ferryboats for the Virginia Ferry Corp., and ships for the Panama Line. Later designs, which are now regarded as American classics, were those for a pencil sharpener (1934),[28] the Greyhound motorcoach (1940), and the Lucky Strike cigarette package (1942).

Norman Bel Geddes did more to popularize the industrial design profession than any of his competitors, despite the fact that almost all of his more outlandish futuristic renderings remained unrealized. His enthusiasm and panache earned him the title of the "P.T. Barnum of Industrial Design."[29]

Born in Adrian, Michigan, in 1893, Geddes attended the Cleveland School of Art and the Art Institute of Chicago before joining the Chicago advertising agency, Barnes-Crosby. He began with poster designs (for General Motors and Packard) and magazine covers (*The Saturday Evening Post* and *Collier's*), but in 1918

Above

Walter Dorwin Teague vase, glass, engraved decoration, for the Steuben Glass Company, c. 1932

Below

Joseph Sinel weighing scale designed for the International Scale Corporation, c. 1927. Illustrated in *Creative Art,* vol. 3, 1928, p. xxxvi; *Annual of American Design 1931,* Ives Washburn, 1931, p. 85; and *The American Architect,* May 1932, p. 42 (collection Mitchell Wolfson, Jr., Miami-Dade Community College)

started a career in New York as a stage set designer.[30] Immediately successful with his designs for Dante's *Inferno* and his staging of *The Miracle* for Max Reinhardt, Geddes did not turn to industrial design until 1927. In that year, he opened his own firm, convinced that industrial design was closer to real life and more vital than his work for the theater.[31]

His early commissions (1929-32) were for domestic products such as furniture for the Simmons Co. (1929), counter scales for the Toledo Scale Co. (1929), and a range of gas stoves for the Standard Gas Equipment Corp. (1932).[32] Geddes showed a comprehension of the needs of machine-age design which matched that of Teague. His prototype House of Tomorrow (1931) and his skyscraper cocktail shaker (1937) proved his easy facility in numerous fields.

It was Geddes's projections of futuristic transportation – streamlined automobiles, ships, and trains – which were widely criticized. Many of these were reproduced in *Horizons,* the book he published in 1932.[33] *Fortune* magazine described him in 1943 as a "bomb thrower" whose designs would cost American industry a billion dollars in retooling.[34] Both the public and numerous corporate executives, however, remained entertained and enchanted by Geddes's romantic vision, which reached its apex in his Futurama "Metropolis of Tomorrow" for the General Motors Highways and Horizons Pavilion at the 1939 New York World's Fair.[35]

Henry Dreyfuss was born in 1904 in New York. Graduating from the Ethical Culture Arts High School in 1922, he enrolled in a stage design class taught by Norman Bel Geddes, then at the height of his theater career. Dreyfuss served a short apprenticeship in stage set design, and in 1927 R.H. Macy offered him work as a product stylist. He declined this on the grounds that it entailed making cosmetic changes to existing products rather than redesigning them. He also preferred to remain independent, so that he could serve several clients rather than one. In 1928 Dreyfuss opened his own New York office, and from the following year his freelance industrial design business quickly bloomed.[36]

Dreyfuss's interest was primarily in the design of utilitarian objects – clocks, stoves, refrigerators, hardware, telephones, etc. His goals were less ambitious and obtrusive than those of Teague and Geddes. In his autobiography, *Designing for People* (1955), Dreyfuss even chose the word "cleanlining" in preference to "streamlining," in order to distance himself from the excesses of the 1930s restyling movement.

An air of understatement, if not self-effacement, pervaded Dreyfuss's designs. To retain his integrity, he consciously limited his clients to roughly fifteen, thus ensuring that he could provide each with a thorough, ongoing design service. Among his major corporate customers were the Bell Telephone Laboratories, the Crane Company (suppliers of bathroom fixtures), General Time, the Hoover Co., John Deere, McCall's, and the New York Central Railroad.

Several American design "classics" bear testimony to the prodigious breadth of Dreyfuss's skills; most notably, the cradle desk telephone (model 300) for Bell Telephone in 1937; the "Democracity" diorama in the Perisphere at the 1939 New York World's Fair; and the vacuum cleaner (model 305) for Hoover in 1940. His most spectacular restyling commission, however, was the Twentieth Century

Limited express train between New York and Chicago which he designed for New York Central in 1938.[37] The locomotive's streamlined exterior combined an impression of speed and power with aerodynamic efficiency. Dreyfuss's career included numerous other restyling commissions, such as his refrigerator for General Electric in 1934 and his Toperator Washer for Sears, Roebuck, in 1933.

The celebrity afforded *Donald Deskey* by his stewardship of the Radio City Music Hall project now seems out of proportion to the importance of the other, lesser-known works with which he was involved in the late 1920s and early 1930s. Product design and development for large American and British corporations was interspersed with architectural, trade fair, and interior design research that evolved on a random, individual basis.[38] From its small beginnings, Deskey's staff grew through the 1930s to 125, as offices in London, Brussels, Milan, Copenhagen, and Stockholm were opened to serve overseas clients.

Among Deskey's more important accomplishments was his pioneership of tubular steel and aluminum furniture, plastics, and packaging. Other innovations included the "Sportshack," a prefabricated weekend house which he introduced in 1933/34, and his invention of "Weldtex," a laminated panel in Douglas fir, as an attractive and durable building material for low-cost housing.[39] Deskey considers among his most important achievements many of the projects which never proceeded beyond the experimental stage: for example, a long-range study for the modernization of the vast Mercantile Mart in Chicago; an environmental control system to filter out all pollutants in the air (a joint venture with Dr. Alvin Barach for the Presbyterian Hospital); a plateless printing system for Westinghouse; and an ongoing project spanning his fifty-year career involving research and development on prefabricated structures and systems in wood, fiberglass, and prestressed concrete.[40]

Born in Lebanon, Ohio, on April 3, 1904, *Russel Wright* was the youngest member of the industrial design movement which evolved in the late 1920s. Graduating from high school in 1920, he moved to New York, where he enrolled at the Art Students League to study painting and, when this proved unsuccessful, sculpture.[41] Wright entered Princeton University in 1921, and in due course joined the Princeton theatrical group, the Triangle Club. This choice of extracurricular activity proved fortunate as Wright met Norman Bel Geddes during the staging of *The Miracle*. Geddes was even then beginning to lean toward industrial rather than theater design, and this influenced the young Wright.

In 1927 Wright married Mary Small Einstein, who played a large part in his career throughout the 1930s, both as an adviser and as a silent partner. His contribution to industrial design, confined largely to the home,[42] was spectacularly successful, especially a series of "stove to table" wares in which he combined two functions: utensils which were sturdy enough for cooking and handsome enough for serving. Wright saw clearly that the Depression led inevitably to informal entertaining. To this end he designed a range of durable dinnerware services in spun aluminum and ceramics. In particular, his aluminum corn sets, tea services, and vases, for the Chase Brass Co., captured the spirit of functional elegance needed in the early 1930s. His 1937 "American Modern" line of ceramic dinnerware, however, shows a more curvilinear, sweeping contour.

Below

Richard Buckminster Fuller "Dymaxion" car for the Gulf Corporation, shown at the 1933 Century of Progress Exposition (photo Hedrich-Blessing)

Wright's designs for furniture – for example, his radio and piano for the Wurlitzer Co. (c.1932) and his range of "Modern Living" furniture for the Heywood-Wakefield Co. (1935) were less distinctive. Infrequent commissions for entire interiors, such as his cocktail lounges for the Restaurant Du Relle on Madison Avenue, New York, also have a nondescript quality.

Harold van Doren is commonly credited with the introduction of industrial design to the Midwest. A former Assistant Director at the Minneapolis Museum of Art, Van Doren went into partnership with John Gordon Rideout before establishing his own business in Toledo, Ohio.[43] One of the first to see the potential of synthetic materials in contemporary design, Van Doren cooperated with industry to increase and sharpen the range of available colors, especially for plastics. The radio case which he and Rideout designed around 1932 for the Airking Products Co. shows an intensity of color and a strong skyscraper influence which yielded within three years to aerodynamic principles which the two designers applied to a range of children's vehicles – pedal cars, snow sleds, wagons, and scooters. Their tricycle design for the American National Co. (c. 1935) emphasized the extremes of the streamline philosophy: the curvilinear steel frame housed teardrop fenders and webbed handlebars evocative of airplane wings. Less flagrantly commercial was the line of factory machinery which Van Doren modernized for the Excello Aircraft & Tool Corp. in Detroit, and his white plastic counter scale for the Holly Carburetor Co.[44] In 1940 Van Doren recorded his ideas and experiences in a book entitled *Industrial Design*.

Joseph Sinel was born in 1889 in New Zealand, and spent his school years there before going to England, where he worked as a designer in Carlisle.[45] Various positions in the London commercial art world followed. After serving in the British Mercantile Marine in World War I, Sinel settled briefly in San Francisco, where he worked as a freelance commercial artist. A few years later in New York Sinel turned increasingly to machine esthetics and the related field of industrial design; in 1924, for example, he published a book on trademarks. A gifted landscape artist in his free time, Sinel applied an easy graphic talent to a wide range of product designs for labels, letterheads, trademarks, and posters. In the 1930s he moved gradually away from the field of advertising towards industrial design: furniture, rugs, gasoline pumps, hearing aids, and weighing scales.[46] His New York office in the mid-1930s was at 132 E. 58th Street.

One of the younger industrial designers, *Robert Heller,* was retained by A. C. Gilbert & Co. around 1927 to modernize their line of household appliances: percolators, refrigerators, mixing machines, electric toasters, and, most notably, the "Airflow" electric fan, which Heller remodeled as an airplane propellor mounted on a streamlined body.[47] Success – quickly gauged by increasing sales – led to Heller's redesigning everything from the firm's advertising booklets and typography to its showrooms. Other clients included the Akron Furniture Co. in Akron, Ohio, and Waterman & Co., a frosted foods firm in New York.

Another to draw sporadic attention in the late 1920s was the architect-designer *Richard Buckminster Fuller,* who in 1927 introduced his revolutionary Dymaxion house as an inexpensive answer to traditional housing.[48] The Dymaxion (the name evolved from a combination of phrases such as "dynamic design" and

"maximum area") consisted of a hexagonal, two-story structure suspended from a central tiered mast. Comprising prefabricated components suitable for any climatic conditions, the model offered industrial, rather than architectural, solutions to the housing problems of the new age; not only could it be assembled in 24 hours, but it was completely self-contained, generating its own central heating, sewerage disposal, and electrical systems. The public's positive response, if only one of curiosity, encouraged Fuller to follow up in the early 1930s with a related venture, the Dymaxion automobile, which he exhibited to an amused though puzzled audience at the 1933 Century of Progress Exposition.[49] The vehicle was shaped like a "falling raindrop" (the ideal streamlined shape), and had only 3 wheels, as "a 4-wheel car can't look like a raindrop without getting too long."[50] Despite the seriousness of Fuller's twin projects, neither advanced much beyond the prototype stage.

John Vassos was born in Greece in 1898. He emigrated to the United States in 1919, settled in New York, and attended the Art Students League from 1921 to 1922. Trained as a commercial artist, Vassos had matured by the early 1930s into a versatile industrial designer. His skills encompassed painting, book illustration and binding, furniture design, lecturing and writing.[51] Among his inventions in the interwar years was a range of modular, multipurpose furniture, which he patented in 1939. In the same year he designed the "Room of Tomorrow" at the New York World's Fair, and the Television Pavilion at the Golden Gate International Exposition.

At least a dozen other designers applied themselves effectively to remodeling American consumer products in the 1930s, among them George Sakier, [52] Gustav Jensen, Lurelle Guild,[53] Nathan George Horwitt, Gilbert Rohde,[54] Frederick Carder, Lucien Bernhard,[55] Egmont Arens, George Switzer,[56] Peter Müller-Munk, Otto Kuhler, and the architectural firm of George Howe and William Lescaze. Other designers have unfortunately remained unidentified under the covering name of the corporation for which they worked.

Below, left

Olson Rug Company Truck and Burlington Zephyr Train shown at the Century of Progress Exposition, Chicago, 1933. Design consultants for exterior of train: Holabird & Root; interior design by Paul P. Cret. The Zephyr was advertised as "the holder of all long distance non-stop railroad records" and "America's 1st Diesel Streamline Train." It was manufactured by the Edward G. Budd Manufacturing Company, Philadelphia, and is now at the Museum of Science and Industry, Chicago (photo Hedrich-Blessing)

Below, right

Edward G. Budd Manufacturing Company "Silver Streak," designed by Colonel E. J. W. Ragsdale of the Rail Car Division, 1934. The interior was designed by Holabird & Root (architects) (photo Hedrich-Blessing)

1 INTRODUCTION

1 For recent efforts to define Art Deco, see issues of The Art Deco Society of New York, newsletter, for example, those from Spring 1983 to Fall 1985
2 See, for example, Richard Striner, "Art Deco: Mediational Design for the Inter-War Decades," unpublished lecture notes, 1985
3 For accounts of German industrial design at the turn of the century, see C. Adolph Glassgold, "The Modern Note in Decorative Arts," The Arts, March 1928, pp.153–67; and Helen Appleton Read, "Twentieth Century Decoration," Vogue, July 15, 1928, p. 74ff.
4 Brian J. R. Blench, The Art Deco Society of New York, newsletter, Spring 1985, p. 2
5 Ralph Flint, "In the World of Architecture," The Art News, October 31, 1925, p. 10
6 Recalled by Wright in "The Tyranny of the Skyscraper," Creative Art, vol. VIII, May 1931, pp. 325-26
7 Ibid., p. 332
8 Quoted by Henry McBride, "The Palette Knife," Creative Art, vol. VIII, May 1931, p. 321
9 See Fortune magazine, December 1936, p. 136 ff.
10 See, for example, a list of the objects which were shown at the Lord & Taylor Exposition of Modern French Decorative Art
11 Helen Appleton Read, "Contemporary Decorative Art in America," Vogue, August 1, 1927, p. 66
12 For a selection of early criticisms of modernism in America, both positive and negative, see Helen Sprackling, "Modern Art and the Artist," House Beautiful, February 1929, p. 151 ff.; A. Frederic Saunders, "From L'Art Nouveau to L'Art Moderne," The Jeweler's Circular, February 21, 1929, pp. 105-09; Good Furniture Magazine, June 1927, p. 277; Donald Haskell, "The American Designers," Creative Art, vol. III, 1929, p. liii; and Ely Jacques Kahn, "The Province of Decoration in Modern Design," Creative Art, vol. IV, December 1929, p. 886
13 The prices given are from America As Americans See It, ed. Fred. J. Ringel, New York, 1932, p. 200
14 Richardson Wright, "The Modernist Taste," House and Garden, October 1925, p. 77
15 Ibid., p. 110
16 Ibid.
17 Mary Fenton Roberts, "Beauty Combined with Convenience in Some Modernistic Rooms," Arts and Decoration, February 1929, p. 72
18 Richard F. Bach, "Styles A-Borning: Musing on Contemporary Industrial Art and Decoration," Creative Art, vol. III, June 1928, No. 6, p. xl
19 Metalcraft, March 1929, p. 132
20 Illustrated in Vogue, August 3, 1929, p. 30 ff.
21 For articles on the Allvine house, see Arts and Decoration, January 1930, p. 52 ff.; New York Sun, November 9, 1928; and Every Week Magazine, December 22, 1929, p. 5
22 Arts and Decoration, January 1930, p. 52 ff.
23 For illustrations of the furniture in the Allvine house, see America's First Modernistic Home, auction catalogue 5005A,

Christie's, New York, October 4, 1980
24 Quoted in E. F. Lougee, "Furniture in the Modern Manner," Modern Plastics 12, December 1934, p. 18
25 At the time of writing there were Art Deco Societies or groups in the following US cities: New York, Chicago, Washington, D.C., Baltimore, Miami Beach, Tulsa, Kansas City, Los Angeles, San Francisco, Philadelphia, and Albuquerque
26 Conversation with the author, March 1985

2 EXHIBITIONS

1 Cervin Robinson and Rosemarie Haag Bletter, Skyscraper Style Art Deco New York, New York 1975, p. 44
2 The Decorative Furnisher, May 1925, p. 81
3 Ibid., p. 82; and The New York Times, February 16, 1925, p. 4; and February 17, 1925, p. 4
4 The Decorative Furnisher, August 1925, p. 75
5 Ibid., p. 91
6 Georges Villa, "Paris Exposition Shows Way to New Art of Future," The American Magazine of Art, vol. XVII, April 1926, No. 4, p. 190
7 The American Magazine of Art, vol. XV, October 1924, No. 10, p. 540
8 Architectural Forum, January 1926, p. 11
9 Charles R. Richards, "In Defense of the Modern Movement in European Industrial Art," The American Magazine of Art, vol. XV, December 1924, No. 12, pp. 631 ff.
10 Ibid., p. 634
11 Architectural Record, March 1923, pp. 266-71; and House and Garden, September 1922, pp. 35 ff.
12 The Newark Museum: A Chronicle of the Founding Years 1909-1934, Newark Museum, 1934
13 The Decorative Furnisher, November 1925, p. 75
14 Joseph Breck, "Modern Decorative Arts: A Loan Exhibition," Bulletin of the Metropolitan Museum of Art, vol. 21, No. 2, February 1926, p. 37. Quoted also in The American Magazine of Art, vol. XVII, April 1926, No. 4, p. 170
15 "A Selected Collection of Objects from the International Exposition of Modern Decorative and Industrial Art Paris 1925," exhibition catalogue, The American Association of Museums, 1926
16 Retailing, November 23, 1929, p. 20
17 The exhibition was discussed in numerous contemporary reviews; for example, Creative Art, vol. II, March 1928, No. 3, pp. XLII-XLV; The Arts, February 1928, pp. 120-21; Good Furniture Magazine, June 1928, pp. 287-90; Architectural Record, May 1928, pp. 461-68; and The American Architect, March 5, 1928, pp. 317-22
18 Letter from Geri Savidge, of Lord & Taylor, dated December 7, 1982, in the possession of Ms. Isabelle Croé
19 "An International Exposition of Art in Industry," exhibition catalogue, R.H. Macy & Co., 1928
20 Ibid., p. 8
21 Good Furniture Magazine, January 1929, p. 40
22 Mary Fenton Roberts, Arts and Decoration, February 1929, p. 72

23 Biographies of members, American Designers' Gallery, Inc., exhibition catalogue, Autumn 1928, unpaginated
24 Good Furniture Magazine, January 1929, p. 45
25 American Designers' Gallery, Inc., exhibition catalogue, 1929, unpaginated; and Creative Art, vol. IV, June 1929, No. 6, pp. xi-xii
26 Retailing, March 23, 1929, p. 13; and Good Furniture Magazine, May 1929, p. 234
27 American Designers' Gallery, Inc., exhibition catalogue, 1929
28 "An Exhibition of Contemporary American Design," exhibition catalogue, The Metropolitan Museum of Art, February 12 – March 24, 1929, extended to September 2, 1929
29 Quoted by Blanche Naylor, Design, November 1929, p. 115
30 It should be noted that, of the group, Solon was not an architect; he was a ceramic designer
31 "An Exhibition of Contemporary American Design," op.cit. See also The American Architect, March 5, 1929, pp. 315-22
32 "The Architects' Modern Rooms at the Metropolitan," Creative Art, vol. IV, June 1929, No. 6, p. xlvii
33 Design, September 1931, p. 85
34 AUDAC, exhibition catalogue, Brooklyn Museum, May-June, 1931, unpaginated
35 Retailing, November 9, 1929, p. 15
36 AUDAC, op.cit. See also C. Adolph Glassgold, "Audac Exhibit," Creative Art, vol. VIII, June 1931, No. 6, pp. 436-40
37 Donald McGregor, "AUDAC in Brooklyn," Good Furniture and Decoration, June 1931, p. 323
38 Contempora Exposition of Art and Industry, exhibition catalogue, Art Center, New York, 1929, unpaginated
39 Retailing, March 30, 1929, p. 15
40 Retailing, June 29, 1929, p. 18
41 See, for example, Matlack Price, "Contempora," Good Furniture Magazine, August 1929, pp. 71-76
42 Contempora Exposition of Art and Industry, op. cit.
43 Architectural Record, August 1933, pp. 113-15
44 Edgar Kaufmann, Jr., "Industrial Design in American Museums," Magazine of Art, May 1949, pp. 179-83
45 Machine Art, exhibition catalogue, The Museum of Modern Art, March 6 – April 30, 1934, unpaginated
46 Architectural Forum, May 1934, pp. 331, 334-35
47 Architectural Forum, December 1934, p. 408
48 Richard F. Bach, "Contemporary Industrial Arts," Design, December 1934, p. 48

3 FURNITURE

1 Helen Appleton Read, "Twentieth-century Decoration," Vogue, July 15, 1928, pp. 74-75
2 For information on Moholy-Nagy and the New Bauhaus, established in Chicago in 1937, see Architectural Forum, October 1937, pp. 22, 82
3 See a bedroom by Bernhard in Retailing, June 29, 1929, p. 18

4   See Bernhard's article in *House and Garden*, "House and Garden's Modern House," January 1929, pp. 68-69. For his designs, see *Architecture*, June 1928, pp. 313-14

5   Illustrated in *Vogue*, July 15, 1928, p. 75; and *The American Architect*, June 20, 1928, p. 826

6   See, for example, "Wood or Metal?", *Creative Art*, vol. IV, January 1929, No. 1, p. 49, for models by Breuer and Mies van der Rohe; and *Architectural Record*, September 1930, pp. 209-13, for tubular examples by Breuer, the Bauhaus, and Le Corbusier

7   René Herbst, *25 Années U.A.M.*, Paris 1956

8   Marta K. Sironen, *A History of American Furniture*, East Stroudsburg, Pa., and New York 1936, p. 119

9   *House and Garden*, February 1927, p. 77

10   Paul T. Frankl, "Furniture of the Fourth Dimension," *House and Garden*, February 1927, p. 140

11   For early examples, see *Vogue*, March 15, 1927, p. 85

12   For examples of Weber's skyscraper designs, see *Decorative Art: The Studio Yearbook of Creative Art 1930*, London 1930, p. 143

13   Paul T. Frankl, *Machine-Made Leisure*, New York 1932, p. 140

14   Charles R. Richards, *Good Furniture Magazine*, January 1929, p. 10

15   Illustrated in Karen Davies, *At Home in Manhattan*, exhibition catalogue, Yale University Art Gallery, 1983, p. 78, Plate 58

16   *House and Garden*, May 1930, p. 134

17   See, for example, *Metalcraft*, March 1929, pp. 132-35

18   Helen Appleton Read, "Modernism in a Museum," *Vogue*, April 27, 1929, p. 75

19   *The American Architect*, January 5, 1929, p. 37

20   See, for example, "Metals in Interior Decoration," *The Metal Arts*, vol. 1, No. 1, November 1928, pp. 39-46

21   Helen Sprackling, "The Growing Use of Metal in Decorative Arts," *House Beautiful*, September 1929, p. 267

22   Paul T. Frankl, *Form and Re-Form*, New York 1930, pp. 143, 145

23   "Metal Furniture on the Upgrade," *Retailing*, August 9, 1930, p. 13

24   See Martha Fischer, "The Exotic Woods of the Modernist Movement," *House Beautiful*, April 1930, pp. 457 ff.

25   Gilbert Seldes, "The Long Road to Roxy," *The New Yorker*, February 25, 1933, p. 22

26   *Ibid.*, p. 24

27   Mary Fenton Roberts, "Beauty Combined with Convenience in Some Modernistic Rooms," *Arts and Decoration*, February 1929, p. 112

28   John Loring, "Above Radio City Music Hall," *Architectural Digest*, July 1984, pp. 66-71

29   Seldes, *op.cit.*, p. 24

30   Unpublished autobiography, courtesy of Paulette Frankl

31   See, for example, three articles by Frankl in *Arts and Decoration* on the Modernist movement: May 1928, pp. 56 ff.; June 1928, pp. 58 ff.; and July 1928, pp. 54 ff. See also *House and Garden*, November 1928, pp. 98-99; and a chapter by Frankl in *Annual of American Design 1931*, New York 1930, pp. 25-27

32   See, for example, Pierre Migennes, "Un Artiste Décorateur Americain Paul Th. Frankl," *Art et Décoration*, January 1928, pp. 49-56

33   See, for example, the dining room in *The Arts*, March 1928, p. 231

34   See, for example, *Vogue*, March 15, 1927, p. 84; and *House and Garden*, February 1927, p. 140

35   For a biography of Schoen, see Davies, *op.cit.*, (n. 15 above), p. 25

36   Nellie C. Sanford, "An Architect-Designer of Modern Furniture," *Good Furniture Magazine*, March 1928, pp. 116-18

37   *Ibid.*, p. 118; see also fine Schoen furniture in *Good Furniture Magazine*, September 1928, p. 129

38   Examples of Schoen furniture are illustrated in *Decorative Art: The Studio Yearbook of Creative Art 1930*, London 1930, p. 148

39   See, for example, *House and Garden*, February 1929, p. 95

40   For lavish examples of Schoen's cabinetry, see *Good Furniture Magazine*, September 1928, p. 129; and March 1928, p. 118

41   For interior views of the RKO Theatre, see *The American Magazine of Art*, vol. XXVI, February 1933, No. 2, pp. 78-79

42   For a biography of Weber, see I. B. Gorham, "Comfort – Convenience – Color, examples from the designs of Kem Weber on the Pacific Coast," *Creative Art*, vol. VII, October 1930, No. 4, pp. 249-53

43   For a comprehensive biography of Weber, see David Gebhard and Harriette von Breton, *Kem Weber, The Moderne in Southern California 1920-1941*, exhibition catalogue, University of California, Santa Barbara, February 11 – March 23, 1969

44   See, for example, Kem Weber, "House and Garden's Modern House," *House and Garden*, December 1928, pp. 76-77, 162

45   See examples in *House Beautiful*, July 1931, pp. 61, 92; and *Creative Art*, vol. VIII, May 1931, No. 5, pp. 377-79

46   *House Beautiful*, July 1931, p. 92

47   *Creative Art*, vol. VIII, May 1931, No. 5, p. 378

48   Gebhard and Von Breton, *op. cit.* (n. 43 above), p. 82

49   For a comprehensive biography of Rohde, see Derek Ostergard and David A. Hanks, "Gilbert Rohde and the Evolution of Modern Design, 1927-1941," *Arts Magazine*, October 1981, pp. 98-107

50   *20th Century Modern Furniture* designed by Gilbert Rohde, sales catalogue, The Herman Miller Furniture Co., 1934; and *Troy Streamline Metal*, sales catalogue, The Troy Sunshade Co., 1934

51   *Architectural Forum*, December 1934, p. 417

52   "Contemporary Quinquennial," *Architectural Forum*, December 1934, p. 409; quoted in Ostergard and Hanks, *op.cit.* (n. 49 above), p. 104

53   Ostergard and Hanks, *op.cit.*, p. 99

54   *Fortune*, November 1935, p. 103

55   *Ibid.* Examples of Kiesler's furniture designs are illustrated in *House and Garden*, December 1933, pp. 8 ff.; see also Frederick Kiesler, *Contemporary Art Applied to the Store and its Display*, New York, 1931, p. 150

56   *House Beautiful*, February 1930, pp. 166, 214

57   The nursery is illustrated in *House Beautiful*, February 1930, p. 214

58   See *Good Furniture Magazine*, May 1929, p. 232; Frankl, *op.cit.* (n. 22 above), p. 34; and *House Beautiful*, July 1929, p. 55

59   John Loring, "American Deco," *Connoisseur*, January 1979, p. 52

60   *Arts and Decoration*, February 1929, p. 73

61   *Good Furniture Magazine*, May 1929, p. 230

62   See, for example, *Arts and Decoration*, January 1934, p. 15

63   *Arts and Decoration*, May 1934, pp. 4-7; *House and Garden*, December 1928, pp. 91-93; and Bouy's studio for Stehli Silk Corp. *Creative Art*, vol. VI, April 1930, No. 4, p. 255

64   Sironen, *op. cit.* (n. 8 above), pp. 140-41

65   See, for example, the dining room in *Good Furniture Magazine*, May 1929, p. 233; and *House Beautiful*, July 1929, p. 55

66   Frankl, *The Annual of American Design 1931*, *op. cit.* (n. 31 above), p. 40

67   See, for example, a cabinet by Hoffmann in *House and Garden*, February 1929, p. 76

68   Article by Wolfgang Hoffmann in *House and Garden*, July 1929, pp. 62-63

69   See, for example, *Retailing*, August 9, 1930, pp. 13, 19; and *House Beautiful*, February 1930, p. 166

70   *Kaleidoscope* was issued between 1928 and 1933

71   For a biography of Lescaze, see Sironen *op. cit.* (n. 8 above), pp. 142-43; and *Architectural Forum*, December 1934, p. 399

72   For an article on Lescaze's style, see Herbert Williams, "The Home of an Uncompromising Modernist," *Arts and Decoration*, April 1940, pp. 5ff.

73   See, for example, R.W. Sexton, *American Apartment Houses, Hotels, and Apartment Hotels of Today*, New York 1929, pp. 283-91; and *The American Architect*, March 5, 1929, p. 312

74   See, for example, *Architectural Forum*, December 1934, pp. 394-97. See also *William Lescaze*, catalogue 16, traveling exhibition catalogue, The Institute for Architecture and Urban Studies, New York 1982, pp. 20, 44, 46-47

75   For a biography of Rosse, see *American Designers' Gallery*, exhibition catalogue, Autumn 1928, unpaginated

76   *Arts and Decoration*, February 1929, p. 73

77   *Good Furniture Magazine*, May 1929, p. 231

78   *Arts and Decoration*, February 1929, p. 73; *House Beautiful*, February 1930, p. 165; *The American Architect*, December 5, 1928, p. 752; for another see *Good Furniture Magazine*, May 1929, p. 230

79   *Architectural Record*, February 1929, pp. 163-66; and *The American Architect*, January 5, 1929, pp. 37, 41-42

80   *Creative Art*, vol. VI, April 1930, No. 4, p. 253

81   For a fine survey of Wright's work, see William J. Hennessey, *Russel Wright: American Designer*, exhibition catalogue, Gallery Association of New York State, 1983

82   *Decorative Art 1935, Yearbook of the Studio*, London 1935, p. 41. Wright also designed furniture for the Conant Ball Company.

83   Wright's piano for the Wurlitzer Company's exhibit at the 1939 New York World's Fair is illustrated in *Arts and Decoration*, September 1933, p. 41; a radio in *House and Garden*, January 1934, p. 54

84   See, for example, *House and Garden*, September 1935, pp. 58-59

85   *Retailing*, November 2, 1929, p. 12; and *House and Garden*, April 1930, p. 83

86   *Retailing*, October 19, 1929, p. 2

87   *House and Garden*, February 1929, p. 77; and February 1930, p. 86

88   See, for example, *House Beautiful*, November 1931, p. 387

89   *House and Garden*, March 1929, pp. 114-15

90   *House and Garden*, February 1929, p. 77

91   *House and Garden*, November 1931, p. 83

92   *Commercial Art and Industry*, January-June 1933, pp. 82 ff.; see also *House Beautiful*, February 1933, pp. 38-39

93   *Decorative Art 1935*, *op. cit.* (n. 82 above), p. 8

94   *House and Garden*, July 1938, p. 83

95   *The Arts*, vol. 13, May 1928, p. 297; and *House and Garden*, July 1938, p. 83

96   For a biography of Kachinsky, see Sironen, *op. cit.* (n. 8 above), pp. 143-44

97   *Decorative Art: the Studio Yearbook of Creative Art 1930*, London 1930, pp. 146-47

98   For a biography of Victor Proetz, see *Architecture and Decorative Arts by Victor Proetz*, exhibition catalogue, City Art Museum, St. Louis, August 19-September 18, 1944; see also *St. Louis Post-Dispatch*, August 22, 1966; and *The Washington Post*, August 23, 1966

99   *Design*, June 1932, p. 34

100   *Architectural Forum*, January 1932, pp. 28-32

101   Helen Sprackling, "Backgrounds Designed for the Furniture," *House Beautiful*, April 1931, pp. 374 ff.

102   See *Good Furniture Magazine*, May 1929, p. 234; and *Henry Varnum Poor 1887-1970*, retrospective exhibition catalogue, Museum of Art, Pennsylvania State University; September 14-November 20, 1983, p. 48, and, furniture for his own house, "Crow House," p. 66

103   Sprackling, *op.cit.* (n. 101 above), p. 377

104   *Good Furniture Magazine*, June 1927, p. 277

105   *Ibid.*

106   Sironen, *op.cit.* (n. 8 above), pp. 120-21

107   *Ibid.*, p. 125

108   *Ibid.*, p. 123

109   *Ibid.*, p. 124

110   Richard F. Bach, "Quantity and Quality," *Good Furniture and Decoration*, February 1931, p. 108

111   Berkey & Gay were later sold to Simmons. See Sironen, *op.cit.* (n. 8 above), p. 133. For a Berkey & Gay advertisement, see *House and Garden*, December 1936, p. 9

112   Sironen, *op.cit.* (n. 8 above), pp. 128, 134-35

113   For an article on Grand Rapids furniture, including the Johnson Furniture Co. and Imperial, see "Style Trends at Grand Rapids," *Good Furniture Magazine*, July 1929, pp. 45 ff.

114   For Dynamique Creations advertisements, see, for example, *Arts and Decoration*, March 1929, p. 41; and *House and Garden*, April 1928, p. 11; August 1928, p. 6; March

1929, p. 22; December 1929, p. 12; December 1930, p. 13; October 1931, p. 11
115 See the advertisement for Rohde's furniture for Heywood-Wakefield in *House and Garden*, October 1931, p. 6
116 For an article on Geddes's furniture for Simmons, see *Retailing*, November 2, 1929, p. 12; and October 19, 1929, p. 2
117 Sironen, *op.cit.* (n. 8 above), p. 137; and advertisements in *Arts and Decoration*, January 1937, p. 3; and October 1936, pp. 6-7. For Deskey's furniture designs for Schmieg, Hungate, & Kotzian, see *House and Garden*, February 1934, p. 47
118 Photographs of the Mallin Furniture Co.'s furniture for Joseph Urban are in the Urban archives at the Butler Library, Columbia University, New York City
119 For examples of W. & J. Sloane's furniture, see *House and Garden*, January 1937, p. 20
120 See *Troy Streamline Metal*, sales catalogue, Troy Sunshade Co. 1934
121 For a history of the Widdicomb Co., see Sironen, *op.cit.* (n. 8 above), p. 133; see also the Deskey designs for Widdicomb in *House and Garden*, February 1934, p. 47
122 The Chicago Historical Society has some of the original Howell Company catalogues. Information courtesy of Sharon Darling. The firm claimed to be the first in the USA to manufacture a selection of Mies van der Rohe chromed tubular models
123 McArthur's address was listed from 1934 as 1 Park Avenue, New York. A factory was later established in Bantam, Connecticut, where airplane seats were manufactured. McArthur died in 1962. Information courtesy of Christopher Wilk
124 For examples of Heller's furniture, see *House and Garden*, June 1931, pp. 58-59; and *Decorative Art 1934: Yearbook of the Studio*, London 1934, p. 62
125 The Reed Shop, Inc., at 13 E. 57th Street, New York, advertised a range of wicker furniture in *House and Garden*, January 1927, p. 35; and October 1928, p. 39
126 An Ypsilanti advertisement for reed furniture is illustrated in *House and Garden*, October 1922, p. 117. See also the editorial in *Retailing*, July 19, 1930, p. 19, on Deskey's furniture designs for Ypsilanti
127 *Retailing*, December 20, 1930, pp. 15, 20
128 See, for example, *Annual of American Design 1931*, *op. cit.* (n. 31 above), p. 30

4 LIGHTING AND CLOCKS

1 "Lighting by Design," *Arts and Decoration*, November 1934, p. 15
2 George B. Hotchkiss, Jr., "Modern Lighting," *Good Furniture and Decoration*, September 1930, p. 166
3 Eugene Clute, "Modern Decorative Light Sources," *Architecture*, August 1931, p. 71
4 For a discussion on American lighting engineers, see R.W. Sexton, "Lighting Fixtures of Today," *Architecture*, June 1930, pp. 323-30
5 For discussions on the various types of illumination, see Eugene Clute, "A New Approach to Lighting Design," *Architecture*, December 1934, p. 306; and Walter W. Kantack, "Fundamentals in Providing for Good Lighting," *The American Architect*, September 1931, pp. 48 ff.
6 For biographical information on Von Nessen, see *At Home in Manhattan*, exhibition catalogue, Yale University Art Gallery, 1983, pp. 24, 111
7 See, for example, *House and Garden*, June 1930, p. 27; and September 1930, p. 37
8 See, for example, *Good Furniture and Decoration*, September 1930, p. 167
9 *House Beautiful*, August 1930, p. 161
10 John Loring, "Above Radio City Music Hall," *Architectural Digest*, July 1984, pp. 66-71
11 *The Kaleidoscope*, April 1929, p. 5
12 See, for example, *Arts and Decoration*, November 1934, p. 18; and *Decorative Art 1934, Yearbook of the Studio*, London 1934, p. 127
13 Examples of Lansha Studios light fixtures are illustrated

in *Arts and Decoration*, March 1928, p. 74; and September 1929, p. 74
14 *The American Architect*, February 20, 1929, pp. 238-39
15 *Architecture*, August 1931, p. 71
16 A selection of Modernist table lamps at Frederick Loeser & Co. is illustrated in *Good Furniture Magazine*, September 1928, p. 132
17 *Good Furniture Magazine*, December 1928, p. 351
18 See, for example, *Decorative Art 1933, Yearbook of the Studio*, London 1933, p. 90
19 See, for example, a Heaton wall sconce illustrated in *Arts and Decoration*, February 1934, p. 42
20 For a comprehensive biography of Rohde, see Derek Ostergard and David A. Hanks, "Gilbert Rohde and the Evolution of Modern Design 1927-1941," *Arts Magazine*, October 1981, pp. 98-107
21 *Ibid.*, p. 106
22 See, for example, *Decorative Art 1936, Yearbook of the Studio*, London 1936, addendum p. III
23 For a selection of Rohde clocks for the Herman Miller Clock Co., see *Arts and Decoration*, September 1934, p. 55
24 *House and Garden*, July 1929, p. 8
25 See, for example, *House and Garden*, February 1929, p. 99; and *House Beautiful*, November 1933, p. 219

5 SILVER

1 *The Jeweler's Circular*, February 27, 1930, pp. 104-05
2 Illustrated in W. Scott Braznell, "The Advent of Modern American Silver," *Antiques*, January 1984, p. 240
3 "Modernistic Influence on Sterling Silver," *Arts and Decoration*, April 1928, p. 52
4 "The Modern Note in Decorative Arts," *The Arts*, April 1928, p. 229
5 A contemporary advertisement of the Apollo Skyscraper line is illustrated in *Antiques*, January 1984, p. 240
6 A. Frederic Saunders, "Modernism in Silverware," *The Jeweler's Circular*, February 27, 1930, p. 103
7 Illustrated in *Arts and Decoration*, April 1928, p. 52
8 Peter Müller-Munk, "Machine-Hand," *Creative Art*, vol. V, October 1929, No. 4, p. 711
9 D.H., *Creative Art*, vol. III, December 1928, p. li
10 A selection of "Spirit of Today" items are illustrated in *Vogue*, July 1, 1928, p. 59
11 For a Modernist tea service by Deskey, see *Art and Industry*, vol. 24, June 1939, p. 232
12 For Reed & Barton, see, for example, *Vogue*, July 1, 1928, p. 59, and *Good Furniture Magazine*, September 1928, p. 130. For examples of Locher's "Modern Classic" pattern, see *House Beautiful*, May 1934, p. 94
13 *Spur Magazine*, August 1933, p. 40
14 For a functionalist dinner service by Smed, see *The Christian Science Monitor*, Boston, May 1, 1937
15 "Machinal Molds Metal," *Interior Architecture and Decoration*, December 1931, pp. 274-75
16 *Chase Chrome*, firm's 1936-37 reprint, Gladys Koch Antiques, December 1978, p. 3
17 *Ibid.*, pp. 44, 51
18 *Ibid.*, p. 6

6 METALWARE

1 *The Decorative Furnisher*, November 1925, p. 91
2 Illustrated in *Art News*, October 1925, p. 10; *The Decorative Furnisher*, November 1925, p. 91; and *Arts and Decoration*, December 1925, p. 74, and April 1927, p. 82
3 See, for example, Alastair Duncan, *Art Deco Furniture*, New York and London 1984, p. 54, III. no. 21
4 *Arts and Decoration*, December 1925, p. 74
5 *Good Furniture Magazine*, February 1927, p. 71
6 *International Studio*, July 1925, p. 264
7 *Chase Chrome*, firm's 1936-37 reprint, Gladys Koch Antiques, December 1978, p. 3
8 *The American Architect*, May 1935, pp. 73-79
9 *Interior Architecture and Decoration*, June 1931, pp. 167-69
10 *Metalcraft*, January 1929, pp. 14-15

11 *The Metal Arts*, vol. II, No. 2, February 1929, p. 107
12 Illustrated in *ibid.*, p. 164
13 See "Decorative Metalwork and Cotton Textiles," exhibition catalogue, Third International Exhibition of Contemporary Industrial Art, The American Federation of Arts, 1930-31, unpaginated
14 For a brief biography of Bach, see *Interior Architecture and Decoration*, May 1931, pp. 100-01
15 *The American Architect*, August 1930, p. 47
16 *Architectural Forum*, October 1932, pp. 352-58; and *Architecture*, October 1934, pp. 203-08
17 See, for example, *Good Furniture Magazine*, August 1930, pp. 89-91, 94
18 See, for example, *The Kaleidoscope*, October 1930, pp. 4, 13
19 *Interior Architecture and Decoration*, March 1931, p. 2; and *The Kaleidoscope*, July 1930, front and back cover illustrations
20 *The Kaleidoscope*, April 1929, p. 6
21 *The Kaleidoscope*, January 1933, cover illustration and p. 4
22 See, for example, *House and Garden*, February 1928, p. 80
23 *International Studio*, June 1929, pp. 170-74
24 *International Studio*, June 1925, p. 170
25 See a "Coursing Hounds" staircase by Diederich in *House and Garden*, September 1927, p. 98
26 See, for example, *Good Furniture and Decoration*, June 1930, p. 311
27 See, for example, *House and Garden*, September 1928, p. 161, and October 1928, p. 167; and *The Metal Arts*, vol. II, No. 1, January 1929, p. 46
28 *The Metal Arts*, vol. II, No. 1, January 1929, pp. 1, 3-4

7 CERAMICS

1 Ross Anderson and Barbara Perry, *The Diversions of Keramos: American Clay Sculpture 1925-50*, exhibition catalogue, Everson Museum of Art, Syracuse, N.Y., 1983
2 *Ibid.*, p. xiv
3 Edna Maria Clark, *Ohio Art and Artists*, Detroit 1975, p. 166
4 Anderson and Perry, *op.cit.*, p. xv
5 "A Selected Collection of Objects from the International Exposition of Modern Decorative and Industrial Art," exhibition catalogue, The American Association of Museums, 1926, artists listed alphabetically
6 "International Exhibition of Ceramic Art," exhibition catalogue, The Metropolitan Museum of Art, New York 1928, artists listed by country. For a review of the exhibition, see also Charles R. Richards, "The International Ceramic Exhibition," *Creative Art*, vol. III, October 1928, No. 4, pp. xlii-xlvii
7 "An International Exposition of Art in Industry," exhibition catalogue, Macy's, New York, May 14-26, 1928, pp. 20-21; and "An Exposition of Modern French Decorative Art," exhibition catalogue, Lord & Taylor, New York, February 1928. See also *House Beautiful*, September 1928, pp. 268-69
8 Douglas Haskell, "The American Designers," *Creative Art*, vol. III, December 1928, No. 7, p. liii
9 *Design*, December 1931, pp. 160-63
10 *Design*, June 1933, p. 6; and Anderson Perry, *op.cit.* (n. 1 above), p. xv
11 *Design*, June 1933, pp. 6-8
12 *Fortune*, vol. 16, December 1937, p. 114
13 Kenneth R. Trapp, *Toward the Modern Style: Rookwood Pottery, The Later Years 1915-1950*, exhibition catalogue, Jordan-Volpe Gallery, New York, March 22-May 14, 1983, p. 26
14 *Ibid.*, p. 23
15 Virginia Hillway Buxton, *Roseville Pottery for Love . . . or Money*, Tymbre Hill, 1977, pp. 172-76, 209. See also *Arts and Decoration*, March 1929, p. 100
16 For examples, see *House and Garden*, November 1929, p. 122; and *Design*, December 1928, p. 122
17 Ethel Brand Wise, *The American Magazine of Art*, vol. XX, February 1929, No. 2, p. 69

18 *Cowan Pottery Museum*, booklet, Rocky River Public Library, 1978, p. 5
19 *Ibid*. Numerous examples of Cowan Pottery are illustrated in *Cowan Pottery*, sales catalogues, 1925-1931
20 *Cowan Pottery Museum*, *op.cit.*, p. 6
21 Anderson and Perry, *op.cit.* (n. 1 above), p. 14
22 Carmie Amata, "An Artist Catches the Essence of an Era," *The Plain Dealer*, Cleveland, August 14, 1983, p. 10
23 *Ibid.*, pp. 14, 16
24 *Design*, November 1936, p. 16; and November 1939, p. 12
25 *Design*, November 1936, p. 20
26 Anderson and Perry, *op.cit.* (n. 1 above), pp. 40-41
27 Vally Wieselthier, "Brief Autobiography," *Arts and Decoration*, February 1936, p. 46
28 *Design*, September 1931, p. 80
29 Two examples of Wieselthier's Contempora groups are illustrated in *Interior Architecture and Decoration*, April 1931, pp. 86-87. For other examples see *Design*, November 1929, pp. 103-05; April 1931, p. 259; and *Vogue*, May 25, 1929, pp. 80-81
30 Henry Varnum Poor, *A Book of Pottery, from Mud into Immortality*, New York 1958, p. 87
31 *Henry Varnum Poor 1887-1970*, retrospective exhibition catalogue, The Museum of Art, The Pennsylvania State University, 1983, p. 40
32 *Ibid.*, p. 41
33 Ben Hecht, "Henry Varnum Poor," *Decorative Art*, vol. 8, 1931, p. 365; and *Vogue*, January 19, 1929, p. 100
34 *Henry Varnum Poor*, *op.cit.*, p. 44
35 Anderson and Perry, *op.cit.* (n. 1 above), p. 86
36 *Ibid.*, pp. 86-95. See also *Design*, October 1937, p. 16
37 *Design*, June 1934, pp. 16-17
38 See, for example, two 1938 examples: *Tiger*, in the Museum of Ogunquit, Maine, and *Cat*, in the Everson Museum of Art, Syracuse
39 *Who's Who in American Art*, 1936-1937, s.v. "Diederich, W. Hunt"

8 GLASS

1 "A Selected Collection of Objects from the International Exposition of Modern Decorative and Industrial Arts," exhibition catalogue, The American Association of Museums, 1926, artists listed alphabetically
2 "An International Exposition of Art in Industry," exhibition catalogue, Macy's, New York, May 14-26, 1928, artists listed by country; and "An Exposition of Modern French Decorative Art," exhibition catalogue, Lord & Taylor, New York, February 1928, pp. 25-28
3 See, for example, *Vogue*, December 8, 1930, pp. 90-91; and *House and Garden*, October 1928, pp. 118-19
4 See, for example, *House Beautiful*, November 1932, p. 315; and *House and Garden*, November 1932, p. 18; December 1932, p. 69; and March 1933, p. 67
5 See a typical engraved vase by Simon Gate in *The American Architect*, February 1930, p. 44
6 1928 advertisement illustrated in Hazel Marie Weatherman, *Colored Glassware of the Depression Era 2*, Springfield, Mo, 1974, p. 48
7 Phoenix Glass Company, undated catalogue (c. 1968), p. 5. A copy exists in the Corning Museum of Glass Library
8 *Ibid.*, p. 6
9 Illustrated in *Pencil Points*, November 1932, p. 741
10 Example of Harriton's glass illustrated in *Retailing – Home Furnishings Edition*, August 3, 1942, p. 37; and *Mechanix Illustrated*, May 1946, p. 87. For examples by Eny Art Inc., see *The American Architect*, February 1930, p. 42
11 Illustrated in *The Glass Industry*, December 1934, p. 280
12 Illustrated in *The Glass Industry*, December 1933, pp. 125-27

9 TEXTILES

1 See, for example, *House and Garden*, October 1925, p. 123, and December 1925, p. 117; *House Beautiful*, September 1928, p. 277; and *International Studio*, May 1930, pp. 58, 62
2 See, for example, *House and Garden*, March 1928, p. 141
3 Louise Bonney, "Modern Fabrics and the American Manufacturer," *Good Furniture and Decoration*, February 1930, p. 86
4 "The Use of Modern French Fabrics," *International Studio*, May 1930, p. 64
5 M.D.C. Crawford, *Annual of American Design 1931*, New York 1930, p. 47
6 Louise Bonney, *op.cit.*, p. 85
7 "Watch the Modern Vogue in Fabrics," *Good Furniture Magazine*, May 1928, p. 235
8 *House Beautiful*, April 1929, p. 490
9 See, for example, *Design*, April 1931, pp. 242-47; and May 1931, pp. 16-17
10 "Exhibition of Contemporary Textiles," exhibition catalogue, W. & J. Sloane, New York, December 1930; see also *The American Magazine of Art*, vol. XXII, January 1931, No. 1, pp. 31-33; and *Good Furniture Magazine*, December 1930, pp. 301-03
11 *Design*, February 1932, p. 215; *Good Furniture and Decoration*, December 1930, p. 282
12 Blanche Naylor, "Guatemala Conquers America," *Design*, May 1935, pp. 9-11, 14; and *House and Garden*, February 1932, p. 68
13 Louise Bonney, *op.cit.* (n. 3 above), p. 89
14 Paul T. Frankl, *Form and Re-Form*, New York, 1930, p. 115
15 For a Ryther Modernist design, see *House Beautiful*, April 1929, p. 491
16 Information on Steichen courtesy of Ulysses G. Dietz, Curator of Decorative Arts, the Newark Museum. Examples of Steichen's fabric designs for Stehli Silks are illustrated in *The Arts*, March 1928, p. 158
17 Louise Bonney, *op.cit.* (n. 3 above), p. 86
18 Katherine Morrison Kahle, "The Desert Comes to Home Decoration," *House and Garden*, April 1931, pp. 73-75, 132
19 See, for example, *House and Garden*, November 1930, p. 131; and *Creative Art*, vol. 9, October 1931, No. 4, p. 322
20 *Retailing*, March 30, 1929, p. 17
21 N.C. Sanford, "Art Moderne Rugs are in Great Demand," *Good Furniture Magazine*, May 1928, p. 246
22 Blanche Naylor, "Significant Designs Enter New Fields," *Design*, June 1930, p. 48
23 "Art Moderne Rugs to the Fore," *Good Furniture Magazine*, September 1928, p. 140
24 *The Arts*, vol. 13, 1928, pp. 299-300
25 *Good Furniture Magazine*, April 1930, pp. 217-18
26 *Design*, June 1930, pp. 46-48
27 N.C. Sanford, "Modernistic Rugs Made in America," *Good Furniture Magazine*, July 1928, p. 38
28 Rug illustrated in *Arts and Decoration*, May 1928, p. 39
29 *Good Furniture Magazine*, July 1928, pp. 40-41
30 "Are You Selling Your Share of Modernistic Rugs?" *Retailing*, January 12, 1929, p. 17
31 Examples of Kauffer's and Dorn's carpets are illustrated in *Creative Art*, vol. IV, January 1929, No. 1, pp. 35-37, 39
32 Sanford, *op.cit.* (n. 27 above), p. 38
33 The Schoen rug is illustrated in *Good Furniture Magazine*, July 1928, p. 39; the Benton rug is referred to in *Creative Art*, vol. IX, July 1931, No. 1, p. 50
34 Illustrated in *The Arts*, March 1928, p. 298; and *Good Furniture Magazine*, September 1928, p. 140
35 *Arts and Decoration*, February 1935, p. 51
36 See, for example, *House Beautiful*, January 1929, pp. 54-55
37 "Modernistic Wall Hangings," *Good Furniture Magazine*, August 1928, pp. 104-06
38 "The Tapestries of Marguerite Zorach," *Design*, June 1936, pp. 3-4
39 See, for example, *Good Furniture Magazine*, August 1928, pp. 108-10; *House and Garden*, October 1929, p. 124; and *Vogue*, August 1, 1927, p. 67

10 ARCHITECTURE

1 For a comprehensive history of the growth of the American skyscraper, see Charles M. Gay, "The Romance of the Skyscraper," *The American Magazine of Art*, vol. XXII, March 1931, No. 3, pp. 209-16; and Paul Goldberger, *The Skyscraper*, New York 1982
2 Goldberger, *op.cit.*, pp. 17 ff.
3 For Frank Lloyd Wright's reminiscences on Sullivan's Wainwright Building, see *Creative Art*, vol. 8, May 1931, No. 5, pp. 325-26
4 Goldberger, *op.cit.*, p. 31
5 For an illustration of the ornamentation on the Guaranty Building, see Goldberger, *op.cit.*, p. 30
6 For a history of the competition, and illustrations of some of the better entries, see Goldberger, *op.cit.*, pp. 51 ff.
7 For Howells and Hood's discussion on their winning design, see "The Tribune Tower, Chicago," *Architectural Forum*, October 1925, pp. 185-90. For an article on other entries, see Irving K. Pond, "High Buildings and Beauty," *Architectural Forum*, February 1923, pp. 41-44, and April 1923, pp. 179-82
8 For a rendering of Saarinen's entry, see Cervin Robinson and Rosemarie Haag Bletter, *Skyscraper Style Art Deco New York*, New York 1975, p. 7
9 For an article on pre-1925 American skyscrapers, see Francis Lorne, "The New Architecture of a Flamboyant Civilization," *Arts and Decoration*, November 1925, pp. 58 ff.
10 R.W. Sexton, "Unifying Architecture in America," *International Studio*, February 1926, p. 43
11 Paul Philippe Cret, "Ten Years of Modernism," *Architectural Forum*, August 1933, p. 91
12 Thomas E. Tallmadge, "Will This Modernism Last?" *House Beautiful*, January 1929, p. 44
13 For articles on the 1916 New York Zoning Law, see *Architectural Forum*, October 1921, pp. 119-34
14 See, for example, Sexton, *op.cit.* (n. 10 above), p. 44
15 For an advertisement for the Northwestern Terra Cotta Company, see *Architectural Record*, December 1928, p. 43
16 For advertisements for the National Terra Cotta Society, see *Architectural Forum*, June 1927, p. 178; and *Architectural Record*, December 1930, p. 99
17 For advertisements for the Atlantic Terra Cotta Company, see *The American Architect*, June 1931, p. 73; and *Architecture*, September 1931, p. 10
18 *Architectural Forum*, Winter Supplement, December 1929, p. xix
19 For an example of cast stone as architectural decoration, see *The American Architect*, May 1931, p. 18
20 Philip N. Youtz, "Architecture Revolts from Education," *The American Magazine of Art*, vol. XXIII, October 1931, No. 4, p. 313
21 *Ibid.*, p. 320
22 For a discussion on the pioneers of the International Style in Europe, see a two-part article by Henry-Russell Hitchcock, Jr., in *Architectural Record*, November 1928, pp. 337-49, and December 1928, pp. 453-60
23 For examples of California International Style architecture, see Pauline Gibling, "Modern California Architects," *Creative Art*, vol. X, February 1932, No. 2, pp. 111-15; for other American exponents, see *Fortune*, October 1935, pp. 59 ff.
24 Hildreth Meiere, "The Question of Decoration," *Architectural Forum*, July 1932, p. 1
25 *William Lescaze*, Institute for Architecture and Urban Studies and Rizzoli Publications, Inc., Catalog No. 16, New York 1982, pp. 34-47
26 "Philadelphia's Fancy," *Fortune*, December 1932, p. 65
27 Illustrated in Marcus Whiffen and Carla Breeze, *Pueblo Deco*, Albuquerque 1983, pp. 92-93
28 For illustrations of the building and its decoration, see *The American Architect*, September 1927, pp. 401-06; and May 1931, pp. 396-99. The Newark Telephone Building is illustrated in *Architectural Forum*, May 1930, pp. 667 ff.
29 *The American Architect*, May 1931, p. 398
30 Sexton, *op.cit.* (n. 10 above), p. 67
31 Executed by L. Del Turco & Bros., Inc. illustrated in *Architecture*, March 1932, p. 142; and *Pencil Points*, July 1929, No. 7, pp. 481, 483
32 For illustrations of buildings by Voorhees, Gmelin & Walker, including the Salvation Army Headquarters building, see *Creative Art*, vol. V, July 1929, No. 1, pp. 461-65. The firm's telephone buildings are illustrated in Ralph T.

Walker, "A New Architecture," *Architectural Forum*, January 1928, pp. 2-4

33 Illustrated in Robinson and Bletter, *op.cit.* (n. 8 above), p. 56

34 *Ibid.*, pp. 16-17

35 For examples of Kahn's lobbies, see *Architecture*, October 1934, pp. 230-31, p. 238; and September 1930, pp. 136-38; *The Metal Arts*, vol. III, No. 6, June 1930, pp. 234-37

36 For articles on the Stewart Building, see *Metalcraft*, November 1929, pp. 202-08; *American Architecture*, December 1929, pp. 48-51, and November 1930, pp. 30-31; and *The Metal Arts*, vol. II, No. 10, November 1929, pp. 498-501, and plate LXVI

37 For a series of articles on the construction of the Chrysler Building, see *Architectural Forum*, October 1930

38 For a discussion on the rivalry between Van Alen and Severance, see Goldberger, (n. 1 above), p. 83

39 William van Alen, "The Structure and Metal Work of the Chrysler Building," *Architectural Forum*, October 1930, p. 494

40 Youtz, *op.cit.* (n. 20 above), p. 318

41 The marble's contrasting grain is clearly seen in *The Metal Arts*, vol. III, No. 6, June 1930, plate XXXVII

42 *Architectural Forum*, October 1930, p. 410

43 Illustrated in *The Metal Arts*, vol. II, No. 7, August 1929, p. 378. The entrance doors in aluminum by Henry Nellissen

44 Promotional booklet, the Empire State Building, Publicity Associates, New York, May 1, 1931, p. 7

45 The construction of the Empire State Building is discussed in *Architectural Forum*, August 1930, pp. 241-46, and February 1931, pp. 229-33; and *Creative Art*, vol. VIII, April 1931, No. 4, pp. 242-44

46 The lobby of 500 Fifth Avenue is illustrated in *Architecture*, October 1934, p. 235

47 *Ibid.*

48 Preliminary sketches of the decoration in the Waldorf-Astoria Hotel are illustrated in *The American Architect*, January 1931, pp. 34-35; and *Architecture*, November 1931, p. 251-53

49 *A Romance with the City: Irwin S. Chanin*, ed. Diana Agrest, New York 1982, p. 13

50 *Metalcraft*, March 1929, pp. 108-09

51 *Ibid.*, pp. 110-13

52 *A Romance with the City*, *op.cit.* pp. 76-84

53 For a comprehensive biography of Hood and his work, see *Raymond Hood*, the Institute for Urban Studies and Rizzoli International Publications, Inc., Catalogue No. 15, New York, 1982

54 G.H. Edgell, "The American Skyscraper of Today," New York 1928, p. 363. For a rendering by Georgia OKeeffe of the building at night, see Goldberger, *op.cit.* (n. 1 above), p. 60

55 For an article by Hood on the Daily News Building, see *Architectural Forum*, February 1935, pp. 126 ff.

56 Quoted in Kenneth M. Murchison, "As I See the News Building," *Architectural Forum*, November 1930, p. 533

57 For a view of the globe and black glass walls, see *Architecture*, October 1934, p. 236

58 The Fagus factory in Alfeld, Germany, is illustrated in *The American Magazine of Art*, vol. XXV, August 1932, No. 2, p. 109

59 *Fortune*, January 1933, p. 67. Only the southeast corner of the property, at 48th Street and Fifth Avenue, was excluded from the 3-block-long parcel of land

60 The French Building was called La Maison Française and the British one The British Empire Building

61 For articles on Rockefeller Center, see, for example, *The Studio*, May 1933, pp. 290-96; *Architectural Forum*, May 1931, pp. 601-04, January 1932, pp. 1-8, and April 1932, pp. 355-60; and *Design*, February 1934, pp. 3-6

62 See *Architectural Forum*, October 1933, pp. 274, 277

63 For illustrations of Hildreth Meiere's three panels, see "The Question of Decoration," *Architectural Forum*, July 1932, pp. 2, 3, and 8

64 Illustrated in *Metalcraft*, December 1931, p. 232

65 For an excellent walking tour of New York's Art Deco buildings, compiled by Tony Robbins, see *Art Deco Week*, The Art Deco Society of New York, newsletter, June 9-17, 1984, unpaginated

66 *Metalcraft*, February 1930, pp. 359-61; and *The*

American Architect, May 1931, pp. 44-45

67 See, for example, David Gebhard and Harriette von Breton's definition in *Kem Weber, The Moderne in Southern California 1920-1941*, exhibition catalogue, University of California, Santa Barbara, February 11-March 23, 1969, pp. 11 ff.

68 *Eastern-Columbia Building*, information leaflet, Cultural Heritage Board, Cultural Affairs Dept., Room 1500, City Hall, Los Angeles, CA 90012

69 For a view of the original exterior and lobby, see *Metalcraft*, November 1930, pp. 214-15; and *Progressive Architecture*, November 1982, pp. 112 ff.

70 *Tower Topics*, anniversary issue, Bullocks Wilshire brochure, September 29, 1970; *Bullocks Wilshire*, reprint, California Arts and Architecture, January 1930; *Architectural Forum*, May 1933, p. 357; and Elizabeth McMillan, *1929/79 A Legend Still: Bullocks Wilshire*, brochure, n.d.

71 *Tower Topics*, *op.cit.*, p. 1

72 Frank Lloyd Wright used textured concrete blocks as early as 1914, on his Midway Gardens, Chicago, and the A.D. German warehouse, Richland Center, Wisconsin, 1915

73 For an article on Wright's Hollyhock house and its textile-block slab construction, see *Architectural Record*, December 1927, pp. 449 ff.

74 For exterior and interior views of the 450 Sutter building, see *Metalcraft*, August 1930, pp. 62-65, 80-81

75 Three Modernist lobbies by Pflueger are illustrated in *Architecture*, October 1934, p. 239

76 Illustrated in *American Architecture*, July 1932, p. 67

77 Susannah Harris Stone, *The Oakland Paramount*, Berkeley, California, 1982, p. 20

78 *Ibid.*, p. 14

79 For an article on Holabird & Root, see *Architectural Forum*, April 1937, pp. 10-11

80 For an article on the Palmolive Building, see Henry J.B. Hoskins, "The Palmolive Building, Chicago," *Architectural Forum*, May 1930, pp. 655-58

81 For an article on the Chicago Daily News Building, see Anne Lee, "The Chicago Daily News Building," *Architectural Forum*, January 1930, pp. 21-32 and plates 8, 11, 13; also *Architecture*, January 1930, p. 32

82 For a view of the exterior of the Michigan Square Building and its shop fronts, see *American Architecture*, November 1933, pp. 28-29

83 Anne Lee, "The Chicago Civic Opera Building," *Architectural Forum*, April 1930, pp. 491-95

84 For views of the interior, see *The Metal Arts*, vol. II, No. 3, April 1929, p. 140

85 *Architectural Forum*, June 1933, pp. 453 ff.; *Fortune*, June 1933, pp. 72 ff.; *Cincinnati Union Terminal Dedication 1933*, souvenir booklet by S. Marsh, Cincinnati, n.d., unpaginated

86 *Metalcraft*, February 1931, pp. 76-80

87 For an article on the new restoration of the hotel's interior, see Jayne Merkel, "Grand Hotel," *Connoisseur*, June 1984, pp. 67-71

88 *Art Deco in Indianapolis*, booklet, Indianapolis Architectural Foundation, Indianapolis 1980, p. 7

89 *Tulsa Art Deco*, The Junior League of Tulsa, Inc., Tulsa 1980, pp. 38-42

90 *Ibid.*, pp. 43-46

91 Laura Cerwinske, *Tropical Deco, The Architecture and Design of Old Miami Beach*, New York 1981

92 Lynn M. Appleton and Bruce London, *Miami Beach's Art Deco Buildings: Resources for Recycling*, Urban Resources, vol. 2, No. 2, Miami

93 "Art Deco Historic District," *Portfolio*, Winter 1985, Miami Beach Preservation League, 1979

94 R.W. Sexton, *American Theaters of Today*, vol. II, Architectural Book Publishing Co., Inc., New York 1927, p. 3

95 For the interior of the Uptown Theater, see *Architecture*, November 1929, pp. 292-94

96 For the interior of the Pickwick Theater, see *The American Architect*, December 1929, pp. 22-24

97 For a view of the auditorium in the St. George Playhouse, see *American Architecture*, April 5, 1928, pp. 454-58

98 For an interior view, see *Metalcraft*, October 1931, pp. 130-35; and *Architectural Forum*, November 1931, pp. 568-70

99 Illustrated in *Architectural Forum*, September 1932, p. 220

100 *Architectural Record*, May 1927, pp. 385 ff.; and *Architectural Forum*, May 1927, pp. 414 ff.

101 *Architectural Forum*, May 1927, p. 416

102 For views of the Central Park Casino, see *Architectural Record*, August 1929, pp. 97-108; and *The Metal Arts*, vol. II, No. 10, November 1929, p. 527

103 Henry McBride, "The Palette Knife," *Creative Art*, vol. VIII, May 1931, No. 5, p. 322

104 For a discussion on the decline of the skyscraper, see Robinson and Bletter, *op.cit.* (n. 8 above), p. 71

II SCULPTURE

1 For a definitive discussion of all aspects of 20th-century American vanguard sculpture, see Joan M. Marter, Roberta K. Tarbell, and Jeffrey Wechsler, *Vanguard American Sculpture 1913-1939*, traveling exhibition catalogue, Rutgers University Art Gallery, Rutgers University, 1979

2 For a biography of Nadelman, see Lincoln Kirsten, *Elie Nadelman*, New York, 1973

3 See Merle Armitage, *Sculpture of Boris Lovet-Lorski*, New York, 1937

4 For fine examples of Lovet-Lorski's sculpture, see *Arts and Decoration*, April 1926, p. 63; *Vogue*, February 15, 1927, p. 82; *The Art News*, January 14, 1928, p. 14; and *Creative Art*, vol. IX, October 1931, p. 335

5 Mary Fenton Roberts, "Art Reviews: A Point of View," *Arts and Decoration*, March 1928, p. 116

6 A model of *Playing Dogs* is in the Brookgreen Gardens collection, South Carolina

7 For biographies of Jennewein, see *Sculpture by Carl Paul Jennewein*, brochure, Brookgreen Gardens, 1937; and Shirley Reiff Howarth, *C. Paul Jennewein*, Tampa, 1980

8 See Howarth, *op.cit.*, pp. 23, 81

9 *Ibid.*, p. 34 ff.

10 Illustrated in *The American Architect*, July 1933, pp. 50-51

11 Howarth, *op.cit.* (n. 7 above), p. 42

12 For a biography of Lachaise, see *Gaston Lachaise*, exhibition catalogue, 50th Anniversary Exhibition, March 5-April 27, 1980, Whitney Museum of American Art, New York, 1980

13 Illustrated in *Architectural Forum*, February 1933, p. 129

14 For biographical sketches of Milles, see *Architectural Forum*, November 1934, pp. 306-09; and Helen Appleton Read, "The Work of Carl Milles," *Vogue*, January 4, 1930, pp. 60-61, 90

15 *Vogue*, January 4, 1930, p. 61

16 For examples of direct carving by Laurent, de Creeft, Gross, and Warneke, see *Arts and Decoration*, December 1934, p. 40

17 Peter Moat, *The Robert Laurent Memorial Exhibition*, exhibition catalogue, University of New Hampshire, 1972-73, p. 18. Fine examples of Laurent's sculpture are illustrated in *Vogue*, May 15, 1928, p. 79; and *Arts and Decoration*, December 1935, p. 39

18 Louise Cross, "William Zorach," *The Studio*, July 1934, p. 80; see also William Zorach, "Tools and Materials," *The American Magazine of Art*, vol. XXVIII, March 1935, No. 3, pp. 156-60

19 For a two-part autobiography by Zorach, see *The American Magazine of Art*, vol. XXXIV, April 1941, No. 4, pp. 162-68, and pp. 234-39

20 For a typical example of Zorach's work, see Helen Appleton Read, "The Contemporary Note in Sculpture," *Vogue*, May 15, 1928, p. 78

21 From a paper given by Manship at the Arts Students League, New York, 1915, Paul Manship Papers, Archives of American Art, Smithsonian Institution, as quoted in *Paul Manship: Changing Taste in America*, exhibition catalogue, 19 May – 18 August, 1985, Minnesota Museum of Art, Landmark Center, Saint Paul, 1985, p. 63

22 Comment by an unnamed artist related by Carl N. Werntz, the Chicago Academy of Fine Arts, 9 November, 1912, American Academy in Rome Papers, as quoted in *Paul Manship: Changing Taste in America*, *op.cit.*, p.63

23 Charles H. Caffin, *American Masters of Sculpture*, New

York, 1913, p. 9

24 For biographical information on Manship, see *Sculpture by Paul Manship*, brochure, Brookgreen Gardens, 1937; *Paul Manship*, retrospective exhibition catalogue, February 23 – March 16, 1958, Smithsonian Institution; and *Paul Manship: Changing Taste in America*, op.cit. (n. 21 above)

25 Leila Mechlin, *Washington Star*, January 9, 1937, quoted in *Paul Manship: Changing Taste in America*, op.cit. (n. 21 above), p. 10

26 *Paul Manship: Changing Taste in America*, op.cit. (n. 21 above), pp. 117-23, and 128-29

27 Illustrated in *Architecture*, September 1934, pp. 133-36

28 e.e. cummings, "Gaston Lachaise," *Dial*, vol. 68, February 1920, pp. 194-95

29 For a biography of Clark, see *Sculpture by Allan Clark*, brochure, Brookgreen Gardens, 1937

30 Illustrated in *Famous Small Bronzes*, exhibition catalogue, The Gorham Company, n.d., pp. 17, 19; and *House Beautiful*, April 1929, pp. 486-87

31 For examples of Waugh's modernist sculpture, see *Sidney Waugh*, American Sculptors Series 6, New York, 1948

32 For biographical information on Amateis, see *Sculpture by Edmond Amateis*, brochure, Brookgreen Gardens, 1937

33 Brookgreen Gardens, in Murrells Inlet, South Carolina, is a large landscaped garden in which are displayed numerous modernist works by the sculptors discussed here; for example, Manship, Jennewein, Lachaise, Diederich, Waugh, Fairbanks, and Gregory. For more information, see Beatrice Gilman Proske, *Brookgreen Gardens Sculpture*, Brookgreen Gardens, 1968; and *A Century of American Sculpture: Treasures from Brookgreen Gardens*, New York, 1981

34 See *The Metal Arts*, May 1929, p. 196

35 For a comprehensive biography of Storrs, see *John Storrs and John Flannagan: Sculpture and Works on Paper*, exhibition catalogue, Sterling and Francine Clark Art Institute, November 7 – December 28, 1980, Williamstown, Mass.

36 *Ibid.*, p. 43

37 *Christian Science Monitor*, February 13, 1928, as quoted in *John Storrs and John Flannagan: Sculpture and Works on Paper*, op.cit., p. 19

38 Illustrated in *Creative Art*, vol. VI, May 1930, No. 6, supplement, p. 117

39 Walter R. Agard, "American Architectural Sculpture," *The American Magazine of Art*, vol. XXIV, March 1932, No. 3, pp. 206-12

40 For a fine summary of contemporary American architectural sculpture, see Agard, op.cit.

41 Chambellan was born September 15, 1893, and died November 29, 1955, in Jersey City, New Jersey. All information on the artist, courtesy of Monroe Denton

42 Information courtesy of Monroe Denton

43 Characteristic examples of Chambellan's style – terracotta spandrels for the Suffolk Title & Guaranty Co. Building in Jamaica, Long Island – are illustrated in *Pencil Points*, January 1929, pp. 8-9

44 See, for example, Hartley Burr Alexander, "The Sculpture of Lee Lawrie," *Architectural Forum*, May 1931, pp. 594-600

45 See, for example, *Architectural Forum*, May 1931, p. 593 ff.; and *The American Architect*, October 1934, pp. 46-47, 75

46 See Hartley Burr Alexander, "The Sculpture of Lee Lawrie," op.cit. (n. 44 above), p. 598

47 For examples of Lawrie's architectural sculpture, see *Architecture*, April 1930, pp. 217-18, and May 1932, p. 281 ff.; and *The American Architect*, July 1933, p. 36, and October 1934, p. 50

48 See, for example, *Architecture*, April 1930, pp. 222-23; and *Architectural Forum*, May 1931, pp. 587-89, 591

49 For a biography of Leo Friedlander, see *The Metal Arts*, April 1929, p. 160

50 See Friedlander's article, "The New Architecture and the Master Sculptor," *Architectural Forum*, January 1927, pp. 1-8

51 See Friedlander's heroic equestrian groups, "Valor" and "Sacrifice" for the Arlington Memorial Bridge,

Washington, D.C., illustrated in *Architectural Forum*, December 1936, pp. 534-36, and March 1933, p. 31

52 *The Metal Arts*, op.cit.

53 Both illustrated in *Architectural Forum*, February 1933, p. 131, and December 1936, pp. 537-38

54 A pair of Friedlander panels, entitled "Leaping over the Miles," for the New York Telephone Building, Buffalo, are illustrated in *Pencil Points*, September 1931, No. 9, p. 679

55 Some panels illustrated in *The American Architect*, August 1930, pp. 36-37

56 For examples of modernist architectural sculpture by Fjelde, Keck, and Meyer, see *Pencil Points*, November 1929, pp. 784-88, 790-91

12 PAINTING AND GRAPHICS

1 For a discussion on the Stieglitz Gallery, see Milton W. Brown, *American Painting: From the Armory Show to the Depression*, Princeton, 1955, p. 39-44

2 For a contemporary review of the Armory Show, see Theo. Le Fitz Simons, "The New Movement in Art," *Arts and Decoration*, March 1913, p. 214 ff; and Frederick James Gregg, "The Attitude of the Americans," pp. 165-67

3 Brown, op.cit., p. 47

4 *Ibid.*, pp. 81-82

5 For skyscraper sketches by O'Keeffe, see *The American Magazine of Art*, vol. XXV, August 1932, No. 8, p. 97

6 See *Architecture*, May 1931, pp. 260-61

7 For a review of Rivera's Rockefeller Center commission, see *Diego Rivera: A Retrospective*, traveling Museum exhibition catalogue, New York, 1986, pp. 294-97

8 For sketches of the Radio Keith Orpheum (the RKO) Theater, see *The American Architect*, December 1932, pp. 51-54

9 For illustrations of the Radio City Music Hall murals, see *Arts and Decoration*, January 1933, pp. 27-29; *The American Magazine of Art*, vol. XXVI, January 1933, No. 1, pp. 80, 82-83, 85; and *Creative Art*, vol. X, January 1933, No. 1, pp. 38-39, 41-43

10 Philippa Gerry Whiting, "Rockefeller Center Debut," *The American Magazine of Art*, vol. XXVI, January 1933, No. 1, p. 86

11 For an assessment of the Radio City Music Hall's loss in revenue, see Roberta Brandes Gratz, "Is Rockefeller Center losing its Heart?," *The Soho Weekly News*, January 12, 1972, pp. 9-11

12 For a biography of Binder, see Dr. Wolfgang Born, "Binder in America," *Arts and Industry*, vol. 27, August 1939, pp. 55-58

13 For a biography of Ilonka Karasz, see Karen Davies, *At Home in Manhattan*, exhibition catalogue, Yale University Art Gallery, 1983, p. 42

14 For biographical sketches on Mariska Karasz, see *Interiors*, September 1960, p. 215; and *Art News*, October 1954, p. 59

15 For a biography of Bistttram, see Tricia Hurst, *Southwest Art*, March 1978, pp. 82-86. Information courtesy of Luise Ross

16 A partial set of *Annual Advertising Art*, published by the Art Directors Club of New York, is in the collection of the Cooper Hewitt Library, New York

17 For packaging designs by Vassos, see Martin Greif, *Depression Modern: The Thirties Style in America*, New York, 1975, p. 86

18 For a comprehensive article on the WPA, see *Fortune*, May 1937, p. 109 ff.

19 The PWA is discussed in "P.W.A.," *Architectural Forum*, November 1933, pp. 339-43; and Forbes Watson, "The Public Works of Art Project," *The American Magazine of Art*, vol. XXVII, January 1934, No. 1, pp. 6-9

20 *Fortune*, May 1937, op.cit., p. 112

21 *Ibid.*, pp. 114-15

22 For a brief review of the WPA and illustrations of completed commissions, see Nora Richter Greer, "Nurturing the Heritage of W.P.A. Art," *Architecture*, December 1983, pp. 26-27

13 JEWELRY

1 Made available to the author in 1985 by John Loring, Director of Design, Tiffany & Co., New York

2 Examples of Modernist jewelry by these firms were illustrated in contemporary fashion magazines. See, in particular, *Vogue* and *House and Garden*

3 For a selection of Modernist jewelry produced by these firms, see February issues of *The Jeweler's Circular*, 1925-33. Information courtesy of Dr. Annella Brown

4 For a summary of the partnership between a jewelry manufacturer and retailer, see Ettagale Blauer, "Oscar Heyman & Brothers – the Jeweler's Jeweler," *Modern Jeweler*, June 1985, pp. 38-41

5 See, for example, *The Jeweler's Circular*, February 2, 1929, pp. 14, 19

6 *The Jeweler's Circular*, February 2, 1927, p. 169

7 See, for example, *The Jeweler's Circular*, February 4, 1925, pp. 155, 163

8 Quoted in J.W. Harrington, "Jewelry Design and Present Style," *The Jeweler's Circular*, February 23, 1928, p. 108

9 See, for example, Ima Thompson, "Adapting Modern Decorative Themes to Jewelry Designing," *The Jeweler's Circular*, February 21, 1929, pp. 99-104

10 *Ibid.*, p. 101

11 *The Jeweler's Circular*, February 27, 1930, pp. 106-07

12 *The Jeweler's Circular*, March 1932, p. 73

14 WORLD FAIRS

1 For a selection of World Fair souvenirs, see *The Encyclopedia of Collectibles: Typewriters to World War Memorabilia*, Virginia, 1980, pp. 120-33

2 The other World Expositions held between the two world wars were not considered memorable. These included the Philadelphia Sesquicentennial International Exposition (1926), the San Diego California-Pacific International Exposition (1935), and the Cleveland Great Lakes Exposition (1936-37)

3 See *Fortune*, October 1930, p. 84

4 See "Official Guide Book of the Fair 1933," A Century of Progress, Administration Building booklet, Chicago, 1933

5 For a comprehensive illustrated review of the Exhibition, see *Architectural Record*, May 1933, pp. 347-74

6 Frank Monoghan, "The Fairs of the Past and the Fair of Tomorrow," *Encyclopedia Britannica*, 1938, p. 22

7 See *Architectural Forum*, August 1931, p. 133, ff.

8 See Paul P. Cret, "The Hall of Science," *Architectural Forum*, October 1932, p. 293 ff.

9 Eugene H. Klaber, "World's Fair Architecture," *The American Magazine of Art*, vol. XXIV, May 1932, No. 5, p. 294

10 See, for example, *Architectural Forum*, October 1931, p. 449 ff.; and *The American Architect*, May 1932, p. 28

11 For examples of sculptural decoration at the Fair, see the weekly newsletter, *Progress*, A Century of Progress, published from January 4, 1933

12 "Centennial News 1836-1936," Texas Centennial Exposition, exhibition newsletter, September 7, 1935

13 For an illustrated history of the Fair site, see "A Guide to Fair Park Dallas," Dallas Historical Society, 1983

14 *Dallas Morning News*, June 7, 1936, p. 1

15 For a comprehensive illustrated review of the World's Fair, see *Dawn of a New Day: The New York World's Fair, 1939/40*, exhibition catalogue, June 21-November 30, 1980, The Queen's Museum, 1980

16 For preliminary sketches of the Trylon and Perisphere, see *Architectural Forum*, May 1937, pp. 392-96; see also *Architectural Design and Construction*, April 1939, London, p. 123 ff.

17 "Building the World of Tomorrow: The New York World's Fair," *Art and Industry*, April 1939

18 "Painting and Sculpture in the World of Tomorrow," Department of Feature Publicity, New York World's Fair 1939, unpaginated

19 *Ibid.*

20 For a review of the Exhibition see Eugene Neuhaus, *The Art of Treasure Island*, University of California, Berkeley, 1936

21 *Ibid.*, especially pp. 9, 29, and 33

22 E.T. Buck Harris, *Magic in the Night*, official souvenir, Golden Gate International Exposition, the Crocker Co., San Francisco, 1939, unpaginated
23 See *Interior Design and Decoration*, May 1939, p. 64

15 INDUSTRIAL DESIGN

1 For a history of industrial design in the US from before World War I, see Edgar Kaufmann, Jr., "Industrial Design in American Museums," *Magazine of Art*, May 1949, pp. 179-83
2 For an excellent analysis of American industrial design, see Jeffrey L. Meikle, *Twentieth Century Limited*, Philadelphia, 1978
3 See Jeffrey L. Meikle, "Celebrated Streamliners," *Architecture*, December 1983, p. 49
4 *Ibid.*
5 Retailers also introduced installment buying (ie. credit), to attract buyers in the late 1920s
6 Gilbert Rohde, "What is Industrial Design?," *Design*, December 1936, p. 3
7 See Gilbert Rohde, "The Design Laboratory," *The American Magazine of Art*, vol. XXIX, October 1936, No. 10, p. 638 ff.
8 For an attempt to place industrial designers in three categories, see *Art and Industry*, vol. 24, June 1938, p. 233
9 Eugene Schoen, "Industrial Design: A New Profession," *The American Magazine of Art*, vol. XXXI, August 1938, No. 8, p. 479
10 For a discussion on what constituted good industrial design, see F.F. Barnes and J.O. Reinecke, "Does it Sell?," *Art and Industry*, vol. 24, April 1938, pp. 146-50
11 Sigfried Giedion, *Mechanization Takes Command*, New York, 1969, p. 610
12 John MacArthur, "Modernistic" and "Streamlined," *The Bulletin of the Museum of Modern Art*, vol. 15, No. 6, December 1938, p. 2
13 *Machine Art*, exhibition catalogue, the Museum of Modern Art, March 6 – April 30, 1934, unpaginated
14 For a discussion on this subject, see John Perreault, *Streamlined Design: How the Future Was*, exhibition catalogue, The Queen's Museum, January 28 – May 6, 1984, unpaginated
15 For an article on the subject, see, for example, Carlton Atherton, "Speed Determines New Forms," *Design*, April 1934, p. 4 ff.
16 MacArthur, *op.cit.*
17 "Design Decade," *Architectural Forum*, October 1940, p. 220
18 See, for example, Kathleen Church Plummer, "The Streamlined Moderne," *Art in America*, January/February 1974, pp. 46-54
19 Sheldon Cheney and Martha Candler Cheney, *Art and the Machine*, New York, 1936, p. 62
20 For an informative article on Teague, see M.S., "A Realist in Industrial Design," *Arts and Decoration*, October 1934, pp. 44-48; for a biography, see also, Meikle, *op.cit.* (n. 3 above), pp. 43-48
21 Quoted in Meikle, *op.cit.* (n. 3 above), p. 43
22 For articles on industrial design by Teague, see "The Cash Value of Design," *Arts and Decoration*, January 1936, p. 34 ff.; and "Industrial Art and Its Future," *Art and Industry*, vol. 22, May 1937, pp. 193-96
23 Teague's Bantam Special camera is illustrated in Donald J. Bush, *The Streamlined Decade*, New York, 1975, p. 19
24 For articles on Loewy, see Richard Pommer, "Design: Loewy and the Industrial Skin Game," *Art in America*, March/April, 1976, pp. 46-47; J.M. Bowles, "Walter Dorwin Teague," *Commercial Art and Industry*, January 1933, pp. 82-88; and Meikle, *op.cit.* (n. 3 above), especially pp. 60-67
25 For illustrations of Loewy's designs, see K.C. Plummer, "The Streamlined Moderne," *Art in America*, January/February 1974, p. 48
26 Loewy's London office was managed by Louis Otto, who published an article on industrial design, "The Designer or Stylist's Place in Industry," *Art and Industry*, vol. 21, July 1936, pp. 26-28
27 Martin Greif, *Depression Modern: The Thirties Style in America*, New York, 1975, pp. 88-89
28 The pencil sharpener is illustrated in John Perreault, "How the Future Was," exhibition catalogue, The Queen's Museum, January 28 – May 6, 1984, unpaginated; and Martin Greif, *Depression Modern: The Thirties Style in America*, New York, p. 79
29 Meikle, *op.cit.* (n. 3 above), p. 48
30 For an article which discusses Geddes's stage sets, see Louis Kalonyme, "Eugene O'Neill's Dithyrambic 'Lazarus Laughed'," *Arts and Decoration*, September 1927, p. 68 ff.
31 For articles on Geddes, see "Bel Geddes," *Fortune*, July 1930, pp. 51-57; Douglas Haskell, "A Stylist's Prospectus," *Creative Art*, February 1933, pp. 126-33; and F.A.M., "Social Progress and the Artist," *Art and Industry*, vol. 27, 1939, pp. 184-88
32 See "Design for Utility," *Arts and Decoration*, November 1933, p. 24
33 Norman Bel Geddes, *Horizons*, Boston, 1932
34 "Both Fish and Fowl," *Fortune*, February 1934, p. 90
35 For an article on a futuristic Geddes metropolis, see "City 1960," *Architectural Forum*, July 1937, pp. 51-61; for illustrations of his Futurama exhibit, see Bush, *op.cit.* (n. 23 above), pp. 159-64
36 For articles on Dreyfuss, see "Henry Dreyfuss," *Design*, January 1935, pp. 4-7; and Meikle, *op.cit.* (n. 3 above), pp. 55-60
37 Illustrated in Perreault, *op.cit.* (n. 28 above), illus. no. 29
38 For a biography of Deskey, see David A. Hanks, *Donald Deskey*, New York 1986
39 Information provided by Deskey, 10 January, 1986
40 Information provided by Deskey, 10 January, 1986
41 For a comprehensive biography of Wright, see William J. Hennessey, *Russel Wright: American Designer*, exhibition catalogue, The Gallery Association of New York State, MIT Press, 1983; see also "A Designer at Home," *House Beautiful*, April 1934, pp. 30-33
42 For an article by Russel Wright on industrial design, see "Unintentional Modern," *Arts and Decoration*, January 1934, p. 51
43 Cheney and Cheney, *op.cit.* (n. 19 above), pp. 54, 84
44 *Ibid.*, p. 239; and *Architectural Forum*, May 1934, p. 334
45 For a biography of Sinel, see Percy Seitlin, "Joseph Sinel," *P.M.* magazine, June 1936, p. 3 ff.
46 Leather desk accessories by Sinel are illustrated in *Design*, September 1932, pp. 82-83; for other items, see *Creative Art*, vol. III, July 1928, No. 7, pp. xxxiii-xxxvii
47 For Heller's designs, see *Art and Industry*, vol. 25, August 1928, pp. 66-70
48 For articles on Fuller's Dymaxion house, see "The Dymaxion House," *Architecture*, June 1929, pp. 335-40; Theodore Morrison, "The House of the Future," *House Beautiful*, September 1929, p. 292 ff.; "Dymaxion House," *Architectural Forum*, March 1932, pp. 285-88; and "The Dymaxion House," *Fortune*, July 1932, pp. 64-65
49 For articles on Fuller's Dymaxion car, see *Fortune*, June 1933, p. 8; and *Architectural Record*, August, 1933, p. 147
50 "Off the Record," *Fortune*, June 1933, p. 9
51 For a brief biography of Vassos, see *Who's Who in America*, 1980/81
52 For Sakier's views on industrial design, "Ten Years From Today – Maybe," *Arts and Decoration*, January 1935, p. 20
53 For a brief biography of Guild, see "Industrial Design," *Art and Industry*, vol. 29, September 1940, p. 89
54 For Rohde's philosophies of industrial design and a discussion of his school of design, see *Architectural Forum*, January 1936, p. 17; see also, "The Modern Designer Considers Floor Plans," *Art and Industry*, vol. 24, May 1938, pp. 175-77
55 For a biography of Bernhard, see "Design Dossier," *Art and Industry*, vol. 26, January 1939, p. 18 ff.
56 For a review of Switzer's designs, see "Pioneering in Design," *Art and Industry*, vol. 24, May 1938, pp. 175-77

⫷BIBLIOGRAPHY

MAGAZINES

American Architect, The, 1925-1938
American Home, 1928-1931
American Magazine of Art, The, 1920-1939
Architectural Forum, 1920-1940
Architectural Record, 1913-1936
Architecture, 1925-1936
Art and Industry, 1936-1940
Art Digest, The, 1926-1939
Arts, The, 1920-1931
Arts and Architecture, 1925-1936
Arts and Decoration, 1924-1939
Commercial Art and Industry, 1932-1935
Country Life, 1920-1937
Creative Art, 1927-1933
Decorative Furnisher, The, 1925
Design, 1920-1940
Fortune, 1930-1940
Good Furniture, 1920-1930
House and Garden, 1920-1937
House Beautiful, 1927-1939
Interior Architecture and Decoration, 1931-1932
Interior Design and Decoration, 1934-1936
International Studio, The, 1925-1928
Jeweler's Circular, The, 1925-1939
Kaleidoscope, The, April 1928-January 1933
Metal Arts, 1928-1930
Metalcraft, 1928-1932
Pencil Points, 1925-1933
Retailing, 1929-1930
Studio Yearbook, The, 1920-1937
Vogue, 1925-1929
Women's Wear Daily, 1920-1940

MAGAZINE ARTICLES

Fields, Mary Durland, "Newcomb Pottery: The Pride of New Orleans," *Collector Editions* — vol. 12, No. 3, Fall 1984, pp. 28-31
Loring, John, "Above Radio City Music Hall," *Architectural Digest*, July 1984, pp. 66-71
O'Connor, Michael, "A Modern Dilemma, Contrasts and Conflicts in Miami Beach's Deco District," *Art and Antiques*, May 1984, p. 43 ff.

EXHIBITION CATALOGUES

Anderson, Ross, and Perry, Barbara, *The Diversions of Keramos American Clay Sculpture 1925-1950*, Everson Museum of Art, Syracuse, N.Y., 9 September-15 April 1984
Darling, Sharon S., *Decorative and Architectural Arts in Chicago 1871-1933, an illustrated guide to the Ceramics and Glass Exhibition*, Chicago Historical Society, Chicago, 1982
Davies, Karen, *At Home in Manhattan: Modern Decorative Arts 1925 to the Depression*, Yale University Art Gallery, New Haven, Conn., 1983
Field, Richard S. and Co., *American Prints 1900-1950*, Yale University Art Gallery, New Haven, Conn., 10 May-31 August 1983
Gardner, Paul V., *Frederick Carder: Portrait of a Glassmaker*, The Corning Museum of Glass, Corning, New York, 20 April-20 October 1985
Harrison, Helen, *Dawn of a New Day: The New York World's Fair 1939-1940*, Queens Museum, New York, 21 June-30 November 1980
Hennessey, William J., *Russel Wright: American Designer*, Gallery Association of New York State, 1983
Keen, Kirsten Hoving, *American Art Pottery 1875-1930*, Delaware Art Museum, Wilmington, Del., 10 March-23 April 1978
Marter, Joan M. and Co., *Vanguard American Sculpture 1913-1939*, Itinerary Exhibition, Rutgers State University Art Gallery, Rutgers, N.Y., 16 September 1979-25 May 1980
Ostergard, Derek E., *Mackintosh to Mollino: Fifty Years of Chair Design*, Barry Friedman Ltd., New York, 1984
Perreault, John, *Streamline Design: How the Future Was*, The Queens Museum, New York, 28 January-6 May 1984
Perrot, Paul N. and Co., *Steuben: Seventy Years of American Glass Making*, Itinerary Exhibition, Toledo, Ohio, 1974

Reynolds, Gary A., *American Bronze Sculpture: 1850 to the Present*, Newark Museum, Newark, N.J., 18 October 1984-3 February 1985
Varian, Elayne H., *American Art Deco Architecture*, Finch College Museum of Art, New York, 6 November 1974-5 January 1975
Carved and Modeled American Sculpture: 1810-1940, Hirschl and Adler Galleries, New York, 20 April-4 June 1982
Design in America: The Cranbrook Vision: 1925-1950, The Detroit Institute of Arts and The Metropolitan Museum of Art, New York, 14 December 1983-17 June 1984
Exhibition of Wall Paper Historical and Contemporary, Buffalo Fine Arts Academy/Albright Art Gallery, Buffalo, New York, 1937
Fifty Years on Fifth: A Retrospective Exhibition of Steuben Glass, Steuben Glass, New York, 1984
Furniture by Architects: Contemporary Chairs, Tables, and Lamps, Hayden Gallery, Massachusetts Institute of Technology, Cambridge, Mass., 16 May-28 June 1981
Gaston Lachaise 50th Anniversary Exhibition Catalogue, Whitney Museum of American Art, New York, 1980
Henry Varnum Poor 1887-1970: A Retrospective Exhibition, Museum of Art, Pennsylvania State University, Pennsylvania, Pa., 14 September 1983-1 July 1984
Kem Weber: The Moderne in Southern California 1920-1941, Art Galleries, University of California, Santa Barbara, 11 February-23 March 1969
Machine Art, The Museum of Modern Art, New York, 6 March-30 April 1934
Paris-Hollywood, Galerie 1900-2000, Paris, December 1981-January 1982
Paul Manship: Changing Taste in America, Minnesota Museum of Art, Saint Paul, Minn., 19 May-18 August 1985
A Retrospective Exhibition of Sculpture by Paul Manship, Smithsonian Institution, Washington, 23 February-16 March 1958
200 Years of American Sculpture, Whitney Museum of American Art, New York, 16 March-26 September 1976

BOOKS

Bush, Donald J., *The Streamlined Decade*, New York, 1975
Cerwinske, Laura, *Tropical Deco: The Architecture and Design of Old Miami Beach*, New York, 1981
Chanin, Irwin S., *A Romance with the City*, New York, 1982
Cheney, Sheldon and Cheney, Martha Candler, *Art and the Machine: An Account of Industrial Design in 20th-Century America*, New York, 1936
Cornell, H., *Carl Milles*, Stockholm, 1963
Cucchiella, S., *Baltimore Deco: An Architectural Survey of Art Deco in Baltimore*, Baltimore, 1984
Darling, Sharon, *Chicago Furniture Art, Craft, and Industry 1833-1933*, New York, 1984
Dietz, Ulysses G., *The Newark Museum Collection of American Art Pottery*, Newark, N.J., 1984
Drexler, Arthur and Daniel, Greta, *Introduction of Twentieth Century Design from the Collection of the Museum of Modern Art*, New York, 1959
Dreyfuss, Henry, *Industrial Design Vol. 5*, New York, 1957
Frankl, Paul T., *Form and Re-Form*, New York, 1930
———, *New Dimensions The Decorative Arts of Today in Words and Pictures*, New York, 1928 (reprinted 1975)
Florence, Gene, *The Collector's Encyclopedia of Depression Glass*, Paducak, Ky., 1977
Gardner, Paul V., *The Glass of Frederick Carder*, New York, 1971
Gebhard, David and Co., *A Catalogue of the Architectural Drawing Collection*, The University Art Museum, University of California, Santa Barbara, Calif., 1983
Gebhard, David and Winter, Robert, *Architecture in Los Angeles: A Complete Guide*, Salt Lake City, Utah, 1985
———, *A Guide to Architecture in Los Angeles and Southern California*, Salt Lake City, Utah, 1982
Gebhard, David, and Halpern, David, *Tulsa Art Deco: An Architectural Era, 1925-1942*, Oklahoma, 1980
Geddes, Norman Bel, *Horizons: A Glimpse into the Not Far-Distant Future*, Boston, Mass., 1932
Goldberger, Paul, *The Skyscraper*, New York, 1982
Greif, Martin, *Depression Modern: The Thirties Style in*

America, New York, 1975
Hanks, David A., *Donald Deskey*, New York, 1986
Hennessey, William J., *Russel Wright: American Designer*, Hamilton, Ontario, 1983
Hillway Buxton, Virginia, *Roseville Pottery for Love . . . or Money*, Atlanta, Ga., 1977
Hirshorn, Paul and Izenour, Steven, *White Towers*, M.I.T., Cambridge, Mass., 1979
Hitchcock, Henry-Russell and Johnson, Philip, *The International Style*, New York and London, 1966
Hubert, Christian and Shapiro, Lindsay Stamm, *William Lescaze*, (IAUS, #16), New York, 1982
June, Glory, *Art Deco in Indianapolis*, Indianapolis, 1980
Koch, Gladys and Rosa, Thomas M., *Chase Chrome*, Stamford, Conn., 1978
Kovel, Ralph and Terry, *The Kovels' Collector's Guide to American Art Pottery*, New York, 1974
Lancaster, Clay and Jacoby, Stephen M., *Architectural Sculpture in New York City*, Toronto, 1975
Lenox, *Lenox China: The Story of Walter Scott Lenox*, Trenton, N.J., n.d.
Lynch, Vincent and Henkin, Bill, *Jukebox: The Golden Age*, Berkeley, Calif., 1981
McGrain, Patrick, *Fostoria . . . The Popular Years*, Frederick, Md., 1982
Meikle, Jeffrey L., *Twentieth Century Limited: Industrial Design in America 1925-1939*, Philadelphia, Pa., 1979
Moore, Patricia Anne, *The Casino Avalon*, Santa Catalina Island, Calif., 1979
Murtha, Edwin, *Paul Manship*, New York, 1957
Neuhaus, Eugene, *The Art of Treasure Island: The Golden Gate International Exposition of 1939*, Berkeley, Calif., 1939
Pevsner, Nikolaus, *Pioneers of Modern Design from William Morris to Walter Gropius*, New York, 1949
———, *The Sources of Modern Architecture and Design*, New York, 1968
Plaut, James S., *Steuben Glass* (Monographs on American Arts and Crafts, Volume 1), New York, 2nd edition, 1951
Porter, Aichele K., *The Wharton Esherick Museum Studio and Collection*, Paoli, Pennsylvania, 1977
Proske, Beatrice Gilman, *Brookgreen Gardens Sculpture*, Brookgreen Gardens, S.C., 1968
Read, Herbert, *Art and Industry: The Principles of Industrial Design*, New York, 1954
Robinson, Cervin and Co., *Skyscraper Style Art Deco New York*, New York, 1975
Rogers, M.R., *Carl Milles: An Interpretation of His Work*, New York, 1973
Sironen, Marta K., *A History of American Furniture*, East Stroudsberg, Pa., and New York, 1936
Stern, Robert A.M. and Catalano, Thomas P., *Raymond Hood* (IAUS, #15), New York, 1982
Stone, Susannah Harris, *The Oakland Paramount*, Berkeley, Calif., 1982
Strombom, S., *Carl Milles*, Stockholm, 1949
Tappannorth, Arthur, *Raymond M. Hood*, New York, 1931
Waugh, Sidney, *Sidney Waugh* (American Sculptors' Series, #6), New York, 1948
Weatherman, H.M., *Colored Glassware of the Depression Era 2*, Springfield, Mo., 1974
———, *Fostoria . . . Its First Fifty Years*, Ozark, Mo., 1972
Whiffen, Marcus and Breeze, Carla, *Pueblo Deco: The Art Deco Architecture of the Southwest*, Albuquerque, N.M., 1984
Whitford, Frank, *Bauhaus*, London, 1984
Wirz, Hans and Striner, Richard, *Washington Deco: Art Deco in the Nation's Capitol*, Washington, D.C., 1984
Wise Keyser, Ernest, *Brookgreen Gardens Sculpture*, Brookgreen Gardens, S.C., 1937
Wixom, Nancy Coe, *Cleveland Institute of Art: The First Hundred Years 1882-1982*, Cleveland, Ohio, 1983
Brave New Worlds: America's Futurist Vision, The Mitchell Wolfson Jr. Collection of Decorative and Propaganda Arts, Miami-Dade Community College, Mitchell Wolfson New World Center Campus, Miami, Fla., 1984
Cincinnati Union Terminal Dedication 1933, Cincinnati, n.d.
Deco Addresses, New York, 1984
Deco America, A Universe '82 Calendar, New York, 1981

APPENDIX

2 EXHIBITIONS

(Location and description)

1922
The Wiener Werkstätte in America Galleries, New York exhibition of Viennese furniture and objects

1925
F. Schumacher & Co., New York room of modernist furniture from the 1925 Exposition Internationale, Paris

1926
Traveling exhibition, Boston, New York, Philadelphia, Cleveland, Detroit, St. Louis, Minneapolis, Pittsburgh "A Selected Collection of Objects from the International Exposition of Modern Decorative and Industrial Art, Paris, 1925"
Waldorf-Astoria Hotel, New York Fifth Annual Exhibition of the Art-in-Trade Club
Zimmermann Studios, Inc., New York 1 modernist bedroom
W. & J. Sloane, New York 1 modernist bedroom

1927
R.H. Macy's & Co., New York Art-in-Trade exhibition
John Wanamaker's, New York "Venturus" exhibition
Barker Bros., Los Angeles "Modes & Manners" shop
Secession, Ltd., Chicago shop with *moderne* interior
Charles A. Stevens & Bros., Chicago shop with *moderne* interior

1928
Abraham & Straus, Brooklyn "The Livable House Transformed" exhibit

Lord & Taylor, New York "An Exposition of Modern French Decorative Art"
R.H. Macy's & Co., New York "An International Exposition of Art in Industry"
American Designers' Gallery, New York Exposition of Contemporary Art in America
L. Bamberger & Co., New York model rooms decorated in the modern style
Gimbel Bros., Pittsburgh model apartments in the modern manner
Kaufmann's, Pittsburgh model apartments in the modern manner
Rich Bros., Atlanta model apartment in the modern manner
Davison-Paxon, Atlanta model apartment in the modern manner
Frederick Loeser & Co., Brooklyn "Art Moderne" interiors
Frederick Nelson, Seattle modern interior
Wolfe Lipman, Portland, Oregon modern interior
John Wanamaker's, New York modern interior
Scruggs-Vandervoort-Barney, St. Louis modern interior
B. Altman & Co., New York "An Exhibition of 20th century Taste in the New Expression of the Arts in Home Furnishings . . ."
Marshall Field & Co., Chicago modern interiors
Helena Rubinstein, Chicago modern shop interior
Milgrim's, New York modern shop interior
Mandel Bros., Chicago modern shop interior

1929
Metropolitan Museum of Art, New York "The Architect and the Industrial Arts: An Exhibition of Contemporary American Design"

Marshall Field & Co., Chicago exhibition of modern interiors
Contempora, Inc., New York Exposition of Art and Industry
Architectural League of New York Architectural & Applied Arts Exposition
American Designers' Gallery, New York 2nd Exposition of Contemporary Art in America
Newark Museum, Newark Modern American Design in Metal
Bullocks Wilshire, Los Angeles "Today" exhibition
Gladding Dry Goods Co., Rhode Island modern interior

1930
Newark Museum, Newark Floor Coverings from Primitive to Modern Times
AUDAC, New York Exhibition of Contemporary Industrial Art

1931
Metropolitan Museum of Art, New York Objects: 1900 and Today
AUDAC, Brooklyn Museum Exhibition of Contemporary Industrial Art
W. & J. Sloane, New York exhibition of modern decorative arts

1933
The Museum of Modern Art, New York Exhibition of Contemporary American Industrial Art

1934
The Museum of Modern Art, New York "Machine Art"
The National Alliance of Art and Industry Inc., New York "The Industrial Arts Exposition"
The Metropolitan Museum of Art, New York Exhibition of Contemporary American Industrial Art

INDEX